FEMINIST ADVOCACY, FAMILY LAW AND VIOLENCE AGAINST WOMEN

Around the world, discriminatory legislation prevents women from accessing their human rights. It can affect almost every aspect of a woman's life, including the right to choose a partner, inherit property, hold a job, and obtain child custody. Often referred to as family law, these laws have contributed to discrimination and to the justification of gender-based violence globally. This book demonstrates how women across the world are contributing to legal reform, helping to shape non-discriminatory policies, and to counter current legal and social justifications for gender-based violence.

The book provides case studies from Brazil, India, Iran, Lebanon, Nigeria, Palestine, Senegal, and Turkey, using them to demonstrate in each case the varied history of family law and the wide variety of issues impacting women's equality in legislation. Interviews with prominent women's rights activists in three additional countries are also included, giving personal accounts of the successes and failures of past reform efforts. Overall, the book provides a complex global picture of current trends and strategies in the fight for a more egalitarian society.

These findings come at a critical moment for change. Across the globe, family law issues are contentious. We are simultaneously witnessing an increased demand for women's equality and the resurgence of fundamentalist forces that impede reform, invoking rules rooted in tradition, culture, and interpretations of religious texts. The outcome of these disputes has enormous ramifications for women's roles in the family and society. This book tackles these complexities head on, and will interest activists, practitioners, students, and scholars working on women's rights and gender-based violence.

Mahnaz Afkhami is Founder and President of Women's Learning Partnership, former Minister for Women's Affairs in Iran, and editor of *Faith and Freedom: Women's Human Rights in the Muslim World*.

Yakın Ertürk is former UN Special Rapporteur on Violence against Women, its causes and consequences, former Director of the Division for the Advancement of Women (DAW), and author of *Violence without Borders: Paradigm, Policy and Praxis Concerning Violence Against Women*.

Ann Elizabeth Mayer is Associate Professor Emeritus of Legal Studies and Business Ethics at the Wharton School of the University of Pennsylvania, USA, and author of *Islam and Human Rights: Tradition and Politics*.

Routledge Studies in Development and Society

For more information about this series, please visit: www.routledge.com/Routledge-Studies-in-Development-and-Society/book-series/SE0317.

FEMINIST ADVOCACY, FAMILY LAW AND VIOLENCE AGAINST WOMEN

International Perspectives

Edited by Mahnaz Afkhami, Yakın Ertürk, and Ann Elizabeth Mayer

Routledge
Taylor & Francis Group

LONDON AND NEW YORK

International Development Research Centre
Ottawa • Amman • Montevideo • Nairobi • New Delhi

First published 2019
by Routledge
2 Park Square, Milton Park, Abingdon, Oxon OX14 4RN

and by Routledge
711 Third Avenue, New York, NY 10017

Routledge is an imprint of the Taylor & Francis Group, an informa business

Co-published with the
International Development Research Centre
PO Box 8500, Ottawa, ON K1G 3H9 Canada
info@idrc.ca / www.idrc.ca

The research presented in this publication was carried out with the
financial assistance of Canada's International Development Research
Centre. The views expressed herein do not necessarily represent those
of IDRC or its Board of Governors.

Trademark notice: Product or corporate names may be trademarks
or registered trademarks, and are used only for identification and
explanation without intent to infringe.

British Library Cataloguing-in-Publication Data
A catalogue record for this book is available from the British Library

Library of Congress Cataloging-in-Publication Data
A catalog record for this book has been requested

ISBN: 978-1-138-34492-1 (hbk)
ISBN: 978-1-138-34493-8 (pbk)
ISBN: 978-0-429-43820-2 (ebk)
ISBN: 978-1-55250-610-3 (IDRC ebk)

Typeset in Bembo
by Swales & Willis Ltd, Exeter, Devon, UK

CONTENTS

CONTRIBUTORS

Editors

Mahnaz Afkhami is Founder and President of the Women's Learning Partnership (WLP), Executive Director of the Foundation for Iranian Studies, and former Minister for Women's Affairs in Iran. Her leadership in the non-governmental, academic, governmental, international, and activist spheres has helped enable women in the Middle East, Africa, and Central Asia to make choices that impact their own lives and the lives of their families and communities. Her publications include *Muslim Women and the Politics of Participation* (1997), *Faith and Freedom: Women's Human Rights in the Muslim World* (1995), *In the Eye of the Storm: Women in Post-Revolutionary Iran* (1994), *Women in Exile* (1994), and *Women and the Law in Iran* (1993). Training manuals she has co-authored include *Victories over Violence: Ensuring Safety for Women and Girls – A Practitioner's Manual* (2012), *Leading to Action: A Political Participation Handbook for Women* (2010), *Leading to Choices: A Leadership Training Handbook for Women* (2001), *and Claiming Our Rights: A Manual for Women's Human Rights Education in Muslim Societies* (1996).

Yakın Ertürk is a Global Visiting Associate at Rutgers University's Center for Women's Global Leadership, and the Institute for Women's Leadership Consortium. She served as a faculty member in the sociology departments of University of Riyadh in Saudi Arabia; Hacettepe University in Ankara, Turkey; and Middle East Technical University in Ankara, Turkey. She has held international positions and human rights mandates, among them Director of International Research and Training Institute for the Advancement of Women (INSTRAW), Santo Domingo, Dominican Republic; Director of Division for the Advancement of Women, UN Headquarters, New York; UN Special Rapporteur on Violence against Women, and member of the European Council's Committee for the Prevention of Torture. In 2016, WLP published the English translation of her book, *Violence without Borders: Paradigm, Policy and Praxis Concerning Violence against Women* as part of WLP's Translation Series.

Ann Elizabeth Mayer is Associate Professor Emeritus of Legal Studies and Business Ethics at the Wharton School of the University of Pennsylvania. She earned a PhD in History from the University of Michigan, a Certificate in Islamic and Comparative Law from the School of Oriental and African Studies at the University of London, and a Juris Doctor from the University of Pennsylvania. Her main research areas include Islamic law in contemporary Middle Eastern and North African countries and international human rights law, with an emphasis on women's international human rights. She has published extensively in journals and edited collections, and her book *Islam and Human Rights* was translated into Persian and published in 2014.

Case study authors

Brazil

Mariana Barsted is a lawyer with post-graduate sensu lato in Civil Procedure Law. She has experience in family law, succession law, human rights, and domestic violence against women and is a member of the Brazilian Bar Association and Brazilian Institute of Family Law. She is a project coordinator at Cidadania, Estudo, Pesquisa, Informação e Ação (CEPIA) and works on issues related to human rights, including training programs for women and youth in sexual and reproductive rights. She has conducted pro bono legal work with low-income populations.

Leila Linhares is Co-Founder and Director of Cidadania, Estudo, Pesquisa, Informação e Ação (CEPIA). She is a lawyer with experience in family law, human rights, and domestic violence against women and is a member of the Brazilian Bar Association and Brazilian Institute of Family Law. She is a member of the Committee of Experts of the MESECVI, which oversees the Implementation of the Inter-American Convention on the Prevention, Punishment, and Eradication of Violence against Women of the Organization of American States. She participated in drafting the text of the Maria da Penha Law and the Femicide Law. She is an Emeritus Professor of Postgraduate Studies in Gender and Law at the School of the Magistrates of Rio de Janeiro and has authored several publications on women's human rights, gender violence, and sexual and reproductive rights.

Jacqueline Pitanguy is a sociologist and Co-Founder and Director of Cidadania, Estudo, Pesquisa, Informação e Ação (CEPIA), a non-governmental organization based in Rio de Janeiro, which works with gender issues and educational programs relating to violence against women and reproductive health. She has been a Professor at the Pontificia Universidade Católica de Rio de Janeiro and at Rutgers University, where she held the Laurie New Jersey Chair in Women's Studies in 1991–92. She held a cabinet position as President of the National Council for Women's Rights (1986–89), designing and implementing public policies to improve conditions for women in Brazil. She was the President of the Brazil Human Rights Fund and is a member of the Board of WLP.

India

Kalpana Kannabiran is a feminist sociologist, legal scholar, and rights advocate, and is currently Professor and Director at the Council for Social Development in Hyderabad, an institute of advanced research in the social sciences supported by the Indian Council of Social Science Research. She was part of the founding faculty of the National Academy of Legal Studies and Research University of Law, where she taught sociology and law, and is Co-Founder of the Asmita Resource Centre for Women, where she led the legal services and outreach program. Her work and publications have focused on questions of constitutionalism and social justice in India, with a specific focus on gender, sexual and religious minorities, caste, indigenous rights, and disability rights.

Iran

Mehrangiz Kar is a writer, attorney, and activist specializing in women's rights and family law. Having practiced law in the Islamic Republic of Iran for twenty-two years, she has published numerous books and articles on issues related to law, gender equality, and democracy in Iran and abroad. She was formerly a visiting scholar at Harvard University, Brown University, University of Virginia, California State University Northridge, University of Cape Town, Wellesley College, and Brookings Institution. Kar has received several international awards for her human rights endeavors, including the Democracy Award from the National Endowment for Democracy, Ludovic-Trarieux International Human Rights Prize, and the Human Rights First Award. Examples of her books published in Iran relevant to the topic of this case study include: *Women's Participation in Politics: Obstacles and Possibilities* (2001), *Violence Against Women in Iran* (2000), *Legal Structure of the Family System in Iran* (1999), and *Elimination of Gender Discrimination: A Comparison of the Convention On Elimination of All Forms of Discrimination Against Women (CEDAW) and Iran's Contemporary Laws* (1999). Her book, *Violence Against Women in Iran* (2000), has become an essential reference for research on VAW in Iran.

Azadeh Pourzand is the Associate Director of Learning and Impact at Small Media Foundation, a London-based media lab that provides research, training, and advocacy solutions to support the work of civil society actors and at-risk communities globally. Prior to joining Small Media, she managed an extensive civil society strengthening program at IREX in Washington, DC. In 2015, she was awarded a fellowship at the National Endowment for Democracy (NED). Azadeh has a Master's degree in Public Policy from the Harvard Kennedy School of Government, and a Master's in Business Administration from Nyenrode Universiteit. Azadeh co-founded Siamak Pourzand Foundation, an organization that promotes freedom of expression in Iran.

Lebanon

Ziyad Baroud is the founding and managing partner at HBD-T Law. He is a graduate of the Université Saint-Joseph of Beirut. He also holds a Master's degree and a diploma in Conflict Resolution and pursued doctoral studies at Paris X Nanterre.

He is a lecturer at the Faculty of Law and Political Science of Université Saint-Joseph. Baroud specializes in litigation before the Lebanese courts and in international arbitration. He is experienced in government relations and administrative contracts. He has been involved in various short- and long-term consultancy missions with UN agencies, the World Bank, ministries, and members of Parliament. He participated actively in elaborating laws and in legislative reforms, headed the governmental commission on decentralization, and served as the Minister of Interior and Municipalities in two consecutive cabinets between 2008 and 2011.

Ghadir El-Alayli is a Lebanese attorney-at-law at the Beirut Bar Association, a consultant, and a researcher specializing in human rights, justice, and regulatory projects setting legal and political reform recommendations for Lebanon and the Arab world. He holds a Master's in Private and Business Law and is a PhD candidate in Public Law at Université Saint-Joseph's Faculty of Law and Political Science, Beirut, Lebanon. He currently teaches law and political philosophy, law and society, and law and history of art. He advised civil society organizations and international organizations on issues related to law, human rights, and politics. El-Alayli wrote a book about the extent of Lebanese women's right to grant Lebanese nationality to their children and has published many policy papers, reports, research papers, and articles on law, human rights, and politics.

Nigeria

Victoria Ibezim-Ohaeri is the Founder and Director of Research and Policy at Spaces for Change, a non-profit organization based in Nigeria. She has studied at Nigeria's University of Uyo, Graduate Institute of International and Development Studies (Geneva), Harvard Law School, and the Said Business School at Oxford University. She heads Spaces for Change's knowledge-building and accountability campaign initiatives around women's rights, defending the civil society space, and urban and energy sectors in Nigeria. She is currently the country team leader of an international multi-year study examining how fossil fuel subsidies and their reform have gender-differentiated impacts. Leveraging the hard evidence gathered through research, policy analysis, community engagements, national-level advocacy, and global interactions, Ohaeri routinely facilitates public policy dialogues, mobilizes citizen participation and civil society engagement in policy development, and engages the Nigerian Parliament on policy regarding specific social and economic issues.

Palestine

Luna Saadeh is an advocate and expert on women's rights, gender, and policy issues and has worked with governments and institutions in Palestine and across the Arab world. With twenty years of experience working in the Middle East with international development agencies and local governments, Saadeh has an accomplished track record in developing and implementing policies and country strategies. Her research on gender mainstreaming and human rights has been published at global conferences and in various publications. She represents the state of Palestine at the Administrative and Legal Affairs Department of the Arab Women Organization. She also sits on various advisory boards and committees in Palestine.

Fidaa Barghouthi is a consultant and researcher with a Master's in Gender, Law, and Development from Birzeit University. She has extensive academic and professional experience in conducting research and analysis on various topics, with a strong focus on women's issues. She has developed several policy papers, training manuals, and fact sheets in the field of women's economic, political, and social rights as well as peacebuilding. She is currently serving as a Gender Consultant/ GIZ (Private Sector Development Program) to support the Gender Unit and the Committee in reviewing the policies, laws, and procedures of the MENA from a gender perspective and to develop and implement an operational plan for the Gender Unit.

Fatmeh Muaqqet is a lawyer and feminist researcher, and holds a Master's degree in Law, Women, and Development from Beirzeit University. She represents the state of Palestine at the legal unit of the Arab Women Organization. She also co-founded the Palestinian Maintenance Fund, where she serves as General Manager, and has championed and lobbied for the adoption of numerous laws and measures to combat violence against women in the state of Palestine. Her publications include pieces on women's accessibility and access to justice, a review of the Palestinian labor law from a gender perspective, and an extensive study of sexual abuse within the family. She has prepared and implemented several training programs on the themes of human rights, economic and social rights, UN Security Council Resolution 1325, and gender-based violence.

Senegal

Alpha Ba is a sociologist and Professor at the University of Thiès in Senegal, and is an Associate Researcher at the Gender Research Group of the Gaston Berger University of Saint-Louis. He has worked for more than ten years on the issue of women's rights in Senegal, particularly the economic rights of rural women.

Aminata Bousso Ly holds a Master's degree in Human Rights. She works at Rencontre Africaine pour la Défense des Droits de l'Homme (RADDHO) in Dakar, Senegal, as a Programme Officer on women's and children's rights.

Turkey

Gökçeçiçek Ayata is a lawyer specializing in human rights. Currently, she is attending the PhD Program in Public Law at Istanbul University. Since 2006, she has worked for the Human Rights Law Research Center of Istanbul Bilgi University as an expert researcher. She has co-authored the books *What and Who is Protected* *by the Law on the Protection of the Family? Narratives of the Judges, Prosecutors and Lawyers* (2011) and *Gender of Justice: Legal Experiences in Combating Male Violence* (2014). She has co-edited the following books: *Women's Rights: International Law and Practice* (2010), *Prohibition of Discrimination: Concepts, Legislation, Monitoring and Documentation* (2011), and *Training Manual on Prohibition of Discrimination* (2011).

Ayşen Candaş holds a PhD in Political Science from Columbia University. She is a full-time faculty member in Boğaziçi University's Political Science and International Relations department. Also affiliated with Boğaziçi University's Social Policy Forum and various civil society organizations, she has published articles on the trajectory of basic rights in Turkey, the impact of social policies on equality and the liberties of various groups, shifts in the aims of social policy in Turkey, constitutional politics in Turkey, and the rights of sexual, ethnic, and religious minorities. Currently, she is a Visiting Professor at Yale University's Department of Political Science and is also affiliated with the MacMillan Center at Yale.

Interviews

Hoda Elsadda is a Professor of English and Comparative Literature at Cairo University and one of five women members of Egypt's fifty-member Constitutional Committee, which drafted the country's 2014 Constitution. She previously held a Chair in the Study of the Contemporary Arab World at Manchester University (UK) and was Co-Director of the Centre for the Advanced Study of the Arab World (UK). In 1997, she co-founded the Women and Memory Forum (www. wmf.org.eg), a research organization that focuses on reading Arab cultural history from a gender-sensitive perspective, and is currently the Chairperson of its Board of Trustees. Her research interests are in the areas of gender studies, cultural studies, comparative literature, oral narratives, and women's writings. Her most recent book is *Gender, Nation and the Arabic Novel: Egypt: 1892–2008* (2012).

Asma Khader is the Executive Director of the Sisterhood Is Global Institute-Jordan (SIGI/J). Since earning her law degree at the University of Damascus in 1977, she has been an advocate for human rights and the empowerment of women and girls. She is a member of the Arab Lawyer's Union, the Arab Organization for Human Rights, the Executive Committee of the International Commission of Jurists, and the Advisory Committee of the Women's Division of Human Rights Watch. She was instrumental in establishing the Jordanian Children's Parliament and in creating legal literacy and assistance programs for Jordanian and Palestinian refugee women. Khader is an expert sought after by national, regional, and international organizations to lead advocacy campaigns, draft laws, recommend policy reforms, and conduct legal analysis and fact-finding missions. Formerly the Minister of Culture for the Hashemite Kingdom and the President of the Jordanian Women's Union, Khader has spearheaded efforts to reform Jordan's family law in her roles as activist, scholar, and policymaker.

Rabéa Naciri is a founding member of the Association Démocratique des Femmes du Maroc (ADFM), one of the largest Moroccan NGOs focused on women's rights, and a member of the National Human Rights Council of Morocco. Previously, she was Executive Director of the Collectif 95 Maghreb Egalité, a network of women's associations and women researchers from Algeria, Morocco, and Tunisia committed to preventing violence against women. She is a renowned scholar and has written extensively on Arab women and poverty, women and Islam, capacity building for women, and strategy development for the promotion of women's rights.

Haleh Vaziri is an expert analyst on global affairs who focuses on the Middle East and North Africa region. She has co-authored and edited several WLP publications, including *Leading to Choices: A Leadership Training Handbook for Women* (2001), *Victories over Violence: Ensuring Safety for Women and Girls* (2012), and *Strategizing for Democracy: Challenges and Opportunities for Women in the MENA Region* (2012). Vaziri founded VRMC, a firm advising a diverse clientele on issues of democratization, international media markets, and public diplomacy vis-à-vis aspects of the research management process—proposal preparation, questionnaire design, analytic writing, presentations, conference planning, and curriculum development. Previously, she was a Research Manager at the InterMedia Survey Institute, where she supervised and trained qualitative and survey field work teams throughout the MENA region. Vaziri holds a PhD in International Relations from Georgetown University.

ACKNOWLEDGMENTS

We are grateful for the generous support provided by Canada's International Development Research Centre (IDRC) to Women's Learning Partnership for Rights, Development, and Peace (WLP) for the research initiative that led to the publication of this anthology. This project has provided an incredibly valuable opportunity to analyze factors contributing to inequality and gender-based violence in societies and to use the knowledge gained to advocate for a better future.

We thank WLP partners in Brazil, Egypt, India, Jordan, Lebanon, Morocco, Nigeria, Palestine, Senegal, and Turkey for hosting and facilitating workshops to reflect on the initial research drafts and provide feedback. We are grateful to those who participated in the workshops and shared their experiences, critiques, and wisdom with WLP to ensure that the research was thorough and accurate. We are indebted to Hoda Elsadda, Asma Khader, and Rabéa Naciri for their insightful and personal accounts of their role in leading change in their countries, and to Haleh Vaziri, who conducted the interviews with these leaders.

We would also like to thank Roula El-Rifai and Nola Haddadian of IDRC and Helena Hurd and Leila Walker of Routledge for their support and guidance throughout the research and publication process. We appreciate Lina Abou-Habib and Kimberly Schor of WLP for coordinating the research process and Allison Horowski of WLP for shepherding the book to publication. We also thank Nanette Pyne for her many hours editing the book.

Finally, we thank WLP and the women activists around the world for their commitment and dedication to advancing equality, justice, and democratic values in their countries and communities who inspired this initiative.

ABOUT WOMEN'S LEARNING PARTNERSHIP

Women's Learning Partnership for Rights, Development, and Peace (WLP) is a coalition of autonomous women's rights organizations working in the Global South that is dedicated to empowering women, strengthening civil society, and advancing democracy. WLP partners develop culturally adapted curriculum, lead transformative workshops, design and implement advocacy initiatives, and promote capacity-building activities. The Partnership uses a sustainable, bottom-up approach to advance human rights, increase political participation, develop robust democratic institutions, and promote leadership that is inclusive, horizontal, and compassionate. WLP's training materials have been published in more than twenty languages, reaching tens of thousands of women in more than fifty countries.

1

INTRODUCTION

Mahnaz Afkhami

Early in my tenure as Secretary General at the Women's Organization of Iran (WOI),[1] I traveled with a small group of women to some forty towns and villages around Iran. We wanted to find out what would be most useful to the women themselves. What were their priorities? What were their most important challenges and needs? In every town or village we went to schools, factories, farms, homes, prisons, city councils, teachers' associations – anywhere to learn about women's lives and the challenges they faced.

The experience was often excruciating, sometimes exhilarating, but always instructive. In Abadan, I talked to a woman of twenty who had killed the sixty-year-old husband who had raped her repeatedly since she had been given to him in marriage at the age of nine. On a dusty, winding street in Yazd, we passed a woman who was crying. We stopped the car and asked her why she was crying. She said she was the legal advisor for the WOI branch in Yazd and her husband had just beaten her, forbidding her to set foot in the WOI center. In Lorestan, a young woman at the WOI center told us she had started a class teaching recitation of the Quran because that was the only subject women in the community were allowed to come to the center to learn: "We first have to get them to come out of the house and into the center before we can bring up anything else."

The most important lesson we learned in all these exchanges was that the path to change was through political power and economic self-sufficiency. I felt the importance of this need – and the injustice of the system – myself after I had returned to Iran, when I went to open a savings account for my child with my own money. The bank manager said, "You can't do that. You can open an account, but your husband has to co-sign, and *he* is the one who will be able to withdraw funds from the account, not *you*." Even though it was *my* money, for *my* child, it took a male to make the decisions.

Each of the examples above shows an aspect of family law that impacts women's lives negatively. This book demonstrates that more attention needs to be paid to the harms caused by family laws that leave women disempowered and vulnerable. Historically, gendered legislation has tended to limit women's choice in almost all aspects of life – from marriage, divorce, custody of children, and control over their bodies, to inheritance, residence, travel, and work. It has invariably undermined women's rights and harbored discrimination and violence against them. Family law has been the most vivid representation of gendered legislation and arguably the most potent justifier of gender-based violence (GBV).

This book is one outcome of the larger Women's Learning Partnership for Rights, Development, and Peace (WLP) Family Law Reform project[2] that aims to support the empowerment of women and other groups to prevent and overcome GBV through locally led research and national advocacy campaigns to reform family laws. The book, a joint project of IDRC and WLP, directs the reader to questions about how women, especially women in Muslim-majority societies, are faring in this life-determining intersection of culture and law at the dawn of the twenty-first century; what factors in culture and law, especially gendered legislation, both religious and secular, have moved us forward and which ones have kept us back; and what women can/should do – strive to do – to bring about positive change.

These questions have been a primary focus of WLP, a partnership of twenty autonomous women's rights organizations in the Middle East, Africa, Asia, and Latin America, since its inception in 2000. This book, based on case studies by local scholars in eight countries in four regions, three in-depth interviews with scholar/activists involved in national advocacy for policy change, a comparative overview of the case studies and discussion of the multiple paths in family law adoption, and a final article on the form and effect of socio-political and religious backlash against women's progress in the past few decades, is an effort to put these questions in context. A brief reference to its history will inform on the scope both of the research and the partnership's activism that has led to this project.

After the groundbreaking family law reform in Morocco in 2004, WLP's partner organization, Association Démocratique des Femmes du Maroc (ADFM), a leading force in the reform process, published the *Guide to Equality in the Family in the Maghreb* (Women's Learning Partnership 2005).[3] In the *Guide*'s foreword, Rabéa Naciri (2005: 3) states "democratization and modernization of the region's countries are closely linked to the issue of relationships between men and women within the family" and refutes the idea that Islam by itself dictates the discrimination embedded in existing family laws that perpetuate the violence women suffer on a daily basis.

The *Guide* presents a carefully crafted advocacy plan that discusses conflicts between discriminatory articles in the family law legislation and major international human rights documents, as well as scientific research on the health consequences of implementing discriminatory features of existing law.

A most helpful and important part of the work involved presentation of different and sometimes conflicting opinions of each of the four schools of Sunni Islam on specific articles of family law that help advocates to demonstrate that there is no definitive version of religious dictates on many of these legislative mandates.

WLP translated the *Guide* into English and launched it at the Association of Women's Rights in Development's (AWID) International Forum in Bangkok, Thailand in 2005, where WLP's annual meeting of the partners was scheduled to take place in parallel with the AWID Forum. WLP also invited ten leading young activists from Iran to participate in a week-long leadership workshop and to dialogue with other partners. Iranians who had lost the advantages of their pre-revolutionary family law immediately after the revolution were eager to learn from the Moroccan experience and the *Guide*, which WLP had translated into Persian.

Back in Iran, in 2006, these activists organized the One Million Signatures Campaign for Reform of Family Laws, expanding the Moroccan advocacy tools by initiating a nationwide campaign that produced a variety of communication strategies, including an active outreach to a global audience through social networking and to local communities through face-to-face campaigning, kitchen-table meetings, door-to-door mobilizing, and widespread networking. Their special focus on including men in the movement achieved their 30 percent participation. Noushin Ahmadi Khorasani, co-founder of the movement, describes the process in *Iranian Women's One Million Signatures Campaign for Equality: The Inside Story*, translated into English and published by WLP in 2009.

In February 2009, Mussawah: Equality and Justice in the Muslim Family, a research and advocacy network for family law reform co-founded by WLP board member Zainah Anwar, was launched in Kuala Lumpur. The ADFM co-founders who had worked with Zainah for two years to prepare for the event, as well as several Iranian activists, joined other WLP partners to participate in the proceedings. The viral spread of concepts and strategies from Morocco to Washington, DC, to Thailand, to Tehran, to Kuala Lumpur, and subsequently around the world demonstrated the potential for creation of a viable global movement for change based on well-researched local activism that can be shared and expanded globally with speed and efficiency.

In 2010, in response to requests from our partners and their networks, WLP began to compile the Corpus of Laws of the countries in the Global South, detailing in several languages the constitutions, family laws, financial laws, penal codes, and related legislation that impacted the status of women and violence against women (VAW). The goal is to provide a legal and advocacy resource center for those engaged in preparing draft legislation and advocacy strategies for legal reform, based on the premise that universal human rights can be realized through contextual strategies for implementation. By categorizing documents by issue (and country), the Corpus will make it easier for scholars, activists, reformers, and citizens to find relevant documents and will provide access to successful reforms in relatively similar cultural conditions.

The activist experience and scholarly research that have culminated in the present volume will be instrumental in taking our work on family laws to the next stage. The case studies were conducted by researchers in Lebanon, India, Iran, Brazil, Senegal, Turkey, Nigeria, and Palestine. They provide a variety of contexts for comparative analysis. Among them are multi-ethnic, multi-religious societies (Lebanon, India), a theocratic state that has come into being in part as a backlash to modernity and expanded rights for women (Iran), a society living under decades of occupation (Palestine), a secular state (Turkey), two countries colonized by two culturally and linguistically distinct European countries (Francophone Senegal and Anglophone Nigeria), and a more developed society with secular laws but influenced by strong religious forces (Brazil).

The first draft of each case study, written by a native scholar, was discussed and evaluated by a group of local activists, religious leaders, media representatives, and policymakers who participated in workshops held in each case study country. The comments and reactions at the workshops were studied and integrated into the final draft. Due to political circumstances, the Iran workshop was held not in Iran but in collaboration with the Association for Middle East Women's Studies (AMEWS) at the Middle East Studies Association's annual conference in Boston, Massachusetts in 2016.

From the case study workshop discussions, we learned that whether the society studied was governed by a secular or religious government; had a Muslim, Catholic, or multi-religious experience; or was more or less affluent, the structure of gender relations were similar. In all cases, the man was seen as the head of the family. Men were seen as the "bread winners" and, in one way or another, controlled women's economic activity and had a say over whether they could take a job outside the informal sector. Almost always, family legislation limited women on whether they could have a voice in their place of residence, guardianship of children, and ability to pass their citizenship rights to their husbands or children born outside their native land.

We also learned that the hierarchical and top–down decision-making characterized by patriarchy are not only shared in families across the world but are replicated in educational institutions, the workplace, and politics. In fact, the structure of the family, the foundational unit of society, is replicated in communities and societies. Some workshop participants pointed to new research that has demonstrated that violence in the family is an indicator of problems in the area of national security and that inequality in gender relations is a valid barometer to measure a nation's stability and security. Some pointed to the role of art, literature, and culture in strengthening the existing patterns. Many pointed to the role women played in perpetuating cultural practices that support patriarchy by implementing these practices in celebratory ceremonies that mask their brutality. Many agreed that both genders are products of centuries of patriarchal indoctrination and that the structures are not created by one gender to abuse the other, but by the exigencies of earlier conditions when life expectancy, reproductive realities, and the economics of survival dictated a division of roles that has long outlived its usefulness.

The workshops helped formulate strategies for raising consciousness among populations and policymakers, not only about the injustice of the existing family laws, but also about their high cost in terms of development, prosperity, and security. They all recommended further research and comparative analysis on law reform efforts, and, equally important, on successful implementation of the laws.

The interviews with Asma Khader of Jordan, Rabéa Naciri of Morocco, and Hoda Elsadda of Egypt offer unique perspectives into the processes, development, and achievements of women's movements with regard to family law reform in each of their countries in the last four decades, as well as lessons learned for the future. The three women share similarities in their careers, although they came to their focus on family law from different professional backgrounds and perspectives. Asma Khader began her career as a lawyer and came to realize that as important as legal aid was, a more vital need was for activist organizations that helped bring support, information, awareness, and agency to women. A lawyer could help a woman get a divorce, but only organized activist work would help her find her voice and gain the skills and the power she needed to sort out her life in marriage and divorce.[4] Asma's subsequent positions as head of the Jordanian Women's Union, Minister of Culture, and Senator helped her weave together the many strands of knowledge, resources, and connections that enabled her to lead the movement for legislative change in Jordan.

Rabéa Naciri of Morocco began her career as an academic sociologist. Her public life began as a member of a progressive/left political party that saw gender discrimination as an integral part of inequality and class difference in society. Her party held that once these problems were solved at the societal level, discrimination against women would be eliminated. In the course of her scholarly work and social activism, she concluded that in fact the reality was the reverse – that addressing the issue of women's inequality was the best route to reaching justice for all members of society. She then moved on to co-found ADFM and focused on family law reform as the underlying cause of discrimination in the private sphere as well as in the community and society.

Hoda Elsadda of Egypt is a Professor of English and Comparative Literature and co-founder of *Hajar*, a women's studies journal in Arabic. She began her work on family law reform in 1993 as a member of a task force to revise the marriage certificate template in Egypt. She founded the Women's Memory Forum, an organization that sought to produce alternative knowledge in history, culture, society, law, economics, and politics to challenge stereotypical discourses about women. These experiences led to her appointment in 2014 as one of five women and forty-five men from a wide range of backgrounds and interests on the committee tasked to draft the new Egyptian Constitution.

Each of these three interviewees participated actively in building the scholarship required to offer viable legal, cultural, socio-political, and economic arguments for the reform of family legislation. Their four decades of struggle led them to emphasize that change in family relations requires a slow and lengthy process. It involves major upheaval in every aspect of life, radical alteration in many familiar and deeply entrenched practices, and the knowledge that only a holistic, all-inclusive approach will bring the desired results. They all refer to knowledge creation as an important, but not exclusive, aspect of the work. They agree that mobilization of men and women is an indispensable part of the effort. They point to the similarities in otherwise diverse societies in the structure of the power relations in the family. Their steadfast and decades-long work demonstrates that family law reform requires culture change that involves a lengthy and carefully crafted, multi-faceted struggle.

Yakın Ertürk's long history of research and advocacy for human and women's rights makes her overview article of special importance. Her cogent analysis of the case studies lends strength to her call for the revitalization and reaffirmation of the interconnectedness of women's resistance movements to achieve a feminist jurisprudence.

In the concluding article, Ann Elizabeth Mayer, Emeritus Professor of Law at The Wharton School, University of Pennsylvania, reviews the backlash to the status of women in four widely diverse countries: Russia, the United States, Iran, and Turkey. She observes that politicization of religion, whether by those with some level of commitment to a faith such as in Turkey and Iran, or by leaders who have shown no such commitment, is a common route to the reversal of rights for women. She also points to the recent developments in the practice of VAW through social networking tools and the use of digital communication as a means of bullying and harassing women.

VAW is a social phenomenon. It is a product of historically rooted gender inequality that has become embedded in culture and law. Culture structures a society's view of life – how it defines values, determines facts, and creates beauty. As in all else, it is a function of social relations and is changeable. Some of the case studies demonstrate how laws reflect the primacy of cultural values; whereas, in others, law can be seen as resulting from power and politics. Law is a manner of decision-making: how a society structures the patterns of relationship among its members. As with culture, law is also changeable: as time moves on, people change; new values, facts, and perceptions emerge; and power relations assume new forms. The interaction of culture and law determines the social structure that frames the condition of social existence, affecting men and women's lives from the time they are born to the time they die. Conversely, men and women can affect and structure the conditions that frame their lives.

The work presented in this anthology reaffirms our decades-long research and advocacy indicating that women, who are half of the population of the world, are by definition half of all races, ethnicities, sexual diversities, religions, cultures, and abilities. Subgroups of women bring to the global experience every other experience of injustice, in addition to what they live with as women. They also create culture and sustain it through their roles as mothers, caretakers, primary educators, and keepers of tradition. History has made the patriarchal system that has ruled the structure of families and the architecture of human relationships obsolete. The struggle for change must begin at the roots. Women and men, whose emotions, personalities, and well-being are limited by the archaic roles assigned to them, must come together to shape a new way of experiencing life, work, and leisure by thinking beyond equality and creating a new shared vision for the future.

Notes

1 The WOI was founded in 1966 by a 5,000-member assembly of Iranian women from diverse backgrounds and regions, gathered through consultation, brainstorming, and negotiation. Its mission was "to raise the cultural, social and economic knowledge of the women of Iran and to make them aware of their family, social and economic rights, duties, and responsibilities." I became the WOI Secretary General in 1970.
2 The project is supported by the International Development Research Centre (IDRC). The project's objectives are to:

- Contribute to the development of locally led research – including the promotion of moderate interpretations of Family Law – on culturally specific and effective strategies to reform Family Law and to prevent and counter gender-based violence (GBV).
- Develop and use comparative knowledge on best practices in Family Law reform to inform advocacy efforts.
- Using the research and knowledge generated on Family Law, build the capacity of local actors to launch national advocacy campaigns.
- Develop a global coalition of activists who can call upon one another's assistance, knowledge, and resources to support efforts toward ending GBV.

3 This innovative advocacy tool for reform of the family law in Muslim-majority societies was the first publication in WLP's Translation Series; WLP translated the *Guide* from the original Arabic to English and Persian. In each of its thematic modules, the *Guide* presents the current state of the law, then proposes religious, human rights, sociological, and domestic legal arguments for reform, well-supported by relevant data.
4 As Asma pointed out in her interview for this volume, the repeal of Article 308 resulted from a long and significant campaign that included research to learn how much people knew about it, its impact on women's lives, and whether they agreed that it should be abolished – as well as advocacy based on the research.

References

Khorasani, Noushin Ahmadi (2009) *Iranian Women's One Million Signatures Campaign for Equality: The Inside Story*, Women's Learning Partnership Translation Series, Bethesda, MD: WLP.

Naciri, Rabéa (2005) "Foreword to the Guide," *Guide to Equality in the Family in the Maghreb*, authorized translation of *Dalil pour l'égalité dans la famille au Maghreb*, Copyright © 2003 by Collectif 95 Maghreb-Egalité, Chari Voss (trans.), Ahmad Kazemi Moussavi (ed.), Women's Learning Partnership Translation Series, Bethesda, MD: WLP.

Women's Learning Partnership (2005) *Guide to Equality in the Family in the Maghreb*, authorized translation of *Dalil pour l'égalité dans la famille au Maghreb*, Copyright © 2003 by Collectif 95 Maghreb-Egalité, Chari Voss (trans.), Ahmad Kazemi Moussavi (ed.), Women's Learning Partnership Translation Series, Bethesda, MD: WLP.

PART I

Country case studies

2

FEMINIST ADVOCACY FOR FAMILY LAW REFORM

Cross-country overview

Yakın Ertürk

Introduction

Discriminatory practices in family life, codified into law, remain a major concern for women's quest for equality and rights worldwide. Amending laws to eradicate patriarchal biases has been a common goal for women's movements, at the international and national levels. Feminist advocacy, women's representation in decision-making, and the international gender equality agenda have been critical to the recent gender-sensitive legislative and judicial advances in family-related matters, in many countries.

In the past decades, contemporary ideals of justice and the human rights framework motivated women in their struggle for equality, and they increasingly identified the family as a nexus in the violation of rights in private and public life and family laws as the legal construction of domination and subordination in both realms. Consequently, legislative and judicial practices governing family relations became contested sites for women globally, particularly in countering violence against women (VAW).

This chapter provides a comparative overview of eight case studies on advocacy-based family law reform, which is the research component of Women's Learning Partnership's (WLP) global campaign for family law reform. The following countries are included in the case studies, which are discussed in the subsequent chapters: Brazil, India, Iran, Lebanon, Palestine, Nigeria, Senegal, and Turkey.[1]

Cognizant that gender inequality manifests in diverse sites, the premise of the research is that family laws are political sites where patriarchal interests and women's subordination are institutionalized, including through violence; therefore, these laws matter. Also known as personal status codes, these laws are linked to national constitutions and other national laws, such as the penal code and VAW laws. Understandings inherent in the respective legislations are often complementary, but they may also diverge or even contradict one another, making them inherently volatile.

The case studies offer a context-specific account of feminist advocacy for family law reform, particularly since the 1970s, when a new feminist agency and mobilization was on the rise. The assessment of the case studies relies on narratives of convergence and divergence in the ways women mobilized, established alliances, and advocated for change in order to identify what worked in the different contexts. Comparing countries according to an "ideal typical" family law or a technical legal analysis of texts is not within the scope of this chapter.[2]

The diversity of laws, their interpretation, and reform initiatives observed in the case studies enables revisiting some of the heated debates concerning women and law, often articulated in oppositional binaries: secular versus religious; unified versus plural; top down versus bottom up, and modern versus traditional. Also important in this debate is the Orientalist gaze that singles out Islam as inherently misogynous. These suggest a number of sociologically relevant questions: Is progress a linear process tending towards modernity? Can reforms motivated by a state agenda serve feminist goals? Are secular laws a guarantee for gender equality? How can women's human rights be advanced under conditions of legal pluralism? What is the most conducive socio-political culture for feminist engagement with the state? What is the likelihood of a broad-based feminist mobilization in politically polarized settings? Answers to these questions are explored throughout this overview.

Family law adoption, in the case studies, has been embedded in diverse trajectories of nation-state building, which reflect sociologically different formations and dynamics of governance; power between the state, community, and individual; cultural, social, and political discourses; levels of development, and varying civil mobilizations, including that of women. As elaborated below, in the course of different periods of the twentieth century, the nation-state building entailed multiple paths in the adoption of family-related laws. In some, personal status systems were replaced with unified secular civil laws; in others, varying patterns of legal pluralism based on ethnicity and religion were maintained. These formations set the stage for later reform initiatives.

The case studies focus on the reform initiatives of the past three decades; however, the discussions are placed within a historical context that narrates the circumstances and particularism of each country experience, which, at the same time, reveals the similarities and the common challenges for feminist advocacy across space and time. Each country experience illustrates the complex web of patriarchy, state, and community relations as well as the competing religious/secular discourses that circumscribe feminist activism, which has prompted some to draw on feminist, secular, and international human rights sources, and others to work within a religious/cultural framework.

This chapter starts with a brief discussion of the multiple paths in family law adoption within the trajectories of modern nation-state formation; this is followed by an assessment of the findings of the case studies on contemporary feminist advocacy for law reform and concludes with reflections on lessons learned and prospects for feminist jurisprudence.

Multiple paths in family law adoption

The countries under consideration are multi-ethnic and multi-religious societies, with patriarchal and patrilineal family traditions; except for Iran and Turkey, the countries also share a historical legacy of colonial rule. Given the inherently complex and diverse socio-political structures inherited by the emerging states, the nation-state building project required a fundamental re-configuring of the relationships between the state, the community, and the individual, thus implanting into the future formations sources of tension and competing demands.

The modernization ideal, which remained more or less intact until the 1960s, favored the subjugation of the hegemonic traditional centers of power (tribe, religious/ethnic) to the authority of the central state. Modernity, designed along Weberian "legal-rational" principles, entailed the creation of rational and secular institutions. It was assumed that traditional formations would wither away in time. This did not happen. The process of de-colonialization radicalized and empowered "traditional" centers of power while at the same time paving the way for the rise of "Third Worldism," which rejected the linear model of development and promoted a revolutionary and socialist world vision, thus contributing to the collapse of the modernization myth. At this juncture, religion became championed in the anti-colonial struggle and occupied a primary place in societal formation and construction of identities.[3]

The twentieth century, therefore, offered different paths for state building, with significant implications for how the controversial issues of religion and personal status laws were to be handled. The particular arrangement adopted at this juncture laid the ground for the legal and institutional parameters for future generations.

Hence, historical heritage, ideological orientation of leadership, and the balance of power among hegemonic groups, intersecting with the dynamics of timing of independence, are critical factors in shaping family-related legislative systems in each country. Over the years, these systems have undergone reform, but their common patriarchal character remained largely intact until the 1970s, when feminist scholarship and activism profoundly challenged the socio-political landscape and public discourse on reform.[4]

For the purposes of this overview, legal adoption in the eight countries during the foundational period of state building is approached within two broad trajectories: unified secular civil codes and plural ethno-religious personal status laws.[5] The two trajectories are meant to provide a basis for distinguishing general trends and tendencies rather than to suggest immutable fixed categories. Iran is taken up somewhat outside of the two paths.

Brazil and Turkey, two countries from remote geographies and different historic and socio-cultural realities, are prototypical of legislative/judicial consolidation.

Significant parallels exist between the two with respect to timing of anti-monarchist nation-state building and a relatively long history in engagement with normative and democratic institutions, although with periodic discontinuities caused by military interventions. Brazil and Turkey are also members of regional human rights systems, which provide additional levels of legal recourse when domestic remedies fail, through the Inter-American and European Human Rights Courts respectively.

The creation of secular republics in Brazil (1890) and Turkey (1923) allowed for the adoption of unified civil codes inspired by the French and the Swiss civil codes respectively, replacing the Portuguese *Filipino* Code in Brazil (1916)[6] and the 1917 Ottoman Law of Family Rights[7] in Turkey.[8] The secular, modern, and Western models that informed the new Civil Codes in Brazil and Turkey were not necessarily egalitarian,[9] as they were typically based on the hierarchical male-headed household principle. The Brazilian and Turkish experiences in codification of family laws, although inherently patriarchal, introduced a trajectory of increased secularization in family matters, offering women in both countries viable entry points to broaden their rights.

The periodization of independence from colonial rule in the remaining countries corresponds more or less to the mid-1990s, when conditions for unified family laws had seriously eroded. The exception to this was Senegal, which was declared a secular republic in 1963, when the government took a bold step to establish a unified legal/judicial system by abolishing separate courts and adopting the secular unified *Code de la Famille*. However, this was short-lived: in 1971, with strong resistance from religious/conservative groups, an exception for the Muslim community under a separate section on Islamic succession law had to be made in the *Code de la Famille*.

The path of legal adoption followed in the other countries shows varying degrees of continuity with the legal/judicial pluralism inherited from the colonial era. Normative fragmentation under colonialism enabled the governance of subject populations and control of property and labor; therefore, it was consistent with the objectives of colonial rulers. However, it is somewhat curious as to why post-colonial states opted for legal pluralism, which obviously challenged consolidation of state power. Also puzzling is why emerging nations with a constitutional commitment to equality before the law would subject their citizens to different standards and laws (Sezgin 2013: 3–5). The socio-political landscape of the mid-twentieth century and the specific circumstances confronting each country account for the choices made: some chose to unify their courts while maintaining normative pluralism or vice versa, and others opted for both normative and institutional fragmentation. In some cases, the choices made at the initial stage were considered as a provisional short-term compromise by the founding fathers, but these arrangements often created durable regulatory paths that resisted change.

Legal pluralism in countries such as India, Lebanon, and Nigeria demarcate religious communities and minority-majority relations. Therefore, radical law reform in such contexts would have been divisive and provocative. In India, for instance, despite constitutional secular democracy and the commitment of the leadership to a unified secular legal system, four main sets of religious personal laws (each internally diverse and contested) – Hindu, Muslim, Christian, and Parsi laws – were codified separately from the main body of the Unified Civil Law (UCC). Civil courts adjudicated all personal status law cases.

Lebanon, on the other hand, maintained both legislative and judicial pluralism; fifteen different codes for the eighteen sects commonly referred to as "confessions" enjoy constitutional recognition, a structure rooted in the state-building projects embarked upon when Lebanon was an Ottoman[10] province and when it was under the French mandate (1920–43). Hence, the state legally marginalized itself in family matters, leaving the experience of Lebanese citizens to kin affiliation and religious descent (Joseph 2000: 130). Religious, legislative, and judicial pluralism in Lebanon is all encompassing, representing not only personal status but also the structure of representation and governance. Since independence, seats in the Parliament and state apparatuses have been allocated according to the distribution of religious sects in the population, which is more or less based on a 1932 census. This has enabled religious leaders to consolidate their influence over social, political, and legal life, creating a strong patriarchal front.

A dual structure at the federal and state levels as well as north–south dichotomy characterizes the Nigerian legislative and judicial system. The north–south dichotomy also corresponds to the cultural and religious diversity of the Muslim north and Christian south. In the latter, a Criminal Code modeled after English law is administered in English-type courts; in the former, separate Sharia court and Islamic law is in force. Discrepancies between English and Islamic law informed the reform of the legal and judicial systems in the northern region, resulting in the enactment of a Penal Code enforceable by all the courts.

The legal pluralism Palestine inherited from its colonial past is exacerbated by Israeli occupation and settler colonialism – a case unlike any other in modern history. Prior to the Israeli occupation, Palestinians lived under Ottoman rule, followed by the British Mandate (1922–47). The 1947 UN Partition Plan, which established Israel, left the West Bank and Gaza Strip to different political rule, the former subject to Jordanian rule and the latter to Egyptian rule. In 1967, following the Six Day War, Israel occupied East Jerusalem, all of the West Bank, Gaza, the Golan Heights, and the Sinai. Each system of governance on Palestinian lands meant that new laws were added to the legal/judicial framework in force, resulting in the coexistence of competing texts and courts, subjecting the Palestinians to an amalgamation of laws inherited from different sources and historical periods: the 1917 Ottoman family law, laws from the British Mandate, Jordanian and Egyptian laws, and Israeli military orders. This multiplicity of laws has naturally led to the lack of a consistent personal status law governing family life and that of Palestinian women, whether Muslim or Christian.

Finally, the trajectory of the Iranian family law adoption – although sharing common trends with the above countries – took a distinct turn in 1979 with the Islamic Revolution, which marks a deviation from the modernist legal reforms that had been put into motion during the Pahlavi era. The Islamic Revolution not only put an end to these reforms, but also was regressive in imposing a strict sex segregation and dress code. Two days before the commemoration of International Women's Day in 1979, Khomeini introduced laws that signaled the rollback in women's rights. The previous reforms were replaced with a Sharia-based family law and special courts, presided over by male religious judges.

In concluding this section, it can be argued that, regardless of the different ways in which states dealt with personal status systems, the implications for women's equal citizenship and enjoyment of universal human rights have been profound – in some cases opening new entry points, in others blocking individual rights and autonomous space. Except for Brazil, the role of Islam and Islamic jurisprudence is a key feature in the trajectories of the countries examined. Given the highly politicized nature of Islam today, a common strategy among women for law reform has become particularly demanding.[11]

The next section explores how women's movements in the case studies have been challenged by and have responded to these trends and tendencies in their family law reform advocacy.

The rise of new feminist agency

The preceding discussion identified the different paths in which regulatory systems concerning family matters evolved in the early and mid-twentieth century in the countries reviewed. Women's rights in the different models of family law, whether secular or religiously based, were either instrumentalized or sacrificed for other priorities in the nation-formation process. States, over the years, continued to engage in law reform; however, while the process was continuous, its direction was rarely linear. Contingent upon changing sociological parameters, reform initiatives showed both progressive and regressive tendencies in all countries, at times expanding, at times limiting women's rights.

In this respect, the Senegal case illustrates how the unified secular family law, initially adopted, was ruptured by demands for a religiously based law for the Muslim community. A more striking example is Turkey, where, after almost a century of laicism and a long proactive phase of feminist activism that resulted in successful reforms, today patriarchy adorned with Islamism is making a major comeback in social policy and law.

The engagement of the global women's movement and the United Nations (UN) has transpired into a comprehensive international regime for women's rights. As women's concerns trickled up from the local to the global, the women's movement diversified and so did the UN gender agenda, which experienced a shift of focus from formal equality to integrating women into development, to women's empowerment, to women's human rights, and to women and peace (Ertürk 2016; Jain 2005; Snyder 2006). This regime encouraged national-level pro-women change – at times modest and at times impressive – in the four corners of the globe.

The adoption of the Convention on the Elimination of All Forms of Discrimination against Women (CEDAW), also known as the Women's International Bill of Rights, although it lacked a focus on VAW, was a major victory in altering international relations. The main breakthrough in women's human rights, however, came in the 1990s: in 1992, CEDAW adopted General Recommendation (GR) 19,[12] defining VAW as a form of discrimination, and, in 1993, the Vienna Conference on human rights officially recognized VAW as a human rights violation.

Unlike previous agendas concerning women, the recognition of VAW as a public policy concern was a powerful force for mobilizing women worldwide as well as for interrogating the taken-for-granted aspects of everyday life and the instigation of violence through legislative and judicial structures. Focus on VAW and the adoption of civil domestic violence bills, in many countries, unmasked the intricate intersectionality[13] between VAW and the property (maintenance and inheritance) regimes of family laws, which ultimately determine women's capacity to escape violence and seek protection under domestic violence legislation.

The VAW agenda, therefore, can be said to have had transformative outcomes, particularly in three areas: (1) conventional understandings of human rights beyond violations perpetuated mainly by state actors in the public sphere; (2) the doctrine of state responsibility to include the actions of private individuals, thus, together with the former, demystifying the public–private dichotomy in law; and (3) the criminal justice systems, with the inclusion of new species of crimes (Ertürk 2016: 133). Today, VAW as a public policy issue is on the agenda of not only women's organizations but also states, which are mandated to address laws governing family relations and women's demands in this regard.

The case studies show how activism for the enactment of VAW laws has provided a strategic ground for the women's movement to coordinate and synergize advocacy around the reform of family laws. For instance, the passage of the Violence Against Persons (Prohibition) Act[14] in Nigeria was the outcome of years of activism, which took off from a legislative advocacy workshop on VAW in 2001, held in Abuja. After the workshop, the Legislative Advocacy Coalition Against Violence Against Women (LACVAW), comprised of fifty local and international organizations and individuals, lobbied for a National Bill prohibiting VAW. The coalition created a broad-based support for the bill through strategic partnerships and alliances with other like-minded actors, including federal agencies and lawmakers. The bill was only finally adopted in 2015, revealing the tolerance for VAW in society.

Lebanese feminists saw sectarian pluralism as a major obstacle in their struggle for gender equality and demanded a uniform civil code to counter the country's social fragmentation. In 1996, the President proposed the optional civil family law and presented it to the cabinet in 1998. The proposed bill had to be shelved indefinitely due to bitter opposition from almost all communities (Joseph 2000; Maktabi 2013). Because the many initiatives to reform the personal status systems have proved to be futile to date, the authors of the Lebanon case study suggest that concentrating efforts to reform the 2014 domestic violence law may, in the long run, be more strategic in dismantling the patriarchal family.[15]

With the exception of Iran, all of the countries reviewed are party to CEDAW. The Convention is used by women's organizations to hold their governments accountable to their treaty obligations, to sensitize the population by disseminating the CEDAW Committee's country recommendations, and to pressure governments to domesticate national laws to comply with international standards. That said, the fact that most states have entered extensive reservations to the Convention, mainly concerning the provisions with respect to family and citizenship, impacts its effective applicability (Arat 2003). Feminists, therefore, launched parallel campaigns aimed at both the removal of the reservations and amendment of discriminatory laws. The case studies offer a rich account of how ratification of CEDAW gave thrust to women's reform initiatives in the States Parties.[16] Women's engagement with the international gender-equality regime has also challenged feminist skepticism towards engagement with the state, as the state and its apparatuses became important sites for women to rally for compliance with international law.

For instance, the breakthrough in the adoption of Brazil's legendary Maria da Penha Law (2006) on VAW was largely achieved by framing women's advocacy campaigns within international instruments: particularly significant were the demands for the Brazilian government to comply with the CEDAW Committee's recommendations. Similarly, the feminist campaigns in India around sexual assault and dowry deaths – both of which were also campaigns for legal reform – owe their success in part to CEDAW.[17] In 1999, the Supreme Court of India cited provisions from CEDAW, the Beijing Declaration, and Article 2 of the Universal Declaration of Human Rights (UDHR) in its judgment on two cases and interpreted the statutory provisions in favor of equal status of the mother and father vis-à-vis a minor child. In 2004, the Turkish Parliament amended the equality provision of the Constitution in line with CEDAW. The amendment introduced a wording on "state responsibility" to ensure equality in practice. The principal of "positive discrimination" as demanded by women's groups was, however, left out.

The initial meeting of 120 women's organizations from seventeen countries in Rabat, spearheaded by the Moroccan feminist organization Association Démocratique des Femmes du Maroc (ADFM), resulted in the 2006 Equality without Reservations Campaign, launched to pressure governments to lift CEDAW reservations, harmonize national laws with its principles, and adopt its Optional Protocol. In 2011, the King withdrew Morocco's reservations to Articles 9(2) and 16; subsequently, the government removed the remaining reservations.

The absence of a sovereign state in Palestine to be held accountable for compliance with international standards makes it a peculiar case for feminist activism. Prior to 2012, due to its international status, the Palestinian National Authority was not entitled to sign and ratify international human rights instruments, yet it unilaterally committed itself to abiding by international law, including CEDAW. This galvanized the women's movement, since they could now use CEDAW as a legal reference point in formulating their proposals for reform of the personal status system.

Despite the many success stories of how CEDAW and other international/regional human rights mechanisms facilitated national standard setting in gender equality, international law concerning women's rights has been highly contested.

The shift towards culture-based identity politics and the growth of religious extremist movements in the post-Cold War era unleashed new assaults on the women's human rights movement. On the other hand, the national security paradigm, with its militarist and nationalist overtones, that gained prominence after 9/11 reduced the enthusiasm and willingness of states to comply with international human rights obligations.

In the case of Iran, after the 1979 Islamic Revolution, human rights became a point of divergence between the regime and the international community on the one hand, and the more liberal-minded Iranians on the other. The new rulers adhered to a cultural relativist position and opted to distance themselves from universal human rights standards, which they defined as Western in nature. This excerpt from an editorial in the *Tehran Times* (6 February 1996), in connection with the visit of the UN Special Rapporteur on the Situation of Human Rights in the Islamic Republic of Iran, reflects the mindset of the officials in Iran at the time:

> Criteria for human rights are respected by everyone; however, any judgment on the situation of human rights in a country should be harmonious with the nation's culture, religion and traditions. The special envoy should not surrender to direct and indirect pressures from the United States and other Western powers whose aims are to use human rights as leverage against Iran.
>
> *(Karabell 2000: 212)*

This is a common sentiment of Islamists and other hard-liners, who, joined by their female allies, have launched an offensive against CEDAW, which they perceive as a coercive and alien encroachment on the family and culture. In the aftermath of the Arab Spring, this discourse became particularly pronounced in eroding the influence of international human rights mechanisms. For instance, in Egypt, Salafi Members of Parliament made a strong appeal to withdraw from the Convention.

While these may appear as extreme examples, the reality remains that in all societies, cultural/religious discourses, strongly upheld by centers of power as part of their political strategy, enjoy popular support – including by some women – either through democratic consensus, repression, or manipulation. Therefore, while gender equality may be a common goal for women at large, there are often irreconcilable differences as to what this means and how it is to be achieved among different women's groups.

On the other hand, beyond culture and religion, legal pluralism often marks minority/majority relations, where personal status laws acquire a communal meaning and become a source of community mobilization for autonomy. In this respect, intertwined with communal, religious, and national concerns, feminist advocacy for legislative change takes place within a highly contested terrain, replete with tension at several levels: between human rights and cultural discourses, individual rights and group rights (as reflected in legal pluralism, e.g., in India and Lebanon), and among various women's groups. However, this complex web of power relations and competing discourses is not static and fixed; it comprises socio-political constructs in a constant state of reconciliation and realignment, requiring feminists to constantly modify their strategies accordingly.

So far, relatively liberal political environments have provided an enabling environment for feminists to use international law as the primary bargaining tool to mobilize support from civil society, including diverse women's groups, and to hold their governments accountable to their treaty obligations.[18] Under more contested and restrictive environments, women, either as a strategic choice or out of conviction, chose to advocate from within established religious norms and values. However, it has been argued that there is a limit to how much feminists can achieve by interpretation of religious texts and that over-reliance on such approaches to reform can "privilege what is outlined in religious texts as the only legitimate framework for claiming rights" (quoted in Sezgin 2013: 217).

Moroccan feminists led a twelve-year campaign for the reform of the highly discriminatory *Mudawana*, by incorporating a progressive reading of religious texts through a broad-based coalition. However, the process was highly polarized:

> support for and opposition to the proposed reforms reached a climax on 12 March 2000, when one march that gathered between 40,000 and 100,000 people supported women's rights, while between 100,000 and 200,000 persons protested against anti-Islamic influences in another counter-march.
>
> *(Maktabi 2013: 292)*

The stalemate was resolved with the endorsement of the new law by the King, who argued that it is consistent with the Sharia.

The success of the Moroccan family law reform has been attributed to three factors: collective feminist action in coalition building, a favorable government, and a global environment that was conducive to women's rights (Moghadam and Roudi-Fahimi 2005: 6). The Moroccan family law of 2004, despite its limitations, is significant in signaling a shift in the balance of power between the attitude in patrilineal tribal networks and state authority in favor of the goals of the women's movement. It also demonstrated that change is possible through collective action in a rather conservative environment.

Given the difficulty of a feminist or human rights-based debate in Iran after the 1979 Revolution, the women's movement strategized from within a religious paradigm by challenging the conservative interpretations of Islamic jurisprudence and engaging with religious scholars. They have, at the same time, also focused on ways to minimize the impact of discriminatory laws on women and engaged in raising awareness programs among both women and men. Inspired by the Moroccan experience, the One Million Signatures Campaign, launched in favor of wholesale family law reform in Iran, was particularly effective in educating women and men about their rights and the limitations of existing laws, as well as in encouraging civil society to pressure the state for reforms.

Where family law is intertwined with multi-ethnic, multi-religious community tensions, feminist advocacy encountered both external and internal confrontations.

For Indian feminists, the debate around the UCC, dating back to the early period of independence, was particularly contentious as it sparked unrest, not so much as a matter of women's rights but rather as an instrument of national unity, sidelining gender concerns. In this respect, the upsurge of communal tensions over the Supreme Court decision on the Shah Bano case (which granted Bano the right to maintenance from her ex-husband) are illustrative of how communal politics are implicated in personal status law, where communal difference finds its ultimate expression. The Muslim community perceived the judgment as an encroachment on Sharia law. The reactions prompted the government to begin parliamentary procedures that overturned the Supreme Court's decision. This case was a milestone in the Muslim women's search for justice and a marker of the political battle over personal law.

The heightening of the crisis in communal politics in the 1980s due to the politicization of family law and the increasing association of the UCC with Hindu hegemony witnessed the hijacking of gender concerns into other realms. Shifts and fragmentations within the women's movement unfolded as the feminist secular consensus broke down. With collective feminist action hampered, negotiations with the system and feminist reform efforts necessarily took a distinctive route in each of the major religions. Nonetheless, despite the majority/minority contestations and Hindu majoritarianism with its specific effects on women's rights, especially from minority groups, the fact that Muslim women, from Shah Bano in the 1980s to Shayara Bano in 2016,[19] "have stood their ground both against Muslim orthodoxy and against Hindutva politics is one that shines the torch on the strength of feminisms in India even in times of siege" (Chapter 4, this volume: 66).

Palestinian feminists, who advocated for a secular state and implementation of a civil personal status law as a long-term goal, have also reported that in the short term there were moments of shift from a secular to a compromising approach in order to achieve their goal, particularly when a coalition with other women's groups is concerned.

Claims for women's universal human rights as a bargaining tool fared better in situations where the state discourse was more receptive towards global and regional human rights institutions, such as in Brazil, which actively engaged with both the UN as well as the Inter-American Human Rights system. The feminist movement in Brazil, largely inspired by its participation in the UN International Women's Year and the First World Conference on Women held in Mexico City (1975), engaged in a long process of advocacy for women's rights that resulted in the recognition of equal rights between men and women in the 1988 Constitution.

According to the Brazil case study, the feminist movement played a key role in countering public and private patriarchy under both dictatorship and democracy. From 1975 until the adoption of the 1988 Constitution (denoting the return to democracy), the feminists, motivated by the human rights paradigm, were a driving force for the changes in discriminatory legislation and the creation of institutional mechanisms for women's advancement. In this context, feminists organized nationwide meetings and forged alliances with various women's groups and deputies to generate a broad-based consensus in support of their agenda, which included a demand that political parties integrate a women´s rights perspective in their programs. According to Pitanguy (Brazil case study), feminist advocacy for women's rights in Brazil had a particularly strong political character in the 1980s, and, as early as 1976, a group of feminists presented Congress with a proposal for amendments to the Civil Code to ensure equality between men and women in matters of family life, which finally materialized in 2002.

International law was also a primary bargaining tool for the Turkish women's movement, which emerged following the transition to democracy after the 1980 military coup that crushed all democratic forces and civil associations in the country. In 1986, seven thousand signatures were collected and submitted to the Parliament in the campaign for the implementation of CEDAW. This was the first mass action since the return to civilian rule in 1982, which led the Turkish feminist Şirin Tekeli to depict the feminist movement as a pioneer in Turkey's democratization (Tekeli 1990: 20).

The Turkish case illustrates how feminists skillfully seized the enabling environment created by Turkey's European Union (EU) accession process to push for their agenda to eliminate discriminatory laws. Focus on legal reform and monitoring of the implementation of CEDAW had already enabled the feminists to build coalitions with other women's groups, which captured public discourse with a vibrant debate on women's rights. Through the media and dialogue with parliamentarians, they highlighted the inherent contradictions of existing laws vis-à-vis Turkey's international obligations, including the requirements under the EU accession process. The removal of the concept of "head of household" and the introduction of an equal property regime in the reformed Civil Code (2002) and recognition of sexual crimes in the new Penal Code (2005) as crimes against women's bodily integrity (as opposed to crimes against public morality) are milestone achievements of feminist advocacy, signifying a deviation from construing women as a legal category in need of protection, thus penetrating the essence of patriarchal relations.

As in the case of feminists in Brazil, the Turkish women's movement drew its legitimacy from fostering solidarity through a coalition of diverse and autonomous women's groups and engagement with the global feminist agenda and gender equality regimes. Regrettably, as aforementioned, the enabling environment that led to a successful reform process is now encountering backlash and political authoritarianism, which is systematically co-opting and marginalizing the feminist agenda and activism, confining civil space in general.

Before closing this section, a brief revisit of the Lebanon case is warranted. As indicated, women's status in Lebanon is bound by fifteen separate personal status codes, making feminist advocacy for family law reform a tricky and risky business. Women's independent legal subjecthood is seriously undermined by the existence of multiple jurisdictions that grant autonomy and power to religious communities. The religious diversity that safeguards the legitimacy of religious pluralism and social heterogeneity at the same time limits the maneuvering space for autonomous feminist activism to pressure for change in family law (Maktabi 2013: 303).

The stalemate in the area of reforming personal status laws places Lebanon behind several Middle East/North Africa countries, measured on various indicators. For example, according to a Freedom House study, Lebanon ranks fifth with respect to non-discrimination and access to justice, coming after Tunisia, Morocco, Algeria, and Egypt (Nazir and Tomppert 2005: 25). Whereas, as Maktabi argues (2013), "Lebanese women enjoy the most extensive forms of freedom of expression in the Middle East, thanks to ease of media exposure and transnational networking" (ibid.: 305). This paradoxical situation of women's status in Lebanon is a striking testimony to the fact that there is no "one size fits all" approach to feminist agency and women's activism.

Concluding comments

The review of the case studies has exposed the dialectical nature of family law reform across regions, marking both victory and backlash for women. They also provide evidence that, despite the regressive trends, feminist agency and demand for equality and justice have become firmly entrenched in public discourse and the public policy landscape. The arduous terrain in which women's human rights struggle takes place has necessitated feminists to adopt diverse strategies across time and space, demonstrating that there is no easy prescription that can be applied or replicated in all contexts. Nonetheless, the feminist law reform initiatives reviewed in the case studies offer lessons learned and insight for the global family law reform campaign:

- Family laws, whether grounded in religious or secular sources, are social and political constructs; therefore they can be changed. Since the meaning and the impact of changes in law as well as the emerging new challenges cannot be fully predetermined, monitoring and scrutiny mechanisms need to be factored into advocacy strategies.
- The secular and religious dichotomy of law can be a fallacy; secular family laws do not presume the equality of women – they can be as patriarchal as laws based on religious sources. That said, the case studies reveal that where extensive reforms of personal status law at the initial period of adoption introduced new parameters to family relations, the patriarchal family experienced a rupture that opened greater legal space for the individual and for women's "emancipation."[20] On the other hand, where law adoption conformed to pre-existing family norms, patriarchal control over women became reinforced, and, in some cases, codification resulted in loss of select rights previously available to women. Laws grounded in religion, by casting an additional layer of "divinity" to the patriarchal foundation of laws, make reform initiatives more difficult.
- Therefore, although a secular legislative system is not an end in itself, it is a requisite for establishing an "equality before the law" principle, which provides a viable legal point of entry for women to seek equal rights as citizens. In this respect, in a secular legal regime, feminists can garner considerable success

by using equality provisions of national constitutions and international human rights law to challenge laws and practices that inherently violate the principle of equality before the law.

- Embracing universal human rights norms while framing gender equality from a progressive reading of religious texts can potentially contribute to coalition building and can diffuse opposition. Such approaches, however, need to be handled with vigilance, since in the long run they may be self-defeating and reinforce the religious framework as the only legitimate source of rights, thus creating an impasse for feminist advocacy and women's rights.

- Legal pluralism marks minority/majority relations, and under this system, family laws acquire a communal meaning. Even when such regimes offer a secular remedy to enable individuals to opt out of the communal track, communal pressure may inhibit a woman from seeking remedy from civil institutions. Under such circumstances, feminist advocacy is faced with the task of building internal consensus within a particular community, risking a deviation from feminist and universal human rights norms – at least in the interim. At the same time, in terms of its demonstration of a wider praxis for feminist legal reform, the indispensability of plural legal spaces and the use of each space to gain more ground for women can be a viable strategy for women's movements.

- Judicial activism has had important impact on case law and court rulings, which in turn have played a role in challenging laws related to marriage, divorce, custody, alimony, etc., prompting significant legislative amendments. A two-track advocacy strategy, entailing both legislative and judicial reform, will not only mutually reinforce each track but will also increase the strategy's impact.

- Reform advocacy initiated by feminists through building coalitions among diverse women's groups and civil society at large and positioning their movement above political party lines will not only be empowering in itself but will also give greater legitimacy to women's demands vis-à-vis the wider society and state authorities. Allies both within and outside the state are key to mobilizing support and diffusing opposition.

- Law reform campaigns that are carried out in isolation from social, political, or cultural contexts will rarely achieve their objectives; therefore, effective strategies require a multi-pronged approach that includes influencing public discourse, gaining allies from among different stakeholders, and building coalitions.

- In this respect, sensitizing mass media and the public discourse on matters related to law, women's human rights, and the state's obligations has exponential benefits, as it will influence the mind-sets of politicians, decision-makers, judges, and law enforcers, as well as ordinary citizens, thus contributing to democratization and rupturing of patriarchal culture. In other words, by engaging in public debate while advocating for legislative change, women's movements are likely to stimulate socio-cultural transformation alongside legal reform.

- Establishing links with international and transnational women's organizations and networking around common issues can contribute to building a conducive international environment and influence national-level public debate and state receptiveness to feminist law reform advocacy.

- Top-down initiatives may have limited impact in their application and run the risk of pacifying feminist agency. However, women-friendly reforms, even if top-down, have proven to be instrumental in opening new space for individual rights and freedoms, which feminists have appropriated in furthering their interests.
- Feminist advocacy to expand civil rights has greater leverage in relatively homogenous settings with unitary court systems (Morocco), as opposed to plural courts catering to multi-religious communities (Lebanon).
- The production and use of sex-disaggregated data are effective advocacy tools for feminists in making women's oppression and its connection with wider socio-economic factors visible and in formulating policy-specific goals and recommendations.
- Where intervention in family laws may prove to be futile, using other laws or civil remedies provides an opportunity to get around the resistance.
- Last but not least, change is not linear but dialectical, requiring revisiting and modifying strategies for change.

The case studies reviewed illustrate the complex web of patriarchy, state, and community relations, as well as competing discourses that circumscribe feminist activism in the struggle to combat violence through law reform, clearly demonstrating that law is a contested site. Therefore, upholding the cultural legitimacy of universal human rights norms while confronting hegemonic cultural/religious discourses remains a challenge for feminist scholarship and activism to achieve equality in laws.

The fragmentations posed by identity politics, the distance of the human rights system to the lives of ordinary people, the popular appeal of cultural/religious discourses, the declining state commitment to human rights, and the backlash provoked by the very advances women have made over the past decades have challenged the legitimacy of universal human rights discourse, thus confronting feminists and women's human rights defenders with some pertinent questions:

> How can the universality of women's rights be best defended and implemented given that the reality of life is based on a variety in moral rules and social institutions? Are human rights universally applicable or, alternatively, are there legitimate cultural divergences from human rights norms? Are universal rights and particular cultures irreconcilable with respect to achieving gender justice?

These are complex questions, and answers can range from absolutist relativism that religion is the only source of a valid moral norm, to absolutist universalism that culture is irrelevant to universal human rights. Today, both positions continue to be defended by women's groups, as well as others. Some of the arguments in which culture and religion are invoked against the universalism of women's rights largely belong to hegemonic centers of power; however, others raise legitimate questions, both epistemologically and ethically, that will continue to occupy feminist theory and praxis (Ertürk 2012). The challenge is to avoid the relativist trap in embracing difference and the diverse cultural/religious positioning of women.

Notions of difference need not be a legitimizing factor of inequality, they should be encompassed by, rather than replace, notions of equality (Yuval-Davis 2006: 281). Absolutist approaches from all camps overlook the politics of resistance, dialogue, and cooperation, which have been inherent to feminist activism inspired by the universal human rights paradigm. Clearly, universal human rights law in itself cannot enable feminist advocacy to achieve equality in law. There are inherent limitations on the ability of external sources to compel change within a given society. Nonetheless, the fact that the international community of states continues to engage in multi-lateral diplomacy grounded in universally agreed norms, including the human rights framework, is encouraging for the defense of universality of human rights values, which is a cultural resource that has not been fully utilized in confronting hegemonic cultural representations.

The pluralism in women's voices, although divisive at times, provides the condition for the construction of a universalism of human rights that accommodates diversity not only between but also within societies, manifestations of which will naturally be context-specific. However, once institutionalized, human rights norms themselves may constitute a political interest that transforms power balances and legitimates the sovereignty of the individual, thus, increasing the demand for broad-based democratization and justice. This will celebrate culture and religion as people's domain that is compatible with human rights culture.

Feminist theory and praxis are at a juncture of a new vision that must respond to these challenges and convincingly integrate into its vision both the moral and the legal force inherent in international human rights law. The interconnectedness of women's resistance movements accounts for the success achieved thus far by the global women's movement in changing national and international laws over the past decades. With the global encroachment of neo-conservative, right-wing politics on women's rights, the force of this interconnectedness needs to be revitalized and the transnational feminist alliances across borders be reaffirmed. Only then can a feminist jurisprudence be realistically envisaged and defended.

In the meanwhile, feminists must insistently assert that if gender equality is an obligation under internationally agreed treaties and upheld in national constitutions, then it should be prioritized over any other legal provision that attempts to rule otherwise.

Notes

1 For a background discussion on the WLP project as well as the case studies, see the Introduction to this volume. Also included in this volume are interviews with feminist activists in Egypt, Jordan, and Morocco.

2 Htun and Weldon (2011) developed a family law index based on thirteen indicators to measure male/female equality in family laws and rank countries accordingly; scores range from 0 (no equality) to 13 (full formal equality). Eight of the case studies/interviews in this volume are included in Htun and Weldon's study, with varying scores: Brazil 13, Turkey 12, Morocco 10, India and Nigeria 9, Jordan 2, and Egypt and Iran 1.

3 For instance, in Turkey, with the termination of the Caliphate, religion was divorced from the nation and subjugated to state authority; whereas, in large parts of the Muslim world, religion played a critical role in the anti-colonial mobilization and state building. Today, identity politics and extremist discourses are embedded in religion.

4 This is not to deny the earlier history of women's agency. Each country has its story of women at the forefront of independence, nation building and struggle for rights – a story that rarely receives recognition in official history accounts and is often sidelined, suppressed, or co-opted for other priorities.

5 For a more nuanced discussion of family law adoption, see Sezgin (2013).

6 The *Filipino* Code granted the husband the right to kill his adulterous wife; whereas, male adultery went unpunished. Although in 1991, the Superior Tribunal of Justice annulled this double standard, the norm remained firmly ingrained in Brazil's cultural consciousness for years.

7 The *Tanzimat* (reorganization) reforms undertaken in the empire in the late eighteenth century also included the adoption of the 1876 *Mecelle*, Ottoman personal status law, which was the first attempt to codify and standardize Islamic law. *Mecelle* served as the basis of the 1917 Ottoman family law.

8 This constitutes the first secular code regulating personal status in a Muslim country that outlawed polygamy and gave women equal rights to inheritance, marriage, divorce, and child custody.

9 France and Switzerland lagged behind these countries in women's suffrage, which in France was 1944 and in Switzerland, 1971; for Brazil and Turkey, it was 1932 and 1934 respectively.

10 The Ottoman Empire (1300–1923) was made up of confessional communities called the *millet*, each governed by their own laws and leaders. *Tanzimat* reforms replaced the *millet* system with European-style secularist governments. Its legacy can be traced in successor states of the Empire.

11 For discussions on Islam and Muslim women, see Afkhami and Friedl (1997); Arat (2003); Mayer (2012); and Welchman (2007).

12 On 14 July 2017, the Committee adopted GR 35 on "gender-based violence against women," updating GR 19.

13 Feminists use "intersectionality" to describe the complex reciprocal attachments and conflicts that confront women both as individuals and collectivities seeking to "navigate" among structures of race, gender, and class, at the intersections of which they face multiple forms of violence (see Cabrera 2010).

14 The bill was rejected in 2003, mainly owing to the women-focused title and provisions; in 2008, the bill was renamed the Violence Against Persons Prohibition Bill.

15 The following custody case (cited in Maktabi 2013: 299) is revealing: in 2006, a civil court decision concerning a mother's appeal for the custody of her child over-ruled the verdict by a Sunni religious court. This case-based example demonstrates how civil courts, by using new laws or new interpretations of existing laws, can get around resistant personal status systems.

16 Regional instruments complement CEDAW: the Maputo Protocol (Protocol to the African Charter on Human and People's Rights on the Rights of Women) in Senegal and Nigeria; Istanbul Convention on VAW and the European Convention on Human Rights (ECHR) in Turkey; and the Convention of Belem do Para and the Inter-American Human Rights System in Brazil. The Inter-American and European Human Rights Courts set significant precedence for women's rights globally. In this respect, two cases are particularly noteworthy. The first is the landmark decision of the former in the *Velásquez Rodríguez v. Honduras* (1988) case, which is the first application of the "due diligence" standard that holds states accountable for violations of women's rights perpetuated by non-state actors (Ertürk 2006). The second is the ruling of the latter in 2009 on a domestic violence case (*Opuz v. Turkey*) brought against the Turkish government for failing to protect a woman from the fatal attack by her husband. The court found that Turkey violated three articles of the ECHR.

17 India signed CEDAW in 1980, but it did not go into force until 1993.
18 Authoritarian/militarist governments also promote pro-women measures, as part of their project to strengthen their control over religious/ethnic centers of power.
19 Shayara Bano was one of five Muslim women to petition the Indian Supreme Court in 2016 to rule on the constitutionality of triple-*talāq*, which allows a Muslim husband to divorce his wife unilaterally by saying "*talāq*" three times (*Shayara Bano v. Union of India*, Writ Petition (Civil) 118 of 2016).
20 Women's "emancipation" refers to the granting of rights to women from above, as part of a broader socio-political project, which is also referred in the literature as "state feminism." While emancipatory measures provide women with equal access to available legal rights, full liberation enables women with the choice of what to do with given rights, including changing them. See, for example, Molyneux (1985) and Kandiyoti (1987).

References

Afkhami, Mahnaz and E. Friedl (eds.) (1997) *Muslim Women and the Politics of Participation*, Syracuse: Syracuse University Press.

Arat, Zehra F. K. (2003) "Promoting Women's Rights against Patriarchal Cultural Claims: The Women's Convention and Reservations by Muslim States," in D. Forsythe and P. McMahon (eds.) *Global Human Rights Norms: Area Studies Revisited*, Lincoln, NE: Nebraska University Press: 231–251.

Cabrera, Patricia M. (2010) *Intersectionalities: A Review of Feminist Theories and Debates on Violence against Women and Poverty in Latin America*, London: Central American Women's Network (CAWN).

Ertürk, Yakın (2006) *The Due Diligence Standard as a Tool for the Elimination of Violence against Women, Report of Special Rapporteur on Violence against Women, its Causes and Consequences*, UN Commission on Human Rights (E/CN.4/2006/61).

——— (2012) "Culture versus Rights Dualism: A Myth or a Reality?" *openDemocracy 50.50*. 25 April, www.opendemocracy.net/5050/yakin-erturk/culture-versus-rights-dualism-myth-or-reality.

——— (2016) *Violence without Borders: Paradigm, Policy and Praxis Concerning Violence Against Women*, Washington, DC: Women's Learning Partnership.

Htun, Mala and S. Laurel Weldon (2011) "State Power, Religion and Women's Rights: A Comparative Analysis of Family Law," *Indiana Journal of Global Legal Studies*, Vol. 18, Issue 1: 145–185.

Jain, Devaki (2005) *Women, Development, and the UN: A Sixty Year-Quest for Equality and Justice*, Bloomington, IN: Indiana University Press.

Joseph, Suad (2000) "Civic Myths, Citizenship, and Gender in Lebanon," in Suad Joseph (ed.) *Gender and Citizenship in the Middle East*, Syracuse, NY: Syracuse University Press: 3–32.

Kandiyoti, Deniz (1987) "Emancipated but Unliberated? Reflections on the Turkish Case," *Feminist Studies*, Vol. 13, No. 2: 317–338.

Karabell, Zachary (2000) "Iran and Human Rights," in David P. Forsythe (ed.), *Human Rights and Comparative Foreign Policy*, Tokyo: United Nations Press: 206–223.

Maktabi, Rania (2013) "Female Citizenship in the Middle East: Comparing Family Law Reform in Morocco, Egypt, Syria and Lebanon," *Middle East and Governance*, Vol. 5: 280–307.

Mayer, Ann E. (2012) *Islam and Human Rights: Tradition and Politics*, 5th ed., Boulder, CO: Westview Press.

Moghadam, Valentine M. and F. Roudi-Fahimi (2005) *Reforming Family Law to Promote Progress in the Middle East and North Africa*, Washington, DC: Population Reference Bureau.

Molyneux, Maxine (1985) "Mobilization without Emancipation? Women's Interests, the State and Revolution in Nicaragua," *Feminist Studies*, Vol. 11, No. 2: 227–254.

Nazir, Sameena and Leigh Tomppert (eds.) (2005) *Women's Rights in the Middle East and North Africa: Citizenship and Justice*, Boulder, CO: Rowman & Littlefield Publisher, Inc.

Sezgin, Yüksel (2013) *Human Rights under State-Enforced Religious Family Laws in Israel, Egypt and India*, Cambridge: Cambridge University Press.

Snyder, Margaret (2006) "Unlikely Godmother: The UN and the Global Women's Movement," in Myra Marx Ferree and Aili Mari Tripp (eds.) *Global Feminism: Transnational Women's Activism, Organizing, and Human Rights*, New York: New York University Press: 24–50.

Tekeli, Şirin (1990) "1980'ler Türkiyesi'nde Kadınlar" [Women in Turkey in the 1980s], in Şirin Tekeli (ed.), *Kadın Bakış Açısından 1980'ler Türkiye'sinde Kadın* (*Women in Turkey in the 1980s from a Woman's Perspective*), İstanbul: İletişim Publishing: 7–41.

Welchman, Lynn (2007) *Women and Muslim Family Laws: A Comparative Overview of Textual Development and Advocacy*, Amsterdam: Amsterdam University Press.

Yuval-Davis, Nira (2006) "Human/Women's Rights and Feminist Transversal Politics," in Myra Marx Ferree and Aili Mari Tripp (eds.) *Global Feminism: Transnational Women's Activism, Organizing, and Human Rights*, New York: New York University Press: 275–295.

3

BRAZIL

*Mariana Barsted, Leila Linhares, and
Jacqueline Pitanguy*

Introduction

This study summarizes the political process of expanding women's rights in
Brazil during the last three decades, when feminists have undertaken efforts to
change discriminatory family laws that allowed the naturalization and conceal-
ment of domestic violence, as well as impunity for perpetrators. It highlights
how changes in laws related to family issues were fundamental for the approval
of laws against gender-based violence (GBV). Other civil legislation, as well
as penal and labor legislation, that contributed to legitimize violence against
women (VAW), are also analyzed. The 1988 Constitution, rooted in equality between men and women, was a landmark in addressing VAW, affecting
women's rights at large.

Laws are deeply connected to political processes. The period covered in this
study includes a military dictatorship (1964–85) and democratization (1985–present).
Operating in these different political contexts, feminists used various strategies to
advocate for the change in discriminatory laws and were key actors in the expansion
of women's rights.

The transition to democracy in Brazil led to the creation of national mechanisms
responsible for the implementation of public policies and non-discriminatory laws.
The National Council for Women's Rights (CNDM), created in 1985 following
the Nairobi Forward Looking Strategies, was a crucial actor in abolishing discriminatory laws. Understanding that there is a synergy between the national and
international context, this study also describes the positive impact of International
Conventions, Treaties, Declarations, and Plans of Action of the UN Conferences
and CEDAW Recommendations concerning family relations and VAW on the
legislative advances that occurred in Brazil.

National context and historical foundations of legal discrimination against women

Brazil is a federative republic and a secular state since its 1891 Constitution.[1] However, there has always been tension between laicism and religion, with the Catholic Church, and more recently with evangelical churches, influencing the legislative, executive, and judiciary powers, particularly on issues related to family relations, and sexual and reproductive rights.

Brazil was colonized by Portugal between 1500 and 1822. Until 1888, its agricultural economy was based on slavery. This pattern of institutionalized violence took place in a context where the family model was rigidly patriarchal, in relation to women, children, and other family members.

After Brazilian independence, Portuguese legislation continued to be adopted, shaping social and moral values, and especially for private life, legitimizing male domination that included VAW. It is important to highlight a particularly discriminatory piece of this legislation, called the Filipino Code, that ascribed punishment for transgressions concerning moral life, domestic coexistence, and marital relations.

The first Brazilian Constitution (1824) after its independence from Portugal considered equality a general principle, although only men with economic resources could exercise political rights. The roles of women and men were distinct and rigidly hierarchical, with women seen as men's property. The crime of adultery was punished only against women, leaving men with full freedom for sexual relations outside marriage. This cultural value had long-lasting influence in jury courts. Until recently, with the argument of legitimate defense of honor, men who committed such crimes were acquitted. In 1991, due to a strong feminist advocacy movement, the Superior Tribunal of Justice rejected the use of this argument.[2]

Slavery was abolished in 1888, and the republican system, overthrowing the monarchy, was adopted in 1890. The republic was strongly influenced by positivist ideology and its Civil Code by the French Civil Code (Napoleonic Code), which kept women subordinate to men. Marriage was considered a sexual contract (Pateman 1988) in which women relinquished their freedom, their self-determination, and their bodies to their husbands' domination and direction. The first Republic Constitution (1890) declared that the state was secular and that unified national laws would apply to all of its citizens, including the legally recognized religious minorities.

The legitimation of VAW, and the legal, cultural, and social mechanisms that justified it, led to a domestic, private, male-dominated family environment. This pattern of masculine domination was often internalized by women, naturalized and rendered invisible by society. Rosa (2004) observes that behaviors apparently dictated by moral norms have often originated in legal orders, acquiring a moral content, even after the legal norms have been abolished.

The struggle for the recognition of women's citizenship rights gained strength at the beginning of the twentieth century, when suffragists started the first wave of feminism.[3] These pioneers expressed the demands of many Brazilian women who, since the nineteenth century, through a feminist press, demanded the right to education, equality in the family, and political rights. Their victory occurred with the approval of the electoral law of 1932, which recognized equal political rights for men and women.

The suffragettes were able to include in the 1934 Constitution women's right to vote and the recognition of equality, without distinction of sex, race, and social origin, but they did not have the power to change the legislation on family, as expressed in the 1916 Civil Code.

Beginning in the 1950s, Brazil's predominantly rural society experienced industrialization, economic growth under the aegis of liberalism, an accelerated process of urbanization, expansion of the middle class, and greater participation of women in the labor market. The patriarchal pattern was, however, manifested in labor laws allowing husbands to terminate their wives' work contracts, if they considered it prejudicial to family care. In the 1960s, European feminist ideas arrived in Brazil, gaining socialist and democratic connotations in the context of the military dictatorship then in power.

To understand the magnitude of the legislative changes that have taken place in Brazil, it is necessary to review the feminist movement's struggle and compare its strategies of advocacy for women's rights before and after the 1988 Constitution, in terms of family rights and confronting gender violence.

Women's rights before and after the 1988 Constitution

In the last fifty years, Brazilian history has been marked by two distinct moments: the periods of dictatorship and democracy. In both contexts, the performance of the feminist movement stands out. Following the suffragettes, there was, in the 1970s and 1980s, a second wave of the feminist movement, which played a key role in raising women's issues as a central question of democracy while the country was under a dictatorship.

Feminists struggled against dictatorship and, at the same time, struggled to bring women's issues to the public arena, building alliances with other movements and associations, labor unions, and universities with an agenda that included civil rights, domestic violence, discriminatory legislation, equal pay in the labor market, social benefits, and reproductive health and rights, including the right to abortion (Pitanguy 2016; Barsted 1992). There was also an intellectual feminist production focused on issues related to women's rights. Pitanguy (2016) points out that in the early 1970s, feminist movements, organized in consciousness-raising groups, study centers, and unions, were demanding an expansive definition of democracy, the recognition of women's equality with men, and advancement of women's full citizenship rights. In the 1970s, Carmen da Silva, an important journalist and feminist, wrote a series of articles on behavioral changes, unequal gender relationships in the family, and the need for divorce regulation, which had great appeal to middle-class women.

Initially, feminist demands for women's rights received little support from men who fought against the dictatorship because they considered that focusing on women's rights weakened the general political struggle. The feminist agenda criticized the values in Brazilian society, which included the patriarchal model, the requirement of virginity only for women, and the pattern of family violence. Feminists denounced how these values justified domestic VAW and the collusion and indifference of the state and society to this problem. They demanded the repeal of discriminatory laws.

The UN International Women's Year, 1975, marked a new phase of the feminist movement. In Rio de Janeiro, feminist groups organized a seminar (considered the landmark of the second feminist wave in Brazil)[4] to discuss the role of women in Brazilian society. One of the speakers, Lélia Gonzales, also introduced the issue of racial discrimination against women in Brazil.[5] Encouraged by the UN International Women's Year and the First World Conference on Women in Mexico City, in which many Brazilian feminists participated, the women's movement made many proposals for legislative changes to implement gender equality.

Barsted (1992) points out that feminists knew how to detect the democratic gaps of a nation that was still under dictatorship, but which already allowed elections to state governments in 1982. Those elections marked the victory of democratic forces in Brazil's main states, opening an avenue for feminists with local executive power to demand the creation of institutional mechanisms, such as state-level councils, for the defense of women's rights.

Since the 1980s, the feminist movement in Brazil has had a strong political character, focused on advocacy for women's rights; as early as 1976, a group of feminist advocates presented Congress with a proposal for a change in the Civil Code, advocating for equality between men and women in matters of family life. The re-democratization of the country's political institutions and, internationally, the UN's call to create governmental mechanisms for the promotion of women (at the 1985 World Conference on Women, Nairobi) influenced Brazilian feminist advocacy.

During the 1980s, Brazil was one of the first countries to establish gender-focused public policy institutions, such as the National Council for Women's Rights (CNDM), the State Councils, the Special Police Stations to Attend to Women Victims of Domestic Violence (DEAMs, which encountered resistance from the official security apparatus), and the Integral Program on Women's Health. At the end of that decade, the first health center for VAW victims was established.

The intense relationship between the social movement and the state is due to a specific configuration of the feminist and women's movement in Brazil, developing a type of "republican" feminism (Sorj 2008) that emphasizes the claims of rights to the state and the demand for state intervention to correct gender inequalities.

The movement adopted a strategy on VAW of outreach to the media showing that the police failed to respond to cases of violence, leading to the death of victims and impunity of the aggressors. The strategy aimed to build bridges with the state and reach the population at large as an ally for creating the DEAMs. The DEAMs resulted from an alliance between women's groups, lawyers' associations, and professionals within the criminal justice system who demonstrated the need for changes in police and judicial responses to domestic violence cases.

Pitanguy (2011) noted that the creation of these institutional structures inaugurated another type of advocacy strategy, involving government agencies, women's movements, and civic organizations with consensus agendas, combining common strategies of action. Another important political advocacy action in the 1980s was the campaign "A Constitution to be worthy has to guarantee women's rights."

Pitanguy (CNDM's President, 1985–89) stated that the CNDM, in partnership with social movements, called on women to submit proposals for the new Constitution. Many proposals were put forward in a process that could be called "mass advocacy." At the end of 1986, the CNDM organized a large national meeting at the National Congress, which was attended by women from all regions of the country and during which the *Letter of Brazilian Women to the Constituents* was approved.

This is an example of an advocacy process based on women's proposals for a new normative order that could bring equality between men and women and that affirms the role of the state in implementing this legal framework. Based on this *Letter*, a long process of advocacy for women's rights was developed, resulting in advancement of the 1988 Constitution, which recognized equal rights between men and women and repudiated violence within the scope of family relationships.

To understand the legislative changes since 1988, it is important to know the content of the legislation that was in force prior to this time, especially in matters of family law, which reinforced practices of VAW. It is remarkable that in only thirteen years, between 1975 and 1988, feminism in Brazil had a huge impact, changing discriminatory legislation and creating institutional mechanisms for the promotion of women's rights. The changes explicitly endorsed in the 1988 Constitution were based on the paradigm of respect for human rights, especially women's human rights.

The situation of women in family law before and after the 1988 Constitution

During the period 1916–88, a Civil Code[6] reflecting sexist patriarchal values provided an ideological basis to control women's sexuality, legitimize sexual violence in marriage, and absolve men who murdered their wives and were defended with the argument of the legitimate defense of honor. It also reinforced the Penal Code's category of "honest" women (meaning those who met prevailing moral behavior standards). Sexual harassment at work was irrelevant, especially for domestic workers and women not aligned with political parties.

The 1916 Civil Code gave men exclusive power in conducting family matters. It also included the requirement of women's virginity before marriage, the possibility of the marriage's annulment if the lack of virginity was not communicated to the husband before marriage, the husband's right to administer the wife's estate, his right to have sex with his wife without her consent, and the right of parents to disinherit their daughters for dishonest behavior. The law treated women, when married, as "relatively incapable," with limited capacity for certain acts. It also dictated that only the father was the legal administrator of the children's assets, a function granted to women only in the absence or impediment of the husband. Women were also forced to adopt their husband's surname and needed their husband's permission to work.

This situation changed in 1962 through the Civil Statute of Married Women, "which provides for the legal status of married women" and recognized women as a collaborator in administering conjugal unity, allowing more decision-making power over their lives; however, men's predominance was not abolished nor was the patriarchal marriage's structure changed.

The Divorce Law created an important change in 1977, when the feminist movement was already a political actor demanding equality in civil laws and the right to divorce. Until the mid-1970s, legally separated women suffered a kind of "social exile" since they were not well accepted in society. The new law allowed legally separated couples the ability to divorce, which was allowed only once. Other changes through the Divorce Law were the end of the obligation to take the husband's family name and changes to the marital property regime, so that it became community property by default (if the spouses did not manifest a different property regime).

With the promulgation of 1988 Constitution, the legal status of women in Brazil underwent a profound change, with equal legal rights to men and women in the public and private spheres. This was made possible by the participation and actions of women's movements in the country's re-democratization process. Feminists emerged as political actors – questioning the power relations, inequalities, and hierarchies that define Brazilian society. Rights are not abstracted from power relations between classes, sexes, and races/ethnicities, particularly in countries like Brazil that are still marked by great inequalities. In this sense, access to the rights declared in the Constitution is still limited by these social characteristics.

The CNDM's 1986 *Letter of Brazilian Women to the Constituents* demanded that the new democracy democratize gender relations. To assure women's rights, the CNDM developed an efficient advocacy program in Congress, known as the "lipstick lobby," which encouraged the female federal deputies elected in 1986 to act together despite their differences, supporting the CNDM's agenda.[7]

This feminist advocacy allowed women to participate and have an innovative impact in the 1988 Constitution, bringing formal equality between men and women in rights and obligations under Article 5:

> All persons are equal before the law, without any distinction whatsoever, Brazilians and foreigners residing in the country being ensured of inviolability of the right to life, to liberty, to equality, to security and to property, on the following terms:
> I – men and women have equal rights and duties under the terms of this Constitution . . . .

Furthermore, Article 226 states that men and women shall exercise the rights and duties of marital union equally. It also states that the family shall enjoy special protection by the state; that religious marriage has civil effects, in accordance with the law; that the stable union between a man and a woman is recognized as a family entity and the law shall facilitate the conversion of such entity into marriage; and that the state shall ensure assistance to the family in the person of each of its members, creating mechanisms to suppress violence within the family.

By recognizing equal rights in the marital union, the 1988 Constitution eliminated from Brazilian law the historical legal discrimination against women and also extended the concept of the family, now also including the stable union as a family entity.

Also relevant are the advancement of international human rights law and the gradual accession of Brazil to these civilizing instruments (Trindade 2002; Lindgren 2001; Bobbio 1992). Although Brazil ratified CEDAW in 1984, the Brazilian state did not recognize all the parts regarding equality in family relations that were incompatible with the 1916 Brazilian Civil Code. These reservations, which were only withdrawn in 1994, were pointed out and denounced by feminists and by the CNDM, which claimed that the country should meet international human rights standards. Many Brazilian feminists participated in the UN World Conferences on Women, exchanging experiences and creating networks that would enable legislative change and pressure on the UN to elaborate CEDAW.

The most important change in legislation since the 1988 Constitution is the new 2002 Civil Code, which eliminated the hierarchies between men and women. The *pater familias* power of the 1916 Civil Code was replaced by the expression of family power to be provided equally by the spouses. It also provided for the duty of mutual assistance between spouses and assistance to children and the elderly.

The norms that regulate family rights are expressed in different legislation, especially in the 1988 Constitution (Articles 226–230), in the 2002 Civil Code (mainly Articles 1.511–1.783-A), in the Labor Code (in various Articles), in the 1940 Penal Code, and especially in Law 11.340/2006, known as "Maria da Penha Law," which addresses domestic VAW. The redefinition of gender roles and the increased participation of women in the labor market, leading to more economic autonomy (Bruschini et al. 2006: 65), were also of fundamental importance in the legal reorganization of family structures.

Sexual and reproductive rights before and after the 1988 Constitution

Since the 1980s in Brazil, two key agendas mobilized feminists in the defense of sexual and reproductive rights: the high incidence of maternal mortality and the criminalization of abortion.

In the early 1960s, the contraceptive pill, although under attack by the Catholic Church, allowed women the possibility of exercising sexuality free from reproduction. Women's main demands in this area were for gender equality, with regard to contraceptive and reproductive responsibilities, access to information, the means to control fertility, and sexual and reproductive freedom, without discrimination, coercion, or violence.

The 1988 Constitution recognized family planning as a right, placing reproduction in human rights parameters. Feminist and CNDM advocacy impeded the inclusion in the Constitution of the "right to life from conception," which would have ensured an absolute ban on abortion.[8]

The 1940 Penal Code, still in force, regulates the right to abortion (called "humanitarian abortion"), permitted only when the mother's life is at risk or the pregnancy is the result of rape. Until 1979, advertising contraceptive methods was prohibited. The recommendations of the UN Conferences of Cairo (1994) and Beijing (1995) to soften laws criminalizing abortion did not lead to modification of Brazilian legislation, which remains very strict (Barsted 1995: 44).

In 1994, in preparation for the Cairo conference, feminist organizations in Brazil, including CEPIA,[9] drafted a law regulating the 1988 Constitutional provision on the right to family planning. In 1996, the Family Planning Law, which regulated access to contraception, sterilization, and guaranteed healthcare, was approved.

Despite intense feminist mobilization for the right to abortion and despite the recommendations of the 1995 Beijing Platform for Action of the Fourth World Conference on Women, the conservatism of the legislative branch prevented any progress on this issue, even threatening setbacks, which would have led to a total ban on abortion.

Progress came when feminist health professionals at the Ministry of Health succeeded in establishing a technical norm (1999) to guide public hospitals when providing assistance to sexual violence victims, including the right to termination of pregnancy in case of rape, access to emergency contraception, and prophylaxis of sexually transmitted diseases (STDs) and HIV/AIDS. This technical standard was expanded in 2011 to include the right to humane care for women having abortions through the public health system.

In 2009, feminist civil society organizations, including CEPIA, developed a strong advocacy campaign to raise public awareness and support for the right to terminate a pregnancy of an anencephalic fetus. This victorious advocacy led, in 2012, to a Supreme Court (STF) ruling, allowing abortion in this circumstance. Since late 2015, women's movements in Brazil have been addressing the STF in the context of the Zika virus, demanding the legality of abortion for women who may have been affected by this epidemic, which can cause, among other problems, microcephaly of the fetus.

The difficulty in decriminalizing abortion signifies the maintenance of rigid control over women's bodies, which are still subjected to a patriarchal pattern that denies their autonomy.

The impact of family laws on coping with gender violence: penal laws

During three centuries of Portuguese colonization, husbands were able to invoke the right to kill their wives, alleging adultery. Although this was formally withdrawn from Brazilian penal law in 1840, Hermann and Barsted (1995) point out that this right still influences sexual moral standards in Brazil.

For a long time, Brazilian society considered that aggression against women in the home was a private affair concerning only family members. Feminists denounced this naturalization of domestic violence, affirming that "the private is political." In the late 1970s, the Brazilian press finally gave visibility to the murders of women by their husbands, who accused them of adultery and were acquitted by juries under the legitimate defense of honor argument. Feminist groups denounced this impunity, using the slogan "those who love do not kill." This campaign, with marches and graffiti, was successful, raising social consciousness on a theme scarcely debated until then.

In the early 1980s, feminist groups created voluntary services (called "SOS Women") to serve victims of sexual and domestic violence. They also started a dialogue with the governors for the creation of DEAMs, based on a feminist model that recommended that the heads of these police stations as well as the police officers should be women. At that same time, shelters for women who were victims of violence, and centers for psychological and legal orientation, were established.

Between 1985 and 1989, the CNDM reinforced the importance of these services, promoted national debates on VAW, and produced videos featuring opinion makers who spoke out against this violence. The *Letter of Brazilian Women to the Constituents* contained the demand for including the theme of violence in the Constitution's chapter on family.

The CNDM promoted the first quantitative survey on VAW, which demonstrated that VAW occurred mainly within the family. In 1989, a national survey conducted by the Brazilian Institute of Geography and Statistics demonstrated that while violence against men occurred in public spaces, for women, crimes occurred in the family, committed mainly by husbands, companions, or boyfriends.

VAW and murders of women continued to occur, and in many cases the perpetrators went unpunished. Feminist demonstrations spread throughout the country, especially protesting the persistence of the notion of the legitimate defense of honor.

By 1988, conservative forces gained strength within the executive branch. The CNDM was seen as too progressive, a menace to traditional values and economic interests. Its victories regarding the Constitution led to antagonism for its political role. After the popular mobilization engendered by democratization and despite a strong feminist movement defending the CNDM's independence, in 1989 conservative forces gained strength over the executive branch and the President weakened the CNDM, leading to the loss of resources and power. In the 1990s, feminist movements organized themselves into national networks and NGOs dialoguing with sectors of the legislative branch and beginning a feminist advocacy focused on the judiciary.

The 1990s saw several important positive steps in the struggle against VAW. In 1991, the Superior Court of Justice, in an historic decision, declared that the argument of legitimate defense of honor had no legal validity and was only an expression of the domination of men over women. In 1992, CEDAW General Recommendation number 12 included VAW in its text as discrimination. The UN approval of CEDAW Recommendation number 19, which expanded the definition of VAW and included Specific Recommendations for action steps, was of great importance strengthening the mobilization of feminists. The Declaration of the World Conference on Human Rights (Vienna, 1993) also considered VAW as a violation of human rights. Paragraphs 18 and 38 of the Declaration and its Program of Action called upon states to eliminate GBV and all forms of sexual abuse and exploitation.

The mobilization for the decriminalization of abortion and the denunciation of impunity in crimes against women could not be supported by a state that adhered to conservative proposals. The dialogue with the federal executive branch was only fully resumed in 2003, when the Secretariat of Policies for Women (SPM) reassumed the dialogue with the feminist movement.

In 1994, feminists applauded the work of the General Assembly of the Organization of American States (OAS) in approving the Convention on the Prevention, Punishment, and Eradication of Violence against Women known as the Convention of Belém do Pará, the content of which is legally binding on the countries that have ratified it. This Convention recognizes VAW as a violation of human rights and defines it as physical, sexual, and psychological violence committed in society, in family relations, and by the state and its agents. It gave enormous assistance to the drafting of the Maria da Penha Law and its approval by the National Congress.

Paradoxically, despite having been ratified by the Brazilian state, the Convention, in practice, was superseded by a national law (Law 9.099) that considered less serious crimes with punishment of less than two years. In these cases, the perpetrator was not arrested and was only obliged to pay a small compensation to the victim. This law encouraged reconciliation between the victim and the aggressor. The scope of this law for crimes of domestic violence was strongly criticized by feminists, who considered it incompatible with the 1994 Convention of Belém do Pará and the 1993 UN Declaration condemning VAW as a violation of human rights. In opposition to feminists, groups of criminal judges and jurists identified with the minimum criminal law theory aimed at eliminating imprisonment for many crimes.

Facing these criticisms, feminists began to mobilize to eliminate all the discriminations still in force in penal law, even after the 1988 Constitution. This included the important work of feminist advocates who analyzed, in the light of the Convention of Belém do Pará, all of the discriminations in the 1940 Penal Code. This involved a dialogue with the federal legislative branch, especially a dialogue with women parliamentarians and senators.

Largely under the 1988 Constitution and international human rights instruments ratified by the Brazilian state, all parts of the 1916 Civil Code related to family matters were repealed by eliminating existing legal discrimination against women. With regard to violence, the 1988 Constitution, in anticipation of Convention of

Belém do Pará, included an important paragraph to Article 226, which deals with the family. This paragraph, written with guidance from the women's movement, recognizes that:

> The family, which is the foundation of society, shall enjoy special protection from the State . . .
>
> § 8° The State shall ensure assistance to the family in the person of each of its members, creating mechanisms to suppress violence within the family.

Even if the constitutional text did not include an explicit reference to VAW, since the 1990s, the infra-constitutional legislation was gradually changed to reflect concern for gender violence. In this process, feminists examined the penal legislation, identifying the various discriminations, and indicating necessary changes. The feminists maintained constant dialogue with the legislative branch and obtained the support of institutions with impeccable social legitimacy, such as the Brazilian Bar Association. Thus, since 1994, the penal law has gradually been amended.[10]

By giving constitutional status to the international conventions and treaties of human rights, the 1988 Constitution is in line with international conventions and treaties recognizing equality between men and women in public and private life, including CEDAW and its Optional Protocol.

In December 1998, through Legislative Decree 89, Brazil's National Congress approved the recognition of the compulsory jurisdiction of the Inter-American Court of Human Rights in all cases concerning the interpretation or application of the American Convention on Human Rights. The same year, the Ministry of Health prepared the *Technical Guidelines for Prevention and Treatment of Injuries Resulting from Sexual Violence against Women and Adolescents*, which also regulates an article of the Penal Code that deals with legal abortion (pregnancy resulting from rape).

Since 2003, some feminist demands have been addressed. The SPM was created, with the status of a Ministry, it maintained a broad dialogue with women's movements, and it formulated Gender Equity Plans and the National Pact to Combat Violence against Women with the inclusion of feminist proposals from NGOs and women's conferences. In that sense, efforts to change penal legislation were successfully undertaken from 2003 to 2015.

In 2003, Law 10.778 established compulsory notification throughout the nation in cases of VAW that are seen in the health services, public or private. This law adopted the definition of VAW contained in the Convention of Belém do Pará.

In 2004, Law 10.886/04 recognized "domestic violence" as a crime, changing the wording of Article 129 of the Penal Code, which deals with personal injury, to include "injury . . . against a forebearer, descendant, sibling, spouse or partner, or one who lives, or has lived, or still lives with the victim, in conditions of domestic relations, cohabitation or hospitality with the victim," and to increase the penalty by one-third.

In 2005, Law 11.106 amended several articles of the Penal Code that were clearly discriminatory. It repealed articles that eliminated punishment for a rapist who married the victim or when the victim married another and did not require the continuation of the investigation or prosecution. It also repealed an article that considered only the abduction of an "honest" woman, a discriminatory expression, to be a crime. Similarly, adultery, which had been culturally used as an argument against women, was no longer considered a crime, and it was repealed.

Amending the Penal Code to a large extent was recommended when the CEDAW Committee reviewed the Brazilian National Report in 2004. A strong advocacy campaign, with significant participation and contributions by CEPIA, was carried out by a coalition of feminist organizations so that the Brazilian state complied with the CEDAW Recommendations. In 2006, an important breakthrough occurred with the adoption and entry into force of the Maria da Penha Law (Law 11.340), which included mechanisms of the Convention of Belém do Pará, considering VAW as a violation of human rights.

The Maria da Penha Law makes punishment more severe for aggressions against women when they occur in the domestic sphere. The legislation changes the Penal Code and makes it possible for offenders against women in the domestic sphere to be arrested *in flagrante delicto* or to have preventive detention ordered. It also increases the maximum detention time from one year to three years.

This law affirmed that, regardless the magnitude of the sentence, VAW is a violation of human rights, as established by the Vienna Declaration (1993) and the Convention of Belém do Pará (1994), and it created a national policy to address VAW. It also defined VAW (physical, sexual, psychological, moral, and patrimonial), created special courts for VAW, and established protective measures for women, including the removal of the offender from the home (if he lives with the woman), directing the offender to avoid contact with the woman, and the woman's right to defense counsel, among other measures of great importance for ensuring the victim's safety. This law does not allow conciliation mechanisms, such as mediation. The perpetrators are prosecuted and, if convicted, can be jailed. Passage of this law had wide social acceptance.

In the intense process of feminist advocacy for the drafting and approval of the Maria da Penha Law developing broad collaboration with key actors having political power was of particular importance. This process also led to a deepening of the public debate about gender violence and the limitations on women's exercise of their citizenship. This advocacy was an example of pressure on the state, which was silent regarding its legislation in relation to women's human rights.[11]

Also important for the success of feminist advocacy was Brazil's ratification of various international instruments for the protection of women's human rights, such as the Vienna Declaration of 1993, the Inter-American Convention on the Prevention, Punishment and Eradication of Violence Against Women "Convention of Belem do Pará" of 1994, and the CEDAW General Recommendations for Brazil, when presenting National Reports for this Committee.[12] Similarly, Brazil's recognition of the jurisdiction of the International Courts of Justice, especially the OAS Inter-American Human Rights Commission and the OAS Inter-American Court of Human Rights, had a strong impact.

The OAS Human Rights Commission accepted the denunciation by human rights organizations of the Brazilian government's failures in relation to prosecuting the two murder attempts on the pharmacist Maria da Penha Fernandes by her husband, who remained free. The Commission's ruling forced Brazil to support the victim, to prosecute the perpetrator, and to draft a law on domestic violence.

The shadow reports, drafted by feminists for the CEDAW Committee, made a decisive contribution as the Committee presented its recommendations to the Brazilian state for the elimination of all forms of discrimination against women, including the elimination of GBV and related legislation.

In her interview for this case study, Leila Barsted, one of the authors of the text used in drafting the Maria da Penha Law, noted that it was the result of a collective action coordinated by a feminist coalition of NGOs,[13] based on the sources mentioned above. This involved feminist women who worked as attorneys, judges, prosecutors, and public defenders and who analyzed Brazilian legislation, family violence laws in several Latin American countries, and Spain's 2004 VAW Act. For Barsted, an important factor in this advocacy process was the existence of reliable statistical data that indicated the high rates of VAW practiced in the context of family relations.

This feminist advocacy took place in a national political context that was favorable to human rights. Under pressure from feminists, the federal government's gender mechanism, the SPM, gained ministerial status in 2003 and began to act in line with feminist movements. In conjunction with the SPM, feminist groups and women parliamentarians drafted a proposal for a law on VAW that was discussed at public hearings throughout the country, strengthening the bill.[14]

The approval of this law had great social repercussions in the media and in different sectors of opinion, demonstrating its acceptance by society. However, it was challenged by some sectors of the judiciary and jurists defending the so-called "theoretical current of critical criminology,"[15] which considered it unconstitutional and discriminatory because it was directed only at women and it broadened the punitive perspective of law. Campos and Carvalho (2011) analyzed the positions of the defenders of critical criminology, presenting the paradigm of a feminist criminology.[16] For them, critical criminology had refused to listen to women, and, when it did, it didn't support or value the feminist project.[17]

Even in the face of these highly professional jurists' criticisms, feminist organizations undertook successful advocacy with the Supreme Court (STF) members, demonstrating that the law was in line with Articles 3 and 23 of CEDAW. In a 2012 unanimous decision based on feminist arguments, the STF considered the law constitutional, obliging the judges to comply.

Since the approval of the Maria da Penha Law in 2006, feminist organizations have worked to monitor its implementation by identifying successful cases, as well as difficulties and obstacles (see Pasinato 2011). However, VAW rates still remain high. This indicates the need for broader women's empowerment policies and efforts by the state and society, especially the educational system and the media, to take action to prevent VAW.

The growth in recent years of a conservative familial ideology endangers the implementation of the Maria da Penha Law. The idea of protecting the family, in this conservative perspective, gives lower priority to a woman's right to a life free of violence. In the National Congress, religious and conservative parliamentarians are presenting many proposals trying to weaken this legislation.[18]

To investigate VAW in Brazil and the allegations of the government's deficiencies in applying the legal instruments to protect women in situations of violence, parliamentarians who favored women's demands for laws relating to VAW established a Parliamentary Inquiry Commission (PIC) on VAW in 2013. Public hearings were held throughout the country, collecting data on VAW. The PIC produced an extensive report and presented a set of recommendations, including the elaboration of the Femicide Law.

Leila Barsted, who participated in advocacy for the approval of the Femicide Law, notes that drafting national laws on femicide was proposed in the OAS's Follow-Up Mechanism to the Belém do Pará Convention (MESECVI). In 2008, the MESECVI issued a declaration on femicide, defining it as the violent death of women on a gender basis, and recommended that OAS member countries incorporate the crime of femicide in their legislation.

In 2012 and 2014, government researchers demonstrated that murders of women in the domestic sphere had increased. The media's dissemination of these data fostered the national debate on femicide. These data, as well as the MESECVI-OAS Declaration on femicide, supported the advocacy actions of women judges and advocates from feminist organizations who submitted a proposal for a femicide law to the PIC.

This proposal was discussed at a meeting, held by the SPM, with feminist groups and with the participation of UN Women Brazil, and forwarded by the SPM to the National Congress, which in 2015 approved Law 13.104, the Femicide Law. An important contribution to the debate on femicide is found in the work of Mello (2016), which includes the experiences of several countries that had already adopted the characterization of this crime. In her interview for this case study, Leila Barsted noted that the final text of the law, under pressure from conservative groups, excluded the word "gender" from the original proposal. This law provides femicide as a qualifying circumstance of murder, with stricter punishment for the murderer.

The advancement of legislation to combat domestic VAW was made possible by the recognition in the 1988 Constitution of the equality between men and women in public life and in family relations. It also recognized the acceptance of international law for women's human rights protection. The family protection provided by the Constitution included protection against VAW within the framework of family relations. Thus, in addition to eliminating the monopoly of men's power in family relations, the Constitution also included the feminist proposal, from the *Letter of Brazilian Women to the Constituents*, in its Article 226, paragraph 8, regarding the state's obligation to create mechanisms to restrain violence within family relations. With this, the sphere of the family ceased to be a space for private justice, reinforcing the feminist slogan that "the private is political." Through successful feminist advocacy, led by the CNDM from 1986 to 1988, it was possible to make the state responsible for the inclusion of confronting VAW in the governmental agenda.

Labor and social security rights before and after the 1988 Constitution

Labor rights have been recognized since 1932 and were consolidated in 1943, targeting urban workers with a specific chapter on women's work. To protect women, the Consolidation of Labor Laws prohibited several activities for women, permitting them only for men.[19] Gradually, many of these impediments were removed, and, with the 1988 Constitution, women have the same opportunities as men, with labor protections for women relating only to reproductive health. In 1964, labor law was extended to rural working men and women.

In 1973, a law was approved that gave certain rights to domestic workers, most of whom are black women, and the 1988 Constitution expanded these rights. The Maria da Penha Law was innovative in obligating employers to maintain the employment of battered women for six months,[20] so that they cannot be punished twice: once via VAW and second with the loss of their jobs.

The law also provides for protection of domestic workers, the largest number of working women in Brazil. However, it is only since 2015 that they have begun to have the same rights as other workers.

Conclusion

Despite Brazil's being a secular country, since 1889 the hierarchical organization of the family has been influenced by religious conservative values that benefited men and relegated women to a subordinate role, restricted to the family. Domestic violence has long been naturalized as a "simple" private issue, where no one outside the family – neither the state nor its institutions – should get involved. The feminist movement has challenged this hierarchy and this "private family law" since the 1970s.

Brazil's political context during the period of re-democratization and, above all, since the return of democracy, allowed the feminist movement, through various strategies, to significantly expand women's rights. However, even during the dictatorship or less democratic contexts, the perception of gaps in state bodies was a way to introduce changes. An example of this was feminists' support for the deputy who introduced the Divorce Law in 1977 and their dialogue with the Ministry of Health for the launch of the Integral Program on Women's Health in 1982.

One of the most efficient strategies was the creation of the CNDM which, from a state power position, elaborated and developed a feminist agenda. A very important articulation took place between the CNDM and members of the National Congress, especially with women parliamentarians, who formed the so-called "lipstick lobby." The dialogue with the legislative branch provided an opportunity to follow up on the bills, reinforcing a practice of monitoring legislation and the feminists' initiatives with Parliament.

Also, producing and using statistical data on the situation of women, especially on VAW, reinforced and gave more legitimization to feminist demands, allowing greater visibility of VAW; in this sense, it made legislative change possible. The feminist movement's involvement and dialogue with the media, especially with opinion makers sensitive to the movement's agenda, throughout the campaigns allowed the feminists' demands to be known throughout society.

The feminists' expertise in following up on the legislative process, their intellectual production, and the importance of having legislation with women's voice and words and a clear understanding of the political conjecture were also a central finding of this study. Therefore, having female representation in the National Congress when the 1988 Constitution was approved was of fundamental importance.

The recognition of the women's movement by society and the state and the feminists' defense of the agendas of other social movements, such as the landless workers' movement, the black movement, and the ecological movement, were important in the formation of a great democratic alliance. The feminists' dialogue with other progressive sectors of society (e.g., the Brazilian Bar Association) led to strengthening democracy with a gender-based perspective, and to the articulation and negotiation of the various women's movements' overcoming disagreements and forming consensus.

The incorporation of international human rights instruments and International Courts in the 1988 Constitution is a landmark in Brazilian legislation, since it is the first time we have a specific Article (considered the most important Article in the 1988 Constitution) highlighting the isonomy principle (the concept of equality before the law of the citizens of a state) in all spheres of life.

In this sense, the feminist movement's expertise in instigating the OAS Human Rights Commission to examine the state's deficiencies in prosecuting the crime of attempted homicide against a woman was of great importance. Their presentation of shadow reports to CEDAW so that this Committee could pressure the Brazilian state to comply with the provisions of the Convention was similarly important.

The Brazilian legal system, in general, also incorporated the international principles of human rights. This recognition has important implications for Brazil's rights and laws, particularly civil law.

Changes in family legislation are fundamental to confronting violence as is the concept that gender equality can also influence the interpretation and implementation of law was more important than the feminists' ability to draft laws.

Another point to highlight is the importance of feminist ideas that have influenced women who are in state posts – in high-level executive, legislative, and legal positions, such as judges, public defenders, prosecutors, and the heads of Councils and Ministries for Women's Rights – who worked from within their institutions, promoting the struggle for gender equality along with the women's movement.

A remaining obstacle is the lack of gender formation in the curriculum of legal training and education, in general. It is also necessary to have instruments that enable the implementation of the law and dialogue with different levels of power and with different audiences.

CEDAW General Recommendation 33 highlights the obligation of states to provide access and all necessary means to ensure that women have access to justice. It has a detailed analysis of the meaning of access to justice for women, notes the main obstacles to be overcome in order to guarantee the rights of women and girls, and indicates ways to that end. Mechanisms to help shorten the distances that can affect women's human rights are of fundamental importance. Among them is the importance of investing in gender training for legal personnel to understand and act according to the needs of women when they appeal for justice, and to interpret the legislative advances correctly, removing prejudices and sexual values.

The importance of the 1988 Constitution as a milestone in advancing women's rights in Brazil is crucial. The current context presents many threats to women's human rights – especially the threat of retreat based on the many advances that have been made. These advances must be defended and appropriated by all, so that we do not let these setbacks destroy so many years of strong and courageous feminist advocacy in the fight against VAW.

It is important to remember that in Brazil the legislative process is not static, but is one full of tension between the growing conservative forces and women's rights advocates. This requires constant feminist advocacy to counter the strength of these conservative sectors that try to weaken women's achievements and curtail women's rights to a life free of violence. In this sense, the mobilization of women by a democratic, secular, and just society must be permanent.

This study highlights suggestions for the reform of family laws and points out that the affirmation of equality should be focused and that the recognition of the equality of "all" is not enough. It is necessary to include the word "woman" in all legislation; critical and attentive reading, with a gender perspective, of all the country's legislation is also necessary.

This study concludes that feminist strategies should be geared towards expanding national, local, and international communications with institutions and movements that advocate for a broad, inclusive secular democracy with respect to differences in gender, race, and ethnicity, among others, with a common agenda that contemplates intersectionality.

It is also essential to maintain a dialogue with the mainstream media, independent of the conservative forces, and to invest heavily in social media by publicizing the need to monitor legislation and public policies, observing and reporting problems that may indicate national and local setbacks.

It is critical to maintain dialogue with national and local state sectors that may be sensitive to defending the rights gained and that refuse the advances of intolerance and conservatism, especially religious conservatism. Another suggestion is to continue investing in dialogue with society as a whole, denouncing retreat attempts and defending the advances made.

It is also important to continue to follow the recommendations of CEDAW and other human rights committees, as well as the Committee of Experts of the Follow-Up Mechanism of the Belém do Pará Convention, and to improve the skills of those presenting complaints to the International Human Rights Courts. It is crucial to have a strong and comprehensive advocacy campaign with the state and society to ensure that the country signs CEDAW and other conventions on women's human rights and to highlight the need to have a comprehensive approach toward VAW while dealing with family law.

Maintaining popular mobilization in the streets and squares, defending democracy and women's rights, as women have been doing in most countries, is also a necessity. This mobilization alerts society as a whole about the importance of real democracy and the need to oppose back-sliding.

The analyses of the past three decades in Brazil reveals the feminist movement's extremely important role in changing discriminatory family laws, with a strong emphasis on laws against VAW. This feminism continues to be active, with great participation of young women's and black women's movements which seek to maintain and expand the achievements in a current context of concern with the danger of major legislative and public policy backlashes.

In contexts that are more refractory to feminist demands, one can proceed step by step, with small, isolated legal achievements and judicial decisions that, in the future, can strengthen broader legislative changes. Reviewing the historical processes, looking at the past and present, and with a perspective focused on the future, it is possible to analyze what worked and to learn from these processes.

Notes

1 Between 1822 and 1889, Brazil was a monarchy. Brazilian legislation does not incorporate religious norms. Albeit predominantly Christian, Brazil is multi-religious.
2 The Tribunal's decision to overturn a jury's decision that acquitted a man who killed his ex-wife held that "Adultery does not place the offended husband in a state of self-defense. Civil law points to the paths of separation and divorce."
3 These women, mostly highly educated and from the upper-middle class, were influenced by English feminism. Many attended meetings with international suffragettes in England. Among them, the biologist and lawyer Bertha Lutz founded the Brazilian Federation for Women's Progress in 1922, to struggle for women's right to vote (Alves 1980).
4 As a result of this seminar, the Brazilian Women's Center was founded in Rio de Janeiro and feminist newspapers were launched.

5 Lélia Gonzales was one of the founders, in 1983, of the group Nzinga – Collective of Black Women.

6 The three pillars of the 1916 Civil Code were family, property, and contract.

7 Anna Maria Rattes, one of the deputies who participated in the constituent process, said in her interview that there was a very heterogeneous range of thoughts, attitudes, actions, and practices among this group and that what brought them together was the fact that they were women.

8 In her interview, Anna Maria Rattes, a Constituent, highlighted the struggle to prevent the 1988 Constitution from restricting or further limiting the right to abortion. The final text of the Constitution makes no reference to abortion.

9 CEPIA is a nongovernmental, nonprofit organization dedicated to developing projects that promote human and citizenship rights; it focuses on issues of health, sexual and reproductive rights, violence and access to justice, poverty and employment, and strengthening the leadership of social movements.

10 Some examples: in 1994, in the face of complaints about the incidence of sexual violence, especially against girls, rape was included among those crimes considered unbuildable (Law 8.930). Law 9.029/95 considered the requirement of a sterilization certificate and a pregnancy test for admission or permanence in employment as criminal. In 1997, psychological violence was included among the crimes of torture (Law 9.455).

11 In her interview, Congresswoman Jandira Feghali, rapporteur of the Maria da Penha Law in the Chamber of Deputies, said that everything they heard in public hearings as demands or suggestions was written down and considered as to how best to insert it in the Law.

12 Secretariat for Policies for Women (SPM) (2008). This publication contains documents on the evaluation process of the Brazil Report to the Committee of the Convention on the Elimination of All Forms of Discrimination against Women – CEDAW/UN Organizations for the period 2001–05.

13 CEPIA participated in this coalition and played an important role in this advocacy process.

14 In her interview, Nilcéa Freire, a former government SPM minister, said, "we must always bear in mind the millstone that is gender inequality in Brazil in all its dimensions. We must never forget from where we are speaking and where women are placed. It is not enough to have a law; it is not enough to have a known law. It is necessary to have instruments that enable its implementation and therefore you have to be open to dialogue with different levels of power and with different audiences. The fight against VAW gave SMP legitimacy as an institutional body before the society."

15 The focus of critical criminology is on locating the genesis of crime and the interpretation of what is "justice" within a structure of class and status inequalities. This critical theory does not, however, incorporate feminist critical theory that points out gender inequalities.

16 In her interview, Jandira Feghali affirmed that "The Maria da Penha Law has much more than just punishing the aggressor. The Law is much more comprehensive; we took advantage of that political moment to fit in a lot of things that did not even exist in the original Project."

17 In her interview, Arlanza Rebello, Public Defender, said, "The Maria da Penha Law was launched, and the media held the law as another punitive law, a law that incriminates men. It was the great stereotype that this law won and which makes it a law not applied today in its enormous grandeur of innovations. We have to do work around what is this figure of women's defense in the LMP [Maria de Penha Law], their right to information, that the woman's history should be not manipulated, that it should be not always interpreted in order to blame her. There needs to be a greater dialogue between the Courts of Domestic Violence and the Family Law Courts. It must be understood that a woman who suffers violence, suffers violence in all spaces where she is going and must be seen."

18 In her interview, Leila Barsted said, "Recently we had a meeting at UN Women with all the representatives of the NGO Consortium that presented the Maria da Penha Law. We came to the conclusion that there are many bills that want to interfere with the Law. We took a consensual stance that we want the law to be fulfilled. If we open the possibility of dealing with the Law, with the current conservative political context and with the current Congress, it is dangerous to give space to them."
19 Such as prohibiting underground work and overtime, among other rules.
20 In her interview, Arlanza Rebello said she has never seen the application of this article, which raises many questions for judges, for example, who will pay the woman's salary if she works for a private company or in a non-formal job?

References

Alves, Branca Moreira (1980) *Ideologia e Feminismo: A luta da mulher pelo voto no Brasil* (*Ideology and Feminism: The Struggle of Women for Voting in Brazil*), Petrópolis, RJ: Ed. Vozes.

Barsted, Leila Linhares (1992) "Legalização e Descriminalização do do Aborto no Brasil: 10 anos de luta feminista" (Legalization and Decriminalization of Abortion in Brazil: 10 Years of Feminist Struggle), in *Estudos Feministas* (*Feminist Studies*), No. 0, Rio de Janeiro: CIEC/ ECO/ UFRJ.

———— (1995) "O movimento feminista e a discriminalização do aborto" ("The Feminist Movement and the Decriminalization of Abortion"), in *Estudos Feministas* (*Feminist Studies*), Rio de Janeiro: ECO/ UFRJ.

Bobbio, Norberto (1992) *A Era dos Direitos* (*The Age of Rights*), translated by Carlos Nelson Coutinho, Rio de Janeiro: Elsevier.

Bruschini, Cristina, Maria Rosa Lombardi, and Sandra Unbehaum (2006) "O Progresso das Mulheres no Brasil" ("The Progress of Women in Brazil"), in CEPIA, *Trabalho, renda e políticas sociais: avanços e desafios* (*Work, Income and Social Policies: Advances and Challenges*), Rio de Janeiro: CEPIA.

Campos, Carmen and Salo Carvalho (2011) "Tensões atuais entre a criminologia feminista e a criminologia crítica: a experiência brasileira" ("Current Tensions Between Feminist Criminology and Critical Criminology: The Brazilian Experience"), in *Lei Maria da Penha: Comentada em uma Perspectiva Jurídico-Feminista* (*Maria da Penha Law Commented on in a Legal-Feminist Perspective*), Rio de Janeiro: Ed. Lumen Júris.

Hermann, Jacqueline and Leila Linhares Barsted (1995) *Violência contra a Mulher: A ordem legal e a (des)ordem familiar* (*Violence Against Women: The Legal Order and the Family (Dis)order*), Rio de Janeiro: CEPIA.

Lindgren Alves, José Augusto (2001) "Relações internacionais e temas sociais: a década das conferências" (International Relations and Social Issues: The Decade of Conferences), Brasília: Funag/Ibri.

Mello, Adriana Ramos de (2016) *Feminicídio, uma análise sociojurídica da violência contra a mulher no Brasil* (*Femicide, A Socio-juridical Analysis of Violence Against Women in Brazil*), Rio de Janeiro: LMJ Mundo Jurídico.

MESECVI-OEA (2008) *Declaração sobre Feminicídio* (*Declaration on Femicide*). www.oas.org/en/mesecvi/docs/DeclaracionFemicidio-EN.pdf.

Organization of American States (1969) *American Convention on Human Rights: Pact of San Jose, Costa Rica*, www.oas.org/dil/treaties_B-32_American_Convention_on_Human_Rights.htm.

—— (1994) *Inter-American Convention on The Prevention, Punishment and Eradication of Violence Against Women "Convention of Belem do Para"*, www.oas.org/juridico/english/treaties/a-61.html.

Pasinato, Wânia (2011) "Avanços e Obstáculos na Implementação da Lei 11.340/2006" (Advances and Obstacles in the Implementation of Law 11.340/2006), in Carmen Campos (org.), *Lei Maria da Penha Comentada em uma Perspectiva Feminista* (The Maria da Penha Law Commented from a Feminist Perspective), Rio de Janeiro: Ed. Lumen Iuris.

Pateman, Carole (1988) *The Sexual Contract*, Cambridge: Polity Press.

Pitanguy, Jacqueline (2011) "Reconceptualizing Peace and Violence Against Women: A Work in Progress," in *Imagine Peace, Signs*, Chicago, IL: University of Chicago Press, Vol. 36, No. 3.

—— (2016) "Women's Human Rights and the Political Arena of Brazil: From dictatorship to democracy," in Ellen Chesler and Theresa McGovern (eds.), *Women and Girls Rising: Progress and Resistance Around the World*, New York: Routledge: 103–119.

Rosa, Felipe Augusto de Miranda (2004) *Sociologia do Direito: o fenômeno jurídico como fato social* (*Sociology of Law: The Legal Phenomenon as a Social Fact*), Rio de Janeiro: Jorge Zahar Editora.

Sorj, Bila (2008) *Estudos Feministas* (*Feminist Studies*), Florianópolis, Vol. 16, No. 1: 129–130.

Trindade, Antonio Augusto Cançado (2002) *O Direito Internacional em um mundo em transformação* (*International Law in a Changing World*), São Paulo and Rio de Janeiro: Renovar.

4

INDIA

Kalpana Kannabiran[1]

Introduction: contextualizing personal laws in India

> The State shall endeavour to secure that marriage shall be based only on the mutual consent of both sexes and shall be maintained through mutual cooperation with the equal rights of husband and wife as a basis. The state shall also recognize that motherhood has a special claim upon its care and protection.
>
> *Draft Article 42 of Constitution of India,*
> *dropped without debate (Rao 1968: 323)*

India is a constitutional, secular democracy, with the principles of equality and secularism written into the Preamble of the Constitution. The fundamental rights chapter (Part III) of the Constitution of India guarantees equality before the law (Article 14), non-discrimination based on sex, religion, caste, race, place of birth, or any other category (Article 15), the right to life and personal liberty (Article 21), and the right to freedom of religion (Article 25).

Alongside this constitutional framework, and intersecting with it, are religious laws that govern matters related to the family (marriage, divorce, inheritance, adoption, maintenance, succession, and guardianship). In the main, there are three sets of religious personal laws – Hindu, Muslim, and Christian – that have figured in public debates and jurisprudence, especially in terms of their specific relationship to the Constitution and other public law (notably criminal law). There is, of course, a diversity within these traditions as well that has been extensively debated in sociological discourse. The important aspect of these three traditions is that they immediately bring into play the question of the rights of minorities and the (written and unwritten) privileges of the majority in the country – rights and privileges that are not restricted to family laws alone but often bleed into the discourse on family law from a larger, often embattled debate on majoritarianism and the disentitlements of minorities in post-colonial, independent, democratic, plural, and multicultural India.

Tracing the historical context of the majority–minority dichotomy in India, Robinson argues that it was introduced by British colonial rulers

> who viewed particularly the Hindus and Muslims essentially through the lens of religion and saw them as bounded and un-differentiated communities ... The application of such categories and of the rigid notion of cultural/communal identity that accompanied them is ... far from the localized, criss-crossing, and overlapping nature of identities that existed prior to British interventions.
>
> *(Robinson 2012: 6)*

The codification of Muslim Personal Law (MPL) (not the *reform* of MPL) was crucial to this process of constructing minority identities (Williams 2012). Scholars have argued that "India's minority rights policies have weakened the capacity of the state to protect the rights of women as equal citizens of a secular democracy" (Robinson 2012: 34) and assert that the state cannot become "an ally of social conservatism" or allow the undermining of its authority to legislate equal rights (Mahajan 1999, cited in Robinson 2012: 34). However, there is also a tendency to fix the aberrational presence on "the case of Muslims" as distinct from "Hindu Personal Law which has been amended from time to time by the state and Christians who have come together to make more gender-just the provisions of Christian Personal Law" (Robinson 2012: 34).

This chapter will focus on violence in the family and the approach of litigants, courts, legislatures, and the political elite to the elimination of such violence and/or neglect, tracing the relationship between laws criminalizing gender-based violence and personal laws that govern the family. To anticipate our argument, the cases and campaigns unravel for us the complexities in the interconnections between women's status across communities irrespective of, or despite, reform – the Muslim woman not really emerging as the oppressed exception in an otherwise fair and equal world for women of other communities. However, there is another field in which gender simultaneously plays out – Muslim women in an increasingly stridently majoritarian society are denied agency and viewed as victims of an oppressive community, as evident from the debates around triple *talāq* and the Uniform Civil Code (UCC).

While acknowledging the vast and complex terrain occupied by the family in women's lives, this chapter focuses on one aspect of feminist struggles in India – struggles against violence against women (VAW) in the family – and traces feminist debates, advocacy, legal reform, and the growth of jurisprudence and public policy (national and international) around the question of domestic violence (DV) and its interlinkages with gender-based discrimination in family laws from the early 1980s to 2016.

Background of women's rights in India: 1970s and beyond

The early 1980s witnessed the rise of new feminist voices in India. This was the period immediately after the State of Emergency of 1975, which also witnessed the growth of struggles for civil liberties and democratic rights across the country. The articulation of women's rights, however, was independent of the dominant human rights discourse, often raising questions of civil and political rights within the state, and, more importantly, within groups – communities, movements, families – and forcing the state to resolve contending claims. As women's rights movements gained momentum, a number of mass movements and democratic rights groups recognized the need to frame women's rights as part of a broader analysis of human rights, such as the Dalit and Adivasi rights movements.

With the rise in right-wing Hindu nationalism and communalism however, especially in the aftermath of the demolition of Babri Masjid in 1992,[2] one witnesses a shift in public discourse and feminist articulations, especially with respect to the rights of women in the family. Shades of strident majoritarianism are of course evident even in the 1980s, consolidating itself in the next decade.

Most women's groups were small, city/town-based, and worked primarily on consciousness raising, campaigns, and individual casework. This period witnessed the rapid growth in women's organizations, and a large number of women of different generations from all walks of life entered activism as a politically conscious choice. Women's rights groups across India, as elsewhere in the world, sprang from the need to reckon with gender discrimination and to find the theoretical tools to do this effectively. Feminist campaigns brought women's issues into public view through a multi-pronged strategy that included media exposure, strategic litigation, case work, public protests, consciousness and awareness raising at the local and national levels, and lobbying for changes in the law. As Gandhi and Shah argue, feminist mobilization on issues of VAW politicized what was up to that point understood as a "social issue" (Gandhi and Shah 1992: 94).

Voices from the struggle

I begin my account of law reform with three voices from the early 1980s, because the women speaking here are women who have had a lasting influence on the articulation of women's rights in the family. Flavia Agnes is one of the leading lawyers for women's rights in the country; Shahnaz Sheikh was the first Muslim woman to challenge triple *talāq* in the Supreme Court of India, while Satyarani Chadha is known as the face of the anti-dowry movement – her fight to have her son-in-law prosecuted for her daughter's murder resulted in far-reaching changes in the criminal law on dowry deaths in the early 1980s:

> The first time he said I'll beat you, I thought he was joking. No one had said these words to me all my life. When he beat me the first time with his hands I was shocked. The second time – with a wooden hanger . . . The third time it was the belt, the buckle hurt the nose and the bridge broke. I was numb not so much with pain, but despair. No one had warned me marriage included this.
>
> *(Agnes 1984: 11).*

Shahnaz Sheikh writes of her experience:

> In 1983, I filed a writ petition in the Supreme Court challenging Muslim Personal Law as being discriminatory to Muslim women. I was divorced by the utterance of triple talaq and thrown out at midnight by my ex-husband. Life was difficult . . . It was [my husband's] word against mine. I consulted five qazis [magistrates or judges of Sharia courts], each of whom gave me a different version of my divorce.
>
> I did not know what my legal marital status was. Was I married or divorced? That was when I decided to hire a lawyer and challenge this form of divorce and Muslim Personal Law in the SC [Supreme Court] on grounds of equality guaranteed by the Constitution. This was the first case of its kind in the Court.
>
> *(Sheikh 2016)*

Satyarani Chadha's twenty-year-old pregnant daughter died of burns within a year of marriage:

> I lost my daughter 35 years ago but in that process I saved thousands and thousands of others. But in the end, what did I get? He is alive, married and absconding, he is not in prison, but my daughter is dead. This disillusionment with law will always stay with me.
>
> *(Jain 2014)*

The debate on social reform, especially as it impacts women's lives, has an old history. While in its earliest phases the debate focused on the subjugation of Hindu women, particularly high-caste Hindu women, the voices of reform that focused on marriage, conjugal practices, and family have arisen from different regions and, within each religion, from different groups.

Yet it is also true that heightened violence during conflict and the anticipation of violence post-conflict do give rise to community-driven spaces of collective mobilization to offer support to survivors. Vahida Nainar observes that advocacy during the conflict phase improves narrating violence and bearing witness. Victim-survivor communities experience a sense of agency (and even empowerment) as they recall each other's experiences of violence – the space of the camp is transformed into a space of community and solidarity.[3] This is indeed the solidarity that Zakia Soman speaks about when she recounts the cascading effect of community-based advocacy post-conflict into homes in an effort to stall the economic violence of eviction from the matrimonial home and dispossession from assets that come with the unilateral pronouncement of divorce under Muslim law.[4]

There are widely divergent experiences of working with survivors of family violence – especially spousal violence – across religious community, caste, region, and class in India. While some advocates observe that the only women who come to them for relief under public law are women from the majority community, suggesting also that Muslim women go either to Muslim lawyers or to Qazi courts, there are others in the same city like the counselors from Shaheen, a women's support group in the Old City of Hyderabad, managed by survivors, that point to the fact that across social locations, the women who have come to them have suffered from very similar problems. This difference in access to constituencies perhaps also derives from (a) spatial location – lines of contact in the new city being drawn in very different ways from lines of contact in the Old City of Hyderabad, and (b) the distinction between professional legal practice on the one hand and cross-community counseling, paralegal services, and victim support on the other. Sultana, from Shaheen, is a survivor of gruesome assault by her husband when she was pregnant; now, fifteen years later, she is a leader in the counseling center, with a keen sense of the practicalities of justice delivery and the indispensability of providing relief to women in difficult circumstances. She observes that polygamy is a problem for Muslim and Hindu Backward Class (BC) women, while severe restrictions on mobility are a problem with Muslim, Hindu BC, and Dalit women. She also notes that from her experience of a decade as counselor, not all women want to opt out of an abusive marriage or relinquish custody of their children. Several want to remain with the family but want the violence to abate, especially the routine sexual violence. In a context where both the men and women are poor, lack regular employment, and are socially vulnerable, the heightened vulnerability of women in the family can sometimes be reduced through counseling services by women's collectives like Shaheen that are able to bring violent husbands to the counseling table, using their goodwill with the Qazi and their presence in the community and neighborhood.[5]

It is useful to recall Solanki's delineation of two approaches to governing the family. The first she calls the "society-centred" approach, which suggests "group autonomy for cultural groups, especially minorities, in the regulation of the family." Here, she cites Chatterjee's view that a "strategic politics of difference" may be invoked whereby "cultural communities can refuse to be homogenized in the name of dominant reasonableness by developing an 'inner democratic forum'" (Solanki 2011: 5). The second approach is "state-centric" with difference relegated to the private sphere – with the state as the only locus of law (ibid.: 5–6).

Feminist reasoning

The significant aspect of the reform initiatives triggered by feminist groups in India is that there were a series of institutional responses – pre-legislative, legislative, and jurisprudential – that brought about a significant shift in the public discourse on VAW in the family. The purpose through this journey into feminist deliberations over thirty years is to understand the ways in which feminist advocacy has interwoven with legislation and statutory interpretation to shift the standards of interpretation of women's place in the family in India – a shift that has immediate implications for public discourse, the treatment of individual women in families, the response of the justice system (formal and community-based), and the political responsibility of elected representatives.

There have been two distinctive strains of feminist legal reasoning in debates around women's rights amidst claims to cultural (and religious) autonomy across the board – from minority to majority religions: the first has argued for a UCC that will govern practitioners irrespective of faith; the second has argued for a robust recognition of religio-cultural diversity, even while posing the question of equality, entitlements, and protections for women within community spaces.

The debates have been complicated by the fact that: (a) in the first set of arguments in favor of the UCC, the most strident appropriation of the debate has happened in the dominant Hindu right-wing political formations, where the separate spheres argument has been challenged as "appeasement of Muslims" by allowing specific practices like polygamy, unilateral divorce (especially the form that has come to be known as triple *talāq*), and maintenance for divorced/separated Muslim women under the Muslim Women's (Protection of Rights on Divorce) Act, 1986, rather than under the standard provision of Section 125 Criminal Procedure Code; (b) on the second track, where democratization of community spaces has been advocated, right-wing, conservative Muslim clergy and political parties (overwhelmingly male) have resisted every move for internal reform that could reduce the vulnerability of women to structural violence in the family, by insisting on the complete autonomy of community spaces under Article 25 of the Constitution of India; and (c) on the third track, where feminists, especially those from the dominant Hindu groups, have set themselves apart from fundamentalist or communal positions on women, there has not been a clear critique of patriarchal biases in Hindu laws of marriage and divorce and also the "hinduization of the Special Marriages Act" (Agnes 2008a: 504–505).

Advocate Albertina Almeida poses pertinent questions in relation to the current debate on the UCC, drawing on the experience of Goa in retaining the uniform code:

> [E]ven as the UCC is being touted as the panacea for the violations of women's rights, nobody asks what really is the UCC in Goa. What is meant when the civil code is said to be "uniform"? Why was it retained in Goa? And how is it working for different sections of women?
>
> *(Almeida 2016)*

Cautioning us that uniformity does not presume equality, that it can mean uniformity of discrimination across all religions, and that treating unequals equally results in inequality in effect, she presents an analysis of the Goan experience with uniform codes, which is quite specific and bears lessons for the ongoing national debate in India (ibid.).

Across all positions, to put it in a nutshell, equality must be understood in a manner that does not suggest uniformity but rather suggests a framework that ensures parity between groups (especially religious groups) and democracy within groups (Solanki 2011).

Dowry deaths, Hindu women, and law reform: the 1980s

The late 1970s witnessed the deaths of large numbers of young women, in their matrimonial homes, especially from burns; these women were recently married (mostly Hindu, in endogamous marriages within their castes), urban for the most part, and educated. The use of kerosene stoves was rapidly expanding across the country and consuming the lives of newly married women. These deaths were being reported by the husbands' families as suicides:

> Satyarani Chadha did not have the benefit of either vernacular or English education, nor the privileges of an elite class. She was a shy, middle class family woman until the tragic death of her 20 year old, six month pregnant daughter Kanchanbala, with 100% burns in her marital home. This event in 1979 . . . changed her into an activist and a relentless crusader for women's rights and justice. Along with the parents of over 20 dowry victims, she spent 27 years of stubborn pursuit and dogged determination, battling legal cases and visiting courts, till she finally got justice when the High Court upheld the conviction of her son-in-law for abetting Kanchanbala's suicide.
>
> Turning her grief into courage and deriving strength from her personal trauma Satyarani embarked on a life long struggle through her organization Shakti Shalini for women survivors facing DV, dowry abuse and harassment in their marital homes. She spent many years guiding, counseling and supporting parents and girls facing harassment and violence at the hands of their husbands and in-laws for dowry.
>
> *(Jain 2014)*

Feminists insisted that dying declarations of women who had "attempted suicide" be treated as evidence and that police procedures be tightened up; protests against these deaths cascaded (see Kumar 1990: 115–126), with demonstrations, street theater, and sustained campaigns. In 1978, a year after the nationwide protests began, the Prime Minister of India, Mr. Charan Singh, assured a women's delegation that "measures to stop the maltreatment of women for dowry" would be introduced in the next Parliamentary session (ibid.: 120).

Following up on the demand by women's rights groups that matrimonial matters need to be adjudicated in a space that "mitigate[s] disequilibrium inherent in marriage relationships by creating new obligations and modifying old ones," family courts were set up under the Family Courts Act, 1984, with jurisdiction over criminal and civil matters relating to the breakdown of marriage: divorce, restitution of conjugal rights, alimony, maintenance, and child custody (Agnes 2008b: 276–277; see also Basu 2014). These courts were structured to create a more easily navigable space for women and were an important part of the structural and institutional changes brought about through feminist lobbying with the government. On another, related, track, India signed CEDAW in 1980 and ratified it in July 1993 with some reservations.

A survey of one hundred reported cases of deaths of women in their matrimonial homes between 1995 and 2004 shows that although there are problems in the interpretation of women's position in the family arising from the patriarchal mind-sets of judges and lawyers, and although the number of women dying in matrimonial homes remains alarmingly high – women being poisoned, burned, battered, drowned, shot, hanged, and strangled within the "safe and harmonious" confines of the family – there is a marginal increase in the rate of convictions in cases where women have died gruesome deaths and a perceptible shift in the judicial conscience.[6] This impact is not as perceptible however in cases where the woman survives and escapes the cruelty of the matrimonial home. In these cases, the hostility to the survivor for not acquiescing to the codes of patriarchal conjugality (which is constituted by spousal violence) is evident in accounts of encounters with the criminal justice system. On another level, while most of the violence that women are subjected to within their matrimonial homes is premeditated and intentional, *mens rea* (criminal intent) is not read into murders of wives in the same way as it is read into murder per se. As Nainar observes, it is very difficult to argue that DV is torture – that is, giving these acts the gravitas that torture has – unless we are able to shift the focus from the actor to the acts.[7] The family relationship is always the mitigating factor in sentencing policy, although the family relationship in fact renders these women more vulnerable to assault.

Still, justice delayed is better than no justice at all, which is demonstrated amply by the judgment in the case of the murder of Satyarani Chadha's daughter in 1979, which triggered the whole movement for criminal law reform. The Delhi High Court ruled that with respect to presumption, Section 113A of the Indian Evidence Act, although it came into force after the incident, "did not create any new offence and as such it does not create any substantial right but it is merely a matter of procedure of evidence and so retrospective in its application."[8]

Through all of this however, the 1980s saw the emergence of a new common sense – in the public domain, the legislature, the executive, and the judiciary – on women's rights and entitlements within the family. The contradictions were deep, but the debate opened up a space for a different level of engagement, and the law forced an institutional engagement with the problem of VAW and an understanding of the crimes within the family that women were subjected to on a daily basis. Despite this, when the Protection of Women from Domestic Violence Act (PWDVA) was being debated two decades later, eminent jurists asked Indira Jaising, "What is this thing called 'domestic violence'? The law recognises no such thing" (Jaising 2013: xv). The thing called domestic violence had to wait till 2006 to be defined in law.

Muslim women organizing around rights in the family, 1986–2016

It is apt to begin the discussion on family laws and Muslim women with the statement issued on 20 October 2016 by over a hundred "Muslims and people of Muslim descent" in India, which opposes triple *talāq*, the UCC, the Hindu right-wing ruling party's (the Bharatiya Janata Party) "new found love for Muslim women," and the appropriation of the Muslim voice by the All India Muslim Personal Law Board.[9] Here I discuss the textures of advocacy on Muslim women's rights in different parts of the country, focusing on the relationship between family laws and the larger political debates and projects on the status of minorities in India.

In the view of noted political scientist Zoya Hasan, religion, feminist politics, and the question of Muslim women's rights need to be understood so that the intersection between minority rights and women's rights is accounted for. A second issue concerns

> the strategies deployed by minority groups to preserve their distinctive identity in response to threats to it, on the one hand and how Muslim women-led networks are challenging the authority of the religious elite to represent the "Muslim community" while reframing the category "Muslim women" in order to assert political agency to enhance women's rights, on the other.
>
> *(Hasan 2014: 264)*

The nuanced articulation of the rights of Muslim women as put forth in Hasan's statement is a core aspect of the recent article by Shahnaz Sheikh, the first Muslim woman to challenge triple *talāq* in the Supreme Court of India, in 1986 (Sheikh 2016).

The single "positive" outcome of the genocidal VAW in Gujarat,[10] according to Zakia Soman, a founder of the BMMA (Bharatiya Muslim Mahila Andolan or Indian Muslim Women's Movement), was that ordinary women came out of their homes to speak about the violence they had witnessed or experienced. There was anger among women. They simply refused to accept the situation and stepped out of their homes to become first-generation activists – 200–300 women in the first instance. In the face of numbing, targeted assault, survivors were not stigmatized or ostracized by their family or community. There was also insecurity in the minds of parents, which led to mass marriages of very young girls – thirteen to sixteen years of age – post-conflict in the relief camps conducted by camp organizers and supported by Muslim organizations. Soman recounts that the act of stepping out and speaking about anti-Muslim violence led quite naturally to women speaking up about injustice and violence in the family – DV, *talāq*, second marriage without informing the first wife, and sudden demands for dowry. While initially they met as Aman Samuday (Peace Coalition), they realized soon that they needed to meet as women, and called meetings under the banner of Niswaan. Soman recounts their first meetings as a women's group:

> I remember a lot of women had come. Some of the women had come in a full-fledged burkha. But once we all got into the room we said, "there's nobody here, we can all be free here, Ab uthar do, ab burkhe ki zaroorat nahi hai" [now you can remove your burkhas, there is no need for burkhas now]. And they had taken off their burkhas. I had seen their faces for the first time; I'd known them otherwise in the burkha, because they were coming for some rally or dharna [protest] over the Gujarat riots – I had only seen them through their eyes.[11]

The first issues that were brought to the group were *talāq* and polygamy. Where women faced violence and needed to be moved out of the matrimonial home, the fact that the organizers were involved in post-conflict support had built trust in the community so they did not face resistance in retrieving a victim's personal belongings from her husband's home. In terms of law, they used a combination of instruments that worked – Muslim personal law, 125 CrPC for maintenance, PWDVA, 498A IPC, and negotiation and mediation with an abusive husband – anything that was just and brought relief to a woman in a particular situation. Most importantly, the BMMA felt both codification of Muslim law and access to public remedies were both necessary and important.

In the context of working with Muslim women, Noorjehan Safia Niaz observed that violence is not just physical – the threat of divorce, polygamy, and denial of child custody are all forms of violence commonly deployed against women.[12] While it may be desirable to use formal legal institutions such as the courts, women have no control over legal proceedings and poor women cannot afford the expenses incurred in court proceedings. Most prefer a settlement in the Women's Sharia Courts set up by the BMMA. Reiterating Zakia Soman's viewpoint, Noorjehan felt that after the demolition of Babri Masjid and the violence across the country against Muslims, there was a rise of Muslim women's organizations and women found their own voice within the community. Looking back on the early cases like Shah Bano,[13] she feels the difference is that in the mid-1980s there were individual women fighting their battles, whereas now, Muslim women's collectives and movements were backing individual women's struggles. Although there is a very vocal opposition to their work (whether on the topics of *talāq* or women's entry into the Haji Ali *dargah* [tomb]), she feels that it is a sign of the tacit support they enjoy that there has been no fatwa issued against them to date. And she does not believe that it will be possible for regressive forces to gain control over them.

Muslim communities in Tamil Nadu are governed by the Jamaat, an all-male body that interprets Sharia law in adjudication of cases related to family law, especially marriage and divorce. Women, by definition, were excluded from the Jamaat and represented by male kin, even when matters directly concerning them were heard by the Jamaat. In 2004, around the same time that Zakia Soman began to work with Muslim women in post-conflict Gujarat, Sherifa Khanum formed the Tamil Nadu Muslim Women's Jamaat in the southern state of Tamil Nadu:

> Whenever the jamaat wanted to subjugate women, they cited Quran as their guide. So we understood that it was the authority they drew from Quran that they used to oppress women. We then read Quran and re-examined our realities as women. This strengthened our resolve. The word that crystallised their actions and their authority was "jamaat" – a word that carried immense weight. And so in the course of our discussions, the idea was born. Why should we not form a jamaat ourselves?[14]

In 2002, Jameela Nishat founded the Shaheen Women's Resource and Welfare Association to work among women in the riot-affected areas of the Old City of Hyderabad. Taking a different route and working with the office of the Qazi alongside courts dealing with family law – rather than setting up women's jamaats or Sharia courts – in an interview Nishat underscored the difficulties of providing relief to women. Straddling criminal courts, family courts, and Qazi courts, Shaheen calibrates the options available to women who want to leave abusive homes. Recounting her work with the office of the Chief Qazi, she pointed out that the Qazi's records show an overwhelming number of cases of *khula*, where the woman asks for divorce and secures it. She cautioned against reading this as an expression of women's freedom.[15] Rather, in the experience of Shaheen, it indicates that there is so much violence that women are unable to bear it and choose to opt out of marriage.

The All India Muslim Women's Personal Law Board (AIMWPLB), led by Shaista Amber, was set up as the women's wing of the All India Muslim Personal Law Board in 2005. It was perhaps born at this precise moment in response to the growing demand for reform by Muslim women across the country:

> The Muslim woman today continues to face the brunt of a discriminatory law. She is divorced either orally, or in writing, and unilaterally, she gets meagre or no mehr[16] amounts, her husband continues to remarry with impunity; her consent is not taken at the time of marriage, she is forced to undergo halala,[17] she faces intolerable restrictions during her iddat[18] and so on. It is a tragedy that while Quran bestows many rights on the Muslim women, they are not able to access them. The Quranic injunctions must be made legally enforceable by adding it to the constitution of India.[19]

AIMWPLB's *Khuli Adalat* (open court), a mobile adjudicatory forum, provides women facing difficult situations, especially in the family, to place their problems for consideration before Islamic scholars.

In general, the experience of Muslim women and the debate on personal law reform vis-à-vis the UCC has resulted in binaries in public discourse that thwart the possibilities of organic solutions emerging and crafted by the women themselves. Despite this, we have seen the various ways in which women have been able to negotiate the system – if the formation of a women's Jamaat is one route, women's Sharia courts and *Khuli Adalats* are another, and working with the Qazi's office to ensure that women get a fair hearing and decent maintenance in the case of *khula* is a third way.

In addressing the question of law reform for Muslims, in 2005 AIMWPLB put out a Model *Nikahnama* (marriage contract), while in 2015 Soman and Niaz circulated a Draft Muslim Family Law for signatures.[20]

What is of particular interest through all these initiatives is the effort expended to integrate the constitutional principles of justice and equality for women with religious law. Within all these moves, there is a cascading feminist common sense across social location that interrogates violence in the family and searches for alternatives – through counseling, dissolution on mutually consensual terms, negotiated settlements for the return of peace, the right to residence, and importantly in the domain of public law, strategic litigation, legislative reform, and legislative impact assessments on a regular ongoing basis, among others. It is with these questions before us that we move to a consideration of case law and problems in statute and interpretation in the three major religious traditions in India – Hindu, Muslim, and Christian.

Family law jurisprudence: an interreligious snapshot

Two discriminatory statutes that governed Hindus were challenged in *Gita Hariharan v. Reserve Bank of India* (AIR 1999, 2 SCC 228) – the Hindu Minority and Guardianship Act, 1956 and Section 19(b) of the Guardians and Wards Act, 1890.[21] In the first petition, Gita Hariharan was refused recognition as her minor son's guardian when she applied for Reserve Bank of India Relief Bonds in his name. In the second petition, Vandana Shiva claimed custody of her minor son, challenging the legal norm of the father as natural guardian to the exclusion of the mother. The Supreme Court reinterpreted the statutory provisions in both these acts in favor of substantively equal status of mother and father vis-à-vis a minor child. In doing this, the court cited provisions from CEDAW, the Beijing Declaration, and Article 2 of the Universal Declaration of Human Rights (UDHR) (see de Alwis and Jaising 2016 for a detailed analysis). It must be stressed that the route to personal law reform has been distinctive in each of the major religions. The reforms around anti-dowry legislations that primarily affected Hindu women were described in an earlier section, as well as the efforts at mobilizing Muslim women around issues of DV, imbuing new meaning to the idea of plural jurisprudence.

Tracking the relationship between legislative and judicial action with respect to family laws, Subramanian observes that the Christian clergy and mobilizers were more inclined to reform in the post-1980s period than were Muslim leaders (Subramanian 2014). As a result, the initiative for Christian law reform came from the legislature, whereas Muslim law reform was pushed through statutory and constitutional interpretation, faced as it was with no legislative initiative and demands by aggrieved women litigants for entitlements, especially on dissolution of marriage. Even prior to the deliberations around reforming the Christian law of divorce, however, the 1986 case of *Mary Roy v. State of Kerala* (1986 AIR 1011, 1986 SCR (1) 371) removed gender-based discrimination in the inheritance of property among Syrian Christians in Kerala, although her lawyer, Indira Jaising, recalls, importantly, that what Mary Roy was primarily asserting was not ownership, but her right to usufruct, in the property of her natal family to whom she returned after her divorce.[22]

Although there was a fair degree of unanimity that Christian law of divorce, the Indian Divorce Act, 1869, provided very limited and unequal grounds for divorce to men and women, legal reform itself was considerably delayed. It was the case of *Mary Sonia Zachariah v. Union of India* (1995 (1) Ker LT 644 (FB)) that saw the coming together of religious organizations and rights organizations, which included two of Kerala's important reformed Orthodox churches, Christian reform organizations, and rights groups such as the Joint Women's Programme.

The specific points on which the court deliberated in *Mary Sonia Zachariah* were the limited grounds for the availability of divorce (denied to women on grounds of cruelty or desertion alone) and the unequal access to divorce for Christian as compared to other religious groups. The latter point, the court felt, defeated the constitutional guarantee to equality and non-discrimination on grounds of religion and gender. The denial of cruelty as a ground for desertion, the court felt, violated women's fundamental right to life and personal liberty.

The second judgment, *Pragati Varghese v. Cyril George Varghese* (AIR 1997 Bom 349), introduced an easier availability of divorce to Christian women than to Christian men, riding on the crest of Christian reform advocacy. It justified such asymmetry by taking recourse to the "muscularly weaker physique of the woman, her general vulnerable physical and social condition and her defensive and non-aggressive nature and role particularly in this country."

The legislative amendment to the Indian Divorce Act in 2001 was comprehensive and equalized the divorce rights of Christian men and women. It (a) made divorce available to men and women upon mutual consent; (b) removed the requirement of high court confirmation of lower court divorce decrees; (c) increased alimony entitlements, and (d) removed the punitive approach to adultery that authorized transfer of the property of adulterous women to their husbands and children on divorce.

Section 125 of the Criminal Procedure Code (New) adopted in 1974 required men to support their dependent ex-wives. For Muslim men, this meant extending support beyond *iddat*, until such time that the ex-wife found support either through employment or through remarriage. Although in deference to pressure from conservative Muslim legislators a qualification was added in Section 127(2)(6) that exempted Muslim husbands from providing support to their ex-wives beyond *iddat*, decisions on maintenance claims by divorced Muslim women varied in applying these two sections between 1974 and 1985. There was a preponderance in the judicial view that husbands were required to pay permanent maintenance – in contrast to decisions involving Hindu or Christian women, where alimony was the norm after 1974. The case that brought the question of maintenance for a divorced Muslim woman to the national stage was the case of Shah Bano, decided by the Constitution Bench of the Supreme Court of India.[23]

While the arguments of Shah Bano's advocate and legal scholar Danial Latifi were crafted with a keen and nuanced understanding of Muslim law, the author of the judgment, Justice Y.V. Chandrachud, rather than building on the arguments presented, interspersed his judgment with statements such as the "fatal point in Islam is the degradation of woman," and called for a UCC (Subramanian 2014).

The furore that followed this judgment, especially among Muslims, led to Shah Bano herself renouncing the alimony that the court had decreed. In response to the demand of conservative sections, the Muslim Women (Protection of Rights on Divorce) Act, 1986 (MWPRDA) was passed. According to this act, the natal family of the woman and community trusts (*waqf*) would bear the responsibility of providing economic support for women beyond *iddat*.

However, the act was ambiguous about the man's responsibility to maintain his ex-wife beyond the *iddat* period – there was no clear statement that men would not be required to support their ex-wives beyond *iddat*. Women therefore continued to seek maintenance both under 125 CrPC and through other plural mechanisms described in the earlier section. Section 125 CrPC itself was amended in 2001 to remove the ceiling of Rs. 500 per month on maintenance.

In 2001, in *Danial Latifi v. Union of India* (2001 (7) SCC 740), lawyers who had represented Shah Bano argued that Muslim men owed their ex-wives permanent alimony even after the passage of the MWPRDA. Without overruling Shah Bano, or the MWPRDA, the Court followed an established standard of judicial construction – construing statutory law in the light of the Constitution – and asserted that it is "difficult to perceive that Muslim Law would place the responsibility for economic support for a divorced woman entirely on people unconnected to the matrimonial relationship" (cited from Subramanian 2014). Also, importantly, by the time the Latifi decision came, the political climate in the country had turned stridently anti-minority. Given its accommodative and careful approach to interpretation, the Latifi judgment came to bear without much resistance from those who had protested against Shah Bano earlier.

Finally, after decades of opposition to the practice of "triple *talāq*" by Muslim women's organizations, in August 2017 the court in *Shayara Bano v Union of India and Others*[24] finally applied the principle of manifest arbitrariness to strike down the practice of triple *talāq*.

Protection of Women from Domestic Violence Act, 2005

The PWDVA came into effect on 26 October 2006, to provide for "more effective protection of the rights of women guaranteed under the Constitution *who are victims of violence of any kind occurring within the family*" (PWDVA, Statement of Objects and Reasons, cited in Jaising 2014: 3, emphasis added). As Senior Advocate Indira Jaising points out, the legislative invocation of the Constitution in a law on DV is testimony to a feminist journey through the rugged patriarchal terrains of law, where we have come full circle from the point where a judge of a high court famously declared that introducing constitutional law in the home is "like introducing a bull in a china shop."[25] The home, under this law, was conceived as a shared space with entitlements to residence that did not flow from ownership. Jaising points out that the idea of "shared household" in PWDVA "is in keeping with the family patterns in India, where married couples continue to live with their parents in homes owned by their parents" (Jaising 2014: 3). DV under this law is not limited to spousal violence, and "matrimonial relationship" is displaced by "domestic relationship."[26] In the history of feminist support to survivors of DV, dispossession from both the natal home on marriage and the matrimonial home through cruelty has not addressed the survivors' needs for sustenance and shelter. The combination of criminal and civil elements in this legislation, therefore, is aimed at ensuring the abatement of violence *and* the securing of other needs of the woman. The fact was that "women were getting relief all under one roof, where they didn't have to run separately for maintenance, separately for custody, separately for compensation, and then the right to residence – which was a big deal."[27]

The PWDVA was enacted after three decades of struggle to end violence in the home, which included legislation, legislative impact assessment, the deliberations of a Parliamentary Standing Committee, and close monitoring and evaluation (Jaising 2014). In fact, it would not be far from the truth to state that the PWDVA is a direct result of these actions.

What is particularly interesting about the trajectory of this legislation is the different institutional realms and practices it has intertwined with. The PWDVA recognizes public health facilities as service providers and addresses for the first time *within a legislation* the issue of violence as a public health concern (Bhate-Deosthali et al. 2012: 67). The significance of this lies in the fact that it is perhaps the first time that redressing VAW has involved a close engagement with the public health-care system – both from the need for evidence gathering in a medico-legal case and to address the need for emergency treatment, care, and trauma counseling.[28] The dominant view until this point was that DV was a "personal" problem, with the healthcare provider only providing symptomatic relief.

Women's experiences of violence exist across a continuum. Several advocates interviewed for this chapter observed that the *Nirbhaya* case has had a marked impact in women naming marital rape and sexual violence as DV – despite the fact that criminal law in India does not recognize the crime of marital rape, and by these accounts the threshold of tolerance for domestic violence has dropped, with natal families in several instances coming out in support of daughters.[29]

Further, approaches to justice are plural – and not all cases go through the public law system. Yet one of the remarkable characteristics of feminist advocacy against violence has been that the cumulative sensibilities that are crystallized in the PWDVA (for example) have in small but significant measure made inroads into spaces of personal law, providing important standard-setting tools in different locales. With the PWDVA itself being central to the thick nesting of activism around CEDAW, international debates, standards, and stories filter through to the smallest initiatives through an array of practices in strategic litigation – the women's Jamaat, the Qazi court, the *biradari panchayat* (informal caste councils), the court of the magistrate, the constitutional court, or the CEDAW sessions that call governments to account.

The most important lesson that this legislation bears for our understanding of the changed position of women in the family, according to Indira Jaising, is that it represents a departure from protectionism by the state and the emergence of the woman's autonomous and inalienable rights within the family – to a life free from both violence and from dispossession.[30]

Conclusions

This study has attempted to provide a bird's-eye view of the intersections in India between feminist struggles against VAW in the family, the rise of feminist legal scholarship, the campaigns for law reform, and the afterlives of feminist engagements with law.

The rise of violent Hindu majoritarianism has had very specific discursive effects on the rights of women, especially from minority groups, both within the courts and in the public domain. The successful challenge in the Supreme Court of India to the practice of triple *talāq* by Muslim women, and the appropriation of this discourse by the ruling party through the enactment criminalizing the pronouncement of triple *talāq* for instance, to serve the Hindutva agenda of stigmatizing minorities for their shabby treatment of "their" women has rendered the pitch extremely difficult to navigate for women generally, but especially for Muslim women who have been fighting for reform within personal law traditions.[31] The observation is poignant and true that witnessing/surviving collective anti-minority violence makes the narration of violence (within the family) possible. This larger context of bitterly contested majority-minority politics within which Muslim women – from Shahnaz Sheikh and Shah Bano in the 1980s to Shayara Bano in 2016[32] – have stood their ground against both Muslim orthodoxy and Hindutva politics is one that shines the torch on the strength of feminism in India even in times of siege.

An important aspect of this engagement is that the resolution of cases has steadily taken place with simultaneous recourse to the courts and to community-based adjudicatory spaces – those driven by women, like the Muslim women's Jamaat (Dhanraj 2011), as well as through creative interventions in Qazi courts.[33] In terms of its demonstration of a wider praxis for feminist legal reform, the indispensability of plural legal spaces, and the calibrated use of each space to wrest more ground for women, is most significant (see Vatuk 2017).

This review has attempted to signpost the various ways in which legal reform efforts have historically taken shape in India. Codification is not always the answer, as we have seen – it could result in the dispossession of women in insidious ways; nor, as Indira Jaising has argued, is the right to property alone the answer. Across communities, women who leave abusive marriages (or are thrown out) find themselves on the edge of survival. Those who anticipate these troubles and stay are often killed. The campaigns for reform of criminal law introducing the new offence of torture and murder for dowry in the 1980s fueled a new turn in feminist mobilization. And yet, two decades later, the CEDAW Committee marked the rise in dowry deaths as a matter of concern and the Law Commission of India (2007) published a second report on dowry deaths recommending the death penalty.

Important lessons from the campaign against domestic violence, however, are: (a) the ways in which we can resurrect older practices of fairness contained in personal laws and ousted through codification, for a new template of justice; and (b) the ways in which feminist interventions in legal reform intersect. The focus in the PWDVA on shared residence, drawing as it does, on the older right to usufruct that women enjoyed, makes a sharp departure from an approach of state protectionism towards women towards their *right* of residence. This was also the basis of the earlier challenge posed by Mary Roy to Christian women's right to inheritance, which focused on Roy's right to *use* the family property.[34] Similarly, several accounts stressed the fact that the uprising against sexual assault in 2012 and the subsequent reform of rape law has reduced the threshold of tolerance for domestic violence,[35] with survivors of marital rape reporting this at public hospitals.[36] While on the subject, the importance of treatment (of physical and psychological injury) and recording of medical evidence of survivors who approach healthcare facilities is rarely discussed as an intrinsic part of law reform on VAW. The case of the Centre for Enquiry into Health and Allied Themes (CEHAT) in Mumbai illuminates this path for us (Bhate-Deosthali et al. 2012 and Bhate-Deosthali et al. 2013).

The core strengths of the feminist movement against violence in India have been the steady emergence of survivors as leaders of the movement to end violence and the intersectional approach to women's rights. This mapping of the trajectories of rights advocacy, legislation, and the rise of new sensibilities and consciousness, we hope, will serve twin purposes: providing a template through which we may begin to understand other social movements, and offering a template to think through transversal politics for women's rights, in which engagements with legal regimes/lawscapes are critical.

Notes

1 I am grateful to Yakın Ertürk and the WLP team for their support and feedback. I gratefully acknowledge the support of Vasanth Kannabiran, Stanley Thangaraj, and Bandana Purkayastha. I thank Jameela Nishat, Shaheda, Sultana, and Suman from Shaheen, Hyderabad; Zakia Soman and Noorjehan Safia Niaz from Bharatiya Muslim Mahila Andolan (Indian Muslim Women's Movement), Ahmedabad and Mumbai; Padma Bhate-Deosthali and Sangeeta Rege from the Centre for Enquiry into Health and Allied Themes (CEHAT), Mumbai; Anuradha Kapoor from Swayam, Kolkata; Advocates Renu Mishra, Anchal Gupta, Priyanka Singh, and Abhay Pratap Singh from the Association for Advocacy and Legal Initiatives (AALI), Lucknow; Vahida Nainar, women's rights and human rights activist, Mumbai; Advocate Vasudha Nagaraj, Hyderabad; and Senior Advocate Indira Jaising, Lawyers Collective, Delhi, for sharing with me their views and valuable materials from their archives.
2 On 6 December 1992, the Vishva Hindu Parishad and the Bharatiya Janata Party organized the demolition of the Babri Mosque in Ayodhya, Uttar Pradesh, involving 150,000 'volunteers'. The crowd overwhelmed security forces and tore down the mosque, resulting in months of heightened communal tension, widespread protests against the demolition, organized violence against Muslims, and the deaths of at least two thousand people.
3 Interview with Vahida Nainar, 23 December 2016.
4 Interview with Zakia Soman, 21 December 2016.
5 Interview with Sultana, Shaheda, and Suman, Shaheen Women's Resource and Welfare Association, 28 December 2016.
6 These are cases reported from various high courts and the Supreme Court. Details are available on file with the author.
7 Vahida Nainar interview, 23 December 2016.
8 *Subhash Chander and Anr. v. State on 16 December 1991*, 46 (1992) Delhi Law Times 366.
9 http://thewire.in/74667/triple-talaq-statement-muslims/. There are many decisions on triple *talāq* and unilateral male repudiation among Muslims. For a detailed list of cases, see Subramanian 2014: n. 98.

10 In 2002, more than a thousand people were killed over the course of two months in genocidal violence against Muslims in Gujarat, a state then led by Narendra Modi, now India's prime minister.

11 Interview with Zakia Soman, 21 December 2016.

12 Interview with Noorjehan Safia Niaz, 2 January 2017.

13 In 1978, Shah Bano, a sixty-two-year-old Muslim mother of five from Madhya Pradesh, was divorced by her husband. She filed suit in India's Supreme Court and won the right to alimony. However, under pressure from Islamic leaders, the Indian Parliament subsequently reversed the judgment.

14 Sherifa Khanum in *Invoking Justice*, a documentary film on the Tamil Nadu Muslim Women's Jamaat directed by Deepa Dhanraj, 2011.

15 Interview with Jameela Nishat, 26 December 2016.

16 *Mehr* (*mehrieh* in Farsi) is a mandatory payment, in the form of money or possessions paid or promised to pay by the groom to the bride at the time of marriage, which legally becomes her property.

17 *Halala* is a situation in which the divorced woman is forced to marry another man and consummate that marriage, divorces that man, and remarries her original husband.

18 *Iddat* is the period a woman must observe after a divorce or the death of her spouse, during which she may not marry again.

19 Website of All Indian Muslim Women Personal Law Board, www.aimwplb.com/about.

20 They also put into circulation a draft legislation on Muslim family law (Soman and Niaz 2015).

21 This discussion of cases, judicial interpretation, and reform in this chapter is based on Subramanian 2014.

22 Interview with Indira Jaising, 5 February 2017.

23 *Mohammad Ahmed Khan v. Shah Bano Begum*, 1985 SCR (3) 844.

24 Writ Petition (Civil) 118 of 2016.

25 *Harvinder Kaur v. Harmander Singh*, AIR 1984 Del 66.

26 Domestic relationship includes "all relationships based on consanguinity, marriage, adoption and even 'relationships in the nature of marriage'" (Jaising 2014: 9).

27 Interview with Anuradha Kapoor, Swayam, Kolkata, 21 December 2016.

28 Interview with Padma Bhate-Deosthali and Sangeeta Rege, 27 December 2016.

29 Interviews with Advocate Vasudha Nagaraj, Hyderabad, 29 December 2016, and Noorjehan S. Niaz, 2 January 2017. The *Nirbhaya* case refers to the sexual assault and murder of a young woman on the streets of Delhi in December 2012 that resulted in amendments to the rape law in 2013.

30 Interview with Indira Jaising, 5 November 2017.

31 Muslim Women (Protection of Rights on Marriage) Act 2017 passed in December 2017, in Section 4 sets out imprisonment for three years and a fine as punishment for men pronouncing triple *talāq*.

32 *Shayara Bano v. Union of India*, Writ Petition (Civil) 118 of 2016.

33 Interviews with Jameela Nishat, 26 December 2016, and Sultana, Shaheda, and Suman, Shaheen Women's Resource and Welfare Association, 28 December 2016.

34 Interview with Indira Jaising, 5 February 2017.

35 Interviews with Vasudha Nagaraj, 29 December 2016, and Renu Mishra and AALI team, 5 January 2017.

36 Interview with Padma Bhate-Deosthali and Sangeeta Rege, 27 December 2017.

References

Agnes, Flavia (1984) *My Story . . . Our Story, of Re-Building Broken Lives*, Bombay: Women's Centre.

———— (2008a) "Women's Movement in a Secular Framework: Redefining the Agendas," in Mary E. John (ed.), *Women's Studies in India*, Delhi: Penguin: 501–508.

———— (2008b) "Family Courts: From the Frying Pan into the Fire?" in Mary E. John (ed.), *Women's Studies in India*, Delhi: Penguin: 272–278.

Almeida, Albertina (2016) "Goa's Civil Code Shows That Uniformity Does Not Always Mean Equality," *The Wire*, 8 August 2016, https://thewire.in/57211/goas-uniform-civil-code-is-not-the-greatest-model-to-follow/.

Basu, Srimati (2014) "Dreaming a Better Court for Women: Adjudication and subjectivity in the Family Court of Kolkata, India," in Ravinder Kaur and Rajni Palriwala (eds.), *Marrying in South Asia: Shifting Concepts, Changing Practices in a Globalising World*, Hyderabad: Orient Blackswan: 351–370.

Bhate-Deosthali, Padma, T.K. Sundari Ravindran, and U. Vindhya (2012) "Addressing Domestic Violence within Healthcare Settings: The Dilaasa Model," *Economic and Political Weekly*, Vol. *XLVII*, No. 17, 28 April: 66–75.

Bhate-Deosthali, Padma, Sangeeta Rege, and Padma Prakash (eds.) (2013) *Feminist Counselling and Domestic Violence in India*, New Delhi: Routledge.

CEDAW (2007) Concluding Comments of the Committee on the Elimination of Discrimination against Women: India, 37th session, 15 January–2 February, www.un.org/womenwatch/daw/cedaw/cedaw25years/content/english/CONCLUDING_COMMENTS/India/India-CO-3.pdf.

———— (2014) "Concluding Observations on the Combined Fourth and Fifth Periodic Reports of India, 1219th and 1220th sessions," CEDAW/C/IND/CO/4-5, 18 July; http://tbinternet.ohchr.org/Treaties/CEDAW/Shared%20Documents/Ind/CEDAW_C_IND_CO_4-5_17678_E.doc.

De Alwis, Rangita de Silva and Indira Jaising (2016) "The Role of Personal Laws in Creating a 'Second Sex,'" *Faculty Scholarship*, Paper 1681, http://scholarship.law.upenn.edu/faculty_scholarship/1681.

Dhanraj, Deepa (2011) (Dir.) *Invoking Justice* (documentary film).

Gandhi, Nandita and Nandita Shah (1992) *The Issues at Stake: Theory and Practice in the Contemporary Women's Movement in India*, New Delhi: Kali for Women.

Hasan, Zoya (2014) "Religion, Feminist Politics and Muslim Women's Rights in India," in Kalpana Kannabiran (ed.), *Women and Law: Critical Feminist Perspectives*, New Delhi: Sage: 264–273.

Jain, Juhi (2014) "A Tribute to Satyarani Chadha, the Face of the Anti Dowry Movement," 7 July 2014, http://feministsindia.com/tribute-satyarani-chadha-face-indias-anti-dowry-movement/.

Jaising, Indira (2013) "Foreword," in Padma Bhate-Deosthali, Sangeeta Rege, and Padma Prakash (eds.), *Feminist Counselling and Domestic Violence in India*, New Delhi: Routledge: xv–xviii.

———— (2014) "Bringing Rights Home: Review of the Campaign for a Law on Domestic Violence," in Kalpana Kannabiran (ed.), *Women and Law: Critical Feminist Perspectives*, Delhi: Sage: 1–31.

Kumar, Radha (1990) *The History of Doing: An Illustrated Account of Movements for Women's Rights and Feminism in India, 1800–1990*, New Delhi: Zubaan.

Law Commission of India (2007) *202nd Report on Proposal to Amend Section 304B of Indian Penal Code.*

Rao, B. Shiva (1968) *The Framing of India's Constitution: A Study*, New Delhi: Indian Institute of Public Administration.

Robinson, Rowena (2012) "Introduction," in Rowena Robinson (ed.), *Minority Studies*, New Delhi: Oxford University Press: 1–48.

Sheikh, Shahnaz (2016) "Why I Took on Triple Talaq and Why I Oppose the Uniform Civil Code," *Indian Express*, 16 November 2016, http://indianexpress.com/article/opinion/columns/triple-talaq-uniform-civil-code-indian-constitution-4377532/.

Solanki, Gopika (2011) *Adjudication in Religious Family Laws: Cultural Accommodation, Legal Pluralism, and Gender Equality in India*, New Delhi: Cambridge University Press.

Soman, Zakia and Noorjehan Safia Niaz (2015) *No More Talaq Talaq Talaq: Muslim Women Call for a Ban on an UnIslamic Practice*, Mumbai: Bharatiya Muslim Mahila Andolan.

Subramanian, Narendra (2014) *Nation and Family: Personal Law, Cultural Pluralism and Gendered Citizenship in India*, Stanford, CA: Stanford University Press. E-book.

Vatuk, Sylvia (2017) *Marriage and its Discontents: Women, Islam and the Law in India*, New Delhi: Women Unlimited.

Williams, Rina Verma (2012) "Making Minority Identities: Gender, State and Muslim Personal Law," in Rowena Robinson (ed.), *Minority Studies*, New Delhi: Oxford University Press: 73–94.

Abbreviations in Case Citations

AIR: *All India Reporter*; Bom: Bombay; Del: Delhi; ILR: Indian Law Reports; Kar LJ: *Karnataka Law Journal*; Ker LT: *Kerala Law Times*; SC: Supreme Court; SCC: Supreme Court Cases; SCR: Supreme Court Reports

5

IRAN

Mehrangiz Kar and Azadeh Pourzand

Introduction

During the reign of Mohammad Reza Shah Pahlavi (1941–79), progress in women's human rights as an historical process gained momentum, patriarchy as culture notably weakened among various social groups, and the government, including the legislative and judicial structures, became far more receptive to the idea that women had an equal claim to rights. Much of this had been achieved step by step by a gradual socio-cultural change that was launched politically by the 1906/1907 Constitutional Revolution, accelerated by the Pahlavi modernization policies, and supported by the educated progressives with moderate and leftist political inclinations who helped spread it to other parts of society. Throughout this history, religious resistance was always a force to be reckoned with and needed to be pacified. Modernizing changes under Reza Shah (1925–41) affected many facets of national life, but not the laws that denied women political participation or governed family relations, although his banning veiling allowed women to access the public square more easily. In the 1940s and 1950s, the opening of the political space paved the way for women to form numerous organizations in various fields of activity. By the 1960s and 1970s, when the new laws following the White Revolution drastically changed women's position in family and society, women had already become a force to be reckoned with in both family and politics. Thus, women's achievement of their rights was not due only to what government bestowed but also to the fact that they had gained a voice and that their demands were heard.

Since the beginning of the Islamic Revolution, women's rights in Iran have been under attack in the private and public spheres of life, as the new regime "speedily and rigorously revitalized the Islamic forms of patriarchy which clerics believed to be undermined by the Pahlavi dynasty" (Honarbini-Holliday 2008: 45). The assertion of religious orthodoxy aimed to enforce a social model where women's role was as devoted mothers, loyal wives, and obedient citizens.

In the face of many setbacks, women's rights advocates, female lawyers, and ordinary women have risen to engage in decades of struggle to reform discriminatory laws while dealing with forceful pushback from the authorities.

This study aims to shed light on how women's rights have regressed, by analyzing women's legal, social, and political status and assessing the relationship between family laws and violence against women (VAW).

This chapter will review literature on family law reform and VAW in Iran as well as relevant laws. It will discuss interviews with scholars, female lawyers, and women's rights advocates. The study also includes insights from the primary author, Mehrangiz Kar, who practiced law in the Islamic Republic (1979–2001), has written extensively on the subject, and is one of the pioneers of women's rights advocacy in Iran. Finally, the study is informed by the discussions that took place at a national workshop (November 2016) where the authors shared initial research findings with a group of prominent scholars. In the process of covering these materials, there will be some duplication and overlap.

A milestone on the way to gender equality: The Family Protection Law (1975)

Founded in 1966, the Women's Organization of Iran (WOI) was run by women who had been educated in Iranian and foreign universities. Soon after its inception, the WOI became a forceful agency for informing, enabling, and motivating the government to address women's issues in the country. The WOI's legal department was in charge of bringing pressing matters, such as the need for reforms in Family Laws and Family Courts, to the attention of the authorities. Against this background, in 1967, the Parliament passed the first Family Protection Law, followed by its final revised version in 1975.

A number of progressive reforms adopted between 1967 and 1975 bypassed Sharia law. For the first time in Iran's legal system, Family Courts were established, with judges who were graduates of law schools. Family Courts handling divorce cases followed a special procedure. According to Mir-Hosseini and colleagues,

> All divorcing couples were required to appear in courts presided over by civil judges, some of them women. In the absence of a mutual consent to divorce, the court would, upon the establishment of certain grounds, issue a certificate referred to as "Impossibility of Reconciliation" ("*adam-e saāzeš*").
> (Mir-Hosseini et al. 1999)

Essentially, registration of divorce without a court certificate became an offense with legal consequences. One of the most progressive developments in Iran's history was for a court to be able to end a marriage even if the husband was unwilling to divorce his wife (Khorasani-Ahmadi 2008).

A more in-depth look into the 1975 Family Protection Law reveals key legal gains for women, including the following improvements:

- Marriage before the minimum age of eighteen for women and twenty for men became illegal (Article 23);
- Men's unilateral right to divorce was abolished – men and women now had rights to divorce and were only allowed to request a divorce in court (Article 8);
- Upon divorce, the court would decide which parent had the competency and financial means to have custody of children (Articles 12, 13, and 14);
- Both maternal and paternal grandfathers were now considered equally for guardianship of children who had lost their fathers, with the court having discretion to delegate the guardianship to the mother in some cases (Article 15);
- Even though a widowed mother would lose the custody of her children upon remarriage, the court could grant the mother or another able relative the custody of the children in cases when the grandfathers were deceased or unfit for the responsibility (Article 15); and
- Polygamy was limited to a second wife, with the consent of the first wife or, in rare and specified circumstances, by the court, or else the parties would face legal consequences, even if the second marriage was performed in accordance with Sharia law (Article 16).

It is interesting to note that the adoption of the Family Protection Law, which provided significant legal safeguards for women, was often labeled and criticized by certain factions of the modern left as "Westoxication" and by the clerics and their conservative allies as "promoting prostitution" and loose morality (Kar 2007: 31). Thus, for Ayatollah Khomeini and his followers, any reform in support of women's rights meant leading women to moral depravity.

Progress towards gender equality in other arenas

The law that came into force in 1969 put nearly one hundred women on the judge's bench. In this era, women also had the right to demand social and legal change through access to media and the freedom to assemble and create independent organizations for women's advancement. Various centers affiliated with the WOI provided women with free reproductive healthcare and contraception. Abortion became legal on demand for unmarried women and with the consent of the husband for married women.

In addition to the gains noted above, by 1978, the revision of the Family Protection Law as well as laws and regulations related to employment had increased women's rights in child rearing and child custody, and women's employment outside the home was supported, including extending paid maternity leave to seven months, part-time work with full-time benefits for mothers until children reached three years of age, and childcare facilities on work premises became obligatory.

In general, women's rights and freedoms expanded in various spheres of life during this time. With the exception of "honor" killing, the law condemned VAW. Social freedoms for men and women had become acceptable and customary – the mingling of the two sexes in public and at private gatherings, parties, ceremonies, restaurants, movie theaters, and sport stadiums was common.

Moreover, prior to the 1979 Revolution, Iran had ratified human rights conventions, including the International Covenant on Civil and Political Rights (ICCPR). According to Article 9 of the Civil Law, which is still in place, these commitments are irrevocable.

The Islamic Revolution: a major setback in women's rights

The 1979 Islamic Revolution was the beginning of a new political, social, economic, cultural, and legal era in Iran, which led to a new chapter in women's lives in particular, and resulted in restrictions on women's organizations. Ever since the Islamic Revolution, the leaders of the Islamic Republic have referred to Islam and values such as honor and dignity to justify their imposition, legalization, and institutionalization of various forms of VAW: "With the rise of Islam as both a spiritual and a political force in the latter part of the twentieth century, Islamist political movements became closely identified with patriarchal notions of gender drawn from classical fiqh" (Mir-Hosseini 2013: 12). The Islamic Revolution's consequences for women's rights did not end with the revocation of the Family Protection Law; there were many other limitations including closing the National Organization for Women and most other professional and rights based women's institutions.

Setbacks to women's rights in the family

Ayatollah Khomeini suspended the Family Protection Law on 26 February 1979, which marked a major setback in the history of women's rights in contemporary Iran. Examples of some of the key losses for women as a result of the revocation include: Family Courts were dissolved, leaving the handling of family-related conflicts once again in the hands of marriage and divorce registry offices (notaries); laws related to marriage came once again under Article 1133 of the Iranian Civil Code of 1931, which gives men an unconditional right to divorce at any time (Kar 2006: 81–87); women no longer enjoyed equal rights with men to divorce; men regained the right to marry up to four permanent and an unlimited number of temporary wives; mothers lost equal rights to child custody, and the minimum legal age for marriage decreased to age fifteen for boys and age nine for girls.

Discrimination in other spheres

The Islamic Penal Code put in place after the Islamic Revolution (1979) treats women unequally when compared to men in numerous instances. According to the code, not wearing Islamic dress is designated as a crime, punishable by law first by flogging or financial penalty, and if repeated, by two months of imprisonment or financial penalty. The age of criminal responsibility is lower for women than men. According to the Islamic Penal Code, the age of criminal responsibility is the same as the age of puberty. The age of puberty for women (considering the lunar calendar) is age nine; meaning nine-year-old girls can be put on trial and punished as adults. And, since the age of puberty for men is deemed to be age fifteen, it means that criminal responsibility would apply to them six years later.

In post-Revolutionary Iran, women from less privileged, impoverished, and marginalized communities, in particular those from ethnic and religious minority groups, face an even higher degree of discrimination and violence than what was briefly described above. While often deprived of socio-economic support, many are also left uninformed about their limited rights, given lower literacy rates and other similar challenges. Sometimes factors such as the inaccessibility of the law in ethnic languages becomes yet another barrier. Moreover, many women from marginalized communities experience a complex web of violence; for them, local and legal patterns of patriarchy are often combined with the Islamic Republic's discriminatory policies against ethnic and religious minority groups. In some cases, women from these communities feel such severe discrimination and seclusion that they go as far as self-immolation, as happens, for example, in provinces such as Ilam, a Kurdish-majority province.

VAW – a complex problem

The roots of VAW in Iran lie in a collection of mutually affecting components, which include forms of violence such as domestic, social, political, and specific interpretations of religion. To understand VAW in Iran, one should not solely focus on the physical form of violence, but on sexual, psychological, financial, and political violence as well. Since the Iranian Revolution, women have experienced new forms of violence in the public and private spheres. These forms can be seen within the framework of the infrastructure of Iran's revolutionary culture and revolutionary laws, which are both rooted in the same religious traditions. They include emphasis on the value of separation of genders on college campuses, prohibition of women's attendance as spectators at men's sports competitions, blocking the appearance of female artists, and other such forms of violence.

In Iran, as in other countries, women are accustomed to concealing the violence in their lives from others. In particular, they often resist seeking help from courts and public service organizations. Iranian women are subject to control by their fathers, brothers, and brothers-in-law, and, after they marry, they are subject to control by their husbands and their husband's relatives. In the workplace, women are subject to control by their male superiors, and, in their social lives, they are held back by misogynist traditions. In this climate, they resign themselves to violence. Men in Iran who commit violence against their spouses feel encouraged by the general tolerance of VAW, believing that violent behavior is a husband's absolute right.

According to the laws of Iran, after divorce women may be left in poverty, which often leads them to decide to stay with violent husbands. They may also make such decisions due to Iran's unfavorable child custody rules, fearing that after a divorce, they will lose custody. Moreover, women contemplating divorce face a situation where society looks down on divorced women. In these circumstances, a woman suffering from violence may choose suicide rather than a divorce.

Also, claiming alimony (*mehrieh*/dower) after divorce, which, according to Iranian laws, belongs to women, may cause violence against women in the home. In some instances, after signing the marriage contract, a man who owes alimony to his spouse will try to convince the woman to give it up, often under pressure from his family and friends. When a woman wants a divorce and the husband resists, he can use privileges given to him by the law, so that the woman, in the long run, has to give up all of her financial rights in order to complete the divorce. Thus, alimony, which theoretically is a base of security for Iranian women, has become a basis of VAW in the major cities of Iran.

Under both internal and international pressures, some Iranian officials have shown concern for VAW. Also, the phenomenon of increasing VAW has engaged Iranian professionals, who are now receptive to the necessity of controlling it. VAW has become a subject of debate in the media, and some incidents have been featured in headlines. In some instances, the press examines social problems that can lead to VAW. The media, however, operates under repressive conditions and cannot necessarily address key points related to cases of VAW.

Both religious and non-religious traditions, mixed with superstitions, justify VAW. Criticizing traditional points of view in religious and secular contexts is essential, but criticizing Iranian traditions is generally difficult, and criticizing Iranian religious traditions is dangerous due to the lack of protections for freedom of expression. The Iranian press, functioning in the relatively liberal atmosphere that was created after the reform in 1997, has started to work on this important task, and even though the press is continuously under the threat of being suspended and shut down, work on this has continued.

Many experts on religion, specialists in Islamic law, and religious figures have joined the movement of criticizing traditions and especially the VAW that Islamic traditions perpetuate. Iranian society needs corrective interpretations of religion in order to make a peaceful transition to a more constructive understanding of religion. In other words, a society with Iran's particular characteristics requires addressing intricate cultural questions in order to combat VAW.

In Iran, unfortunately, precise statistics on the phenomenon of spousal abuse are lacking. Iranian laws do not provide any specific punishments for men guilty of using VAW in the family, and law enforcement often delays dealing with incidents of VAW. Members of law enforcement believe that family quarrels should be resolved within the limits of the home. It is considered improper for a woman to go to the police or other legal authorities, and, when desperate women do so, they are often reproached. In some instances, the authorities pre-judge and then dismiss their complaints, and even in cases when a woman claims that her life has been threatened by a man, the authorities often remain indifferent.

The dismissive attitudes towards abused women, the lack of shelters for women, and the deficiencies of Iranian laws indicate that the government is not familiar with its responsibility in this area. Therefore, it is important to remind the government of the duties it has to protect the rights of half of its citizens.

Creating an understanding of women's rights and correcting the mistaken belief that women are second-class citizens is a necessary step, one that would mark progress (Kar 2000).

Reform initiatives in the Islamic Republic

The domestic political fragmentations and rivalries within the Islamic Republic have created an imperfect discourse of reform that has had implications for the women's rights movement even when no actual reforms are being achieved. Sometimes this situation has given temporary spaces for women's organizations to grow in the face of repressive laws, but at other times the fragmentation and rivalries have reduced the minimal space for women's rights advocacy. This section provides a quick overview of the key structural obstacles to legal reforms in Iran, as well as some of the characteristics of the women's movement towards reforms.

Iranian authorities claim that the Islamic Republic is a political structure founded on Islamic laws and principles (Kar 2008: 390). And, as Ertürk notes, "The governance structure of Iran is male-dominated, with a strong conservative character . . . [T]he authorities in Iran do not regard this situation as negotiable; therefore, prospects for intervention and change are rather limited" (Ertürk 2016: 230).

With the current non-democratic legislative structure, which gives veto power to an unelected Guardian Council, as well as with the vague conditions of Islamic criteria mentioned in the Constitution of the Islamic Republic, even minimal change seems impossible (Pourzand 2010: 59). The Islamic Consultative Assembly, the *Majles*, does not have independence (Article 94 of the Constitution of the Islamic Republic of Iran). The Guardian Council, which consists of six high-ranking clerical and six non-clerical members, has the power to veto any legislation by the *Majles* (Article 91 of the Constitution of the Islamic Republic of Iran). There is also the Expediency Council, composed of thirty-one members appointed by the Supreme Leader, which is empowered to resolve legislative deadlocks between the *Majles* and the Guardian Council.

Thus, on the one hand, the Islamic Republic's legislative system may not allow democratic laws to pass, relying on the excuse that these laws are in contradiction with Islam. On the other hand, even though the Islamic Republic has not ratified CEDAW, deeming it incompatible with Islamic norms, the Iranian government has entered into significant international human rights obligations that in many instances it fails to meet. In addition to the human rights conventions ratified during the Pahlavi era, the Islamic Republic also ratified the Convention on the Rights of the Child (CRC) in 1994, although with reservations on some articles as being incompatible with Islamic laws.

Characterizing family law reforms in today's Iran

Research and interviews with Iranian women's rights advocates for this case study demonstrate a few key contributing factors to consider when studying ongoing attempts for legal reforms towards gender equality in post-Revolutionary Iran.[1]

First, women continuously seek ways to overcome the barriers the law puts before them. While their efforts to overcome some of these legal forms of discrimination may not have led to substantial legal reforms, they have, however, contributed to creating new contradictions in society and becoming a force of social pressure against the Islamic Republic's discriminatory laws and policies. Women are seeking a way around discriminatory laws, for example by engaging in so-called "white marriages" – in which couples choose to live together outside of marriage, which is a rising phenomenon in today's Iran. One also sees increasing rates of divorce and a high number of female university graduates. Such trends will likely continue to challenge the discriminatory laws as new realities and societal norms transcend legal discriminations and traditional restrictions.

Second, there have been instances when women's rights advocates were successful in engaging more moderate decision-makers of the Islamic Republic in pushing for reforms. In these cases where state officials and/or representatives finally took a step, even if small, to begin the process of legal reforms, the hardline institutions appointed by the Supreme Leader created major barriers to appropriate legislation. For example, the Guardian Council vetoed the Sixth Islamic Consultative Assembly's (*Majles*) decision to ratify CEDAW.

Third, a close look at the attempts to improve women's conditions in the Islamic Republic reveals the importance of Islamic jurisprudence and *fatwa*s (religious edicts). In most cases where the law was at least slightly revised in favor of women (e.g., divorce, child custody for martyrs' widows, abortion), jurisprudence and/or *fatwas* made by high-ranking clerics allowed for a more moderate reading of the Islamic law, justified in line with the conditions of time and place. Essentially, in today's Iran the only source for legislation is "Islamic *ahkam* [rules] and Shi'a *Fiqh* [Islamic jurisprudence]" (Article 4 of the Constitution of the Islamic Republic). In this context, legal reform to improve the circumstances of women is not possible without reliance on the *fatwa*s and jurisprudence of high-ranking clerics within the ruling elite of the Islamic Republic.

Evolving policies on women and the Islamic Republic's political dynamics

Soon after the Islamic Revolution, the Iran–Iraq War (1981–89) broke out and lasted for eight bloody years. Although the general environment of the country was quite repressive, the condition of women was even more repressed than during the earlier years of the Revolution. Islamic dress rules were harshly enforced, as the Islamic Republic emphasized that maintaining the image of the "chaste woman" was women's single most important duty because it symbolically protected the nation against the enemy by honoring the blood of the nation's martyrs.

Ironically, the war was not entirely damaging for women's rights. Many of the widows of the martyrs (but also their mothers, sisters, and daughters) approached the Martyr Foundation demanding direct access to their widow allowance and to the custody of their children. The efforts of these women, many of whom had emerged from revolutionary families, ultimately resulted in an important exception to the law when Ayatollah Khomeini issued a *fatwa* granting widows of martyrs the right to direct access to the government-sponsored monthly children's allowance, as well as giving them custody of the children rather than giving it to paternal relatives.

Following the end of the war and the death of Ayatollah Khomeini, Ali Akbar Hashemi Rafsanjani (President of the Islamic Republic, 1989–97) attempted to move the country in a more pragmatic direction by ending Iran's isolation. During this time, the most notable event in the context of legal reforms towards gender equality was the Law of Amendment to Divorce Regulations, passed in 1992 (Boe 2015: 154). While this amendment was a positive step, it was still far behind the Family Protection Act that had been in place prior to the Islamic Revolution. This amendment tightened the requirement for the registration of divorce, requiring a court certification, which could only be obtained after arbitration, even when the couple consented to the divorce (Zubaida 2003: 217).

In 1995, the law outlining the criteria for the selection of judges, which was passed in 1984 and barred women from serving as judges, was revised. Under pressure from female lawyers and female law students, the government allowed women to serve as investigative judges, advisors to judges, and advisors within the judiciary system. Nevertheless, despite these gains, women were still not allowed to make final decisions on court cases.

In 1997, Seyed Mohammad Khatami came to power and inspired millions of Iranians with his promises of reform. However, despite promises and efforts, the new president and his cabinet were not able to amend the laws of the Islamic Republic to address the fundamental challenges women face. Reformists did try to create some institutional space for women by allowing non-governmental associations to be legally registered and actively work toward advancing women's rights in Iran. They also found the space to establish networks resulting in important women's rights advocacy campaigns, such as the One Million Signatures for Reform of Discriminatory Family Laws (Women's Learning Partnership (n.d.)) and the "No to Stoning" campaign. Nonetheless, women continued to experience many legal challenges, as well as targeted attacks by hardliners against the visibility of women's rights issues in the press.

In 2003, the Sixth *Majles* (2000–04) passed legislation granting custody of both male and female children until the age of seven to the mother. After this age, the custody decision was left to the opinion of the Family Courts, which after their initial post-Revolutionary abolition had become effectively reconstituted by the judiciary.

The Sixth *Majles* was much less successful in its attempt to persuade the Islamic Republic government to ratify CEDAW. For the first time in the history of the Islamic Republic, the women representatives in the *Majles*, all reformists, went to the offices and homes of high-ranking Shi'a clerics, especially grand ayatollahs, to discuss discriminatory laws against women. Their goal in engaging the clerics in an unprecedented dialogue was to persuade them to issue a *fatwa* that would take into consideration the conditions of modern Iranian society in favor of eliminating legal discrimination against women. But these attempts faced systematic conservative resistance (Kar and Pourzand 2016: 216).

The reform movement ended in 2005, when the hardliner Mahmood Ahmadinejad became the President of the Islamic Republic. During this time, considered one of the darkest eras of the Islamic Republic, there were several key events regarding family law and VAW. The new cabinet of hardliners was determined to crack down on any institutions or campaigns launched to work on gender equality in Iran. Multiple repressive methods, such as long detentions and persecutions, led to the ultimate dissolution of the One Million Signatures Campaign, whose members had set out to raise public awareness about discriminatory laws. The government also closed down the Women's Cultural Center, the organization that was behind the launch of the One Million Signatures Campaign.

Additionally during this time, gender segregation in universities intensified, a quota was introduced for women's admission to universities not to exceed 50 percent, and more restrictions were imposed for obtaining publishing licenses for books that directly or indirectly addressed women's rights (Sadeghi 2010: 38).

In 2013, Hassan Rouhani, who made promises during his campaign in favor of women's rights, became the President of the Islamic Republic, but he has not managed to carry out his program. During Rouhani's presidency, high-ranking clerics, Friday prayer Imams in their lectures, and the Supreme Leader have insisted on policies that are inherently disempowering for women, such as encouraging women to stay at home and to have more children, while limiting employment opportunities for women. In these circumstances, VAW continues.

On a positive note, the new cabinet appointed, as deputy for women's affairs, a woman who belongs to the religious segment of the women's rights movement. Compared to other female public officials in today's Iran, she is visionary and courageous. Her office has tried to push for improvements in the legal and social aspects of women's rights within the principles of the Islamic Republic. However, the security forces, with their influential elements in the judiciary and the hardliner press, have stopped this office from realizing its mission.

Still lacking are major legal reforms to address the realities women face in today's Iran, such as domestic violence, high rates of divorce, women's addiction, child labor, men and women refraining from marriage, and other challenges. Meanwhile, despite the discriminatory and punitive measures included in the law, extra-marital sexual relations and white marriages are growing fast. Nevertheless, against all odds, women continue to work hard and to advocate for their rights in various arenas, including the family, universities, arts, the job market, and beyond.

Examples of struggles for reforms towards gender equality

Less than half of the women's rights advocates and experts that the authors interviewed for this case study do not believe that any positive amendments worth discussing have been made to the country's laws. For a more comprehensive study, one should analyze a longer list of desirable reforms concerning women's rights, such as ending polygamy, assuring equal rights in marriage, allowing the marriage of a Muslim woman with a non-Muslim man, permitting the marriage of an Iranian woman with a foreign national, ending temporary marriage, revising inheritance and blood money rules, etc. However, covering all these topics and more is beyond the scope of this case study. The list provided here is based on the insights of those who believed there were a number of relative and minimal successes in legal reforms toward gender equality in the Islamic Republic of Iran. The improvements that have been made that were mentioned in the interviews were:

(1) an increase in the minimum legal age of marriage for girls from age nine (lunar years) to age thirteen (lunar years) of age,
(2) custody and limited guardianship rights for women over their children, and the right of Iran–Iraq War widows to control their children's finances,
(3) a directive by the judiciary for insurance companies to pay equal compensation (blood money) to women and men in case of bodily harm or death resulting from accidents,
(4) allowing women to inherit the price of land from their husbands, and
(5) permitting women, known as female family counselors or advisors, to participate as judges – although without the authority to issue and sign a final ruling.

Some of these relative improvements are elaborated upon below to illustrate how discriminatory elements remain even after reforms.

Minimum legal age for marriage: After the Islamic Revolution, the minimum legal age for marriage was lowered from age eighteen to age nine for girls. Additionally, the law granted the father and the paternal grandfather of girls younger than age nine the right to marry them off, with the condition that the husband will abstain from sexual relations until the girl-child reaches the legal age of marriage. In 2002, during the Sixth *Majles*, which insisted on increasing the minimum to age eighteen, a new minimum age of thirteen was ultimately approved by the Guardian Council (Birnbaum et al. 2014). However, the amended law (Article 1041 of the Civil Code) also granted the guardian (father or paternal grandfather) permission to marry off younger girls upon the approval of the relevant court. As such, even when amended, the law determining the minimum legal age for marriage remains discriminatory, violating the rights of women and children.

Child custody and guardianship: Following the Islamic Revolution, the law changed so that widowed women were no longer allowed to manage their children's financial affairs. By relying on this provision, paternal grandfathers had the right to manage their grandchildren's financial affairs, and they often used their authority to manipulate the finances to their own advantage. During the Iran–Iraq War, with the granting of a special stipend for the children of martyrs and the increase in the number of widows, this situation posed a serious challenge to the system. Mothers, who had no authority over the management of their children's inheritance or the special stipend, began pressuring the Martyr Foundation. The pressure was so severe that the Foundation requested assistance from the judiciary, which managed to convince Ayatollah Khomeini to issue a *fatwa*. The *fatwa*, which later passed into law on 28 July 1985, limited the paternal grandfather's authority to the child's inheritance. As a result of this *fatwa*, any financial assistance provided by the government to the child would be managed by the rightful custodian of the child, who in many cases was the mother (Kar 2007: 96–97). This *fatwa* marks the first relative victory that came about with women's resistance against gender-based discriminatory laws in the Islamic Republic of Iran.

In the years that followed, the Sixth *Majles* (2000–04) was able to reform aspects of the child custody law in favor of women, bringing the law closer to the principles of Article 3(1) of the Convention on the Rights of the Child. However, even the amended law is not on a par with the Family Protection Act (1975) that was in place before the Revolution. Further, under the current Islamic law, guardianship rules continue to disregard the best interest of the child, according to a legal review by the Centre for Supporters of Human Rights (Impact Iran 2015: 27).

In the case of divorce, where child custody is at stake, Article 1169 of the Civil Code specifies that mothers are the preferred legal custodian for children age seven or younger. After age seven, custody is automatically transferred to the father, if claimed by him in the family court. When a mother remarries, she loses the right to custody of the child even below age seven; this is not the case when a father remarries.

However, legal amendments that emerged during the reform era in 2003 require the court to decide on custody on the basis of the child's best interest. When a child reaches the age of legal majority, the court is obliged to seek his or her opinion prior to determining a custody arrangement based on the child's best interest. In this context, a girl can decide at a younger age than a boy, at age nine (lunar years), with which parent she prefers to live.

It is important to note here that according to Iranian law, custody and guardianship work differently. In other words, legal guardianship is not necessarily based on the best interests of the child. Essentially, while custody can be granted to the mother of a child under age seven or based upon the best interests of the child, the father or the paternal grandfather maintains guardianship, even when the mother has legal custody. In most cases, in the absence of a father or paternal grandfather, a mother will be granted legal guardianship. Much power rests with the guardians, since under the law their approval is required on a variety of legal transactions for their wards, such as signing contracts on behalf of the child, opening bank accounts, accessing legal remedies in court, or granting permission to travel outside the country (Impact Iran 2015: 27).

Divorce: Suspending the Family Protection Act and closing down the Family Courts after the Islamic Revolution was a major setback for women. During this time, requests for divorce, especially by men, increased. The government had to find ways to at least temporarily relieve the escalating apprehension among women. For instance, as a measure of awareness-raising, the government agreed to publish twelve conditions of *aqd* (Islamic marriage) in the marriage contract form. This way, at the time of the marriage, women were able to ask for the permission of their husband-to-be to include these conditions as their rights within the marriage, rights that would improve their position. These conditions were not new and were compatible with Islamic rules. However, the Islamic Republic took advantage of Iranian society's ignorance about these conditions, making it seem as though they were its original measures to protect women's rights in marriage.

In any case, it did not take long for women to realize that such conditions do not replace equal rights in marriage that would guarantee women's rights without the need to obtain the man's signature. Meanwhile, in order to control the chaos that was now occurring, the Islamic Republic created "Special Civic Courts" to process familial disputes. These courts did not change anything in favor of women, and in fact the judges of these courts would refer to some of the interpretations of Islamic law most unfavorable to women.

The Law of Amendment to Divorce Regulations emphasized: (1) Men and women had to refer to the Special Civil Courts to address their marriage disputes. Divorce Offices no longer had the right to register divorces for which the couple had not obtained a ruling from the Special Civil Court that ruled out any possibility for conflict resolution; (2) If necessary, Special Civil Courts could now choose from and bring in eligible female advisors. While a positive step forward, this amendment still did not fully restore the right of women to become judges able to render final decisions, a right that women enjoyed before the Islamic Revolution; (3) When divorce is initiated by the man and there is no evidence of the fault of the woman during the marriage, the husband is obliged to pay a certain amount determined by the court to her, as payment for the housework that she performed while married. This concept, called "*ojrat-ol-mesl*," was originally included in the Islamic law within the context of work compensation, but it was not a concept legally applied to marriage and family law. Even though *ojrat-ol-mesl* was added to the family law after the Islamic Revolution to offset the equal rights taken away from women, the compensation it obliges the husband seeking divorce to provide is typically so minimal that does not cover the wife's living expenses. Additionally, women have limited rights to divorce.

In this context, those women seeking a divorce without the consent of their husband usually forgo any monetary payments due. This is the case both in terms of *ojrat-ol-mesl* and dower (*mehrieh*). On occasion, women seeking divorce are forced not only to give up their monetary claims, but they also resort to paying sums of money or giving property to their husbands in an effort to secure his agreement to divorce.

Moreover, in 1982, the jurists of the Guardian Council requested a *fatwa* from Ayatollah Khomeini. The question posed was: "Does the court have the right to grant a divorce to a woman when it is clear to the court that his behavior towards her is unbearable?" The text of the *fatwa* that was issued is: "In the name of the Exalted, the cautious way is to convince the husband to divorce his wife, but if he was not willing, the court can issue the divorce. If I had the audacity, there is another way that is easier." The clause "If I had the audacity" in the Ayatollah's text clearly shows that the clerics had so limited women's rights in Iran that even such a powerful political and religious figure as Ayatollah Khomeini was worried about the reaction of certain clerics who were against any form of women's rights and who justified their patriarchal mindset with their own extremist interpretations of Islam. This shows that the clash within the Islamic Republic's governance was present from the beginning of the Revolution, with the radicals ultimately succeeding to impose their point of view (Mehrpour 1992–93: 301).

Ultimately, in 1982, Article 1130 of the Civil Code was amended to give judges the authority to grant or withhold divorce requested by women. Article 1130 was again amended in 2002, further empowering judges to issue a divorce requested by the woman if she could establish that the continuation of the marriage would cause intolerable suffering or hardship (Sawma 2015).

Regardless, men continue to enjoy the absolute right to divorce despite the minor adjustments and amendments of post-Revolutionary laws in place. The Sixth *Majles* tried to address this inequality in the context of divorce and managed to amend Article 1133 of the Civil Code, inserting the need to demonstrate "adherence to constituted conditions" for men who seek divorce without the consent of the wife. These conditions include the payment of any maintenance not yet paid to the wife, as well as subsistence for three months and ten days, the payment of dower (taking into consideration inflation), and the *ojrat-ol-mesl* confirmation, based on an expert opinion regarding the amount owed or an agreement between the couple.

All in all, even if these amendments to the law are considered steps in the right direction, the law still has a long way to go to ensure gender equality. The man still has the absolute right to divorce in practice and can put the woman in such difficult circumstances and force her to give up all her financial rights in the marriage, making it possible for the man to gain a divorce that the woman did not originally consent to.

Denial of women's right to become judges with full authority: The right to become a judge was one of the most fundamental rights that women gained in 1969. Immediately after the Revolution, it was announced that, according to Islam, women have no right to become judges. At a meeting of a Delegation of Ministers of the Interim Government of Islamic Republic of Iran on 6 October 1979, a ministerial decision reduced the rank of women judges to an administrative one. After the *Majles* was established in 1982, a single Article was added that said "Judges will be selected from among qualified men" (Resolution of Delegation of Ministers of the Interim Government of the Islamic Republic of Iran 1979 and Qualification of Judges Act 1982).

Today, despite the fact that a large number of Iranian women have studied law and become jurists, they are yet to regain the right they once had. Even though there have been some reforms in women's rights that give them judicial ranks, they still do not have the right to declare or sign off on a final verdict – this right is still exclusive to men. In 1995, a legislation titled "Reforming Article 5 of Addendum 5 of Qualification of Judges Act of 1984" was passed. However, it was but a short and incomplete step toward an attempt to return the position of women to where they once stood before the Revolution. According to this minor legal reform, women with judicial qualifications can now be hired as advisors at the Court of Administrative Justice, Special Civil Courts, Office of Guardianship of Minors, or as examining magistrates and research assistants in any judicial office that requires legal studies and research. However, to date, they are still not allowed to be judges and serve with the full power of a judge.

Women's rights movement: achievements and challenges

The persistence, courage, agility, and hard work of women's rights advocates and ordinary women's demand for gender equality stand out as an important social force throughout history of contemporary Iran. As Tohidi writes:

> [T]he women's resistance and agency on daily basis, and especially the women's rights movement in its semi-organized network format along with its well-framed feminist discourse has been a key agent of change toward a shift in Iran's political culture, resulting in a "post-Islamist" era in Iran.
>
> *(Tohidi 2014)*

This study has benefited from the contributions of fifteen women's rights advocates, lawyers, journalists, and scholars, many of whom have first-hand experiences of activism in the Islamic Republic and some of whom have paid a high price for their work. They have been detained, taken to court, or exiled as a result of their activism. Some still remain in Iran and continue their work against all odds. Those abroad support the work of in-country advocates through research, publication, and digital and offline communication. As such, rather than providing a survey of the wealth of existing literature on the women's rights movement in Iran, this section provides a brief summary of the insights the interviewees have shared with the authors. When asked about the role of the civil society and women's rights movement, all the interviewees stated that women's rights advocates of varying backgrounds have played a key role in bringing about modest but significant revisions to the law.

The interviewees credit ordinary women, women's rights advocates, female lawyers, journalists, authors, publishers, artists, informal groups, women's organizations, women's rights campaigns, and occasionally certain decision-makers within Iran's undemocratic political structure for playing roles in raising issues of concern and in pushing for reforms towards gender equality.

The interviewees warn that civil society in Iran is indeed weak due primarily to state-imposed restrictions and repressive measures that the Islamic Republic has historically and notoriously taken against civil society. Maintaining continuity in the work being done is a challenge. The Islamic Republic strategically follows women's rights initiatives and shuts down advocacy campaigns, putting pressure on their members. Yet another challenge is the fact that many women's rights advocates have had to leave the country or have been exiled, creating a gap in terms of the exchange of ideas and lessons learned among various generations.

Women's rights advocates have used even the smallest opportunities and possibilities for advocacy in order to make their demands known to the Islamic Republic and society at large. In recent years, they have heavily, but not exclusively, relied on cyber activism, utilizing digital advocacy as a tool to continuously engage the public, to pressure the decision-makers for legal reforms, and to connect with women's rights advocates and organizations beyond the borders of Iran. Whenever they have seen a small opening, they have engaged in on-the-ground advocacy work across the country. In the absence of access to registered independent organizations, they have formed informal groups for collective advocacy. Whenever the state has tried to completely shut down their activities, they have sought new ways to continue their work, essentially playing cat-and-mouse with the Islamic Republic.

The interviewees drew attention to multiple layers of women's rights advocacy in Iran: (a) ordinary Iranian women who challenge gender-based discrimination such as the mandatory Islamic veil and gender segregation in their daily lives; (b) individual female professionals such as lawyers and publishers, among them many with advocacy experience *before* the advent of the Islamic Republic and thus quick to identify specific areas of law that are discriminatory against women and to demand reforms through their writing and work; (c) collective semi-organized and organized women's groups and organizations, whether as informal local and grassroots groups across the country, charity organizations dedicated to addressing women's challenges, or more well-defined campaigns advocating for women's rights; and (d) a handful of decision-makers within the state apparatuses of the Islamic Republic who have at times advocated for gender equality, risking their official status. Examples of the early generations of women's rights advocates in the Islamic Republic include: Nobel Peace Prize Laureate (2003) Shirin Ebadi and Mehrangiz Kar (both of whom were lawyers in Iran), as well as women in other arenas such as Shahla Lahiji (founder of Roshangaran Publishing House dedicated to women's voices) and Shahla Sherkat (editor-in-chief of *Women's Magazine* [*Zanan*]). Examples of women's rights campaigns include: One Million Signatures Campaign for Reform of Discriminatory Laws, also known as the One Million Signatures Campaign for Equality (2006); Stop Stoning Forever Campaign (2006); The White Scarf Women (2005); and Banning Domestic Violence Campaign (2016). Examples of decision-makers who have advocated for women in their capacity as officials include: Fatemeh Haghighatjoo, Member of the Sixth *Majles,* and Shahindokht Molaverdi, Vice President on Women and Family Affairs during President Hassan Rouhani's first administration (at the time of writing this study).

As some of the interviewees have pointed out, ironically women's resistance and courageous efforts to obtain gender equality have deepened the Islamic Republic's historical fear of women. By now, the authorities know well that women and women's rights advocates are among the most difficult segment of the population to silence, even if by using force. At the same time, the international community's attention to women's rights in Iran makes it even more difficult for the Islamic Republic to continue its repressive measures against advocates.

It has become increasingly difficult for the state to maintain the discriminatory laws against women while trying to gain legitimacy within the international community as a modern Islamic state.

While continuing to pressure the Islamic Republic to reform laws, women's rights advocates have also focused on raising awareness among women and men in Iranian society and have sought alternative ways to minimize the impact of discriminatory laws on women.

One of the most important aspects of women's rights advocacy in Iran is the ability and willingness of the movement and its advocates to reflect on and learn from previous experiences and shortcomings. For instance, many members of the One Million Signatures Campaign believe that had they engaged the grass-roots in advocacy and awareness-raising more inclusively and in more provinces, they would have achieved better results. Similarly, the interviewees suggest that a key to success for Iran's women's rights movement is to expand its ability to identify the intersections whereby they can reach various segments of the population, ranging from women and child workers to socially influential professionals such as teachers and social workers. The aim here should be not only to seek support for the movement, but also to better understand the population's concerns and to offer solidarity and assistance as appropriate.

Another lesson learned from the pre-revolutionary decades of women's rights advocacy is the importance of engaging domestic media and maintaining dialogue with national and subnational decision-makers. In doing so, women's rights advocates can indirectly provide them with tools, guidelines, and solutions for reforms and improvement of women's status in the law and society, even if minimally, and thus actually help women rather than solely criticize the state.

The fact is, however, that despite almost four decades of women's rights advocacy demanding gender equality in the Islamic Republic, little has been achieved in legal reform. Women and women's rights advocates are still left with a long and rocky road ahead to achieve legal reforms and gender equality in contemporary Iran.

Conclusion

The consequences of gender-based discriminatory laws deeply affect today's Iranian society. In addition to the discriminatory family laws, numerous forms of gender-based discrimination are also embedded in other laws of the country. Although the Islamic Revolution has led to the imposition of discriminatory rules, the basic barrier that Iranian women have been facing is not Islam, which is susceptible to different interpretations depending on time, place, and circumstance, but the nature of the Islamic Republic: the theocratic system created by the political and legal fusion of government and religion.

In concluding, it is critical to note that Iranian women have not surrendered to the country's discriminatory laws. While they have long suffered from gender-based discriminatory laws in the Islamic Republic, calling them victims would be an underestimation of their courage, innovation, persistence, endurance, and agility in their struggles towards gender equality. Legal reforms have been minimal in the Islamic Republic. Yet, even the most minimal of legal reforms in favor of women would not have been possible without the tireless efforts and the courage of women and women's rights advocates in Iran.

Note

1 Scholars, lawyers, and women's rights advocates interviewed in December 2016 for this case study include: Nasrin Afzali, Dr. Leila Alikarami, Zohreh Asadpour, Sahar Beit Mashal, Faranak Farid, Dr. Shahla Haeri, Ava Homa, Banafsheh Jamili, Jelveh Jayaheri, Shahla Lahiji, Dr. Fatemeh Moghadam, Forough Samee'nia, Mona Silavi, and Sussan Tahmasebi. An additional interviewee has requested to remain anonymous.

References

Birnbaum, Lili, Cetinkaya Hasret, and Elizabeth Harper (2014) *Children in Iran: Crime, Marriage, Legal Recognition and International Treaty Obligations*, University of Essex, UK: Human Rights in Iran Unit, www.essex.ac.uk/hri/documents/brief-children-in-iran. pdf.

Boe, Marianne (2015) *Family Law in Contemporary Iran: Women's Rights Activism and Sharia*, London: I.B. Tauris & Co. Ltd.

Ertürk, Yakın (2016) *Violence without Borders: Paradigm, Policy and Praxis Concerning Violence Against Women*, Bethesda, MD: Women's Learning Partnership.

Honarbini-Holliday, Mehri (2008) *Becoming Visible in Iran: Women in Contemporary Iranian Society*, New York: Tauris Academic Studies.

Impact Iran (2015) "Rights of the Child in Iran," www.crin.org/sites/default/files/iran_joint_submission_to_crc_committee_0.pdf.

Kar, Mehrangiz (2000) *Pazhuhishi dar Barih yi Khushunat 'alayh Zanan dar Iran* (*Violence Against Women in Iran*), Tehran: Roshangaran.

——— (2006) *Shooresh* (*Rebellion*), Stockholm, Sweden: Baran Publishing.

——— (2007) *Crossing the Red Line: The Struggles for Human Rights in Iran*, Costa Mesa, CA: Mazda Publishers/Blind Owl Press.

——— (2008) "Islam, Democracy and Post-9/11 Nation Building: Is the Islamic Republic of Iran Compatible with the Principles of Democracy and Human Rights," in *Regent Journal of International Law*, Vol. 6, Issue 2, Virginia Beach, VA: Regent University School of Law.

——— and Azadeh Pourzand (2016) "The Rule of Law and Conflict in the Reform Era," in Daniel Brumberg and Farideh Farhi (eds.), *Power and Change in Iran: Politics of Contention and Conciliation*, Bloomington, IN: Indiana University Press.

Khorasani-Ahmadi, Nooshin (2008) "Reform and Regression: The Fate of the Family Protection Law: Interview with Mahnaz Afkhami," Tehran, Iran: The Feminist School, http://fis-iran.org/en/women/articles/reform-and-regression.

Mehrpour, Hossein (1992–93) *Nazarat-e Showrayeh Negahban* (*Opinions of the Guardian Council*), Vol. 1, Tehran: Kayhan Publication.

Mir-Hosseini, Ziba, Mansour Shaki, and Jeanette Wakin (1999) "Family Law," in *Encyclopaedia Iranica*, www.iranicaonline.org/articles/family-law#iii.

Mir-Hosseini, Ziba (2013) "Justice, Equality and Muslim Family Laws: New Ideas, New Prospects," in Ziba Mir-Hosseini, Kari Vogt, Lena Larsen, and Christian Moe (eds.), *Gender and Equality in Muslim Family Law: Justice and Ethics in the Islamic Legal Tradition*, New York: I.B. Tauris & Co. Ltd.

Pourzand, Lily (2010) "Family Law and Gender Equality in Iran: Challenges, Obstacles and Opportunities," Toronto: York University's Graduate Program in Higher Education [A Major Research Paper Submitted to the Faculty of Graduate Studies].

Sadeghi, Fatemeh (2010) "Bypassing Islamism and Feminism: Women's Resistance and Rebellion in Post-revolutionary Iran" in *Revue des mondes musulmans et de la Méditerranée* (*Review of the Muslim Worlds and the Mediterranean*) [online], http://remmm.revues.org/6936.

Sawma, Gabriel (2015) "The Law of Marriage in Iran," http://gabrielsawma.blogspot.co.uk/2015/01/the-law-of-marriage-in-iran.html.

Tohidi, Nayereh (2014), "The Women's Rights Movement and Feminist in Post Islamist Iran," California State University Northridge, www.cmes.ucsb.edu/conference/Gallagher%20Paper%20Summaries/Nayereh%20Tohidi.pdf.

Women's Learning Partnership (n.d.) "Iran's One Million Signatures Campaign," www.learningpartnership.org/iran-oms.

Zubaida, Sami (2003) *Law and Power in the Islamic World*, London: I.B. Tauris & Co. Ltd.

6

LEBANON

Ziyad Baroud and Ghadir El-Alayli

Introduction

Reforming family laws to challenge gender-based violence (GBV) in Lebanon is currently not possible due to objections made by political and religious authorities as well as citizens. Hence, the focus for now should be on reforming law No. 293 on the protection of women and other family members from domestic violence, adopted on 7 May 2014 (referred to hereinafter as "the 2014 Law" or "the Law"). As discussed below, this will allow for filling in its gaps and overcoming shortcomings, pitfalls, and flaws. An amended domestic violence law will also challenge the discriminatory family laws in the long run.

Therefore, the main objective of this study is to assess the 2014 Law, its implementation, and its impact, as well as reforms suggested over the past years and the resistance to such initiatives. In addition, we will also examine the criminal law provisions related to gender-based family violence (Legislative Decree No. 340 of 1 March 1943). As noted below, some religious authorities were especially against the 2014 Law or had serious reservations about its major provisions, which they perceived as "contradictory" with respective religious provisions.

Without going into the details of the numerous religious laws in force in Lebanon, this chapter will provide a general review of their substance, with the aim of understanding their mutual convergence and divergence with the 2014 Law. Due to Lebanon's several religious confessions, there are many texts of family law. The family laws related to the two largest religious communities are the Catholic Personal Status Law of 22 February 1949, which applies to the largest category of Christians, and the Ottoman Family Law of 25 October 1917, which applies to Sunni, Ja'fari (i.e., Shi'a), and Alawi Muslims.

This case study assesses the legal tools related to family law reform to challenge GBV in both theory and practice, notably from a human rights point of view and based on international standards and good practices. Although this study is mainly concerned with legal texts, it bears in mind the linkage between law and other social and human sciences, notably sociology, and the importance of a transversal and multidisciplinary approach, in order to ensure the best interests of the victims of domestic GBV, especially women and children. The article points to clear and targeted recommendations for legal reform where needed.

In addition to prominent references available at academic and professional Lebanese legal libraries, as well as relevant news, articles, press conferences, and investigative reports published in local newspapers, this study also includes interviews with individuals at the most effective special center for rehabilitation against violence, i.e., KAFA: (Enough) Violence & Exploitation Organization.[1]

The national context

A detailed introduction to the Lebanese legislative and socio-political system is necessary to understand the Lebanese laws related to family and domestic GBV.

Therefore, we will first review Lebanon's engagements for human rights to address the need for reform of religious laws and regulations and examine the debate on secularism vs. confessionalism.[2] Later, we will describe the struggle for a civil, i.e., secular, family law. Finally, we will analyze Lebanon's achievement in 2014 by promulgating a special law on the protection of women and other family members from domestic violence.

Lebanon's engagements for human rights

Lebanon has ratified all major UN Conventions, including the Convention on the Elimination of All Forms of Discrimination against Women (CEDAW) (with reservations). In light of the principles of international law provisions, international standards, and good practices, as well as of justice, equality, and fairness, and of natural law, reforming the civil personal status, i.e., family legislation, in Lebanon is a must because currently these are sectarian laws that are often discriminatory (G. El-Alayli 2008; Zalzal 2014: 72).

Religious reforms

To guarantee the respect of fundamental rights, bold and remarkable reform efforts have been made from within religions, both Christianity and Islam (A. El-Alayli 1992; Shamseddine 2006 and 2014; Nasr 2012: 499). Regarding Islam, the calls to re-open *'ijtihad*[3] – which was unfortunately closed – are a good example of the above, based on changing times and circumstances. In fact, there are two conceptions of *'ijtihad*. In the first, *'ijtihad* means derivation of Shar'i *hukm* [law, regulation, or command] through personal judgement and *ray* [personal judgment] for an issue for which the *mujtahid* [person who is using *'ijtihad*] does not find any express text in the Qur'an or the Sunnah [sayings and deeds of the Prophet Muhammad].

(www.al-islam.org)

In the second,

'ijtihad means deduction of the *ahkam* [plural of *hukm*] from the reliable sources (the Quran, the Sunnah, *ijma'* [consensus, or an opinion in which Islamic scholars are unanimous in their ruling], and *'aql* [intellect or intelligence]).

(www.al-islam.org)

Secularism vs. confessionalism

This study asserts that the Lebanese state should promulgate a common civil law for all Lebanese citizens regardless of their religious confessions and beliefs. It is hoped this would ensure fundamental rights on both theoretical and practical levels. However, Lebanese law concerning personal status matters is sectarian, with eighteen legally recognized religious confessions (i.e., sects) in Lebanon belonging to the three monotheist religions. Lebanon has only one non-sectarian family law, entitled "Law on Inheritance of non-Mahometans,"[4] meaning non-Muslims. But this only relates to inheritance matters and is mainly applied to Christians, Jews, and other non-Muslims.

As mentioned above, Lebanon is party to many international human rights treaties. Paragraph B of the Preamble of the Constitution provides that Lebanon is "a founding and active member of the United Nations Organization and abides by its covenants and by the Universal Declaration of Human Rights. The State shall embody these principles in all fields and areas without exception." In addition, Article 7 of the Constitution states that "All Lebanese shall be equal before the law. They shall equally enjoy civil and political rights and shall equally be bound by public obligations and duties without any distinction."

Moreover, Article 9 of the Constitution explicitly guarantees

The freedom of conscience is absolute. The state in rendering homage to the God Almighty respects all religions and creeds and guarantees, under its protection, the free exercise of all religious rites provided that public order is not disturbed. It also guarantees that the personal status and religious interests of the population, to whatever religious sect they belong, shall be respected.

Thus, it is clear that the Lebanese legal system is characterized by its legislative and judicial pluralism regarding personal status matters. Based on Article 9, historical religious communities (as listed in Decree 60 L.R. adopted on 13 March

1936, promulgated under the French mandate) have been granted legislative and jurisdictional powers in matters related to marriage, divorce, adoption, and custody. However, as per Decree 53 L.R. dated 30 March 1939, Muslims have been withdrawn from the scope of Decree 60 L.R. because they refused the provisions of the former, which lead to the promulgation of the latter after only three years.

The legislative and jurisdictional powers granted to religious communities are: the law of 2 April 1951, defining the prerogatives of the Christian and Jewish communities; the Druze personal status law of 24 February 1948, defining the prerogatives of the Druze community (which is technically a Mahometan, i.e., Muslim confession); and the law of 16 July 1962, on the Regulation of Sunni and Ja'fari Justice, defining the prerogatives of the Sunni and Ja'fari communities (the two major Muslim communities). In addition to all of these prerogatives, Muslim communities are granted jurisdiction over inheritance and wills. Regarding other personal status matters,[5] the civil courts have jurisdiction and civil law is applicable (Frontiers Ruwad 2016).

However, it is important to point out that the civil law on non-Mahometans' inheritance rights could technically be extended to all Lebanese who do not wish to be religiously flagged but simply treated as citizens. Increasingly, activists are trying to base their secular discourse on this idea. In fact, Article 9 (see above) of the Lebanese Constitution protects freedom of belief as being absolute. This means that legally each Lebanese person should have the right to choose and change his/her religion or sect. And Decree 60 L.R. (see above) grants the right to each individual to be affiliated with a "common right community" (i.e., a community that would not be flagged under any of Lebanon's eighteen religious sects) or not to be affiliated with any religious group at all, and submits such an individual to a civil code in personal status matters. However, in practice, no "common right community" has been implemented by the state and no civil code in personal status matters has been adopted (Frontiers Ruwad 2016).

Most of the confessional laws are inherently unequal concerning gender relations, and in matters such as the marriage of minors, adoption, and alimony.[6] And the Lebanese Court of Cassation has a limited oversight of decisions of the religious courts, in cases in which such decisions are final and in violation of the religious communities' jurisdiction or in violation of substantial procedural rules considered as pertaining to the public order.[7]

Gender inequality exists in several other laws in Lebanon, some of which are civil (i.e., secular), such as Decree No. 15 dated 19 January 1925, regarding Lebanese nationality (G. El-Alayli 2011 and 2015), and Decree No. 13955 dated 26 September 1963, concerning social security.

What about a civil law?

Historically, civil society, including women's groups, have initiated draft bill proposals to reform the personal status (i.e., family) laws, but to date, none has been adopted. In this respect, many policy papers have also been drafted. This indicates that secular issues, which are linked to women's rights (see below), are not a priority in Lebanon (Musawah 2015: 3), especially for the authorities.

On the one hand, some authors, activists, and NGOs, including feminists, have called for a mandatory civil law applicable to all Lebanese citizens, which would make the religious personal status laws optional and the confessional jurisdictions laws exceptional. For instance, this is KAFA's (Enough) point of view.[8] Others prefer an optional civil personal status law, or, even more nuanced, an optional law that would be limited to civil marriage, leaving the remaining matters of family law to personal choice.

In fact, "civil legislation can help citizens create new social values, redefine their loyalties and widen their scopes of civic participation" (Chartouni 1993). A relatively recent example of such measures was the circular of the former Minister of Interior Ziyad Baroud (co-author of this case study) dated 11 February 2009, which says that to safeguard the "absolute freedom of conscience"[9] (conjunction of Article 9 of the Constitution (see above) and international treaties that have constitutional value for human rights and non-discrimination), citizens may require that the administrative authorities remove the reference to any religious community from the official registers.

This would lead to a legal gap, since Lebanese citizens currently have no legal existence outside their respective religious communities, whether on the level of personal status or of national elections and political representation. Hence, this would push legislators to create civil (i.e., secular) legislation regulating this situation. Unfortunately, the Parliament has remained inert on this, and, once again, confessionalism is stronger than secular reforms. Some activists and politicians refer to the 1990 amendment of the Constitution, which invites Lebanese to surpass confessionalism. Unfortunately, together the political and socio-economic establishment, as well as religious authorities, are stronger than secular reforms.

The 2014 achievement

For the reasons explained here, the relatively new 2014 Law was not formulated as a *direct* reform to family laws. However, the drafting and the adoption of this law to protect children and women from domestic violence opened, for the first time in Lebanon, a serious breach in the general legal system regulating family issues.[10] This is why this law was very controversial and was opposed mainly by religious authorities because they were afraid of losing their source of revenue if they gave up the privileges they enjoy by virtue of the current laws.

All of this is the result of the Lebanese demographic, social, cultural, and political situation in which religious communities play a major role on all levels, especially since not only is the Lebanese legislative system confessional, but the political system is also sectarian.[11] Despite all of the above, the promulgation of the 2014 Law happened thanks to feminist NGOs and human rights activists' lobbying in a context of rising public demand to address the growing number of severe cases of domestic violence. This law's approval was a watershed legislative event regarding family law matters related to GBV.

The 2014 Law and family law-related matters

Violence against women (VAW) is a general problem that faces Lebanese society in all its different categories, regardless of people's faith, region, economic situation, background, etc. (Wilson Center 2013).

As aforementioned, the approval on 7 May 2014, of the Law for the Protection of Women and Family Members against Domestic Violence was a major event in Lebanese society, both legislatively and in public discourse.[12] The law was implemented just two weeks after its entry into force in a decision issued by the Judge of Urgent Matters in Beirut (31 May 2014).[13]

As will be discussed below, the defects of the Law "reflect the absence of political will to explicitly condemn VAW, and the adoption of red lines that are not in the *interest of the family* but reveal a desire to maintain the gender gap" (Zalzal 2014: 60; emphasis added).

It should be noted that the approval of the 2014 Law did not *directly* reform family laws. In fact, the Law provided that all contrary or inconsistent provisions shall be annulled, *except for* the rules of jurisdiction of the Personal Status Courts, the provisions on personal status that remain exclusively applicable in their respective fields, and the law on the protection of juveniles who are in conflict with the law or at risk (Article 22).[14] And neither the latter nor the 2014 Law explicitly addresses

> how to resolve conflicts that may arise between civil court rulings over religious court rulings. While the Court of Cassation has tried to resolve this issue in cases regarding child protection measures, there are still no clear conflict rules allowing for the state courts to refuse the implementation of religious court orders not complying with fundamental individual rights.
>
> *(Frontiers Ruwad 2016)*

Although the 2014 Law did not *specifically* and *directly* reform family laws, it did seriously affect the family law system. Reforming the religious personal status laws is, for the time being, not practically acceptable to most of the Lebanese stakeholders. Therefore, currently in Lebanon, the most pragmatic, realistic, and efficacious way to challenge GBV would be to amend some of the 2014 Law's provisions in order to cover their shortcomings.

One of the aspects and results of gender discrimination in religious family laws is domestic violence. Progressive religious leaders believe that any literal interpretations of religious texts that advocate or condone the beating of a person, notably a family member and especially women, should firmly be rejected. Many of these texts originally outlined the personal opinions held by some religious scholars and acquired varying degrees of religious sanctity in the years that followed. Over time, those personal opinions were viewed as religious literature that was impervious to debate of any kind. The very strong opinions advanced by those scholars of the past have clearly influenced the customs, traditions and concepts held today in certain communities.

(El-Amili 2011)

But these interpretations should be surpassed, which would not be in contradiction with the relevant religions, because they are the result of extremist interpretations of religion that are "blatantly insensitive to religion and offensive to women. Ultimately, however, such notions have no religious orientation whatsoever and certainly do not complement its essence" (El-Amili 2011). In fact, the substance of religions (notably Christianity and Islam, the main religions in Lebanon) is based on *moral and ethical values*, which reject or at least do not encourage VAW.

There is also a need to reform religious family laws in the matter related to age of marriage (see above), which is sometimes related to gender-based domestic violence. Some progressive religious leaders believe that Sharia law does not allow minor girls to be married before they reach the age of religious responsibility (*sinn at-takleef*). However, minors *are* currently being exploited by being married before they are mentally and physically ready – especially in some communities that use religious texts to justify this practice. Given contemporary circumstances, challenging the religious texts that advocate early marriage means the essence of such legislation must change as well. In fact, a Sharia rule provides that "Provisions may change with time." Feminist/women's NGOs, including ABAAD (Dimensions), and human rights activists are also lobbying against child marriage and base their arguments *inter alia* on international law.

Therefore, religious scholars should "advance and build on their understanding of contemporary reality. They should not continue to advocate the use of *fatwas* deemed only valid in certain communities" under certain circumstances more than a thousand years ago (El-Amili 2013). Laws that apply to households as well as to the socio-political sphere need to be reflective of the present era and compatible with universal human rights standards (El-Amili 2011).

The 2014 Law starts by defining the category it aims to protect, namely the family (Article 2, paragraph 1). By the family, the Law means any of the spouses, their mothers and fathers, their brothers, sisters, ascendants, descendants (legal or illegal), as well as persons related thereto by adoption, alliance up to the second degree, guardianship or custody, *takafful* (sponsorship) of orphans, or stepfathers or stepmothers.

However, as noted by some feminists and lawyers, the Law does not cover the case of former spouses, although it should (Zalzal 2016; Ghosoub 2016) because these, namely wives, often remain threatened by their former husbands. The Law also does not cover cohabitation or extra-marital relationships, although it should do so in order to protect all women and victims regardless of the nature of their marital status (KAFA 2014b: 4). This is due to Lebanese official policy, which is, in general, traditional and conservative. In fact, cohabitation and other types of extra-marital relationships are not legally recognized in Lebanon. Moreover, the abovementioned legal definition of "family" is not very clear: it starts by defining it from the spouses' point of view, but it seems to end by defining it from the children's point of view when it mentions stepfathers or stepmothers. This confusion might lead the courts to enlarge the category of family members by including stepfathers and stepmothers of the spouses themselves. Of course, this would further guarantee victims' rights and interests, but it needs to be clarified in the text itself in order to avoid contradictory judicial verdicts that would create insecurity and inequality in the legal status of victims depending on the court presiding over the case.

The Law defines its object, i.e., domestic violence (Article 2, paragraph 2), which includes every act of violence, abstinence, or threat thereof committed by one family member against one or more of its members, encompassing one of the crimes stated below, the consequences of which may cause death or physical, psychological, sexual, or economic injury. We may compare this definition to CEDAW GR 19 on VAW, adopted by the Committee in 1992, which states:

> The Convention [CEDAW] in Article 1 defines discrimination against women. The definition of discrimination includes gender-based violence, that is, violence directed against a woman because she is a woman or that affects women disproportionately. It includes acts that inflict physical, mental or sexual harm or suffering, threats of such acts, coercion and other deprivations of liberty.

The 2014 Law added to this the economic dimension of violence, while GR 19 explicitly refers to "deprivations of liberty," which is not mentioned in the 2014 Law.

It is worth indicating that the Law contains both criminal and protectionist provisions: the first are amendments and additions to the pre-existing penal laws, while the second are special provisions stipulated in order to protect the victim, his/her children, and persons living with him/her from domestic violence. The latter provisions need to be enhanced in order to guarantee efficient and full protection to the categories it defends.

Before analyzing the content of the 2014 Law, it is worth mentioning here two main questions that are usually raised, whether theoretically by scholars and researchers or in judicial practice, concerning domestic violence in relation to religious family laws.

The first concerns under which conditions the victim of domestic violence, i.e. mainly women, would be allowed to leave the marital home with her children without being considered a "dissonant" wife; and what legal procedures she needs to undertake upon leaving the marital home. Here again, a slight distinction should be made between Christians and Muslims.

For Christians, a wife may leave the marital home when the couple's life becomes unbearable or when her stay at the home puts her life and the lives of the children at risk. She must, upon leaving her marital home, file penal proceedings if her husband inflicted physical harm upon her prior to her departure, or she may initiate separation or dissolution proceedings before the relevant religious court.

For Muslims, a wife may leave the marital home when the couple's life becomes impossible or when her stay at home puts her life and the lives of the children at risk. Upon leaving her marital home, she must file penal proceedings if her husband inflicted physical harm upon her prior to her departure, or she may initiate divorce or dissolution "*tafrik*" proceedings before the relevant Sharia or Community courts (www.kafa.org.lb).

The other important question is whether the court may grant custody to the spouse who mistreats the children. Although Christians and Muslims are governed by different legal provisions, as explained above, the procedure and outcomes are sometimes similar. For Christians, child abuse by the parent is one of the main reasons for which his/her right to custody extinguishes because, in this case, the custodian does not preserve the child's safety. For Muslims, where the custodian abuses the children and inflicts physical, psychological, or educational harm upon them, this spouse shall be deemed unworthy of their custody and therefore may lose custody (www.kafa.org.lb).

Now that we have explained the objectives of the 2014 Law and showed the complexity of family law-related matters, we will turn to the new institutional framework related to domestic violence that was established by the 2014 Law.

New institutional entities specializing in domestic violence

In order to implement its protective and criminal provisions, the 2014 Law established innovative official entities specializing in domestic violence.

First, the Law provides that the State Prosecutor shall appoint one public attorney or more in the *Mohafaza* (district or governorate) and entrust him/her with receiving complaints on domestic violence and following up on the same (Article 4).

The Law also provides that a special unit on domestic violence shall be established at the Directorate General of the Internal Security Forces (ISF). It shall have duties similar to the judiciary police and shall examine the complaints submitted before the same and referred thereto. The unit shall be established as per the laws and regulations governing the ISF so as to cover the entire Lebanese territories. It shall have women among its members, all of whom shall be adequately trained to solve conflicts and provide social guidance. Unit members shall implement investigations in the presence of social assistants[15] who are acquainted with domestic affairs and conflict resolution and who shall be selected from a list prepared by the Ministry of Social Affairs. Recently, this list of social assistants has been drafted: all of them are women who have been trained. This list is only awaiting the signature of the Minister of Social Affairs.

The special unit shall have jurisdiction in the event of complicity.[16] Unit members may inspect the crime scene where necessary, within the restrictions provided by the applicable laws (Article 5). A major problem with this is that the Lebanese government has not yet identified where the unit will be physically located, and it has been unreasonably delaying this issue, although it is important in order to move forward with the unit's work and objectives.[17]

Furthermore, a special fund with a moral character and financial and administrative autonomy shall be established to assist the victims of domestic violence, provide them with the care and means necessary to limit the crimes of domestic violence, prevent the same, and rehabilitate the perpetrators thereof. The fund shall be financed by state contributions, for which a credit shall be established in the yearly budget of the Ministry of Social Affairs, and by donations. The fund's structure shall be determined by Cabinet decree, upon the suggestion of the Ministers of Justice and Social Affairs.

Unfortunately, this decree has not yet been promulgated, although KAFA is working with the Ministry of Social Affairs on suggestions in order to elaborate a draft decree.[18] The fund shall be subject to the general legislation regarding Public Institutions[19] and under the guardianship of the Minister of Social Affairs (Article 21).

In the following section, the 2014 Law will be interrogated further in order to flag provisions that need to be reformed.

Substantive and procedural innovations and limitations

The 2014 Law created several important legal innovations, both to criminalize perpetrators and to protect victims, their children, and people living with the victims. However, some of these need to be amended, as per our recommendations below. These recommendations reflect the ongoing demands of feminist NGOs and human rights activists, including women.

First of all, the 2014 Law introduced some modifications to Articles of the Lebanese Penal Code. As per the provisions of the 2014 Law (Article 3), crimes of domestic violence shall be punished as follows.

The amended version of Article 618 of the Penal Code stipulates that whoever incites a minor (a person less than age eighteen) to begging shall be sentenced to a term of imprisonment of no less than six months and no more than two years and shall be subject to a fine of no less than the minimum wage and no more than double its amount.

The modified version of Article 523 of the Penal Code provides that whoever instigates one person or more, whether male or female, who has not reached the age of twenty-one to engage in prostitution or corruption, and whoever facilitates the same or aids him/her therein, shall be sentenced to imprisonment between one month and one year and shall be subject to a fine varying between the minimum wage (675,000 LBP, equivalent to 450 USD)[20] and three times the same. Whoever is involved in illegal prostitution or engages in the facilitation thereof shall be subject to the same sentence. Without prejudice to other relevant criminal provisions, the sentence shall be increased where the crime is committed within the family, regardless of the age of the person against whom the crime is committed.

The new version of Article 527 of the Penal Code includes a new paragraph regarding whoever relies on the prostitution of a third party to gain his/her living, whether fully or partially. The perpetrator shall be sentenced to a term of imprisonment of no less than six months and no more than two years and shall be fined not less than the minimum wage and not more double its amount. Also without prejudice to other relevant provisions of the Penal Code, the sentence shall be increased where the crime is committed within the family and shall be doubled where it involves violence or threat.

An additional paragraph was also added to Article 547 of the Penal Code which now provides that whoever commits willful homicide shall be sentenced to between fifteen and twenty years of hard labor. The sentence shall vary between twenty and twenty-five years where homicide is committed by a spouse against the other. Furthermore, Article 559 of the Penal Code has been amended by increasing the sentences regarding the harm of persons where the offense is committed in one of the cases of willful homicide.[21]

In addition, the 2014 Law also modified Articles 487, 488, and 489 of the Penal Code. Henceforth, Article 487 provides that adultery committed by one of the spouses shall be sentenced to a term of imprisonment of no less than three months and no more than two years. The same sentence shall apply to the partner in adultery where he/she is married; otherwise he/she shall be sentenced to imprisonment for not less than one month and not more than one year. Article 488 stipulates that the spouse shall be punished by imprisonment for not less than one month and not more than one year where he/she takes a lover anywhere in public.[22] The partner in this shall be subject to the same sentence. And Article 489 provides that adultery shall only be prosecuted upon the complaint of one of the spouses and where the plaintiff personally participates in a court action with the public prosecutor. Partners or accomplices shall only be prosecuted together with the adulterer. A complaint filed by a spouse having given his/her consent to the adultery shall be null. A complaint filed three months after the plaintiff became informed of the crime shall not be accepted. The fact of depriving the spouse of his/her right results in annulling public and private actions against the offenders. If the plaintiff accepts resuming life in common with the spouse, the charge shall be dropped.

The 2014 Law provides additional provisions (Article 3.7) to those already existing in the Penal Code. Among those, it stipulates that whoever, with the intent of redeeming "marital rights" to intercourse or because of the same, beats the spouse or inflicts harm thereto, shall be subject to one of the sentences regarding the harm of persons.[23] Where beating or harming recurs, the sanction shall be increased. Where the plaintiff drops the charges, public action shall be refuted only in case the harm damages the person for a period of twenty days or less.[24] Provisions governing recidivism shall remain applicable, where conditions are satisfied. Also, whoever shall, with the intent of redeeming "marital rights" to intercourse or because of the same, threaten the spouse, that person shall be subject to one of the sentences regarding threatening.[25] Where the threat reoccurs, the sanction shall be increased. Where the plaintiff drops the charges, public action subject to some threats[26] shall be refuted. Provisions governing recidivism shall remain applicable, where conditions are satisfied.

The expression "marital rights" to intercourse is derived from the sectarian personal status laws (Zalzal 2014: 68), more specifically from some Muslim jurists who explicitly consider that "intercourse at any time – even when the wife does not feel like – is one of the husband's shar'i rights" (El-Amili 2011: 9)! As recommended by the National Coalition for Legislating the Protection of Women from Domestic Violence, instead of thereby "regulating" "marital rape" in one way or another, the 2014 Law should have vetoed it.[27] Rape, even if it is marital, is a violation of human rights and of the Constitution,[28] which guarantees fundamental rights, notably freedom and equality between citizens.

In fact, the 2014 Law should have amended Articles 503 and 522 of the Lebanese Penal Code which provide that whoever, with violence and threat, coerces a person, *other than his spouse*, to sexual intercourse, is punished with hard labor for no less than five years and no less than seven years if the victim is fifteen years old or younger; in the event a legal marriage is concluded between the perpetrator and the victim, prosecution shall be stopped; and if a decision is rendered in such a case, the execution of such decision shall be suspended against the person who was subject to it. Prosecution or the execution of the penalty shall be resumed before the lapse of three years in cases of misdemeanors and five years in cases of felonies, in the event such marriage ends by the divorce of the woman without a legitimate reason or by a divorce, which is decided by court in favor of the woman.

In addition to territorial jurisdiction governed by the general rules, the victim shall have the right to initiate proceedings in his/her temporary or permanent domicile (Article 6). Without prejudice to the measures to be taken by the Judicial Police in connection with offenses discovered at the time of their commission or immediately afterwards,[29] the Judicial Police shall, without delay, go to the crime scene where domestic violence is committed, after informing the competent Public Attorney in the two following cases: where a witnessed domestic violence crime is committed or where the police are informed that a restraining order relevant to domestic violence has been violated (Article 7).

The 2014 Law ensures the victim's protection from even the Judicial Police: Any of the latter who attempt, by means of coercion, to force the victim of violence or exert pressure thereupon to drop charges shall be subject to the relevant sentence set out in the Penal Code.[30] Any neglect by the judiciary agent to deal with the complaint and information related to domestic violence shall be considered a major offense (as per the provisions of the Law organizing the ISF[31]) and the offender shall appear before the Disciplinary Council (Article 8).

Upon receiving complaints and information and upon the review of the Attorney General entrusted with matters of domestic violence and under the supervision of the latter, the Judicial Police shall listen to the victim and suspect upon their wish in presence of the social assistant.[32] It shall also inform them of this right as well

as all their other rights[33] and listen to all witnesses of domestic violence, including minor children, in presence of the social assistant, as per the provisions of the
law on the protection of juveniles (Article 9). The Judicial Police shall inform the
victim of all his/her rights,[34] including the right to obtain a restraining order (as
detailed below) and to assign an attorney if he/she so wishes (Article 10).

The Public Attorney may receive all complaints related to domestic violence.
He/she may, prior to the issuing of the restraining order by the relevant authority,
entrust the Judicial Police under his/her supervision to take one of the following
measures:

- First, to ensure that the defendant agrees to refrain from causing harm to the
  victim, his/her children, and other persons living with the victim, or refrains
  from instigating anyone to cause them harm. If the defendant refuses, he/she
  shall be prohibited from accessing the household for a period of forty-eight
  hours (renewable once).
- And/or: second, where the same persons are exposed to violence, the defendant may be prohibited from accessing the household for a period of forty-eight
  hours (renewable once), if no other means are available to protect the victim,
  his/her children, and the persons living with him/her. The importance of
  this period is to give the victim the opportunity to obtain a restraining order
  (Lebanese Internal Security Forces 2016: 9). The defendant may also be held
  in custody,[35] and the victim, his/her children, and the persons living with
  him/her may, upon their request, be transferred to a safe place at the expense
  of the defendant and with due consideration of the latter's means.
- And/or: third, where violence results in medical or hospital treatment, the
  victims of violence shall be transferred to hospital, provided the defendant pays
  for treatment expenses in advance. Where the defendant abstains from paying
  the treatment expenses in advance, he/she shall be subject to the provisions
  applicable to alimony in the Code of Civil Procedures, except that the decision to imprison the defendant who has abstained from paying the expenses
  shall be made by the Public Prosecution (Article 11).
- A restraining order is a temporary measure made by the relevant judicial
  authority in the course of examining the cases of domestic violence, in order
  to protect the victim and his/her children. Other descendants and persons living with the victim shall also benefit from the restraining order in case they
  are in danger. Social assistants, witnesses, and any other person providing the
  victim with assistance shall also benefit from the restraining order in order to
  prevent violence or the threat thereof from continuing or recurring. Children
  involved in the restraining order are those children who are in the age of legal
  custody as per the provisions of the respective religious confessions' Codes on
  Personal Statute and other applicable laws (Article 12).

As recommended by several references, whether from lawyers' or activists' point
of view, notably the National Coalition for Legislating the Protection of Women

from Family Violence, the provision above should be amended in order to include the protection of the victim's children regardless of age of custody (KAFA 2014b: 6; Ghosoub 2016: 6). In fact, the age may be different for a boy from that of a girl of the same confession, which leads to the inclusion of some of the victim's children in the restraining order while others are excluded, although they may all have been present with the victim during the occurrence of violence (Zalzal 2014: 71).

The request to obtain a restraining order shall be filed before the investigating judge who is entrusted with the lawsuit, or the Penal Court entrusted with the same, and shall be examined in the deliberation room. The request may also be submitted to the judge in chambers as voluntary jurisdiction in undisputed matters. In both cases, the decision shall be rendered within no more than forty-eight hours. The decision made by the investigating judge or the single judge may be appealed.[36] The decision made by the judge in chambers may be appealed as per the general provisions regarding voluntary jurisdiction in undisputed matters.[37] Lodging an appeal to challenge the decision relevant to the restraining order shall not stop implementation thereof unless the relevant court decides otherwise. The latter is a protective provision especially made in order to ensure that the victim, his/her children, and people living with her/him are sufficiently safeguarded. The decision issued by any of the aforementioned legal authorities shall not be repealed (Article 13).

The National Coalition for Legislating the Protection of Women from Family Violence recommends that the above should be modified. In order to facilitate victims and women's access to justice and save them from many complications, the Law should also allow them to request to obtain restraining orders from the public prosecution (KAFA 2014a: 6 *in fine*; KAFA 2014b: 10).

The restraining order shall compel the defendant to take one or more of the nine following measures:

- First, refrain from prejudicing the victim, his/her children, and persons living with the latter or instigating the same.
- Second, refrain from prejudicing to the continued presence of the victim and persons living with him/her who are covered by the restraining order in the household.
- Third, compel the offender to leave the house temporarily, and for a period determined by the relevant authority, when the victim is found to be in danger.
- Fourth, move the victim and his/her cohabitants who are covered by the restraining order outside the house when they are believed to be in danger and subject to a threat that could be the result of a continued presence in the household, and transfer them to a temporary safe and convenient residency. When the victim moves out, children who are of the age of legal custody shall move out with him/her along with any other children or cohabitants who are at risk. The defendant shall pay the accommodation fees in advance according to his/her means.

- Fifth, compel the defendant, with due consideration of his/her capacities, to pay in advance an amount of money adequate to cover the fees for food, clothing, and education for those of whom he/she is obligated.
- Sixth, compel the defendant, as per his/her capacities, to pay the fees necessary for medical treatment or hospitalization of the victim, his/her children, and persons living with the victim, where violence resulted in the need for treatment.
- Seventh, refrain from prejudicing to any of the private assets of the victim or the persons included in the restraining order.
- Eighth, refrain from prejudicing to furniture and/or movable joint funds, and prohibit any right to dispose thereof.
- And/or ninth, enable the victim, or whomever he/she might delegate, when leaving the house, to access the house and recover personal belongings against acknowledgment of receipt.

For any temporary advance payment, the victim or the defendant may resort to competent jurisdiction to obtain a ruling adequate to the applicable rules. The payment of alimony as decided by competent courts shall end the payment established in the restraining order (Article 14).

Filing a restraining request does not prevent the victim or defendant from filing or pursuing legal actions before courts of all kinds and jurisdictions (Article 15). The request for the restraining order does not need to be submitted by a lawyer and is not subject to any judicial fees or expenses (Article 16). The restraining order issued by the judge in chambers shall be automatically effective, whereas the appellate public prosecution shall implement the one issued by the criminal court. The victim, the parties benefiting from the restraining order, and/or the defendant may request the authority that issued the restraining order, or from the relevant court, to cancel or amend the order upon discovering new facts. Such decision of cancellation or amendment shall be subject to the aforementioned review mechanism (Article 17).[38]

Whoever violates the restraining order shall be subject to imprisonment of up to three months and shall be fined no less than double the minimum wage or shall be subject to one of these two sanctions. Where the violation is accompanied by the use of violence, the offender shall be subject to imprisonment up to one year and shall be fined no more than four-fold the minimum wage. If the offense reoccurs, the sentence shall be doubled (Article 18).

The trial shall be held secretly before the relevant authorities specialized in domestic violence (Article 19). In addition to all and any of the abovementioned sanctions, the tribunal may compel the offender to take batterer's counseling sessions at specialized rehabilitation centers (Article 20). This is one of the most essential provisions of the 2014 Law, since it guarantees a sustainable solution to the sensitive domestic problem faced by concerned families.

Currently, in the absence of such public state-owned shelters and other centers, civil society, mainly KAFA, is playing this crucial role. In fact, judicial decisions regularly refer to KAFA in that regard. However, the responsibility to establish public centers for refuge of victims of violence and rehabilitation lies with the state, delegating this obligation to private or civil entities should never be a long-term solution. It is worth indicating that civil society, notably KAFA, is also training lawyers on domestic violence laws and legal procedures, in order to provide them with the information needed and to put their names on the Judicial Aid Committee's list of lawyers as specialists in this field.[39]

Civil society

Many stakeholders in Lebanese civil society are active in fighting GBV. Below are some of the main NGOs that have lobbied and still struggle for challenging such violence. Secular and progressive human rights and feminist organizations frequently cross communities, religions, and ideologies. However, Lebanese civil society seems to be fragmented, as some of its "stakeholders" are confessionalist and therefore have objectives that substantially differ from the ones above.

KAFA Violence & Exploitation Organization, the main feminist, secular, non-profit, non-governmental national civil society organization, was founded in 2005 and seeks to create a society that is free of social, economic, and legal patriarchal structures that discriminate against women. KAFA aims to eliminate all forms of exploitation and VAW (www.kafa.org.lb/).

The Lebanese Democratic Women's Gathering (RDFL), founded in 1976, actively lobbies as a secular non-governmental women's organization. It works with the democratic forces and represents a part of the secular democratic women's movement. It bases its work on international pacts and treaties, as well as the Universal Declaration of Human Rights and the Declaration on the Elimination of Violence Against Women. The RDFL's objectives are to promote women's status and participation and to empower them. It aims to achieve full equality between both sexes (www.daleel-madani.org).

The Collective for Research and Training on Development-Action (CRTD-A) is an NGO founded in 2003. CRTD-A's activism is not limited to Lebanon; the organization collaborates with partners in Algeria, Bahrain, Egypt, Jordan, Morocco, Syria, and Tunisia. It seeks to contribute to citizenship, social justice, and gender equality (www.crtda.org.lb).

ABAAD (Dimensions) – Resource Center for Gender Equality is a NGO founded in 2011. ABAAD is a non-profit, non-politically affiliated and non-religious civil association that aims to achieve gender equality as an essential condition for sustainable social and economic development in the MENA region. ABAAD seeks to promote women's equality and participation through policy development, legal reform, gender mainstreaming, engaging men, eliminating discrimination, and advancing and empowering women to participate effectively and fully in their communities. ABAAD also supports and collaborates with civil society organizations that are involved in gender-equality programs and advocacy campaigns (www.abaadmena.org).

The National Coalition for Legislating the Protection of Women from Family Violence was founded in 2008 in order to coordinate the efforts of Lebanese civil society's relevant components. KAFA took the initiative to establish this coalition and played a major role in activating it. Lately, the Coalition has concretely proved its efficiency, notably regarding a domestic GBV case.[40]

The Lebanese Women's Council, formerly the Lebanese Arab Women's Union (which was founded on 6 November 1952), is a feminist NGO. The Council and the Coalition show the possibilities of collaboration between NGOs in general, and feminist ones in particular. But until now, such coordination has been strictly limited to a case-by-case scenario and suffers from the lack of a continuous and fixed practical action plan framework.[41]

There are other, individual, initiatives of Lebanese women and youth aiming to educate, enlighten, and lobby for legislative reform (El-Yafi 2012; Ghandour 2012 and 2014). But unfortunately, Lebanese civil society (whether associations or individuals) generally has limited resources (Immigration and Refugee Board of Canada n.d.), which sometimes limits the efficiency of its activities and, hence, achieving its objectives. Moreover, it suffers from the lack of responsibility and straightforwardness in the Lebanese public administration, especially in matters related to women's rights.[42]

Conclusion and recommendations

In conclusion, the aim of legislative reform in Lebanon should be the wider scope of the recommendations as explained in the Introduction to this case study – i.e., establishing a mandatory civil law on personal status that achieves the international law standards of freedom, equality, non-discrimination,[43] and fundamental rights to life, security, and safety, in addition to guaranteeing children's best interests (Lebanese Internal Security Forces 2012: 15–16).

However, as already stated, unfortunately this objective is *currently* not attainable, owing to the resistance of several political and religious authorities and even the general public. Hence, for now, reform initiatives need to concentrate on amending the 2014 Law on the protection of women and other family members from domestic violence, in order to fill its several gaps and overcome its shortcomings and flaws. This goal is crucial because only a few countries in the Arab world, notably Jordan, have comprehensive laws on family violence (Human Rights Watch 2011). So Lebanon should be pioneering this message to the region (Ghosoub 2016: 7).

The recommendations made by this case study are:

1. The Lebanese Parliament should amend the 2014 Law in order:

    - To cover the case of former spouses, cohabitation, and any extra-marital relationships.
    - To clarify the legal definition of the "family."

- To explicitly cover "deprivations of liberty."
- To amend Articles 503 and 522 of the Lebanese Penal Code in order to cover the spouse.
- To include the protection of the victim's children regardless of age of custody.
- To allow victims and women to request obtaining restraining orders from the public prosecution.

2. The Lebanese Cabinet, upon the suggestion of the Ministers of Justice and Social Affairs, should determine the structure of the Fund that aims to fight domestic violence by issuing the relevant decree of implementation.
3. The Lebanese state should establish public centers for rehabilitating not only domestic violence offenders, but also those with other disorders such as addictions.
4. Lebanese civil society should be more united and consolidate its efforts to reform family laws and challenge GBV.
5. The international community should enhance its efforts towards Lebanese civil society and its recommendations to the Lebanese government to reform family laws in order to fight GBV.

Furthermore, we recommend the amendment of all Lebanese laws and regulations in which gender discrimination exists, in such a way to remove any signs of such discrimination from the entire Lebanese legislative system. We mention notably the regulations concerning nationality and social security, as well as some criminal provisions other than those explained above and that cannot be detailed in this brief case study.

In addition to the above, a major recommendation is to also reform education. Domestic violence, and violence in general, is not only a legal matter but also a matter of culture, stereotyped roles, habits, and traditional attitudes regarding women as subordinate or submissive to men, which needs to be changed (Hajali 2015: 6 *in limine*; Bramley 2014).

Notes

1 For information on KAFA, see below.
2 See Ertürk, this volume, for confessionalism in Lebanon.
3 'Ijtihad in Islamic jurisprudence refers to using independent judgment in a legal or theoretical matter.
4 Law dated 23 June 1959.
5 Article 86 of the Civil Procedure Code.
6 Interviews with KAFA staff, Ms. Zoya Rouhana and Ms. Layla Awada, 29 September 2016.
7 Article 95-4 of the Lebanese Code of Civil Procedure.
8 Interviews with KAFA staff, 2016.
9 As per the literal wording of Article 9 of the Lebanese Constitution.
10 Ibid.
11 In addition, Lebanon has a history of civil wars having religious/sectarian aspects and reasons.

12 The Law entered into force (as per Article 23) upon its publication in the Official Gazette on 15 May 2014. Since the official version of the Law is in Arabic, the authors have made an unofficial translation. They also referred to KAFA's unofficial English translation, published on its website: www.kafa.org.lb.

13 For more details regarding the implementation of the law, see KAFA 2014a: 7 *in limine*.

14 Article 34 of Law 422, dated 6 June 2002.

15 Social assistants are parallel to social workers in the US.

16 Meaning when there is an accomplice in a crime.

17 Interview with KAFA staff, 2016.

18 Ibid.

19 Decree No. 4517/1972 dated 13 December 1972.

20 Decree No. 7426 dated 25 January 2012.

21 Stated in the abovementioned new paragraph 2 of Article 547, and in Articles 548 and 549 of the Criminal Law.

22 This refers to a Lebanese legal provision prohibiting spouses' infidelity in public.

23 Articles 554 to 559 of the Penal Code.

24 As per Articles 554 and 555 of the Penal Code.

25 Established in Articles 573 to 578 of the Penal Code.

26 Mentioned in Articles 577 and 578 of the Penal Code.

27 This was also recommended by other civil society actors (e.g., KAFA, 2014a: 6 *in fine*; KAFA 2014b: 1; and The A Project, 2015: 2 *in fine* and 3. For further details about marital rape, see Human Rights Watch 2011 and 2014).

28 Notably its Article 7.

29 Article 41 of the Code of Criminal Proceedings (CCP).

30 Article 376 thereof.

31 Article 130, Paragraph 2 of the Law No. 17, dated 6 September 1990.

32 Please refer to Article 5 regarding this social assistant.

33 As per Article 47 of the CCP.

34 Article 47 of the CCP.

35 As per Article 47 of the CCP.

36 As per the CCP provisions.

37 Ibid.

38 See the provisions of Article 13, above.

39 Interview with KAFA staff, 2016.

40 The case of Manal Assi, who died in Tarik El-Jdideh in Beirut on 4 February 2014, www.maharat-news.com/News.

41 Interview with KAFA staff, 2016.

42 Ibid.

43 About these standards, see Musawah 2015: 10.

References

The A Project, Center for Reproductive Rights (2015) "Sexual Rights Initiative," UN Periodic Review of Lebanon.

El-Alayli, Ghadir (2008) *Personal Status and Monotheist Religions in Lebanon*.

———— (2011) "De l'acquisition de la nationalité libanaise en vertu de l'article 4 *in fine* de l'arrêté 15 S./1925," ("The Acquisition of Lebanese Nationality by Virtue of Article 4 *in fine* of Decision 15 S./1925"), 1st ed.: Masters' Thesis, Université Saint-Joseph, Faculté de Droit et des Sciences Politiques, Beirut.

———— (2015) *Le droit de la femme libanaise d'accorder sa nationalité à ses enfants* (*Lebanese Women's Right to Grant Their Nationality to Their Children*), 2nd ed., Beirut: HBDT.

El-Alayli, Sheikh Abdallah (1992) *Ayna AlKhata'? (Where's the Error?)*, 2nd ed., Beirut: Dar Eljadid.

El-Amili, Sheikh Muhamad Ali El-Hage (2011) *Mutala'a shar'iya . . .* (*Protecting Women From Domestic Violence*), Lebanon: Addar Al'amiliya.

———— (2013) *Tazwij alkasirat* (*Marriage of Minors*), Lebanon: Addar Al'amiliya.

Bramley, Ellie Violet (2014) "Why Does Lebanese Bill on Domestic Violence Fila to Tackle Marital Rape?," 9 April 2014, www.theguardian.com/global-development/2014/apr/09/lebanese-bill-domestic-violence-marital-rape.

Chartouni, Charles E. (1993) *Conflict Resolution in Lebanon, Myth and Reality*, Beirut: Foundation for Human Rights.

Frontiers Ruwad (Youmna Makhlouf, Layal Sakr, Ghadir El-Alayli, and Lara Zgheib) (2016) "Bill Proposals and Policy Papers on Lebanese Personal Status and Nationality," Beirut (not published).

Ghandour, Dala (2012), "The Young Women Arab Leaders: The Voice of the Future," September 2012, The Arab International Women's Forum Conference at the Lebanese American University – Beirut.

———— (2014) "Connecting the Next Generation of Young Arab Women Leaders: Reflections on Leadership," 24 October 2014, The Arab International Women's Forum Conference, London.

Ghosoub, Abdo (2016) *Qanun raqm . . .* (*Law No. 293/2014*), Beirut: KAFA.

Hajali, Majd (2015) "Reproducing Violence through Reconstructing the Hymen?" Thesis: Roehampton, Gothenburg, and Tromsø Universities.

Human Rights Watch (2011) "Lebanon: Enact Family Violence Bill to Protect Women," www.hrw.org/news/2011/07/06/lebanon-enact-family-violence-bill-protect-women.

———— (2014) "Lebanon: Domestic Violence Law Good, But Incomplete," www.hrw.org/news/2014/04/03/lebanon-domestic-violence-law-good-incomplete.

KAFA (n.d.) "Zalfa's Questions on the Personal Status Laws," www.kafa.org.lb.

———— (2014a) "Annual Report," www.kafa.org.lb.

———— (2014b) "Zalfa's Questions on the Law to Protect Women and Other Family Members from Family Violence."

Lebanese Internal Security Forces (2012) *Dawr Qiwa Al-Amn . . .* (*Internal Security Forces' Role Challenging Domestic Violence*).

———— (2016) *Dalil As'ila wa 'ajwiba . . .* (*Q&As about Law No. 293*).

Musawah (2015) "Muslim Family Law: Lebanon, Report," www.musawah.org/sites/default/files/MusawahThematicReportLebanon62_0.pdf.

Nasr, Father Maroun (2012), *Al-ahwal as-shaksiya . . .* (*Personal Status: a Lebanese Matter*), Majallit Al-Machrek, July–December 2012, No. 489–502.

Shamseddine, Imam Sheikh Mhamad (2006) *Al-wasaya* (*Wills*), 2nd ed., Beirut: Dar Almada,

———— (2014) Nahwa Mashrou' Hadary . . . (Towards a Civilized Project of Arab and Muslim Renaissance), 1st ed., Beirut: Mouassasat Imam Shamseddine.

Wilson Center (2013) "Gender-based Violence and International Women's Day," 6 March 2013, www.wilsoncenter.org/article/part-ii-gender-based-violence-and-intl-womens-day.

El-Yafi, Ghada (2012) "Quelques Réflexions autour de l'Islam" ("Some Reflections About Islam"), Conference (5 December, 2011): *Golias Magazine*, February 2012.

Zalzal, Marie Rose (2014) "Protection of Women from Domestic Violence under 'The Bill for the Protection of Women and Family Members against Domestic Violence,'" *Al-Raida*, No. 145/146/147, Part 2, Spring/Summer/Fall *2014*: 59–74.

———— (2016) *Qanun raqm . . .* (*Law No. 293/2014*), Beirut: KAFA.

7

NIGERIA

Victoria Ibezim-Ohaeri

Introduction

What aspects or strategies for the reform of family and gender-discriminatory laws have worked, or not worked, for women and girls in Nigeria? What are the dominant influences and factors militating against the success of policy and legislative reforms that now must be countered in order to strengthen legal protection against gender-based violence (GBV)? This research not only seeks to provide answers to these two research questions, but also adopts an advocacy stance whereby findings reveal the extent and quality of legal protection that women and girls enjoy in Nigeria's two major regions – the south and the north[1] – highlighting new opportunities for reform.

For this study, a literature review was conducted, looking back through recent research on GBV, identifying potential links between discriminatory family laws and VAW in Nigeria. Data was collected from a variety of secondary literature that was sourced both locally and internationally. The second phase of research charted the spatial distribution of GBV in Nigeria's north and south, paying particular attention to the formal and religious governance arrangements that regulate gender and family relations.

The final phase of the research involved stakeholder interviews. Those interviewed include state officials, leaders of women- and children-focused non-governmental organizations (NGOs), members of the religious community, researchers, academics, journalists, and legal practitioners, seeking their inputs and learning.[2] At a workshop held in Lagos on 14 February 2017, the researcher presented her findings to a broad spectrum of gender experts and stakeholders in the equality campaign movement in Nigeria, drawn from both the public and private sectors.[3] The opinions, observations, and experiences shared at the seminar lend depth and meaning to this case study, in describing the painful reality of VAW while highlighting the gaps in law enforcement that need to be closed.

Family law reforms and the challenge of implementation

Overview of the Nigerian legal system

Nigeria's 1999 Constitution sits at the apex of its legal system and prescribes binary structures of legislative authority at the state and federal levels. Accordingly, the legal system encompasses the federal and state law-making structures that operate in the country's thirty-six constituent states, including the Federal Capital Territory (FCT) Abuja. Similarly, disparate enforcement mechanisms are established at both levels to interpret and administer the enactments, consistent with the requirements of due process expressed in the constitutional order. A special court (the Federal High Court[4]) enforces federal laws and exercises jurisdiction throughout the country on a number of issues. The various State High Courts perform this function at the state level. Parties aggrieved by the verdicts of the various states and federal court can approach the appellate courts for a judicial review.

Inspired by deep-seated ideological differences, a striking dichotomy exists between the legislative architecture and the administration of justice systems in Nigeria's northern and southern parts. Nothing exemplifies this north–south dichotomy more than the establishment of two distinct federal enactments for the administration of criminal justice in the northern and the southern regions: the Criminal Code is enforced in the southern part of Nigeria, populated mainly by Christians, while the Penal Code applies to northern Nigeria, predominantly populated by Muslims.

Customary laws vary from place to place, particularly among ethnic groups. Although the Constitution proclaims the country's secularity, religious laws, such as Sharia law (or codes), are popular and widely enforced in the northern part of the country. Sharia law prescribes a standard of social conduct, especially in the realm of family relations, and draws on the customary and religious heritages of the localities where it is enforced.

Post-independence: the era of human rights and legal reforms

Reform of the inherited colonial laws was inevitable after Nigeria gained independence in October 1960. At independence, the Criminal Code, modeled after English criminal law, was administered in English-type courts in southern Nigeria, while Islamic law and procedures were applied in the Area Courts of northern Nigeria. This system of administration was particularly resented in the north. According to one author (Gwangndi 2016: 65), there was popular disenchantment with the prevailing judicial system, especially the criminal justice system, which in the view of ordinary Muslims did not work and was not rooted in their most cherished norms. Discrepancies between English criminal law and Islamic law informed the reform of the legal and judicial systems in the northern region, culminating in the enactment of a Penal Code enforceable by all the courts in the northern region and applicable to all classes of persons who live there. The south, to a large extent, retained the administrative structures of justice delivery borrowed from Western legal traditions.

Since its independence from colonial rule, Nigeria has ratified a wide range of regional and international treaties and aligned itself with policy documents that concern the rights of women and girls, including CEDAW.[5] At the regional level, Nigeria has signed on to and domesticated[6] the African Charter on Human and Peoples' Rights.[7] Nigeria is also one of the thirty-six countries that have signed and ratified the Protocol to the African Charter on Human and People's Rights on the Rights of Women (Protocol to the African Charter).[8] Article 2 of the Protocol to the African Charter obligates States Parties to combat all forms of discrimination against women through appropriate legislative, institutional, and other measures. This provision resonates with Article 16 of CEDAW, which requires States Parties to take all appropriate measures to eliminate discrimination against women in all matters relating to marriage and family relations.

Constitutional limitations, however, affect the validity and application of international treaties in the domestic arena. By virtue of the dualist principle enunciated in Section 12 of the Nigerian 1999 Constitution, international treaties only become enforceable when a corresponding domestic law has been enacted by the Nigerian Federal Parliament. The effect is that the plethora of treaties Nigeria has ratified have no force of law and may not be subject to judicial action until such domestication takes place. Nigeria has domesticated and enforced as local legislation the African Charter on Human and Peoples' Rights (Ratification and Enforcement) Act Cap A9 LFN 2004.

Consistent with Article 2 of the Protocol to the African Charter, legislation provides a solid foundation for effective, coordinated, legal action against VAW. Legislative measures adopted at the national level often build on the legislative models proposed by international and regional institutions and instruments. A variety of legislative measures have therefore been adopted at the federal and state levels to provide a legal basis for addressing VAW. Where state parliaments enact laws prohibiting VAW, the statutory developments apply only to the legislating states or provinces. The legislative measures, for the most part, addressed VAW through the criminalization of local customs deemed harmful to women's rights and interests. In some cases, they focused on reforming state legal institutions, redefining relations in the family, and expanding the scope of official authority to intervene in the private sphere to either prevent or punish violations of women's human rights.

The Criminal Code, the Penal Code, Sharia law, and GBV in the family

The Criminal Code (enforced in the south), derived from the Queensland Criminal Code of Australia, is modeled after the Western concepts of justice and equity and is enforced by English-type adjudicatory bodies. The Penal Code (enforced in the north), derived from the Sudan Penal Code 1899, was also based on the Indian Penal Code of 1834, where the British had enacted the code for populations similar to those in northern Nigeria. Learning from their experience in Sudan and India, the British incorporated the principles of Islamic law into the Penal Code, taking into consideration prevailing local circumstances after conducting extensive consultations with the religious establishment in the region.

Despite the full operation and applicability of the Penal Code in the northern states and the FCT, Sharia law became popular in the region in the late 1990s. What actually constitutes the rules of Sharia law is contested, since interpretations of the relevant passages of the Quran vary, as do assessments of the Sunna, or customs of the Prophet Muhammad. The influence and spread of Sharia law has, over the years, grown phenomenally, with strong implications on family relations. With this phenomenon, Sharia law runs in parallel with the Penal Code, often leading to uncertainty as to which law applies in a given situation. One author notes that the introduction of Sharia law has led to the imposition of sentences that are either more severe than those provided for under the Penal Code, or in some cases provisions that have never been made under the Penal Code (Gwangndi 2016: 62). It has also led to the establishment of offenses that are not found in any penal law in Nigeria, such as adultery, which carries the penalty of death by stoning instead of two years' imprisonment, fine, or both under the Penal Code (ibid.: 62).

The Criminal Code and the Penal Code criminalize certain types of conduct occurring in the public and private spheres. They both lay down legal rules, procedures, and conditionalities for the collection of evidence, the establishment of guilt, and the imposition of legal remedies for specific offenses. Entrenched in those statutes are several provisions that manifestly discriminate against women, perpetuating cultural practices that regard women as inferior to men. For example, there is a sharp distinction in the legal weight attached to acts of criminality towards males and females. By Section 353 of the Criminal Code Act, "any person who unlawfully and indecently assaults any male person is guilty of a felony, and is liable to imprisonment for three years. The offender cannot be arrested without warrant."[9] On the other hand, Section 360 provides that "any person who unlawfully and indecently assaults a woman or girl is guilty of a misdemeanor, and is liable to imprisonment for two years." What this means is that unlawful or indecent assault on a man is statutorily considered to be of greater severity, attracting stiffer penalties than a similar attack on a woman. This disparity has attracted criticism, heightening calls for reform. Prescribing different statutory penalties for similar offenses affecting men and women further breaches the non-discrimination provisions enshrined in Nigeria's 1999 Constitution.

As a second example, domestic violence is often viewed as socially acceptable (Bazza 2010: 176; Ozo-Eson 2008: 292). This acceptability has also permeated legislative enactments that have been applied in a manner that not only discriminates against women, but also legitimizes acts that are consistent with domestic and sexual violence. Section 55(1)(d) of the Penal Code provides:

> Nothing is an offence, which does not amount to the infliction of grievous harm upon any person and which is done by a husband for the purpose of correcting his wife, such husband and wife being subject to any natural law or custom in which such correction is recognized as lawful.

This represents the boldest statutory validation of a culture of tolerance towards VAW in matrimonial relationships. The implication is that a man who inflicts bodily harm on his wife, no matter how grievous, would be absolved from guilt and punishment. The husband's ability to prove the existence of a valid marriage relationship is the highest requirement needed for establishing his innocence. Giving the power of correction to the man/husband entrenches inequality in spousal relationships and contravenes the principles of non-discrimination espoused in the Constitution and a number of international and regional human rights instruments that Nigeria has ratified and domesticated.

The third example is the emergence of Sharia religious principles as state law in many northern states, without deference to the constitutional declaration of secularity enshrined in Section 10 of Nigeria's 1999 Constitution. First adopted in Zamfara State in 1999,[10] the nomenclature changed from Sharia/Islamic principles to the Sharia Penal Code or State Penal Code following its adoption and codification as state law in many northern states. This transformation particularly altered its status from that of mere religious injunctions applicable only to Islamic adherents to legislative commands with state-wide force of law. The popularity of the Sharia Penal Code spread so rapidly that, by the end of 2000, eleven other states in northern Nigeria had embraced and also had begun to enforce it, differing only in approach and details. The Sharia state laws established Sharia Courts and empowered them to determine both civil and criminal proceedings in accordance with Islamic law.

Certain provisions of Sharia Penal Codes have attracted the fury of women's rights advocates and activists. The case of Amina Lawal drew local and international attention to the gender-based prejudices characterizing the Islamic procedures for the establishment of guilt in adultery cases, also known as *zina*. Arrested along with an accomplice, Yahayya Mohammed, and arraigned before the lower Sharia Court in Bakori on 15 January 2002, on a charge of adultery, Amina Lawal was eventually sentenced to death by stoning (Women Living under Muslim Laws 2002). The court discharged and acquitted Yahayya and proceeded to convict Amina on the circumstantial evidence of her pregnancy and the birth of a child outside legal marriage (Bello 2009: 5).

The offence of *zina* is defined as

> whoever, being a man or a woman, fully responsible, has sexual intercourse through the genitals of a person over whom he has no sexual rights and in circumstances in which no doubt exists as to illegality of the act, is guilty of the offence of *zina* (adultery).[11]

The punishment prescribed for *zina* for unmarried offenders is one hundred lashes and imprisonment for one year. Married offenders are liable to stoning to death (*rajm*). *Zina* is recognized as a crime only in northern Nigeria – it is not recognized as a crime in the Criminal Code applicable to the southern part of the country. Both the Kano and Niger State Penal Codes require *zina* (including rape) to be proved only by the confession of the accused or testimony by four witnesses. While the Kano State Code prescribes the need for four male or eight female witnesses, the Niger State Penal Code stipulates that the testimony of men is of greater value than that of women in proving *zina*. The discrepancy in the evidential weight attached to the testimonies of male and female witnesses raises the presumption of men`s intellectual superiority over women and constitutes a marked violation of the constitutional prohibition of non-discrimination on the basis of gender.

An observable trend from the long-standing application of Sharia law in the north is that the men implicated in criminal trials involving unlawful sexual relations between unmarried Muslims (either as co-perpetrators of unlawful sexual relations or as rapists of accused women) usually go free, supposedly due to "lack of evidence." Women, on the other hand, are sentenced to stoning or whipping, or may be sent to jail despite evidentiary insufficiencies. Amina Lawal's case is significantly similar to the case of Safiya Husseini, who was sentenced to death by stoning by a Sharia Court in Sokoto State, while her alleged sexual partner went unpunished. In Zamfara State, Bariya Ibrahim Magazu, a thirteen-year-old girl who became pregnant from a gang-rape, was sentenced to a hundred lashes for unlawful sexual relations and eighty lashes for false accusation, while the three perpetrators were acquitted due to "lack of evidence." On appeal, the lashes for false accusation were revoked, but the other sentence was carried out shortly after her child was born.

Several provisions of the Penal Code apparently depart from the constitutional guarantee of gender equality. Years after their enactment, the Sharia Penal Codes remain publicly criticized, yet legally unchallenged, at least, on the basis of inconsistency with the Constitution. Unlike the customary laws operative in the southern part of the country, the provisions of Sharia Penal Code have hardly been tested for their repugnancy[12] to natural justice, equity, and good conscience.[13]

Due to the irreconcilable differences between Sharia law on one hand and the concepts of women's human rights enunciated in the Nigerian Constitution, CEDAW, and a host of human rights instruments on the other, perception is growing that the full equality of the sexes is incompatible with Islamic doctrine. The glaring inconsistencies have specifically engendered a scenario whereby offenders organize their defense by cherry-picking from the pool of state legislation that afford them greater legal protection either in the form of lesser punishments or total absolution from guilt. The legal developments in Nigeria reinforce the 2005 and the 2010 reviews of the Beijing Platform of Action which concluded that *de jure* and *de facto* equality had not been achieved in any country in the world (United Nations 2014). The 2010 review specifically recognized that even where legal reforms had taken place, they were often ineffectively enforced (ibid.). In this regard, the confusion resulting from the conflicting maze of provisions in the Sharia law and the Criminal and Penal codes widens the gaps between *de jure* and *de facto* equality, presenting additional hurdles for victims, survivors, and implementers. A comprehensive overhaul of statutory provisions governing relations within the family, including those that regulate intimate relationships, is necessary to eradicate the inherent biases women face in the family, harmonize evidential requirements, and make them less confusing.

Understanding the motivation(s) for the reform of family laws

Globally, the 1990s was a period of extraordinary activism for the realization of women's human rights. Nigeria, as with many parts of the globe, was influenced by legal and policy developments resulting from the UN World Conferences on Women. For instance, the 1995 Beijing Platform for Action adopted at the UN Fourth World Conference on Women listed violence against women (VAW) (and girls) as one of twelve areas for priority action, outlining specific actions governments must take to prevent and respond to VAW.[14] Apart from the Beijing document, a number of international and regional instruments – such as CEDAW and the Protocol to the African Charter – expounded on the areas of priority action, highlighting how ending VAW is inextricably linked with the advancement of women.

The shift towards legislating against GBV in Nigeria did not start automatically. In April 2000, Nigeria adopted a national policy on gender equality and the empowerment of women, called the National Policy on Women, followed by a National Gender Policy in 2006. These policy developments responded to entrenched patriarchal ideologies across the country which saw male children preferred over the female, men dominating all spheres of women's lives, and women in a subordinate position, particularly at the community and household levels. Beyond the adoption of a national policy for women, the agency – the National Commission for Women – that was then responsible for coordinating the government's equality pursuits was transformed into an independent, full-fledged Ministry of Women Affairs. A plan of action was developed to support its implementation, and key government departments – such as the Planning, Research and Statistics Department in the Ministry of Women Affairs – were empowered to monitor the progress of implementation. In order to strengthen monitoring across the states and the FCT, a National Consultative Coordinating Committee was established, which involved the participation of the Ministries of Women Affairs from all thirty-six states, civil society organizations, and NGOs to review reports and strategize on the way forward.

The international discourse around the pursuit of equality continued at the national arena, and then trickled down to the various states in workshops, seminars, and other promotional activities. Issues concerning gender inequalities and the status of women in the public and private spheres dominated these discussions at various forums, while producing significant coalitions and networks committed to women's human rights. NGOs played a vital role at these events and in facilitating the emergence of these coalitions, since at that time NGOs provided most of the support services, including shelters, for victims of domestic violence.[15]

Legislative protection for women's rights in Nigeria blossomed in the 2000s, beginning primarily with the southern states. Political commitments, principally in the form of international treaties and regional charters on women's rights, provided a model framework and the normative content for legislation on VAW. For instance, CEDAW provisions, though not domesticated, influenced the promulgation of laws that prohibited harmful practices towards women in the various states (Federal Ministry of Women Affairs 2004: 4). NGOs and other liberal advocates working at the national level drew inspiration and guidance from these model frameworks to push for legal reforms.

The first set of these laws paid attention to the prohibition of traditional practices, including widowhood practices and female genital cutting. The results of the National Survey on Harmful Traditional Practices, conducted by the Federal Ministry of Women Affairs in conjunction with the UN Development Programme, provided data for legislation to review such practices (ibid.: 10). The Cross River State Parliament enacted the Cross River State Girl-Child Marriages & Female Circumcision (Prohibition) Law (2000) just as Ogun State enacted the Ogun State Female Circumcision & Genital Mutilation (Prohibition) Law (2000). As more and more states, especially in the south, adopted or revised legislation on VAW, the more conservative and predominantly Muslim states in northern Nigeria followed.

Although the enactment of state laws to address and punish all forms of VAW and girls aligns with the commitments in regional and international human rights standards, these domestic enactments materially followed the reform approach witnessed in the pre-independence era. The legislations mainly contained provisions criminalizing VAW and punishing perpetrators. Law reform was unsupported with a corresponding effort to reform the customary legal systems and the patriarchal structures that reinforce GBV. Consequently, legal reforms were, more often than not, perceived as imposed Western ideology rather than genuine efforts to transform the customary practices undermining the guarantee of gender equality. As we shall see, while protecting women from violations committed by both the state and third parties is a necessary prerequisite, the ultimate challenge lies in overturning the ingrained cultural prejudices and compromised legal systems shielding GBV from the scrutiny of established mechanisms of accountability.

The case-study of the Violence Against Persons Prohibition (VAPP) Act

The enactment of the Violence Against Persons (Prohibition) Act (the "VAPP Act") represents one of the boldest efforts to coordinate and synergize advocacy around the reform of family laws at the national level. The fourteen-year-long civil society-led activism culminating in the passage of the VAPP law began at a legislative advocacy workshop on VAW in 2001, in Abuja. After the workshop, the Legislative Advocacy Coalition Against Violence Against Women (LACVAW), comprising about fifty local and international organizations and individuals, formed, with the objective of "pushing for a National Bill prohibiting violence against women" (Mahdi 2010). In 2010, LACVAW conducted research to determine the prevalence of GBV in eighteen states[16] across Nigeria's six geo-political zones.

Moved by LACVAW's research findings, partnerships were formed with other strategic stakeholders, alliances were built with key federal legislators, and technical assistance was sought from development partners. LACVAW, for instance, partnered with the Gender Technical Unit of the National Assembly to track and push for the legislative processes. Campaigning activities and solidarity action peaked as LACVAW expanded its collaborations with key local and international actors, while enjoying broad-based stakeholder support especially from federal lawmakers, agencies, and departments, such as the National Human Rights Commission, Ministry of Women Affairs and Social Development, and the Nigerian Police Force, among others.

The bill to proscribe GBV was first presented to the lower Parliament, the House of Representatives, in May 2002. Initially titled the Violence Against Women Bill, it was sponsored by a female federal lawmaker, Mrs. Florence Aya, the then-chairperson of the House of Representatives' Committee on Women. At first, campaign efforts yielded slow, insubstantial results, including the rejection of the bill in 2003. The delay in the passage of the bill was initially attributed to the women-focused title and women-specific language of its provisions. This led to renaming the bill as the Violence Against Persons Prohibition Bill in 2008.

LACVAW's collaboration with female federal lawmakers was not only strategic, but produced results that would have been otherwise unattainable. For instance, in 2005, the then-chairperson of the House Committee on Women's Affairs and Youth Development, the Hon. Saudatu Sani, convened a meeting for LACVAW members, the Technical Committee on legislative matters, and other stakeholders, to deliberate on the procedures for the passage of the bill.[17] They decided to harmonize the draft bill with other related bills on GBV, given that some of the contents were already addressed in both extant legislation and other bills that were also awaiting parliamentary assent. By April 2008, the harmonization of the bill with eight other bills on GBV that had been seeking parliamentary consideration between 1999 to 2008 was completed, culminating in the emergence of the Violence Against Persons (Prohibition) Bill (VAPP Bill). These harmonization activities, led by groups such as the Women's Right Advancement and Protection Alternative (WRAPA) and the International Federation of Women Lawyers (FIDA), helped address the duplication concerns.

Interestingly, the VAPP Bill also enjoyed the overwhelming support of Muslim women organizations. Groups such as the Federation of Muslim Women Association of Nigeria (FOMWAN) hosted sensitization workshops where they urged other Muslim women to embrace the VAPP Bill (Akinbobola 2015). FIDA and WRAPA consolidated these efforts, leading sustained advocacy action and enjoining the Senate to hasten the passage of VAPP Bill. International development partners such as the UN Population Fund also played a critical role in the passage process, by providing technical and financial support to LACVAW.

The Senate Committee on Judiciary, Human Rights, and Legal Matters conducted a public hearing on the VAPP Bill on 2 March 2015, receiving submissions from the public and from women's rights stakeholders. After fourteen long years of activism by women's rights groups, former President Goodluck Jonathan signed the Violence against Persons Prohibition Bill (2013) into law in May 2015, criminalizing various forms of violence against women and men in Nigeria. As LACVAW (2015) noted, the length of time it took to secure the bill's passage is an indication of how deeply VAW is tolerated in the society.

The VAPP Law broadens the scope of existing sexual offenses while also criminalizing a number of harmful acts within the family that could endanger lives or increase a person's vulnerability to violence. For instance, it extends the definition of rape beyond intentional penetration of the vagina without consent, as defined in Section 357 of the Criminal Code Act. In line with modern realities, the VAPP Bill broadened the definition of rape to include penetration of the mouth or anus or any part of the body without consent. In the same vein, the Bill criminalizes spousal battery, redefining it to include the intentional and unlawful use of force or violence on a person, unlawful touching, beating, or striking of another person against his or her will with the intention of causing bodily harm. Similarly, it criminalizes incest; emotional or psychological pain such as genital mutilation of the girl-child or abandonment of children, spouse, children, and other dependents without sustenance; economic abuse in the form of forced financial dependence; denial of inheritance rights; deprivation of resources for necessaries, and repeated insults and name calling, among others.

The VAPP Law's legal coverage encompasses a diversity of harmful acts that could endanger the lives of women and girls in the private sphere. Harmful substances are often administered to the girl-child or women during genital mutilation rituals or in the performance of widowhood rites. Prior to the reforms, law enforcement authorities regarded the majority of these actions as private matters, and interfering with them was regarded as potentially breaching individual or marital privacy. Another feature that makes the VAPP Bill progressive and ingeniously different from other enactments is the array of progressive legal remedies for victims. For the first time, rape victims are entitled to compensation, while the offenders are now listed in a sex offenders register. Another innovation is the provision of a protection order, without any time limit and effective throughout the Federal Republic of Nigeria, notwithstanding the limited jurisdiction of the Bill.

In light of the above, the VAPP Law represents a major "homegrown" response to GBV. It was enacted at a time when violence towards women and girls in the home was largely (and continues to be) considered a private matter to be settled within the family. The thick walls built around issues of violence within the family discourage women from seeking legal redress. As we saw in the previous sections, the provisions of Nigeria's Criminal and Penal Codes relating to violence in the private sphere perpetuated discrimination and offered inadequate protection to victims. Recognizing these challenges, the VAPP Bill not only filled in the gaps in existing laws, but also covered new ground on neglected areas of domestic violence (Onyemelukwe 2016: 4).

Selected case studies: a typology of GBV in northern and southern Nigeria

Consistent with the differences in the socio-cultural and religious contexts between the regions, key disparities also exist in the scale and typology of the GBV prevailing in the two regions. In this section, we shall use a number of case studies to illustrate these disparities, highlighting the dichotomy (if any) in the extent or quality of legal protection against discrimination, especially in the family, available to women and girls in the north and south. Spotlighting the most consequential issues demanding action is necessary both to improve understanding of the magnitude and nature of the problem(s) at the regional level and to develop holistic responses and measures to combat discrimination against women and girls in Nigeria.

Case study 1: abduction and forced (child) marriages in northern Nigeria

Of all the religiously sanctioned practices that affect full equality between men and women, child marriage has emerged as the primary issue because of its high frequency and the critical need for action.[18] The prevalence of child marriage varies widely from one region to another, with figures as high as 76 percent in the North West Zone and as low as 10 percent in the South East.[19] Child marriage is the act of giving a female child for marriage at a very tender age, mostly without her consent,[20] and more recently, also without parental consent. Of the 43 percent of girls married off in Nigeria before their eighteenth birthday, 17 percent were married before they turned fifteen.[21] Illiteracy, poverty, and religious traditions rank high among the major drivers of child marriages: about 82 percent of women who were married before age eighteen[22] had no education.

Although the Nigerian Constitution does not establish a minimum age for marriage, the Child Rights Act, passed in 2003, fixed the age of marriage at eighteen. Only twenty-four out of Nigeria's thirty-six states have, so far, replicated the Child Rights Act as state law, laying the groundwork for implementing the minimum age of marriage in their respective states. The twenty-four adopting states are mainly from the south, and they rely primarily on international human rights law to derive the normative contents of state legislation. In contrast, the marriage age set by legal rules is at variance with powerful traditional and religious practices that predominate in the north, further widening the gap between local culture and the standards set by international human rights norms. Consider the case of Ese Oruru:

Sometime in August 2015, Ese Rita Oruru, 14, was abducted from her home state in Bayelsa, South-South Nigeria by an adult male, Mr. Yinusa Dahiru, a northern Muslim. She was taken away and relocated to Kano State where she stayed for several months before she was rescued and reunited with her parents in June 2016. Charged for abduction, child trafficking, illicit sex, sexual exploitation, and unlawful carnal knowledge, her abductor Yinusa Dahiru is currently facing a criminal trial.

(TheNEWS *2016*)

Ese Oruru's case is just one of numerous cases of girl-child abduction and child marriages in the north. One recurrent feature in all of these cases is that the victims involved were legal minors, wrongfully abducted by adult male Muslims in different parts of Nigeria, converted to Islam, and forced into marriages, pregnancy, and childbirth without their parents' consent. These abductions evoke sad memories of the April 2014 infamous kidnapping of 219 girls from their secondary school hostel in Chibok, Borno State, in northern Nigeria.

Deep-rooted religious practices and traditional institutions that support child marriage have a strong influence on the way the legal system responds to incidents of child marriage. When Ese's mother discovered her daughter's whereabouts in Kano, she journeyed from her Bayelsa base to Kano several times in an effort to rescue her daughter. In both Kano and Bayelsa states, she filed reports with the police authorities. She also petitioned Kano's highest traditional establishment, the Kano Emirate Council. These efforts yielded no positive results. The notion that Islamic law approves of child marriage is so widespread that traditional and law enforcement institutions are often unwilling to respond to such complaints.

The case of Habiba Isiyaku in August 2016 and her forced marriage to the Emir of Katsina illustrates the long-standing unwillingness of the religious/traditional establishment to embrace family law reforms. When Habiba's father – Mr. Isiyaku Tanko of Katsina State – demanded the return of his fourteen-year-old daughter, the Katsina Emirate Council justified the abduction on the basis of Islamic teachings. According to the Council, the legal minor's conversion to Islam and the marriage to the Emir were voluntary, and on that basis, the marriage was declared "irreversible." As with Ese Oruru's case, the petitions to the police authorities were not acted upon (THISDAYLIVE 2016). Public appeals for her release have fallen on deaf ears.

Ese's and Habiba's case studies suggest that some unpopular acts like child abductions and rapes can be justified by Islamic references. And, once clothed with a religious shell, women's rights violations that occur in the guise of applying Islamic law are harder to challenge or resolve using the instrumentality of the law. This means that the failure to act on the part of the political and legal systems is not just because they lack the capacity or resources to do so. Rather, political and systemic inaction flows from the consistency of the harmful acts with a social order where upholding Sharia law is valued. Political and legal intervention would mean authorities straying into an arena that is clearly outside the purview of "formal law," and therefore beyond their scrutiny. Any legal or political action that is shorn of deference to the divine teachings is not just frowned upon, but vehemently resisted.

Case study 2: domestic violence in southern Nigeria

VAW in Nigeria is common practice and cuts across all socio-economic and cultural backgrounds. Just as the practice of child marriage is popular in the northern region, overwhelming statistical data evince unprecedented rates of violence within the family, especially in intimate partnerships and marriage relationships, in the southern region. Statistics from the National Bureau of Statistics show that

> one in five women has experienced some form of physical violence . . . The highest proportion of women who experience physical violence is found in the South-West and South-South. The North-East and North-West report relatively fewer cases of domestic violence, although this could be an indication that violence in households is under-reported.
>
> *(Bazza 2010: 130–136)*

Consolidating the findings of previous studies, a 2016 survey by NOIPolls reiterated with concern an upsurge in the rates of domestic violence, with the highest statistics recorded in Nigeria's South-West Zone at 86 percent, and the lowest in the South-South Zone at about 70 percent.[23]

Nigeria's constituent states, principally in the south, have taken bold steps toward criminalizing all forms of violence based on gender. Notwithstanding the diversity of family reform laws and protective mechanisms in place, policy and legislative reforms that have been passed have not yet shifted the ingrained religious beliefs, social prejudices, and attitudes that reinforce VAW in the family. Accordingly, VAW is still a daily occurrence, with trends showing an increasing number of domestic violence cases that have resulted in the death or near-death of women. About 4,000 GBV cases, ranging from rape, child abuse, sexual assault and sexual abuse to defilement and other matrimonial issues, were reported in Lagos State alone in 2015 (Sesan 2016). The grim statistics buttress the severity of abuse.[24]

Feminist conversations on the impediments to reforms in southern Nigeria

A combination of factors accounts for the weakness of legislative responses to VAW. Onyemelukwe (2016) contends that domestic violence is not taken seriously in Nigeria and that many, even educated people, still consider it justifiable.[25] Many, including implementers – judiciary, police, and even civil society organizations— are not aware of the laws and those whom the law seeks to protect.[26] In contrast, FIDA's Ngozi Ogbolu argues that nothing is wrong with the legal system,[27] rather that the problem lies with the administration of the criminal justice system, especially the deficit in trust that citizens accord the machineries for justice delivery. For instance, all police stations in Lagos State have human rights desks; however, awareness of these sections is not high, with corresponding low levels of access and usage.

A local NGO maintains a website[28] dedicated to increasing awareness of legislation and other resources that proscribe domestic violence. Educational intervention for the general public is also essential, not only to raise awareness, but to sensitize the public on those behaviors sanctioned by culture that are now proscribed by law. Public enlightenment has also enabled more women to become aware of the provisions that afford them legal protection and the mechanisms through which they can seek help. "Seeking legal protection often involves litigation services procured at great expense. Thus, even where there is awareness, there are few resources, such as legal aid and financial assistance available to victims," Onyemelukwe adds.[29]

Reforms often address legal rules and not the poor environment for enabling legal effectiveness. For that reason, women cannot take advantage of the law even if they know the rights and protections available thereunder. Another local advocate agrees that laws and court systems alone are not enough to address VAW. "Yes, there a few landmark cases, but an influx of cases shows that family law reform legislation is not working," says Princess Olufemi Kayode of MEDIACON.[30] After working on the issue of domestic violence for over two decades, she finds that

> not many women actually want to leave their husbands. Women just want the violence or whatever that is causing it to end, but not an end to their marriages, with most preferring mediation rather than dispute-resolution methods that are adversarial and lead to divorce or separation.[31]

The Reverend Sr. Anastacia Njoku strongly agrees with this, noting that some women are scared about the formal channels of legal redress or repelled by the adversarial posturing of formal courts. She says that those who are afraid to pursue litigation for violence for whatever reason could resort to alternative dispute resolution procedures that are accessible formally or informally.[32]

As Kayode's and Njoku's views show, VAW cases continue to be dealt with through religious and/or customarily established procedures and mechanisms of dispute resolution that emphasize tolerance, forgiveness, and reconciliation. The emphasis on forgiveness and tolerance is problematic because it both ignores criminal accountability and de-emphasizes providing redress to the victims or survivors of violence. In addition, the principles adopted by the religious and/or customary reconciliatory mechanisms are not based on law, but rather are often rooted in doctrinal instructions according to either Christian or Islamic texts. In many instances, resorting to these informal mechanisms of dispute resolution precludes victims from seeking redress within the formal justice systems. This substantiates Joy Ngwakwe's contention that women who seek legal redress for violence against them face societal stigma.[33] According to Chibogu Obinwa, one way to overcome that stigma is by sensitizing or encouraging families to welcome their abused daughter back home, especially when she flees from spousal battery and abuse.[34] The anticipation of rejection from their families often forces victims of domestic violence to remain in abusive relationships.

In Nigeria, where both Christianity and Islam hold enormous influence in the conduct of relations in the private sphere, the confidence in the dispute resolution mechanisms that each religion offers continues to soar. Accordingly, integrating these religious and customary dispute resolution methods into the formal justice system has been recommended (United Nations 2010: 16). According to Ngwakwe,[35] the integration will build the capacity of such bodies to administer VAW complaints in accordance with human rights and gender-equality standards under national and international human rights law. WLP workshop participants[36] agreed that the number of domestic violence victims seeking solace in religious institutions is increasing because of the spiritual strength and trust that religious institutions promise their adherents. Therefore, the religious community can no longer be ignored or excluded in conversations around family law reform. As public trust in religious institutions heightens, abused women will benefit from civil society advocacy influencing the religious community to shift from merely providing spiritual and marriage counseling to building shelters for battered women.[37]

Activists such as Princess Olufemi Kayode strongly recommend that the focus on punishment should be de-emphasized. Instead, increasing the legal protection for women and girls should be accompanied by other realistic incentives, including providing medical support services to both perpetrators and survivors. For instance, anger management, treatment of depression, and marriage counseling may present some antidotes to the causative factors of VAW. Offering these antidotes to perpetrators and survivors rests on the recognition that laws and punishments are not enough to address their psychological and psychiatric needs. The alternatives therefore seek to address the root cause of violent act, rather than punish violent behavior that is likely to be repeated over and again.

Furthermore, under-reporting aggravates the social and health risks associated with domestic violence. Public reporting of VAW has several advantages. It helps to reveal gaps in the scope and effectiveness of the law. It also feeds into the statistical data generation and information-gathering efforts of different stakeholders to inform legal development and to strengthen the knowledge base on all forms of VAW.

Exploring new opportunities for reform

Changes driven by public pressure

Legal reforms alone may not be able to unseat religiously sanctioned practices pertaining to the personal status and family relationships that entrench gender inequality. Several conventional and unconventional reactions to gender inequality have demonstrated the potential to induce the official establishments to consider reforms. Public pressure represents one example of an untapped opportunity. For instance, the growing evidence of victims of child marriages resorting to unlawful methods to regain their freedom has triggered angry public reactions and deeply polarizing debates, including international pressure. The ensuing pressure and public debates wield enormous influence on legal and judicial processes, often leading to a reconsideration of the alleged violations using the prism of international human rights norms.

In Ese Oruru's case cited above, intense pressure from media groups, social critics, analysts, civil society groups, and NGOs working on women and children's rights forced the intervention of federal authorities to secure Ese's release and arrest her abductor. Ese returned to her parents pregnant and had a baby girl few months later. In another case, in April 2014, Wasila Tasi'u, age fourteen, was given in marriage to Umar Sani, thirty-five, in Gezawa, outside the northern city of Kano. Seventeen days into the marriage, Wasila allegedly poisoned Umar and three of his friends at her own wedding party. Soon after she was arrested and charged with killing her husband, Wasila disclosed she had been tied to the bed and raped by Sani on their wedding night. She further alleged that it was a forced marriage to a man she did not love and did not want to have a relationship with (Pickles and Bloom 2015). Initially, a motion by defense lawyers to have the case moved to juvenile court was rejected, despite human rights activists' claims that she was too young to stand trial for murder in a High Court. Charges against Wasila were later dropped only after intense pressure and campaigning efforts by civic groups.

As Wasila's case and other related incidents of self-help demonstrate,[38] social pressure matters. The pressure comes through mostly nonviolent actions and legal activities such as organized street protests, internet campaigns, press statements, social commentaries on TV and radio, petitions to authorities, amicus submissions to court, and public interest litigation, among others. The ultimate aim of these actions is to influence changes in policies, practices, and government behavior. As with Ese's and Wasila's cases, pressure on social media led by activists, NGOs, and active citizens has a profound impact on government and individual behavior. For instance, the changes in judicial decisions in Wasila's case were not unconnected to social pressure, and social pressure helped to facilitate Ese's return to her parents. Social pressure is more meaningful and sustainable when the actors applying the pressure are empowered, have knowledge of existing laws and regulations, and use that knowledge to publicly interrogate or challenge acts that contradict applicable enactments on VAW.

Thanks to the advancements in information and communication technology, messages now travel faster, across distances, especially through the use of social networks. With this speed of dissemination, public pressure may be activated and amplified with limited resources. It may or may not be intentional or even coordinated by anyone. It is important to emphasize that social pressure thrives on publicity and public participation. Absent that publicity component, the chance of igniting public resistance and opprobrium to the offending conduct is significantly hampered. Despite this shortcoming, public pressure has helped to bring about change in a number of complex family law situations and holds enormous potential for opening the closed doors of religious laws to implementable reforms.

Changes compelled by maternal health considerations

The negative health impacts of child marriages on the girl-child may present another trigger for reforms. According to the World Health Organization (WHO), many health problems are especially associated with pregnancy during adolescence, such as anemia, malaria, HIV and other sexually transmitted infections, postpartum hemorrhage, and mental disorders, such as depression. Up to 65 percent of women with obstetric fistula[39] develop this as adolescents, with dire consequences (WHO 2015). Deaths during the baby's first month of life are 50 to 100 percent more frequent if the mother is an adolescent versus an older female; and the younger the mother, the higher the risk (WHO 2015).

Weak healthcare systems in Nigeria increase the vulnerabilities that child brides face during pregnancy and childbirth. In 2012, Nigeria accounted for 10 percent of the world's maternal deaths and under-5 mortality rates, with the highest maternal mortality ratio (1,549) found in the North-East and the lowest (165) found in the South-West zones of the country.[40] As of 2013, the Nigeria Demographic and Health Survey showed that for every 100,000 pregnant women who give birth, about 576 will die. The same survey also found that Jigawa State topped the list of teenage mothers, with 78 percent of its girls between the ages of fifteen to nineteen in early marriage, closely followed by Katsina, Zamfara, Bauchi, and Sokoto states, all in the northern part of Nigeria.

The religious cover that child marriages enjoy within conservative localities makes it difficult to challenge and overturn them. However, the statistical evidence of the negative health impacts associated with child marriage can be used to encourage and justify the need for reforms. Chances of reform are heightened when advocacy targets and secures the support of traditional authorities and the official religious establishments. Consistent with this approach, a leading adherent of the northern politico-religious establishment has called on the Muslim *Umma* (community) to ban child marriages in Nigeria, following the tradition in similarly situated contexts such as Morocco, Egypt, and Malaysia, where the marriage age is seventeen, eighteen, and nineteen respectively.[41] Speaking at a workshop organized by the Northern Islamic Forum in Kano in May 2016, the Emir of Kano, Emir Muhammad Sanusi Lamido, advocated a ban on marriage of women below the age of eighteen, stating that most of the women suffering from reproductive health challenges were in such marriages.

The Emir is now spearheading family law reforms in Kano State, which is famed for its extremely conservative stance on Islamic teachings on gender relations in the family. According to a statement, "the (new) law will address what Islam says on marriage, outlaw forced marriages, make domestic violence illegal, and put in conditions that you need to fulfil before you can marry a second wife" (*The Punch Newspapers* 2017). This new campaign is now gaining momentum in policy circles, generating debates in social media, and attracting the consensus of a broad spectrum of stakeholders. In Kano State, initiatives bringing together experts in Islamic law from Bayero University have been launched to deliberate on the possibilities of codifying Sharia law in family issues such as early marriage, girl-child education, and reproductive health.

Enthused by the recent developments, gender experts and advocates agree that engaging the gatekeepers of local customs and religious teachings is a productive reform path to explore and follow.[42] There is more than enough evidence now to warrant a serious review of family laws based on the social costs of child marriages and domestic violence, whether in the north or the south. Collaborative problem solving and strategic engagement with traditional and religious leaders in policy reform discussions is key, not only because of the overwhelming influence they wield in their localities, but also in recognition that they often serve as first responders in family crisis situations.

Changes piloted by education and promotional activities

Because of the religious character that surrounds the practice of child marriage, the social acquiescence to, or the cultural acceptance of, the practice has also grown, despite the negative impacts on children's physical development and wellbeing. As a young girl disclosed, "if a girl is 15 years old and she is not married, people will start complaining" (Girls in their own voices 2016). Addressing cultural acquiescence is another unconventional option (in addition to public pressure and maternal health considerations) that has enormous potential through education and promotional activities to introduce new behavioral norms and lifestyle changes for women and girls, thereby reducing the incidences of child marriage. An interesting example is the new educational and lifestyle exposure offered to twenty-four girls who escaped from Boko Haram abduction. They were given full scholarships at the American University of Nigeria in the North-East state of Adamawa (BBC News 2016). The girls, now women, are flourishing in a program designed especially to address their academic, psychological, social, and emotional challenges.

Illiteracy contributes to a woman's powerlessness with respect to sexuality and reproductive health, while lowering her socio-economic status within the family. who finds that low education levels are also closely associated with early childbearing (WHO 2015). Thus beyond legal reforms, increasing access to education for women and girls can help reduce cultural acceptance of, and acquiescence to, child marriage. Education can also help modify individual and group behavior indirectly by stimulating changes in perceptions of social or cultural norms. Legislative interventions designed to improve girls' access to education and delay marriage are important, but empowering communities to change deeply held (religious) beliefs that justify violent behavior is imperative.

Considerations along these lines probably informed the recent admonition by the foremost Islamic leader and monarch, Emir Muhammad Sanusi Lamido. He strongly recommended the conversion of mosques to primary schools to boost girl-child enrollment and bring education to the doorsteps of citizens at less cost. In his words, "educating the girl-child was more important than building mosques."[43] He further advised that donations for building of mosques should be channeled towards building schools.

In a region where religious conservatism flourishes, serious opposition or mixed reactions from other members of the northern religious establishment was to be expected. His suggestion was regarded as mischievous in some quarters,[44] but was applauded in others.[45] Sanusi Lamido insists that converting mosques to schools is a radical solution to fix the problem of denying access to education (especially for girls) and declining school enrollment, which has been linked to the rise of Islamic terrorist movements in the region. In progressive countries in the Arab world such as Morocco, Muslim worship centers have been efficiently utilized to spread knowledge. Sanusi Lamido's influential politico-religious status means that his ideas may spark serious debates about educational reforms, which can help to potentially put the region on a more progressive and modern path.

Changes impelled by religious differences and tension

Finally, the recurring abduction of young girls from Christian backgrounds and their forced conversion to Islam as a prelude to marriage to much-older Muslim males have also become an additional source of religious tension in the country. Statistical evidence shows a shocking increase in the spate of abductions, religious conversions, and forced marriages of Christian girls in northern Nigeria, where the practice of Sharia law is widespread. In the last five years, in Kano State alone more than forty Christian girls have been abducted, converted to Islam, and married off to Muslims (World Watch 2016). The figures may be higher, given that such conduct within the private sphere is seldom reported. Parents seeking the release of abducted daughters usually meet a brick wall, while law enforcement agencies fail to act because of the powerful influence of religion on the socio-political systems in those states.

In several public statements and press releases, Christian associational bodies in Nigeria's nineteen northern states have criticized cases of Christian minors in the north who are forced into marriages to adult male Muslims. Condemning the spate of abductions of Christian girls in Nigeria, a leader of the Christian Association of Nigeria told *The Punch*:

> I don't know where it is in the religion that teaches that they can take someone's daughter, convert her from Christianity to Islam and marry her off . . . if it were Christians doing this to Muslim girls, Nigerians would have been burnt to ashes. So, to me, it is a total disrespect and a complete disobedience of the law of the land and the law of God.[46]

That young Muslims girls are not subjected to the same ordeal makes the practice of forced conversion particularly objectionable. The "cloud of crisis" (World Watch 2016) generated from this Christian/Muslim dissension is important because of its intrinsic potential to provoke the sort of inter-religious debate and cross-sectoral engagement needed to bridge the ideological divides on gender equality.

Digitally enabled feminist interventions against domestic violence

Feminist positions are not new in Nigeria, dating back to the pre-colonial traditional societies. These women may not have called their own ideologies of equality "feminism," but they contributed to establishing a world where women were empowered (Brittle Paper 2016). Contemporary Nigerian feminist movements and women's rights organizations have stepped up the tempo in changing hearts and minds to ensure that the next generation does not experience the inequities that women and girls are currently facing.

Digital technology has been significantly useful to advance feminist positions in Nigeria. Leaders of leading women's rights organizations and feminist movements such as Josephine Chukwuma of Project Alert and Betty Abah of CEE-HOPE are among those playing a key role in using social media to campaign against pervasive inequality in the private sphere. Regularly, they initiate public debates about inclusivity, creating new understandings of gender relations, winning new converts, or pulling in other independent feminist thinkers in their social interrogations of the structures of inequality. Lately, the initial backlash or the predominant attributions of "man-hating" that often greet feminist statements are gradually softening, leading to greater tolerance and constructive dialogue on contentious issues regarding gender, sexuality, and family relations.

Conclusion

Although the social and politico-legal contexts prevailing in northern and southern Nigeria are characteristically dissimilar, the transgressions against women in both areas are evidently similar. In Nigeria's northern region, the family laws as well as civil and criminal statutes codify certain socio-cultural and religious traditions that provide legal and social justifications for VAW. Women and girls living in the region would benefit from urgent legal reforms. In the southern part, where significant legal reforms designed to counter gendered inequalities have taken place, they have not resulted in achieving substantive equality in practice. In other words, the reform of laws impacting women in the family has neither overturned the disproportionate ways that cultural norms affect women, nor uprooted the ingrained patriarchal ideologies that lower women's status and decrease their autonomy.

There is evidence of clear conflict between the constitutional guarantees of gender equality and the prevailing social practices that engender power imbalances between men and women. Deeply entrenched patriarchal ideologies have permeated the disparate legal and justice delivery systems in both regions of the country, placing obstacles in the path of many women. These obstacles continue to feed on the historical constructs of social and power relations in the family and society. Consequently, the quality of legal protection for women and girls differs along the lines of geographical location and socio-legal contexts. A real cultural shift is needed to protect the most vulnerable citizens from violent abuse (Chinedu 2015).

Although important gaps remain, much progress has been made in shifting the ideological orientations that engender power imbalances between men and women. As the accomplishments of LACVAW and the case studies involving Ese Oruru and Wasila Tasi'u demonstrate, women's rights organizations and feminist movements have made giant strides in creating advocacy networks around specific issues and influencing federal gender policies. Their organizing successes have yielded a cycle of substantive gains. From the enlightenment campaigns to providing legal representation to victims of GBV or litigating in the public interest, these efforts have facilitated the instrumentalization of feminist and equality rhetorics in both national policy frameworks and family law jurisprudence. Winning influential converts such as powerful Islamic monarchs and clerics to the feminists' side has also enabled very conservative regions to suspend their unwillingness to take issues of gender and family relations very seriously. Despite the absence of a nationally centralized body of women's rights movements, advocates have managed to work together, successfully deploying an array of strategies to draw political and legislative attention to gender issues. Even recent campaigns around newer categories of rights, such as lesbian, gay, bisexual, and transgender rights, are tapping into the energies of feminists and gender-justice advocates. In turn, these actions are producing shifts in collective thinking and understandings of gender and family relations in both the public and private sphere and resulting in legal reforms in a more organic fashion.

Learning from the best practices and progress that has been made, future advocacy and reform interventions need to explicitly acknowledge that the reform of family laws should transcend more than just changes to legal provisions, systems, and institutions. Beyond securing changes to legal rules and policies, actors and advocates need to gear up for the more difficult task of changing hearts and minds. The analysis contained in this study is not exhaustive, but it is expected that many of these challenges facing the protection of women's rights remain central to the reform discourse. It is hoped that this study will elevate their visibility and help sustain a dialogue on their resolution.

Notes

1 Nigeria has six geopolitical zones: the North-Central Zone includes the states of Benue, Federal Capital Territory, Kogi, Kwara, Nassarawa, and Plateau; the North-East Zone includes the states of Adamawa, Bauchi, Borno, Gombe, Taraba, and Yobe; the North-West Zone includes the states of Jigawa, Kaduna, Kano, Kebbi, Sokoto, and Zamfara; the South-East Zone includes the states of Abia, Anambra, Ebonyi, Enugu, and Imo; the South-South Zone includes the states of Akwa Ibom, Bayelsa, Cross River, Delta, Edo, and River; the South-West Zone includes the states of Ekiti, Lagos, Ogun, Ondo, Osun, and Oyo.

2 The interviewees include: Cheluchi Onyemelukwe, Executive Director, Center for Health Ethics Law and Development (CHELD), 27 December 2016, e-mail; Josephine Chukwuma, Executive Director, Project Alert, 26 December 2016, e-mail/social media; Betty Abah, Executive Director, Centre for Children's Health Education, Orientation and Protection (CEE-HOPE), 5 December 2016, telephone; Princess Olufemi-Kayode, Executive Director, MEDIA Concern Initiative (MEDIACON), 30 December 2016, e-mail/social media; Joy Ngwake, Executive Director, Centre for Advancement of Development Rights (CEADER), 6 January 2017, e-mail; and Lola Vivour-Adeniyi, Coordinator, Domestic and Sexual Violence Response Team (DSVRT), Lagos State Government, 7 December 2016, in-person meeting.

3 Participants at the Research Presentation Workshop, held on 14 February 2017, were: Ms. Ngozi Ogbolu and Ms. Nnenna Eze, International Federation of Women Lawyers (FIDA), Nigeria; Dr. Angela Daniel, Women Entrepreneurs Association of Nigeria (WEAN); Ms. Ajanma Esen, MEDIACON; Rev. Sr. Dr. Anastacia Njoku and Rev. Sr. Grace John-Emezi, Ancilla Catholic Hospital, Iju, Lagos State; Ms. Obiangbanso Nkechi, Women Advocates Research and Documentation Centre (WARDC); Mr. Victor Ocheja, DSVRT, Lagos State Government; Kate Duru, Echoes of Women in Africa; Ms. Betty Abah, Executive Director, CEE-HOPE; Ms. Ngozi Iwere, Community Life Project (CLP); Ms. Bose Ironsi, Women's Rights and Health Project (WRAHP); Ms. Nneka Nwaneri, *The Nation* newspaper; Ms. Chibogu Obinwa and Ms. Anne Lawal, Women's Learning Partnership (WLP) Global Facilitators; Ms. Uduak Eddy Orok, National Youth Service Corps (NYSC) member; Ms. Francisca Anaeme, Good Women Association (GWA); Ms. Joy Ngwakwe and Ms. Rosemary Nwachukwu, CEADER; and Ms. Victoria Ohaeri and Ms. Aizighode Obinyan, Spaces for Change.

4 There is only one Federal High Court, but with distinct divisions established all over the country, across the geographical zones.

5 Nigeria ratified CEDAW in 1985.

6 Domestication is a legal process through which an international instrument is incorporated into Nigerian law. This parliamentary process transforms the international instrument into a local legislation that can be enforced locally by domestic courts and other law enforcement bodies.

7 The Charter was adopted in 1981 by the then-Organization of African Unity, now known as the African Union.

8 The Protocol to the African Charter was adopted in 2003. It came into force on 25 November 2005, when it received its fifteenth ratification.

9 Criminal Code Act, Chapter C39, Laws of the Federal Republic of Nigeria 2004.

10 See the Sharia Courts (Administration of Justice and Certain Consequential Changes) Law, No. 5 of 1999.

11 Kano State Penal Code S. 127.

12 The repugnancy doctrine sits at the core of Nigerian jurisprudence on native law and customs. Different customs apply from locality to locality. A custom that is acceptable in one locality may be repulsive in another. Judges are required to apply this doctrine to determine the fairness of the customs. Also invoked under the Nigerian law of evidence, the repugnancy test is mainly used to measure the consistency of native customs with the principles of natural justice, equity, and good conscience. The philosophies undergirding the tripartite concept of natural justice, equity, and good conscience are consistent with the contemporary dictates of international human rights.

13 Many customs that apply in the south have been tested for repugnancy. Please see: *Edet v. Esien* (1932) 11 N.L.R. 47; *Danmole v. Dawodu* (1958) 3 F.S.C.46; *Okoriko v. Otobo* (1961) W.N.L.R. 48; *Effiong Okon Ata* (1930) 10 N.L.R. 65; *Asogbon v. Odutan* (1935) 12 N.L.R. 7.

14 The Beijing Platform for Action can be accessed at: www.un.org/womenwatch/daw/beijing/pdf/BDPfA%20E.pdf.

15 For instance, in 2001, an NGO called Project Alert established a shelter that has since provided accommodation to hundreds of women and girls.

16 The Federal Capital Territory (FCT), Kaduna, Kano, Zamfara, Sokoto, Adamawa, Borno, Abia, Imo, Edo, Delta, Cross River, Rivers, Akwa Ibom, Lagos, Ekiti, Osun, and Ogun states were specifically covered.
17 See Solidarity for African Women's Rights, LACVAW, www.soawr.org/blog/legislative-advocacy-coalition-violence-against-women-lacvaw.
18 Notorious incidents such as the 14 April 2014 abduction of over two hundred secondary schoolgirls in Chibok village, Borno State, by Boko Haram insurgents attests to the persistence of child marriages. In May 2016, one of the abducted Chibok girls was found, with her four-month-old baby, fathered by one of her abductors.
19 Girls Not Brides Foundation, www.girlsnotbrides.org/child-marriage/nigeria/.
20 It should be noted that children are unable to "give consent" in a legal sense, and such consent if given may well have been coerced.
21 Girls Not Brides Foundation, ibid.
22 Ibid.
23 Project Alert and NOIPolls (2016).
24 A state-sponsored documentation of domestic violence that resulted in death found that the issues triggering the violent acts typically range from allegations of the wife's infidelity, the wife's demands for house upkeep allowance, the wife's denial of conjugal rights, parent-child grievance, child-parent grievance, and sibling-sibling grievance to disputes between lovers. A common feature of these incidents is that they resulted in the death of the female party (Temilola 2015: 12).
25 Interview with Cheluchi Onyemelukwe, Executive Director, CHELD, 27 December 2016.
26 Ibid.
27 WLP Seminar held 14 February 2017 in Lagos.
28 www.domesticviolence.com.ng, Center for Health Ethics Law and Development (CHELD).
29 Interview with Cheluchi Onyemelukwe, 27 December 2016.
30 Interview with Princess Olufemi Kayode, 30 December 2016.
31 Ibid.
32 WLP Seminar, 14 February 2017 in Lagos.
33 Interview with Joy Ngwakwe, CEADER, 6 January 2017.
34 WLP Seminar, 14 February 2017 in Lagos.
35 Joy Ngwakwe interview, 6 January 2017
36 WLP Seminar, 14 February 2017 in Lagos.
37 Ibid.
38 "Self-help" in local parlance means taking the law into your hands.
39 An obstetric fistula is a hole between the vagina and rectum or bladder that is caused by prolonged obstructed labor, leaving a woman incontinent of urine or feces or both.
40 Working Draft, Government of Nigeria, Launching the SURE-P Maternal and Child Health (MCH) Initiative, p. 7.
41 The named countries are significant because Nigerian Muslims also practice the same Maliki School of jurisprudence that applies in Morocco, Egypt, and Malaysia.
42 WLP Seminar, 14 February 2017, in Lagos.
43 Sanusi Lamido spoke during the graduation ceremony of 2,500 Post Graduate Diploma and NCE teachers during Kano Basic Education week; see *Vanguard Newspaper* (2017).
44 By Dr. Junaid Mohammed and former Lagos State Commissioner of Police, Alhaji Abubakar Tsav.
45 By the second Republic governor of old Kaduna State, Alhaji Balarabe Musa, and National President of the Arewa Youth Consultative Forum, AYCF, Alhaji Shettima Usman Yerima. See *Vanguard Newspaper* (2017).
46 www.worldwatchmonitor.org/2016/11/child-marriage-becoming-a-cloud-of-crisis-n-nigerian-christian-leaders-warn-president/.

References

Akinbobola, Hajiah Raliat (2015) "FOMWAN, Fresh Push for Passage of Violence Against Persons Bill by Beta Nwosu," *The Guardian*, 16 February 2015, http://guardian.ng/features/focus/fresh-push-for-passage-of-violence-against-persons-bill/.

Bazza, Hadiza Iza (2010) "Domestic Violence and Women's Rights in Nigeria," *Societies Without Borders*, Vol. 4, No. 2: 175–192, http://scholarlycommons.law.case.edu/swb/vol4/iss2/6.

Bello, Aminu Adamu (2009) "Zina (Adultery) Under Islamic Law in Nigeria: The Gender Issues in Amina Lawal's Case," www.academia.edu/5142730/Zina_Adultery_Under_Islamic_Law_in_Nigeria_The_Gender_Issues_in_Amina_Lawals_Case.

BBC News (2016) "How to Protect the Chibok Girls From Reliving Their Horror," 29 October 2016, www.bbc.com/news/world-africa-37750983.

Brittle Paper (2016) "This is Why Adichie Believes Her Great-grandmother was a Feminist," 26 September 2016, http://brittlepaper.com/2016/09/adichie-video/

Chinedu, Anarado (2015) "Why Nigeria's New Violence against Person's (Prohibition) Bill is only the beginning," *Ventures Africa*, 15 June 2015, http://venturesafrica.com/why-nigerias-new-violence-against-persons-prohibition-act-is-only-the-beginning/.

Federal Ministry of Women Affairs (2004) *Nigeria National Report on Progress Made in the Implementation of the Beijing Platform for Action (Beijing +10)*, August 2004.

Girls in their own voices (2016) "IF A GIRL IS 15 YEARS OLD AND SHE IS NOT MARRIED, PEOPLE WILL START COMPLAINING," 20 April 2016, www.girlsnotbrides.org/girls-voices/nigeria-if-a-girl-is-15-years-old-and-she-is-not-married-people-will-start-complaining/.

Gwangndi, Maryam Ishaku (2016) "The Socio-Legal Context of the Nigerian Legal System and the Shariah Controversy: An Analysis of Its Impact on Some Aspects of Nigerian Women's Rights," *Journal of Law, Policy and Globalization*, Vol. 45: 60–66.

LACVAW (2015) 26 May 2015, www.v4c-nigeria.com/wp-content/uploads/2014/09/PressRelease26052015.pdf.

Mahdi, Saudatu (2010) "LACVAW, Overview & Analysis of Gender Based Violence in Nigeria (January–June 2010)," http://wrapanigeria.org/wp-content/uploads/2016/12/Overview-of-GBV-2010-Report-Final.pdf.

Onyemelukwe, Cheluchi (2016), "Legislating on Violence Against Women: A Critical Analysis of Nigeria's Recent Violence Against Persons (Prohibition) Act, 2015," *De Paul Journal of Women, Gender & Law*, Vol. 5, Issue 2.

Ozo-Eson, Philomena I. (2008) "Law, Women and Health in Nigeria," *Journal of International Women's Studies*, Vol. 9, No. 3: 285–299.

Pickles, Kate and Dan Bloom (2015) "Murder charges against 15-year-old girl accused of using rat poison to kill a 35-year-old man she was forced to marry are dropped by Nigerian court," *Mail Online (Daily Mail*, UK), 20 May, www.dailymail.co.uk/news/article-3089417/Murder-charges-against-15-year-old-girl-accused-using-rat-poison-kill-35-year-old-man-forced-marry-dropped-Nigerian-court.html#ixzz4NWfQK2QY.

Project Alert and NOIPolls (2016) "Domestic Violence, Poll Report, July 2016," www.noi-polls.com/documents/Domestic_Violence_In_Nigeria_Final__3_._Illustration_pdf.pdf.

The Punch Newspapers (2017) "Sanusi Plans Law Barring Poor Kano Men From Polygamy," 20 February 2017, http://punchng.com/sanusi-plans-law-barring-poor-kano-men-from-polygamy/.

Sesan, Olufowobi (2016) "Domestic Violence, 4,000 Cases Recorded in 1 Year-LASG," 1 June 2016, www.punchng.com/domestic-violence-4000-cases-recorded-1year-lasg/.

Temilola, George (2015) *Lethal Violence against Women in Nigeria (2006–2014)*, IFRA-Nigeria Working Paper Series, N43, 15 January 2015.

TheNEWS (2016) "Ese Oruru: Abductor Docked in Yenagoa," 8 March, http://thenews nigeria.com.ng/2016/03/ese-oruru-abductor-docked-in-yenagoa.

THISDAYLIVE (2016) "Family Accuses Emir of Katsina of Abducting, Forcefully Marrying a Christian Minor," 13 October 2016, www.thisdaylive.com/index. php/2016/10/13/family-accuses-emir-of-katsina-of-abducting-forcefully-marrying-a-christian-minor-2/.

United Nations (2010) *United Nations Handbook for Legislation on Violence against Women*, New York: United Nations.

———— (2014) *Women's Rights are Human Rights*, Office of the High Commissioner for Human Rights (HR/PUB/14/2 United Nations Publication).

Vanguard Newspaper (2017) "Sanusi Lamido's Statement on Converting Mosques to Schools is Mischievous," 8 February 2017, www.vanguardngr.com/2017/02/sanusis-statement-converting-mosques-schools-mischievous-junaid/.

WHO (World Health Organization) (2015) "Reproductive, Maternal, Newborn, Child and Adolescent Health," fact sheets available at www.wpro.who.int/reproductive_ maternal_newborn_child_adolescent/en/.

Women Living under Muslim Laws in Nigeria (2002) "Nigeria: Amina Lawal – Summary of Appeal," www.wluml.org/node/924.

World Watch (2016) "Child Marriage Becoming a 'Cloud of Crisis' – N. Nigerian Christian Leaders Warn President," 15 November 2016, www.worldwatchmonitor. org/2016/11/4727148/.

8

PALESTINE

Luna Saadeh, Fidaa Barghouthi, and
Fatmeh Muaqqet

Introduction

The Palestinian women's movement is faced with layers of complexities related to colonization and occupation on the one hand and a patriarchal society on the other, both of which pose challenges in combating violence against women (VAW). The prolonged and continuing Israeli occupation deprives Palestinians from enjoying their right to liberation and self-determination. Palestinians confront a cycle of violence that includes institutionalized policy-level violations that discriminate against a people at large, particularly burdening women's daily lives.

This chapter[1] examines the women's rights campaigns in Palestine of the past three decades. Due to the absence of a sovereign Palestinian state, political liberation has constituted the priority for Palestinian women. The women's movement has advocated for legal reform from a human rights perspective in order to ensure participation in the state-building process and the institutionalization of the principles of equality and social justice. Reforming the Personal Status Law (PSL), as a tool to combat violence and discrimination against women, is central to the work of the women's organizations. This chapter addresses the debate and discourse among women activists in working to amend the PSL (family law) and the Penal Code. It also highlights the strengths and weaknesses of the campaigns for legal reform initiated by the Palestinian women's movement.

The political situation

Lack of space precludes full coverage of Palestinian political and legal history here, but it must be noted that Palestine is different from the other case study countries in terms of its population living under the longest colonial rule and foreign occupation, the most recent being Israeli occupation and settler colonialism. Palestinian law exhibits diversity, reflecting its colonial history, starting from Ottoman rule, then the British Mandate, Arab rule[2] for the West Bank and Gaza, the military administration of the Israeli occupation of the West Bank and Gaza since 1967, and culminating with the establishment of the Palestinian National Authority (PNA) following the Oslo Accords.

In 1967, after the Israeli occupation forces took control of Gaza, the West Bank, and East Jerusalem, all the laws in the occupied territories that were found contradictory to orders issued by the occupation administration were cancelled. In 1993, some judicial and legal powers were transferred from the Israeli military administration to the PNA in parts of the occupied West Bank and Gaza, in accordance with the Oslo *Declaration of Principles* and the arrangements of the transitional autonomic government of 1993. Accordingly, the head of the PNA issued his first decision on 20 May 1994, which stipulated that laws and legislations that were valid before 1967 in West Bank and Gaza would remain valid. However, in 1994, the PNA assumed the powers of issuing legislation, with the aim of systematizing aspects of individual and public life, in addition to creating uniformity of laws between the West Bank and Gaza.

The period between 1996 and 1998 witnessed political and legal developments within Palestinian society following the signing of the Oslo Accords, subsequent agreements between the PLO and Israel, and the PNA's first presidential and legislative elections in January 1996. These developments motivated the Palestinian feminist movement to develop new methodologies and strategies to address the existing inequalities in Palestinian society and to realize women's human rights by adopting equal, non-discriminatory laws and legislation based on respect for human rights.

The social and cultural situation

Palestinian social structure is based on a patriarchal ideology. Despite social shifts in the Palestinian family from an extended to a nuclear family structure, cultural values traditionally inherited in Palestinian society continue to exist. The most important aspects of these values continue to uphold the inequality between men and women.

A core element within Palestinian society is the family. Individual self-identity is woven into a larger, more complex setting – that of the extended family. The individual's loyalty is measured by the extent to which he/she maintains the traditions of family and their local community. Loyalty leads to benefits from the extended family, mainly protection (Haj-Yahia 2002).

VAW in Palestine is based on complex international- (Israeli occupation) and national- (State of Palestine) level factors. By applying "security measures," the State of Israel has violated and continues to violate all aspects of Palestinians' life and security. Women are subjugated to violence from dual sources – from both the Israeli occupation as well as the local authorities and society.

Palestine is a leader in the Arab world in conducting studies about VAW. The Palestinian Central Bureau of Statistics (PCBS) conducted two surveys on VAW:

the first, the "Domestic Violence Survey," was published in 2005; the second, "Violence Survey in the Palestinian Society," in 2011. Both surveys were conducted at the request of donors, Palestinian ministries, and NGOs in order to acquire further data and information to inform national strategies and policy-level frameworks. However, these surveys were not institutionalized as a core and/or strategic responsibility of the PCBS. Both surveys showed that a woman's marital status, level of education, place of residence, age, size of family, and extended family influence were all factors in the rates of VAW. Data indicate that the extended family controls the family income and increases its control over women. The surveys also show that women who have been married are exposed to violence in its various forms by different relatives, such as a father, siblings, and in-laws (Haj-Yahia 2013). A study carried out by the Bisan Center for Research and Development (Haj-Yahia 1998) found that married women are subject to different types of violence and abuse by their husbands and that women in refugee camps and rural areas were more exposed to violence.

Extended families – tribes – are considered as a primary reference for violence within the family and VAW. Tribes (mainly led by men considered of high religious and social standing) follow patriarchal traditions, which enable male control and defend the role of males in both the family and Palestinian society (Shalhoub-Kevorkian 2001, 2009). Tribal understanding claims neutrality in resolving disputes and conflicts; however, this neutrality also enables and reinforces male dominance over the lives of women.

Notwithstanding the negative role of tribes in dealing with issues of VAW, these traditional, "non-formal" bodies are considered a main resource for women demanding protection. This is due to two factors: the first is the prevailing social order in Palestinian society, which is based on family affiliation and the importance of the person's identity within the family structure. The second is women's dissatisfaction with the performance of governmental organizations in providing protection services (UNDPA 2011) – the reasons for which include violence and retribution by employees, long and complicated procedures, and lack of privacy from the institutions that receive reports or cases related to violence.

Legal reforms to protect women's rights

Legal reform in Palestine began in 1993 with the establishment of the PNA. Prior to this, given the absence of an independent state to hold accountable and in which to advocate for legal reform to protect women's rights (and hold duty-bearers to account), women activists mainly directed their work to welfare interventions rather than human rights (Kazi 2013; Sayigh 1981; Palestine National Assembly-Research Centre 1975).

Between 1920 and the onset of the first Intifada (1987), women's participation was mainly focused on contributing to the national struggle, which continues to be the priority for all Palestinian political factions and has resulted in deferring consideration of social issues until after self-determination is achieved.

During the first Intifada (1987–93), women's participation expanded to include active engagement in political factions. Women began leading movements within the overarching national struggle, demonstrated for both feminism and the national struggle in Palestine's streets in unprecedented numbers, and played pivotal roles politically and economically. However, social issues such as divorce, violence, and early marriage, among others, continued to be secondary to the national struggle for self-determination. In the absence of an independent state and rule of law, political factions, along with tribal committees,[3] continued to play an important role in adjudicating social disputes in the private sphere. However, during the second Intifada (2000–05) and due to women activists' highlighting and shifting women's issues from the private to public sphere, individual citizenship began to shape into political and social citizenship (Giacaman et al. 2006).

This section focuses on the articles that discriminate against women in the main laws that impact women's lives in Palestine – the PSL and Penal Code.

The Personal Status Law

Gender-sensitive justice and legal reform have always been the Palestinian women's movement's major priorities (Johnson 2004). Upon the emergence of the PNA and the first legislative elections in 1996, amending the PSL became and remains one of the most prominent priorities for women's rights advocates. Palestinian Basic Law states in Article 4 that Islam is the official religion in Palestine, that respect for the sanctity of all other divine religions shall be maintained, and that the principles of Islamic Sharia shall be a principal source of legislation. The PSL, which is based on Sharia law, regulates rights in marriage, divorce, custody, and inheritance. For Christians, each denomination follows its own provisions, yet they all regulate marital and family relations and their obligations and duties. For inheritance, Islamic inheritance law is applied to Christians. Because Islam is the official religion and Christians are a minority, the women's organizations' focus was limited to amending the PSL (family law, based on Sharia), rather than addressing the gender gaps in the Christian laws.

The PSL in Palestine is comprised of two different laws: the Jordanian Personal Status Law of 1976 (in force in the West Bank) and the Egyptian Law of Family Rights of 1954 (in force in Gaza), both of which are discriminatory against women (Chaban 2011). Sharia courts handle PSL cases, yet tribal and customary laws, which also are discriminatory, have increasingly dealt with family disputes.

International human rights and CEDAW were the main legal references used by women's organizations in drafting new laws and legal amendments to protect women's rights. The main issues they have consistently raised are discussed below.

Age of marriage

The law in Gaza requires a female to be seventeen years old and a male to be eighteen. However, according to a 1996 directive issued by the Chief Sharia Judge, a female is allowed to marry at fourteen years and seven months and a male at fifteen years and seven months. The law in the West Bank stipulates that a female must be fifteen years old and a male must be sixteen. However, Article 18 (Jordanian Personal Status Law No. 61 (1976)) of the same law defines "year" as the lunar Hijri year, meaning that in Gregorian years, the minimum age of marriage for a female is fourteen years and six months. The two laws are not only in violation of CEDAW, they also contravene new Palestinian legislation such as the Palestinian Child Law No. 7 of 2004, which specifies a minimum age of eighteen.

Guardianship

Jordanian Personal Status Law and the Egyptian Family Rights Law both require that a woman must obtain the consent of a male guardian (*wali*) in order to marry for the first time, regardless of her age, abilities, educational background, or social and mental capabilities. When a male guardian is not available, a judge is permitted to act as a guardian. The paradox of the situation is that a woman can be a judge, a representative in the Palestinian Legislative Council (PLC), or a businesswoman, or assume other high-level decision-making positions, yet she is prevented from the right to enter into marriage without a male guardian (Jallad 2012). Men, of course, are not subject to the same obligation (ibid.).

The Jordanian Personal Status Law differentiates between a female virgin who has never married and a woman who has previously been married. Accordingly, a woman who is eighteen years old and divorced can agree to a marriage without a male guardian, while the marriage of a female virgin who is fifty years old is conditioned on the approval of her male guardian. Men are not subject to a similar condition; they are allowed to marry and remarry without legal contractual constraint. These specific articles reinforce perceptions of females as incapable of assuming responsibility for their lives, while defining unmarried women of any age as children.

Polygamy

Polygamy is allowed under the PSL in the West Bank and Gaza. Males are allowed to marry up to four wives on the "condition" that they ensure justice and equality between the wives. The PSL in both places does not require that the husband inform his first wife of his intent to marry another woman, nor does it require consent of the wife in her husband's decision (Al-Botmeh 2012).

Husband's unqualified right to divorce

Palestinian Muslim husbands have the ultimate right to dissolve their marriage by saying a divorce formula without any consideration of the wife's consent, and the divorce can occur in the wife's absence. In practice, this means that a man can divorce his wife without informing her and without her consent. A husband's ultimate right to divorce without his wife's consent is a cause of great insecurity (both emotional and economic) for women.

Although a husband faces no legal obstacles to divorcing his wife, a woman can only secure this right by inserting a clause to that effect into the marriage contract. Women are also required to show proof of "why" they request a divorce and must surrender the dower or *mahr* (the payment owing to the wife from the husband) as well as any claim to financial maintenance during their "waiting period" (Azzouni 2010). Accordingly, women may seek divorce within very restricted conditions, such as *mukhala'a* divorce (Jordanian Personal Status Law No. 61 (1976), which requires that a woman absolve her husband of his contractual financial obligations. Upon meeting these requirements, the husband has the choice to declare the divorce effective or not.

Under Jordanian Personal Status Law and Egyptian Family Law, a woman can invoke her right to divorce for several reasons:

- The husband's failure to provide alimony (*nafaqa*);
- His prolonged and unjustified absence (for a year or more), if she has been "harmed" by his absence;
- Discord and strife (which both men and women may invoke);
- When any condition of the marriage contract has been breached;
- The husband's long imprisonment;
- The husband is disabled; and
- If the husband suffers from a mental illness.

The existing system in Palestine does not grant women the right to seek unilateral divorce, or *khul'a*. At the time of writing, the Sharia Supreme Council is considering issuing an administrative decision to permit *khul'a* for women in only one case – if the marriage has not been consummated (in the case of "*katb el-kitab*," i.e., a contract without consummation). Nevertheless, the requirements for obtaining *khul'a* are discriminatory, because the wife must waive her financial claims against her husband, giving up her right to money otherwise owing to her.

Child custody

Women are also disadvantaged by child custody law. According to the applicable legal framework, divorced mothers are entitled to custody over their children. However, this right is severely restricted (Article 154-166: Jordanian Personal Status Law No. 61 (1976)). As a result, the child's best interest is often overlooked when courts rule on custody issues. Instead, custody matters are based on the rights of adults.

In the West Bank, the mother is awarded custody of male and female children until they reach the age of puberty, after which custody is granted to the father. In Gaza, the mother is awarded custody of girls under the age of eleven, after which the father is granted custody. The mother is granted custody of boys until they reach the age of seven; a judge must decide upon custody for boys between the ages of seven and nine, in their best interests. Custody of boys over the age of nine is awarded to the father. However, a law issued by PLC Hamas members in Gaza in 2009 allows unmarried widows to retain custody of boys until the age of fifteen and girls until adulthood (Article 118: Egyptian Family Law No. 303 (1954)). In both the West Bank and Gaza, a divorced mother who remarries automatically loses custody of her children, in clear violation of the right to non-discrimination.

Marital property

The concept of shared marital property does not exist in the PSL in the West Bank or Gaza. Husbands and wives maintain discrete and separate financial identities through-out the marriage, with the husband taking responsibility for meeting the wife's basic needs. Thus, upon the end of a marriage, a wife's contribution to the accumulation of marital assets through work carried out within or outside of the home is not rec-ognized unless it is documented. The Family Law Coalition is seeking to change this law, which will grant women the right to assets to which they contributed during the marriage, including through work inside the home. It will also raise women's status in the private domain through their participation in decision-making on an individual and family level (Almuaqat 2009).

Property rights

While legislation and Sharia provide women with the right to own and dispose of property independently, women are hindered from enjoying such rights due to legal, cultural, and societal barriers. For example, a woman who inherits property may be pressured by male relatives to relinquish her interests and rights, citing the preservation of family wealth as a pretext.

The Penal Code in Palestine and violence against women and girls

In Palestine, two penal codes prevail: the 1960 Jordanian Penal Code (JPC) in the West Bank, and the 1936 Egyptian Penal Code (EPC) in Gaza. Both codes contain problematic articles that affect the status and security of women and girls, especially articles that deal with sexual crimes. The code applicable in the West Bank dif-ferentiates between three sexual crimes: rape, sexual assault, and sexual harassment. The code in Gaza addresses only rape and sexual assault (Jallad 2012). Provisions of the Penal Code in force in both the West Bank and Gaza contain discriminatory provisions for women in relation to rape, sexual assault, sexual harassment, domes-tic violence, adultery, sexual crimes and case dismissal, murdering women under the pretext of "honor," and the criminalization of abortion.

Rape

The definition of rape currently applicable in the West Bank (Article 292(1): JPC 1960) discriminates against girls and women. By defining rape as the non-consensual vaginal penetration of non-wife females, the law limits the scope of protection and does not recognize marital rape. And by defining rape as vaginal penetration, any other form of sexual aggression (including non-vaginal penetration) is not considered rape. Such acts are classified as sexual assault, warranting a lesser punishment.

In Gaza, the Penal Code (Article 152: EPC No. 74 (1936)) defines rape as "unlawful sexual intercourse with a female against her will," sodomy with any person (male or female) under threat, and unlawful sexual intercourse or sodomy with a youth (male or female) under sixteen years old. All acts are defined as felonies. However, a lighter sentence may prevail if the perpetrator convinces the court that, in the case of a female youth, she was perceived as being older than sixteen years of age.

Sexual assault

The term "sexual assault" applicable in the West Bank (Article 296(1): JPC No. 16 (1960)) draws on social and conceptual understandings of "honor." Articles 292(1) and 296(1) classify unwanted sexual contact other than vaginal penetration as sexual assault, regardless of its gravity or harm. Similarly to Article 292, Article 296(2) prescribes a greater punishment for sexual assault only when the victim is a minor, below the age of fifteen. Many of the same concerns with the Penal Code's response to rape exist with its response to sexual assault.

Sexual assault is not explicitly defined in the 1936 EPC. Rather, sexual assault appears to be labeled as an "indecent act" in Articles 157, 158, and 159, leaving a vague, and potentially harmful, interpretation of the offenses.

Sexual harassment

In the West Bank, Article 305: JPC No. 16 (1960) prohibits sexual harassment, termed "immoral advances," against both females and males. However, the law does not use the term "harassment." This concept of "immoral advances" is vague and rooted in a culture of "honor," rather than administering non-discriminatory justice. Such ambiguity leads to violating women's rights, which in turn may result in discrediting the victim and social retribution and legitimizes sexual offenses against her.

Domestic violence

Defining and penalizing family violence remains one of the main challenges in the Palestinian legal system. The Jordanian and Egyptian penal codes are silent on domestic violence; thus women in violent or life-threatening marriages have two legal options: pressing charges for spousal abuse or initiating a divorce on the basis of physical harm. Both require evidence of extreme violence and impose a high evidentiary burden on the victim. Adult victims of violence must rely on the general penal provisions on assault when pressing charges. These laws provide little remedy to victims unless they suffer the most extreme forms of injury. The penal code applicable in the West Bank (Article 33: JPC No. 16 (1960)) outlines the penalties for violence based on the number of days the victim is hospitalized.

Similar to other assault cases, if the victim requires fewer than ten days of hospitalization, a judge has the authority to discard the case at his/her own discretion as a "minor offense" (Article 33: JPC No. 16 (1960)). In such cases, the public prosecutors may attempt to reconcile the parties rather than press charges, leading to further problems since the root causes of domestic violence and the perpetrator's accountability are not addressed. The law permits a judge to impose a slightly higher sentence when the victim is hospitalized between ten and twenty days; mandatory prosecution is required only in cases where the victim is hospitalized for more than twenty days (Article 33: JPC No. 16 (1960)). Since domestic violence victims may be admitted to the hospital several times to treat their injuries, with no intention at those times of pressing formal charges, they may have no medical records or legal recourse to support claims of long-term abuse, should they later decide to press charges or seek a divorce.

Adultery

In cases of adultery, the court does not consider any case without a prior complaint from the "victim," as is stipulated in the penal code applicable in the West Bank (Articles 284: JPC No. 16 (1960)). The 1936 Penal Code does not criminalize adultery. However, Egyptian Order No. 260 (1953), which is applicable in Gaza, criminalizes adultery and refers to the EPC. Article 3 of that Code states that adultery can only be prosecuted if the "victim" files a complaint. As such, if women or girls are not able to provide evidence of "force," "threats," and/or "deception" to support rape claims, they risk being criminalized for "adultery."

Incest

To establish a case of incest, a relative (up to the fourth degree) of one of the persons involved must file a complaint for the court to consider a case (Article 286: JPC No. 16 (1960)).

Sexual crimes and case dismissal

The Penal Code applicable in West Bank (Article 308: JPC No. 16 (1960)) permits the dismissal of a case or, if a judgment is issued, the suspension of its implementation if the perpetrator of rape, sexual assault, or sexual harassment marries his victim. Conversely, a female victim of rape may be pressured to marry her aggressor in order to preserve her family's "honor." This arrangement neglects the status of the female as the victim of a brutal assault and rewards the perpetrator. Consequently, the victim of a sexual crime is victimized twice – once by the perpetrator and again by the system. In practice, the police and other actors sometimes use this article as a means to allow perpetrators to evade punishment for sexual crimes against women.

Killing women in the name of "honor"/femicide

Penal Code laws applicable in the West Bank and Gaza (Article 152: EPC No. 74 (1936)) facilitate "honor" crimes and implicitly legitimize the killing of a female for what is considered "improper conduct" as a way to "restore the family's honor." These include laws that provide lenient sentences and exemptions from punishment to men who attack female relatives committing adultery (Abu-Odeh 2000: 363–380) and laws that allow judges to halve a perpetrator's sentence if the family of a victim chooses not to file a complaint.

The Penal Code applicable in the West Bank (Article 340) and the Penal Code in Gaza (Article 18) stipulate that a male who kills or attacks his wife or any of his female relatives on suspicion that she is committing adultery is exempt from punishment. Men who kill women who are "caught" in an "unlawful bed" may receive a reduced sentence. The Penal Code applicable in the West Bank (Article 98) mandates reduction in penalty for a perpetrator (of either gender) who commits a crime in a "state of great fury resulting from an unlawful and dangerous act on the part of the victim." It does not require any standard of evidence of female indiscretion. In Gaza, the EPC also provides for a reduction in penalty for murder of a woman by her husband in circumstances of adultery. It categorizes the murder of a wife (but not a husband) in the act of committing adultery as an extenuating circumstance, thereby reducing the crime of murder to the level of a misdemeanor (Article 237: EPC No. 74 (1936)).

Observing these articles through a gender lens, it is evident that there is a lack of clarity in what constitutes an "illegitimate act." However, the four articles clearly provide legal recourse and protection for men, while lacking any form of legal protection for women. This asymmetry contributes to furthering women's oppression in the private and public spheres and most importantly, embeds structural VAW. This also applies to the reduction in punishment for men who murder women – so-called "honor" crimes against women, or femicide. Conversely, these mitigating factors do not apply to a female perpetrator. These articles contradict Articles 9 and 10 of the Amended Basic Law (2003) that stipulates, "Palestinians shall be equal before the law and the judiciary" and "Basic human rights and liberties shall be protected and respected."

The criminalization of abortion

Abortion is criminalized under the two penal codes applicable in Palestine (Articles 321 through 325: JPC No. 19 (1960) and Articles 175 through 177: EPC (1936)).

Penalties are extended not only to the pregnant woman, but also to all individuals and medical staff who assist her in performing the abortion. This ominous legal approach deprives a woman of her right to a secure and safe abortion if a pregnancy resulted from a sexual crime or an unwanted pregnancy and forces her to resort to the risky act of inducing a miscarriage.

The majority of amendments to the Penal Codes applicable in West Bank and in Gaza remain unaccomplished as of this writing, despite the fact that the suggested amendments on both laws were drafted in 1996. The only achievement, the result of a Presidential Decree, was the abolition of Penal Code Articles 380 (West Bank) and 18 (Gaza). Nevertheless, the various coalitions, women's organizations, and advocacy groups continue to demand the realization of legal reform.

Women's rights campaigns to eliminate discrimination against women

With the advent of the PNA and the approach towards Palestinian state-building, women's organizations and institutions began to organize themselves as a unified movement in order to engage in the state-building process. This included initiatives in advocating for reform in laws and legislative processes from a women's rights perspective. These initiatives and their processes aimed to achieve a secular state based on the respect for all in Palestinian society, without discrimination, and to ensure fundamental freedoms of social justice.

National studies (Jad 2003; Jones et al. 2016; Chaban 2011) indicate that there is no consensus among the women's movement on the discourse of a secular state. Three different feminist trends can be identified based on their discourse: first, a compromise between religion and the law; second, the secular approach, which calls for separation between religion and state; and third, the application of Islamic law.

The majority of women's organizations developed different scenarios to initiate legal reforms to modify or amend local laws. The first was based on the long-term strategy that advocated for a secular state and the implementation of civil personal status laws. The women's organizations' focus on PSL was based on its direct relation to and impact on social relations. The proposed Basic Law calls for full equality of rights for all women without discrimination on the basis of religion or ethnicity. The second scenario was to focus on women's practical needs in order to achieve their strategic needs. Women's organizations aimed to achieve a secular state by working on the existing laws, and based on this approach, numerous amendments were drafted and introduced to the Penal Code, PSL, civil law, election law, and laws regarding VAW, in line with a comprehensive vision for women's rights as stipulated in CEDAW.

Local studies indicated that the efforts by the women's movement via the first scenario failed due to "no unified Palestinian feminist movement with the same orientation and principles working towards the realization of unified demands on women's rights" (Jad 2008). Thus, a struggle ensued during and following the formation of the Palestinian Model Parliament (PMP) (see below) whereby women activists noted that the resistance they encountered was due to the lack of representation of women's demands. The majority of actors in the women's movement approved the articles addressed in the section on legal reforms (see the section "Legal reforms to protect women's rights" above). However, this came with consequences, including the shifting of demands from a secular lens to a compromising approach[4] that was adopted in order to reach the women's movement's ultimate goal. Based on the suggested demands, various campaigns were organized to protect women's rights and prevent discrimination by focusing on the harmonization of domestic laws with CEDAW.

The following section reviews the key campaigns to date for reforming the main laws to eliminate discrimination and VAW in Palestine.

Basic law: women activists in drafting the law

Women's organizations focused their efforts on various initiatives to ensure consistency between local laws and the Basic Law (Chaban 2011) and also to advocate for human rights and equality. Actors in the women's movement actively participated in the various discussions that deliberated the first draft of the Basic Law and they worked towards integrating the core principles of equality and justice into the spirit of the law. Thus, the Declaration shaped a legal framework based on equality and justice for women – on the legitimacy of human rights for all – that does not conflict with Islamic law and international conventions. However, as it was adopted, the Palestinian Basic Law lacks this same or similar terminology to uphold rights of both women and men in a secular and pluralistic society.

The Palestinian Model Parliament: the feminist movement's experience in changing laws and legislations

The PMP is considered the first leading Palestinian feminist initiative between 1997 and 1999 in the West Bank and Gaza since the Oslo Accords. During this period, the Palestinian women's movement and women's organizations directed their efforts to benefit from the new political reality, which included an interim government and democratic elections (albeit under Israeli occupation). The movement led initiatives to ensure continued discourse and debate on women's political, social, and legal rights, focusing on legal issues that discriminate against women, especially the PSL and the Penal Code. The PMP, initiated by the Women's Center for Legal Aid and Counseling (WCLAC) in partnership with feminist and human rights institutions and civil society organizations (CSOs), aimed to mobilize the women's movement, lobby decision-makers and legislators, and advocate for laws and policies based on equality and respect for women's rights within the overall context of human rights. This led to drafting various legal frameworks and policies based on human rights and the rule of law, as enshrined in international standards and conventions.

The PMP conducted comprehensive surveys on the validity of legislation and laws in the West Bank and Gaza. The surveys analyzed and critiqued legal texts, highlighting strengths and shortfalls with regard to women's rights, especially articles within the PSL. The PMP also drafted and proposed national legislation that was in accord with international treaties and charters, to press for legal reform and unification of the PSL in the areas controlled by the PNA. On a parallel level, the PMP mobilized the community in order to stimulate public dialogue and promote legal awareness-raising activities, including national media campaigns, to advocate for non-discriminatory legislation based on respect for human rights on the one hand, and specialized training for legal and human right advocates and experts to address gender-based discrimination in legal frameworks and legislation, including the PSL, on the other.

To reach the community at large, as well as decision-makers and policymakers, and legislators, with the goal of reforming existing laws and legislation, the PMP drafted a unified document in clear and simple terms. Since this was the Palestinians' first experience in drafting legislation, the PMP reached out to women and organizations across the Arab world for their expertise, to enrich the PMP's knowledge in the realm of political, social, and legal developments.

These efforts culminated in holding the two-day central PMP in 1998 under the patronage of President Yasser Arafat. The PMP sessions drew wide attendance and participation from the Palestinian community, as well as Arab women activists from several feminist and human rights organizations. The importance of reforming laws related to women, the family, and society using a rights approach was discussed and debated. The PMP's final recommendations were shared with PLC members, the government, and agencies.

The demands varied between the West Bank and Gaza on some crucial issues. The West Bank demands were perceived as more radical in regards to banning polygamy, requiring divorce to be in court, increasing the age of marriage to eighteen, increasing the age of custody of children to eighteen, cancelling guardianship laws, either spouse's monetary rights after marriage, joint property rights following divorce, and equal inheritance rights between males and females. In Gaza, the feminist movement's demands remained within a religious framework, with minimal amendments that would limit but not end discrimination against women. Their priorities were: increasing the age of marriage for males and females to nineteen, removing the requirement for male guardianship in marriage, monetary rights to be applied for both parties following marriage, the equal division of property following divorce, alimony to be paid upon the date of separation, inheritance laws and regulations to be rephrased to protect women and ensure their rights to inheritance in accordance with Sharia law, requiring a court order in cases of polygamy including the right of the wife to request a divorce, divorce not to be allowed on a unilateral basis and to take place in court, and a mother's right to retain custody of her children until they turn eighteen. In the case of divorce or re-marriage, the court should decide which parent will maintain custody of the child in accordance to the best interests of the child (Nashwan 1998).

These initiatives of the feminist movement sparked controversy, debate, and discussion within Palestinian society in the West Bank and Gaza. This major "social" debate on the PSL also led to counter-campaigns launched by traditional, religious, and political parties. For example, during the PMP's 1998 event, Sheikh Bitawi, head of the West Bank Sharia Court of Appeals, challenged the right of the PMP and its members to address the PSL and criticized and challenged the right of individuals, especially secular women, to debate fundamental aspects of religion and law. Sheikh Bitawi's criticism sparked yet further attacks by the larger Islamic community on the Parliament and members of the women's movement. The Islamists' main focus was not an issue in the PSL itself, but on proposals calling for reforming the Penal Code that addressed the issue of sexuality, morality, and family – in their view, adultery.

In addition to the attack by Islamic clergy, Palestinian community members accused PMP members of being disconnected from Palestinian society, and the PMP's efforts to involve the public in the debates and discussions were downplayed. The PMP was accused of being unable to reach the Palestinian community and raise its awareness on the proposed issues (Siniora 2000).

Another issue was the feminist movement's disjointed approach in addressing legal reforms to the PSL. While debate and discussions were widespread, the pace and centralization of initiatives remained a challenge. For example, some feminist activists led the call for change by promoting and adopting international treaties and charters as a foundation for discussion, others depended on personal experiences, while others relied on feminist literature (Shehada 2005). The PMP's limitations also hindered a wider platform for discussing gender relations within the broader context of the national ambitions to achieve independence and self-determination. Nevertheless, many of the women involved in these processes were experienced in law, jurisprudence, and Sharia, and were active members in the national movement during the Intifada.

Initiatives towards a new family law: developments and strategies after the PMP

After the PMP, Islamic religious institutions began to distance themselves from Islamists attacks against the PMP and made public statements supporting Sharia reform. They formed three committees (with no women members) to draft family law. By 2001, the committees had drafted, but not presented to the government, a unified family law. Differences emerged among the religious establishment. The Supreme Court on Religious Ruling "*Fatwa*" emphasized legitimacy of registration of marriage, insisting that this ensures the optimum proof of a marriage and was necessary to protect the rights of wives, and the Islamic Supreme Council recommended increasing criminal sanctions for not legally registering marriage. In contrast, a *fatwa* (Islamic legal pronouncement) issued in 2000 held to the traditional Sunni jurists' doctrines in terms of the legality of minors to marry, which contradicted the Islamic Supreme Council's action on raising the age of marriage in Gaza.

PMP organizers wanting a family law based on equality realized the need to increase allies and partners from political parties and human rights organizations. In 1998, a preparatory committee was formed composed of representatives from women's rights organizations to work on the documents. Two divergent strategies arose. The first focused on legal reform towards civil law and reform within Sharia law. The second focused on identifying the most prominent discriminatory issues in the PSL that, unlike inheritance law, had no clear or explicit text in Islamic law. An outcome document completed in 2000 constituted a compromise between the two approaches, yet clearly illustrated the principles of respect for human dignity and non-discrimination.

A separate document that addressed the suggested revisions to the PSL was developed, notwithstanding differences on several issues such as polygamy and inheritance. The main points of this document are:

- The full participation of husband and wife in the family, as reflected in a marriage contract between two parties equal in rights and obligations;
- The right of women within the family to self-determination and to be their own guardian after legal marriage, which occurs at eighteen years of age;
- A minimum age of eighteen for marriage for men and women;
- Divorce as a judicial proceeding and not an individual unilateral decision in the presence of the two parties, and divorce to be initiated at the request of either party;
- Establishing a maintenance fund and alimony in the case of arbitrary divorce;
- Guaranteeing equality between men and women when the marriage ends, including in custody and guardianship of children and divisions of property and wealth from the period of married life, taking into consideration that women's work at home and in child rearing is productive; and
- Joint responsibility in the maintenance of the family and children.

In 1998, President Yasser Arafat formed a committee headed by the Supreme Judicial Council to draft the PSL. This committee was formed of judges, academics, and professors from the faculties of law, but no women activists. The proposed draft law led to continued discontent and thus advocacy, given that discrimination against women remained embedded in this document. In 2000, as an initiative from the women's movement and women's organizations, a separate draft document based on civil law and the recommendations of the PMP was produced. However, the process to move forward was hindered and postponed as a result of Israeli tactics and policies (the second Intifada), including the shelling of Palestinian institutions (Abu Hayya 2011).

The Personal Status Law coalition

In 2006, a coalition was formed specifically to address the Palestinian PSL, and the redrafting began that same year. The coalition is comprised of members from women's and human rights organizations, in addition to women's rights activists and legal experts. These organizations and individuals worked to draft a PSL that is more gender-sensitive as well as reflective of contemporary Palestinian social values. Upon completion of the draft and following meetings with religious leaders and legal experts for feedback, the coalition submitted the document to the Palestinian President and Prime Minister for review in 2010.

The new draft law was, as were the previous initiatives, a compromise between women's demands based on civil rights and religion. Women's organizations adopted the approach of modifying the existing PSL as a new strategy in their advocacy work towards ending VAW. Seven main discrimination issues against women were identified by the coalition (see the section "Legal reforms to protect women's rights" above).

A national consensus was reached on the need to raise the age of marriage to eighteen. However, there was no agreement as to whether and under which circumstances an exception to the minimum age law could be made.

The drafters of the Women's Rights Charter called for polygamy to be restricted to exceptional circumstances. Both the Charter's drafters and the coalition also called for requiring prior judicial consent to a polygamous marriage and for current and potential additional wives to have the right to be informed about the existence of the other in advance of a polygamous marriage. The coalition went a step further by calling for the consent of existing wives to a polygamous marriage to be made mandatory and supported the inclusion of polygamous marriage as automatic grounds for divorce, with all financial rights reserved. Currently, the taking of an additional wife is grounds for divorce only if an additional clause to that effect has been inserted into the marriage contract. The reform proposals of the Office of the Chief Justice are more limited in scope; the draft law proposed by his office merely confers upon existing and potential additional wives the right to be informed about the existence of the other in advance of a polygamous marriage.

In April 2011, the Head of the Sharia Supreme Council issued a decision stating that a man must inform his wife of his interest in taking another wife. This raises two concerns. First, such an administrative decision could be easily changed or canceled. As it is stands, it is a regulatory decision that is not incorporated in the law or by-laws. Second, the decision requires informing the wife, but does not require her consent.

Maintenance fund

Palestinian feminists are engaged in ongoing dialogue and debate about the financial aspects of the PSL, such as the dower and maintenance. Proponents argue that it is necessary for women to stipulate in the marriage contract the mutual ownership of financial resources, given the patriarchal culture that reinforces the inferior status of women.

Due to the stagnation in executing maintenance rulings, leaving women and children deprived of their basic economic rights, in 2002, the WCLAC and the General Union of Palestinian Women took the initiative to create the Palestinian Maintenance Fund (PMF). The political will represented by the Supreme Judicial

Department prompted the creation of the fund as part of the Maintenance Fund Law No. 6 of 2005. The PMF's establishing law equalized all Palestinians, regardless of their religion. According to the PMF's data, Christian women as well as Muslim women benefit from its services.

The PMF worked in partnership with beneficiaries, using a study conducted by the PMF on the social and economic situation of beneficiaries, of which women form the majority, and which the amendments were based on, to raise awareness among the community and policymakers to change the stereotypical perception of maintenance. Moreover, the PMF organized a media campaign to launch the discussion on the importance and concept of maintenance and its beneficiaries in the society, especially with decision-makers and policymakers. The PMF addressed decision-makers who were against, with, and neutral, in order to neutralize opponents through building a legal, economic, and social discourse to support the amendment. The PMF also used the voices of the beneficiaries, who formed part of the media campaign, such as in a documentary film about the beneficiaries' stories and in radio talk shows.

Coalition of the Palestinian Penal Codes

In the early 1990s, the WCLAC began raising awareness of Palestinian laws and their impact on women through legal literacy groups. During that same period, the WCLAC drafted an inventory of all Palestinian laws, in consultation with women and women's organizations during workshops. This was followed by meeting with the government to outline the impact of the legal framework on women.

In 1996, following the first elections of the newly formed PNA, the WCLAC held additional workshops to discuss the legal inventory and reform. The WCLAC conducted a study of the Penal Codes, proposing specific articles for revision.

In 2003, the Ministry of Justice submitted a Penal Code draft to the PLC. The draft was criticized by legal experts and the Palestinian women's movement for its non-alignment with international standards (Jallad 2012). In May 2005, approximately 300 Palestinian women held a demonstration in Ramallah calling for a legislative amendment (Article 242: Palestinian Draft Penal Law (2003)) to protect women from "honor" crimes, or femicide, after three women were murdered within one week. A coalition led by the WCLAC was formed in 2005 to address and propose alternatives to the Penal Code. As with the draft PSL, the draft Penal Code continues to be under review.

Women have proposed the following specific demands, which conform to international standards:

- To annul provisions that allow individuals who claim to have perpetrated a murder "in the name of family honor" to be exempted from judicial penalty or to receive a reduced sentence, and to ensure that the perpetrators of murder receive appropriate judicial penalties;
- To increase the sentences of individuals convicted of rape and sexual assault, in order to promote deterrence;
- To criminalize marital rape;

- To create specialized procedures to deal with cases of suspected sexual abuse;
- To establish a new offense, "violence in a domestic context," and/or enact a specific domestic violence law that takes into account the unique nature of violence perpetrated within the family, since at present, domestic violence is prosecuted under the general rules on assault;
- To create a new offense of sexual harassment; and
- To revoke the requirement that a minor under the age of fifteen obtain the consent of a guardian in order to file a complaint.

The most recent draft of the Penal Code, prepared in 2010–11 by the National Committee of Penal Code (comprised of representatives of the Ministry of Justice, the Ministry of Women's Affairs (MoWA), the Attorney General's Office, and women's and human rights organizations), while not flawless, has received a warm reception from the human rights community. The protections enshrined in the latest draft code are testimony to the efforts of women's rights advocates. Indeed, many see the new draft as a critical step forward towards women's rights in Palestine (Al-Botmeh 2012).

The recent draft criminalizes sexual harassment and domestic violence; creates new rules to protect women from violence, including rape and sexual assault; creates special procedures to address crimes perpetrated against children, including sexual abuse; institutes penalties for marrying an individual under the age of eighteen unless the consent of a judge and the minor's guardian has been obtained; and makes no provision for exempting from judicial punishment persons convicted of murder who claim to have acted to preserve "family honor." It also institutes a minimum five-year sentence for murder. However, the Penal Code draft does allow a murderer to benefit from a reduced penalty if the murder was carried out subsequent to discovering the victim committing adultery. It also expands on the list of individuals who can benefit from "mitigating circumstances" in this context to include fathers, brothers, and sons.

Organizations and advocacy groups working in the women's movement realized from their direct work with women victims of violence that there were major problems in the Penal Code and therefore, an urgent need to draft the Family Protection Law, which would decrease violence within the family. In working directly with women seeking protection, women's organizations realized that while the amendments addressed immediate family (nuclear) members, VAW was also committed by members of the extended family, which the Penal Code and its procedures did not address. As a result, in 2005, the WCLAC in partnership with the Al-Muntada Forum to Combat Violence against Women drafted the Family Protection Law.

The Family Protection Law

The Family Protection Law was considered one of the women's organizations' main priorities due to the increase in women victims of violence within the family. The revision to the law stipulated that the abuser must leave the home and gave victims the right to make a complaint without the approval of a male guardian, who in many cases was the abuser.

In December 2008, the WCLAC worked in partnership with the Al-Muntada Forum to propose the law to the MoWA, which is leading a National Committee to Combat Violence against Women (NCCVAW). In 2012, a national conference in partnership between CSOs and the MoWA was held to announce the draft Family Protection Law and to engage the Palestinian community in further discussions on the basis of international and Arab experiences. The NCCVAW adopted the draft law and in 2012 the MoWA and the Ministry of Social Development (MoSD) conveyed the law to the Palestinian Cabinet. In 2013, the Cabinet referred the law to three ministries – MoWA, MoSD, and the Ministry of Justice – for comments and feedback. To date there have been no further developments on this matter.

The Right to Inheritance Campaign

The Right to Inheritance Campaign was initiated in 2012 and led by the WCLAC, with the YMCA Women's Affairs Center in Gaza and the Palestinian Bar Association in the West Bank. The campaign's approach was to adopt the religious texts as stipulated in Sharia law; its goal was to raise awareness of women's rights in inheritance as based on the PSL. The campaign's demands differed from the proposed changes by the women's movement from 1995 to 2006, especially the PMP, as discussed previously. Women's rights organizations were demanding equal rights to property and inheritance and, at that time, a secular state.

To prevent any conflicts with the local and religious culture, the campaign did not challenge the text of inheritance as stated in the Sharia. Yet on a parallel level, these organizations utilized the Inheritance Law (based on Sharia and applying to Muslims and Christians) as a means of legal recourse, as a short-term strategy to protect women's economic rights and enable them to access their rights to inheritance.

Lessons learned: strengths and weaknesses in the women's rights campaigns

The following lessons emerge from the Palestinian women's rights campaigns experience:

Strengths in the women's rights campaigns:

- They were significant in helping to create widespread discussion in Palestinian society.
- They provided a valuable opportunity to assess the dynamics of Palestinian political and social power, especially concerning gender equality, and the level of societal readiness to address such issues.
- They demonstrated the feminist movement's strengths and weaknesses, the political and social supports for women's causes, and the importance of the active participation of political parties in bringing about a significant change in gender equality.

- They gained the attention of media outlets.
- They promoted positive public participation that made evident people's commitment to civil society and democratic practices.
- Leaders of various political parties made numerous statements supporting women's rights.
- Women's rights groups gained experience on how to address resistance and backlash to women's rights from religious fundamentalist and conservative elements.

Weaknesses in the women's rights campaigns:

- The lack of consensus among organizations and political parties supporting the women's rights campaigns was a serious limitation.
- The campaigns highlighted the different views and frames of reference among the Palestinian women's movement. A unified feminist movement with a single feminist discourse was unfeasible, since this does not reflect the diversity and complexity that occurs in a national democratic liberation phase.
- Feminists and women's organizations cannot work in isolation from Palestinian organizations and political forces that share the same vision and interests.
- The participation of some prestigious political figures and their support for the women's rights campaigns were an expression of their personal attitudes towards women's legal issues rather than reflecting their parties' positions.
- Political parties and organizations did not go beyond verbal commitments – there was no adoption of binding positions on women's issues, translation of these commitments to policy-level initiatives, clear action plans, or programs with measurable indicators of change.
- During the preparation and planning phase, women activists involved in the legal reform initiatives did not pay great attention to the conflicts of interest between political parties.
- Feminists who led the women's rights campaigns did not discuss the possibility of involving the Islamists or their Muslim women sympathizers in this process. Feminist leaders assumed that these forces would not support the initiatives, believing that they have "a fixed and rigid" position that contradicts the perspectives of the legal reform initiatives.
- The feminist leaders did not analyze Palestinian realities through an in-depth reading of political, social, and cultural factors, or consider the power dynamics in the Palestinian political arena and how these factors could impact the legal reform initiative, whether positively or negatively.

Recommendations

Based on the feminist experience in the Palestinian context, when preparing for legal reform campaigns it is important to consider the following:

- Identify short-, medium-, and long-term goals for legal reform campaigns in order to develop applicable action plans within the changing political and social variables.
- Analyze the political, social, economic, and legal realities in partnership with the concerned parties.
- Analyze the balance of power, identify the advocates and opponents, and propose plans and alternatives that comply with the stances of the different political powers.
- Collect qualitative and quantitative data to provide social, political, economic, and legal evidence, justifications, and documents to rely on.
- Identify the legal gaps in the laws and legislation along with their origins and their influence on the community, without limiting such influences to women, to create community awareness that supports the process of change and can propose solutions that serve the interests and needs of all community groups.
- Mobilize the media by illustrating the importance of the campaign and to what extent social issues can be reflected in the community structure as a whole.
- Involve various specialized experts who enjoy community acceptance and have exceptional advocacy skills in order to gain support at the decision-making level.
- Target people who can influence decision-makers, to guarantee mobilization towards the desired change in addition to mobilizing political will.
- Follow reform campaigns with monitoring with clear indicators, institution-alize follow-up and assessment processes in order to identify weaknesses and strengths, and establish feedback loops for continued input.
- Invest in capabilities, potentials, and human resources to serve the campaigns' goals and motivate volunteerism in order to set general national demands and to detach them from foreign financing agendas that can be used as a tool to attack the feminist movement's demands.
- Position feminist demands for legal reform among the national priority demands.

Conclusions

Women's rights campaigns that are carried out in isolation from the social, political, or cultural context will rarely achieve their objectives. Women's rights campaigns' efforts should be accompanied and reinforced by socio-economic programming, where linking and networking among all actors is paramount, to shield initiatives from backlash or pushback and to maintain progress for social justice. Feminist intellectual activists can infuse mainstream liberation movements and struggles with ideas, aspirations, and reminders regarding the necessity to always adhere to truly democratic principles that ensure that women and women's interests are consistently acknowledged and represented as essential elements to achieving true justice, peace, and security for all. Toward this end, feminists bear a profound historical responsibility to maintain the principles of justice and democracy, while simultaneously maintaining open lines of communication and building coalitions with women's groups and social actors to gain support for the struggle within their parties. They must combat both oppressive forces within Palestinian society and those of the Israeli occupation. In this context, feminists must be tactical in alliances with other social actors, but should never compromise long-term principles, since those are what keep us relevant, make us credible within our society, and, most importantly, are the basis on which future generations will judge us.

Notes

1 The research included a review of available literature, reports, and statistics, and interviews with Mrs. Zahira Kamal, Secretary General of the FIDA party and a former Minister of Women's Affairs; Judge Daoud Derawi; Attorney Zainab Alghounami; Attorney Ashraf Abu Hayya; activist Randa Siniora; and activist Amal Khreshe.
2 In 1948, three-quarters of Palestinian land and people came under full Israeli control. For lands that remained unoccupied (the 1967 areas), Jordan took administrative control of the West Bank while Gaza was under Egyptian control. The laws that were valid in the West Bank at the end of the British Mandate remained valid until replaced by Jordanian laws. In 1949, the Jordanian civil administration returned the civil rule regime to the West Bank based on the general administration law over Palestine. In 1950, the two banks of Jordan River were officially unified.
3 Reconciliation/tribal committees are part of the Palestinian cultural and legal system.
4 The "compromising" approach is one that seeks harmonization between Sharia law and civil law in order to be accepted in the context of Palestine as a conservative society.

References

Abu Hayya, Ashraf (2011) *Tajrubat Qanon al Ahwal al-shakhsiyya fi Alaradi Alfalstenyia* (*The Experience of Personal Status Law in OPT*), Ramallah: Women's Centre for Legal Aid and Counseling.
Abu-Odeh, Lama (2000) "Crimes of Passion and Construction in Arab Societies," in Pinar Ilkkaracan (ed.), *Women and Sexuality in the Muslim Societies*, Istanbul: Women for Women's Human Rights – New Ways: 363–380.
Al-Botmeh, Reem (2012) *A Review of Palestinian Legislation from a Women's Rights Perspective*, UNDP, www.ps.undp.org/content/dam/papp/docs/Publications/UNDP-papp-research-Legislative%20english.pdf.
Almuaqat, Fatmeh (2009) *Alnisa' Alfalstenyiat wa Qanon al Ahwal al-shakhsiyya Mataleb wa Tawajouhat* (*Palestinian Women and Personal Status Law Demands and Approaches*), Ramallah: Women's Centre for Legal Aid and Counseling.
Azzouni, S. (2010) "Palestine," in S. Kelly and J. Breslin (eds.), *Women's Rights in the Middle East and North Africa: Progress Amid Resistance*, New York: Freedom House: 359–397.
Chaban, Stephanie (2011) "Promoting Gender-Sensitive Justice and Legal Reform in the Palestinian Territories: Perspectives of Palestinian Services Providers," *Journal of International Women's Studies*, Vol. 12, Issue 3, Arab Women and Their Struggles for Socio-economic and Political Rights: 150–167.
Giacaman, Rita, Islah Jad, and Penny Johnson (2006) "Gender, Social Citizenship, and the Women's Movement in Palestine," in Joel Beinin and Rebecca L. Stein (eds.), *The

Struggle for Sovereignty: Palestine and Israel, 1993–2005, Stanford, CA: Stanford University Press: 94–105.

Haj-Yahia, M. (1998) "Beliefs About Wife-beating Among Palestinian Women: The Influence of Their Patriarchal Ideology," *Violence against Women*, 4(5): 533–558.

—— (2002) "Attitudes of Arab Women Toward Different Patterns of Coping With Wife Abuse," *Journal of Interpersonal Violence*, Vol. 17: 721–745.

—— (2013) *Violence against Women in Palestinian Society. Survey Presentation and Analysis*, The Palestinian Initiative for the Promotion of Global Dialogue and Democracy (MIFTAH), Ramallah.

Islah, Jad, Penny Johnson, and Rita Giacaman, "Gender and Citizenship under the Palestinian Authority,", in Suad Joseph, ed., *Gender and Citizenship in the Middle East*, Syracuse, NY: Syracuse University Press.

—— (2008) "The Demobilization of Women's Movements: The case of Palestine," in Srilatha Batliwala (ed.), *Changing their World*, Scholar Associate, AWID: 1–7, 14–16.

Jallad, Zeina (2012) "Palestinian Women and Security: A Legal Analysis," The Geneva Centre for the Democratic Control of Armed Forces (DCAF), Ramallah, Palestine: 3–14.

Johnson, P. (2004) "Agents for Reform: The Women's Movement, Social Politics and Family Law Reform," in Lynn Welchman (ed.), *Women's Rights and Islamic Family Law: Perspectives on Reform*, London: Zed Books: 144–163.

Jones, Nicola and Bassam Abu-Hamad with Georgia Plank (February 2016) *Report on Women and Power. How Women Leaders Negotiate Reality*, Overseas Development Institute: 19–26.

Kazi, Hamida (2013) "Palestinian Women and the National Liberation Movement: A Social Perspective," posted on 13 November 2013, https://libcom.org/library/palestinian-women-national-liberation-movement-social-perspective-hamida-kazi.

Nashwan, K. (1998) *Miswaddatmuqtadayāt li-qānūnahwāl al-shakhsiyyafilastīnīmuwahhad* (*Draft Requirements for a Unified Palestinian Law of Personal Status*), Gaza: Discussion Paper from the Palestinian Model Parliament: Women and Legislation.

Palestine National Assembly-Research Centre (September 1975) "The Struggle of Palestinian Women," Palestine Liberation Organization, Beirut: 5–14.

Sayigh, R. (1981) "Encounters with Palestinian Women under Occupation," *Journal of Palestine Studies*, Vol. 10, No. 4: 3–26.

Shalhoob-Kevorkian, Nadera (2001) *Femicide in the Palestinian Society*, Ramallah: Women's Centre for Legal Aid and Counselling.

—— (2009) *Militarization and Violence against Women in Conflict Zones in the Middle East: A Palestinian Case-study*, Cambridge Studies in Law and Society.

Shehada, Nahda (2005) "Debating Islamic Family Law in Palestine: Citizenship, Gender and 'Islamic' Idioms,": 1–28, https://repub.eur.nl/pub/32934/Metis_174383.pdf.

Siniora, Randa (2000) "Al Daghet wal Tatheer min Ajel Qanon Usra Falasteni: Tajrubat Alparlaman Alfalsteni Alsuawri: Almr'a wal Tchreaat" ("Advocacy and Lobbying for a Palestinian Family Law: Palestinian Model Parliament Experience"), paper presented in the International Conference on: Islamic Family Law in the Middle East and South Africa, Theory, Practice and Opportunities of Reforms.

UNDPA (United Nation Development of Political Affairs) (2011) "Review of Palestinian Legislation From a Women's Rights Perspective," September 2011: 20–31.

9

SENEGAL

Alpha Ba and Aminata Bousso Ly

Introduction

Violence against women (VAW) has received increased attention from the international community in the face of strong evidence and documentation of the injustices that women experience worldwide. Despite the existing international, regional, and domestic legal frameworks protecting women from violence, millions of women still contend with cultural and religious arguments that are used to justify the various forms of violence they face. Examples are early or forced marriage, domestic violence, female genital mutilation (FGM), etc. This leaves women vulnerable to a constant risk of violations of their most fundamental and basic rights, such as their right to life, security of the person, physical integrity, and equality, among others. Such violence starts in households and communities and is reproduced in the wider society.

This chapter focuses on feminist law reform advocacy that aims to eliminate VAW and enhance gender equality in Senegal. It starts with a brief overview of the context and the scope of VAW in Senegal. The second section analyzes the implementation of Senegal's domestic legal framework concerning VAW, the measures taken by the state, and the initiatives of the women's movement to combat VAW. The third section traces the reform processes of family law over the past thirty years by highlighting the different roles played by women and political and religious leaders, the issues that were at stake, and the strategies used. The fourth section provides an analysis of the implementation of international law relating to VAW. Finally, we draw conclusions and highlight lessons learned from the Senegalese family law reform experience and make recommendations for change at the global level.

The study entailed both a review of the relevant literature, including reports and scholarly articles, and interviews with key actors in the struggle for women's rights and the eradication of VAW.[1]

The context and scope of VAW in Senegal

This section aims to explain the social dynamics that contribute to perpetrating VAW in Senegal and to show that, due to gender inequality, violence starts in the family and is sustained throughout society through the processes of socialization and education. As has been well noted, an extreme expression of male control and power over women often "begins at infancy and may accompany a woman throughout her life to old age, through various relationships as daughter, sister, intimate partner, wife and mother" (Ministry of Family and Female Entrepreneurship 2015).

Across the different ethnic groups (Wolof, Pulaar, Serer, Djola, and Mandingue, among others) that comprise Senegalese society, the family is the fundamental unit through which socialization is achieved, values are transmitted, and the different roles of men and women are assigned. The values that govern the relationships inside the family are transmitted from generation to generation and determine behaviors in social relationships. Despite the differences in beliefs and cultural practices within different ethnic groups, deeply rooted gender inequality commonly governs female and male roles within the family, which is translated into relations in public life as well.

The male head of household model, as determined by Senegal's patriarchal culture, is provided for in Article 152 of the Family Code and gives men power and authority over all important matters in the family while reinforcing the subordination of women. Male and female roles are distinct and hierarchical: men are delegated power and control while women are granted child-rearing and domestic responsibilities.

These values are transmitted through a variety of mechanisms, such as local proverbs. Penda Mbow (2001), historian and activist, illustrates this with an example from the Wolof (the cultural majority in Senegal) proverb, *"ligeey y ndey añu dom"* ("the work of the mother in the household makes the success of her children"). Indeed, such sayings refer to the obedience and submissiveness that women owe to their husbands in order to have successful children. Mbow refers to a commonly accepted belief that a child is a reflection of his mother's behavior towards her husband and society. Therefore, women must be devoted body and soul to their husbands, in order to have good offspring, even if it means that they must suffer ill treatment from their husbands. Thus, it is common to praise female figures, such as mothers of religious guides (founders of brotherhoods) as exemplary wives and role models for other women, who demonstrate patience, generosity, obedience, and devotion to their spouses.

According to the latest studies (GESTES[2] 2014; UN Women 2012), the prevalence of violence in Senegalese households is 55.3 percent. These studies estimate that 50 percent of the victims are twenty to forty years old and 32.7 percent are forty to sixty years old. The forms of violence most frequently observed are: verbal (46.5 percent), physical (27.6 percent), and psychological (12.5 percent). Gender-based violence (GBV) in households has different and varied causes, depending on the context and the actors. It results both from socially anchored and discriminating realities and practices towards women on the one hand, and from adverse economic conditions on the other. These include early and/or forced marriages and FGM. With some differences, the roles and status of women often place them in discriminating and unfavorable postures. The persistence of customs and socio-cultural burdens in the practice of GBV is reflected in the words of Penda Seck Diouf,[3] a leader in the struggle against VAW: "The pillar of violence is social gender inequality, gender stereotypes, sexist beliefs and, more or less, the tendency to interpret religion" (interview).

In addition to social factors, economic deprivation is also identified as a cause of GBV. According to Ndèye Astou Diop,[4] "Most of the violence is caused by poverty, because living in precarious situations can cause someone to do things that are not at all desirable."

The GESTES (2014) study found that the most obvious consequences of GBV are: frustration (44.2 percent), trauma (24.4 percent), insomnia (21.4 percent), and loss of appetite (20.3 percent). Physical (27.6 percent) and sexual (2.4 percent) violence are the most pernicious forms of GBV, due to their impact on the integrity of individuals and the health consequences. Yet, perpetrators of GBV in the domestic sphere often go unpunished.

Research shows that, in Senegal, the greatest challenge in the fight against GBV is to "break the silence." Indeed, recourse to the judicial system in the treatment of GBV within households gives an opportunity for endogenous strategies for managing the violence. It is often the lack of a formal GBV management structure or lack of knowledge at the community level that encourages such behaviors. Faced with the limitations of formal GBV management mechanisms, communities develop informal, endogenous mechanisms to cope with them.

Therefore, the injustices that Senegalese women endure in the family have been attributed to (and justified through) their duty of obedience and self-abnegation to men (especially their husbands). The authority of men and subordination of women are translated into the different institutions and spheres of life, such as marriage.

Implementation of laws regarding VAW

Senegal has codified the norms that regulate family issues through the Family Code, which was adopted in 1972 and promulgated in 1973. The country does not have legislation that specifically addresses VAW in an exhaustive way; however, the Penal Code (1965), the Family Code (1972), Law No. 99-05 of

29 January 1999 amending the Penal Code and repressing some forms of VAW, and the Constitution (2001) can be considered the overall domestic legislation giving Senegalese women protection from violence. Here, we will focus on the 1972 Family Code and the 1999 law repressing diverse forms of VAW as we discuss the issue of VAW; other laws will be cited as needed.

At the national level, non-state structures, including civil society organizations, such as the African Network for Integral Development (RADI), the Committee to Combat Violence against Women (CLVF), and the Association of Female Senegalese Lawyers (AJS), are very active in combating VAW by providing different services through orientation, legal support to victims of violence, and advocacy. As part of their advocacy, these organizations often translate the legal framework into local languages and they rely on opinion leaders (religious figures and artists) to denounce VAW and demand that the state adopt new laws. The struggle led by the CLVF with the support of other women's organizations and opinion leaders has led to the adoption of laws including the above-mentioned Law No. 99-05 of 29 January 1999 amending certain provisions of the Penal Code which punishes FGM, sexual harassment, and domestic violence. This complements Articles 294–297, 299, and 305 of the Penal Code, which punish physical violence (e.g., voluntary assault, abortion, excision, murder, assassination). Sexual violence such as rape, indecent assault, incest, procuring, incitement to sexual debauchery, and sexual harassment are also punishable by the Penal Code (Articles 302, 318, 319 *bis*, 320, 321, 322, 323, and 324). Family abuses such as moral and material abandonment, abandonment of families, adultery, bigamy, and forced marriage are punishable by the same Code (Articles 300, 329, 330, 333, and 350).

The Family Code, when adopted in 1972, provided an appreciable level of protection to women in the family in revoking repudiation – the prohibition of the moral and material abandonment of a wife by her husband. Fatou Diop, the vice president of the CLVF, welcomed the Family Code as a sign of political commitment and will on the part of Senegal, at a time when most African countries did not even think of having one; she noted that a list of types of violence prevalent in Senegalese society (e.g., repudiation and economic violence, due to husbands abandoning their wives) was included in the law, which contributed to reducing such violence or at best to raising awareness around the problem.

However, since 1972, the role of women in society has changed considerably. Women fought against perceptions that depicted them as simply wives, mothers, and housekeepers. They have proven to be as capable as men in schools and workplaces. The international legal framework has strengthened that shift by promoting equality between the sexes and equal opportunities for all. Consequently, the Family Code no longer responds to women's current status and aspirations, nor to the universal principles of equality and non-discrimination. Article 152 of the Code sustains the notion of women's subordination and tutelage by their husbands. It provides that "the husband is the head of the family; he exercises this power in the common interest of the couple and the children." This provision, according to Diop, embodies the spirit of the Family Code, against which women should vigorously fight (interview).

In Chapter 1 (on marriage) of the Family Code, the first section deals with engagement; according to Article 107, if the woman breaks the engagement without legitimate reason, she must return the gifts she received, otherwise the man can oppose her marriage to someone else. However, if the man breaks the engagement, while he cannot reclaim gifts he gave, the woman has no discretion over his remarriage. This again highlights the discriminatory nature of the Family Code.

On the issue of polygamy, it remains the sole discretion of the man to subscribe to regime of monogamy or polygamy (Articles 133 and 134 of the Family Code). While this is clearly rooted in Islamic law, the fact that Islam grants the first wife the right to oppose her husband's marriage to a second wife is not acknowledged in the Family Code. This supports the widespread perception that Islamic law inspired those who drafted the Family Code only in instances when it favored men.

The choice of the domicile is also the husband's prerogative (Article 153 of the Family Code). In case of divorce, all the furniture of the main house is presumed to belong to the husband, unless otherwise proven. The furnishings of additional dwellings kept by the husband are deemed to belong to the wife occupying it. In such situations, the wife who lives in the main dwelling – usually the first wife – is disadvantaged compared to the other wives, since she may be totally dispossessed in case of a divorce.

Law No. 99-05 (29 January 1999) provides for punishment of some forms of VAW; however, whether it reduced violence is questionable. A 2012 UN Women report shows that rape is the form of violence most reported either to the judicial system or to the healthcare sector, amounting to 60 percent of the cases registered between 2006 and 2010, and, in a five-year span, reporting of rape, incest, and domestic abuse has doubled. Most of the cases were recorded in healthcare settings, where women have easier access. In Senegalese jurisprudence, rape is not considered a crime but an offense; in cases of pedophilia or incest, judges often have recourse to impose lower sentences than what the law sets (AJS 2013).[5]

It is also noteworthy that despite the criminalization of domestic violence through the 1999 law on VAW, it continues to occur frequently. Such cases are rarely reported to the legal system; they are mostly recorded at hospitals or women's rights NGOs or made public in the media. Of the very few cases that are brought to court, even fewer result in convictions – and with lower sentences than what should apply. All forms of violence that occur in the family, whether it is a father abusing his child or a man beating his wife, are tolerated and perceived to be legitimate by the society. Secrecy is at the heart of the widespread culture of impunity in domestic violence cases.

In incest or domestic abuse cases, the victim or members of their family are often reluctant to seek justice; for diverse reasons, such as preserving the marriage or protecting the husband and the integrity of the family, they often prefer a "friendly" solution. Furthermore, the victims' economic dependency on the perpetrator often leaves them with no choice but to tolerate the abuse in silence. Marital rape is not recognized as a criminal offense punishable by law; even if it

were, religious norms prohibit women from refusing to have sex with their husbands unless they are having their menstrual period or are ill. Therefore, Senegalese
women have no recourse when suffering this type of violence.

Despite the repression of early or forced marriage, it is believed to be widespread at around 33 percent. The Constitution (Article 18) provides that "forced
marriage is a violation of individual freedom. It shall be prohibited and punishable
under the conditions laid down by law." The Penal Code (Article 300) provides
for two to five years of imprisonment to anyone who engages in the consummation
of a customary marriage and performs or attempts to perform sexual intercourse
with a child below the age of thirteen. However, this offers very little protection to minors, since it only protects girls below the age of thirteen and does not
clearly stipulate that early and forced marriage of children is prohibited. Perhaps
one of the Code's most problematic provisions concerns the legal age of marriage
(Article 111), which states "marriage can only be contracted between a man above
eighteen and a girl above sixteen unless age dispensation is accorded on serious
grounds by the President of a regional tribunal." Thus, it can be argued that the
language of the Family Code supports early marriage instead of preventing it.

Overall, VAW cases are not treated with the seriousness the problem warrants.
This highlights several obstacles to the effective implementation of the national
legislation, such as:

- There is a general tendency to hide VAW that occurs within family or
  community and to opt for informal methods of mediation. This encourages
  further VAW.
- The reluctance of the judiciary to apply the law and rigorously sanction
  perpetrators perpetuates a culture of impunity.
- The lack of adequate sensitization from the state on women's rights reinforces
  the discriminatory interpretation and application of law.
- Incoherence in the overall legislative and judicial framework increases women's
  vulnerability to violence.

Family Code reform processes

Since independence, Senegal has engaged in legal reform to adapt laws inherited
from colonization to its current concerns. The first reform began under the supervision of Mamadou Dia (President of the Council) with the 12 April 1961 decree.
This decree established a study committee through the Codification Commission
to propose a Family Code which, while respecting the secular character of the
state, had to take into account the different religions and customs practiced in the
country. Its members disseminated a questionnaire to identify, record, and study
all the customs and practices in Senegal concerning the management of family
relations. For four years, the Commission was not able to produce a document. In
1965, a Committee of Options[6] was set up by then-President Senghor to expedite
the work of the Commission in producing a draft law.

These deliberations were marked by the absence of organizations in defense of women's rights. The debates focused mainly on the place of religion in the codification of the family law. The following guidelines were to be used by the Committee in drafting the law:[7]

- A single Code for a single Nation.
- Factor in exceptions where uniformity may not be possible.
- While responding to conditions of modern life, provisions of the law should be inspired by customs.
- Compromise should be found where traditional and contemporary values collide, and distinguish the genuine religious norms from those based on misrepresentation or distortions.
- With respect to Islamic law, observe what is prescribed by the Quran.

Without questioning certain Islamic religious principles, state representatives succeeded in obtaining religious concessions to achieve a consensual code in 1973.[8] It must be stressed that this period coincided with a unique party system that monopolized power, which increased its influence during the post-colonial regime. The Family Code reflected the idea of modernity that the government wanted to adopt, following the philosophies of Senghor and other intellectuals, but it also acknowledged religion and, to a certain extent, custom. Its main characteristics are the unification of the law, the affirmation of the secular character of the society, recognition of the principles of individual rights, and the principle of equality of all citizens.

The process was quite delicate due to the coexistence of the various normative frameworks that had to be consulted, namely customary law, Muslim law (Sharia), and modern law rooted in the French system. This was done carefully: four hundred headings were included in the questionnaires that were distributed to gather the views of the respondents,[9] and it took eleven years to reach consensus. This initiative attests to the political will to ensure a result that was inclusive of the voices and concerns of everyone.

However, debates on the creation of the Family Code were confined to the circle of government elites, parliamentarians, and appointed members of the Commission and Committee of Options. This post-colonial era was dominated by a one-party system through the Senegalese Progressive Union (UPS),[10] which controlled the political arena. Thus, after the UPS validated the draft law, it was sent to the Parliament for vote. It can be argued in that sense that the Family Code was the product of a confined circle, composed mostly of state agents (M. Ndiaye 2012).

The debates on the Family Code continued, with a wider and more inclusive public debate and the emergence of two main actors that dominated the debates: the feminists and the pro-Islamists. While the former was mainly manifested through the women's rights movement, the second was expressed through the Reform Movement for Social Development (MPRS) (an Islamic political party) and later in the 1990s with the Islamic Committee for the Reform of the Family Code in

Senegal (CIRCOFS).[11] The latter was made possible because of the regime change, with the Socialist Party in power, and the emergence of a multi-party system in Senegal. On the tenth anniversary of the Family Code, the government opened a debate; the proposal of the women's movement for the establishment of monogamy as the common legal regime was blocked by strong pro-Islamist opposition.

In 1989, despite the state's lack of political will and resistance from religious groups, the feminists, with the help of female parliamentarians such as Caroline Diop,[12] managed to achieve the abrogation of Article 154 of the Family Code, which put women's ability to engage in a profession at the sole discretion of the husband. They also obtained the obligation of alimony and the sanctioning of laws on family abandonment.

In 1996, encouraged by the Fourth World Conference on Women in Beijing, the women's movement continued to work on other reform prospects, proposing the substitution of parental authority for paternal power. This also coincided with the Islamic Higher Council in Senegal setting up CIRCOFS. This committee, unlike the women's and human rights organizations, strongly criticized the Family Code and proposed a personal status Code that would reinforce patriarchy in Senegalese society, with the re-establishment of repudiation, the elimination of the inheritance of the so-called "natural" child, and the maintenance of the husband's authority.

The debates on limiting polygamy, on parental authority, and on the fight against VAW, which were introduced by human rights organizations in Senegal, particularly feminist organizations such as AJS and the Réseau Siguil Jigueen (RSJ) network, were supported by the United Nations Fund for Population (UNFPA) with parliamentarians in 1998 and revived reflection on the role of Islam as an ideology and the place of CIRCOFS. Debates on the Family Code during the 1990s were dominated by the pro-Islamists' proposing a personal status Code and a total repeal of the 1972 Family Code. In 2004, CIRCOFS submitted a draft law to the President with such a proposition (Brossier 2005).

This generated major political and social tension, with women's rights movements on one side and religious conformists on the other, and the state in the middle as mediator. The debates did not lead to reform, since plurality of status was favored over unity and social cohesion (Mbaye 1970). The state preferred to remain neutral on the issue because of its fragile authority and electoral issues. S. Diop, President of RSJ and a leading actor of the women's movement, noted, "the President took the best decision by rejecting both claims because they would threaten the national unity and even make the women's movement vulnerable and it is not in our interest to have such influential people against us."[13]

The national legal framework reveals the many achievements that resulted from the mobilization of women's rights organizations. These struggles relied heavily on campaigns in local languages and strong advocacy with policymakers. To advance women's rights, civil society organizations[14] used women in political parties extensively. Their demands, supported by the UN system and technical and financial partners, resulted in the following changes:

- Women's increased access to law enforcement and the security sector (police, peacekeepers, military personnel in the health service, gendarmerie, customs);
- Amendments to the Family Code regarding equality of rights, with Law No. 89-01 of 17 January 1989, amending certain provisions of the Family Code (Article 13 – Legal establishment of domicile; Article 19 amended with a view to include the possibility for a married woman to be the legal administrator of the property of her absent spouse; repeal of section 154 which allowed the husband to prohibit his wife from practicing a profession);
- Taking into account the rights of women and mothers in Act No. 97-17 of 1 December 1997, on the Labor Code (Article L. 105 equal pay for equal work; Article L. 143 maternity leave; Article L. 144 breastfeeding time);
- Strengthening the repression of VAW with Law 99-05 of 29 January 1999, Repression of violence against women in the home and in society (O.J. 27 February 1999, p. 832);
- Law No. 2005-06 of 10 May 2005, on combating trafficking in persons and similar practices and the protection of victims (O.J. No. 6223 of Monday, 30 May 2005);
- Ministerial Order No. 10545 of 10 December 2008, establishing the Reflection Committee on Violence Against Women and Children;
- Decree No. 2004-426 of 14 April 2004, establishing the National Fund for the Promotion of Women's Entrepreneurship;
- Law No. 2005-18 of 5 August 2005, on reproductive health (O.J. No. 6245 of 8 October 2005);
- Development of the national strategy for gender equality and equity;
- Suppression of medical care of the spouse and children of the employed woman in 2006 (Decree No. 2006-1331 of 23 November 2006); repealing and replacing Articles 32 and 33 of Decree No. 74-347 of 12 April 1974, on special arrangements for non-civil servants of the state (O.J. No. 6319, 19 January 2007); Decree No. 2006-1310 of 23 November 2006, repealing and replacing Articles 1 and 8 of Decree No. 75-895 of 14 August 1975, on the organization of occupational or inter-company health insurance schemes and compulsory creation of the said institutions (O.J. No. 6319 of 19 January 2007);
- Establishment of tax equality – General Tax Code Act 2008-01 of 8 January 2008, amending certain provisions of the General Tax Code and on equality of tax treatment (O.J. No. 6387 of 21 January 2008);
- Establishment of absolute parity between men and women in totally or partially elected institutions of the Republic with Law No. 2010-11 of 28 May 2010 (O.J. No. 6544 of 4 September 2010); Decree No. 2011-309 on the establishment, organization, and operation of the National Observatory on Gender Equality;
- Law No. 2010/03 of 9 April 2010, on HIV and AIDS (O.J. No. 6535 of 10 July 2010)
- Law No. 2010-15 of 6 July 2010, on the promotion and protection of the rights of persons with disabilities (O.J. No. 6553, 30 October 2010)

The international legal framework

As in many countries with a Muslim-majority population, the legal system in Senegal is pluralistic in nature; therefore women's rights are constrained by the mingling of modern law, Muslim law, and customary law. This is often an impediment to women's effective enjoyment of their rights in general, particularly within the family. However, Senegal has affirmed its commitment to human rights and the principle of equality since its 1959 Constitution. The preamble of the most recent Constitution (2001) affirms the recognition of international human rights standards and refers to several international instruments, including the Convention on the Elimination of All Forms of Discrimination against Women (CEDAW).[15]

Indeed, in addition to its domestic legal framework, Senegal has also subscribed to an extensive list of international and regional treaties that protect women from violence. Senegal is party to the core international treaties most relevant for women's rights: the International Covenant on Civil and Political Rights (ICCPR), its Optional Protocol, and the International Covenant on Economic Social and Cultural Rights (ICESCR) (1978); CEDAW (1985) and its Optional Protocol (2001); Convention on the Rights of the Child (CRC) (1990); as well as the African Charter on Human and Peoples' Rights (1981) and its protocol on the Rights of Women in Africa, known as the Maputo Protocol (2005). Therefore, Senegal has an obligation to undertake all necessary action, including judicial, legislative, and administrative, to ensure the rights enshrined in these instruments.

The next sections focus on CEDAW and the Maputo Protocol, since they are the two international and regional human rights instruments that exclusively address women's rights.

CEDAW

CEDAW does not explicitly refer to VAW; in 1992, the committee monitoring the implementation of the Convention adopted General Recommendation (GR) 19 to rectify this shortcoming, contending that VAW is a form of discrimination that seriously inhibits women's ability to enjoy rights and freedoms on a basis of equality with men.[16]

In the spirit of CEDAW, Senegal's Constitution (Article 7) also proclaims the principle of equality between men and women in all spheres of life.[17] Senegal follows a monist regime, whereby international treaties directly form part of the legal order and supersede domestic laws.

Therefore, these human rights instruments are key to the civil society movement – both human rights and women's rights organizations – to promote women's rights in Senegal. These organizations use these instruments to develop their advocacy strategies to promote women's rights, especially their right to be free from all types of violence. One of the main strategies used for the latter is the argument of harmonizing Senegal's national legislation on women with its commitments deriving from CEDAW and the Maputo Protocol. Women's rights organizations such as the CLVF, RSJ, and AJS use these two instruments as their main advocacy tools to achieve women's rights in Senegal.

In an interview, Fatou Diop, Vice President of the CLVF, stated that one of the main gaps in the Senegalese legislation on VAW is that the domestic laws are not harmonized with the international norms to which the country has subscribed. Therefore, women's rights organizations see their role as initiating advocacy campaigns on the need to harmonize the legal frameworks protecting women. They have organized several sensitization workshops for women in both urban and rural areas to enable them to know their rights. Along with these, the organizations submit shadow reports through the civil society network both to the international and regional systems.

AJS is one of the leading women's rights organizations to use CEDAW and the Maputo Protocol. They disseminate these documents to women and the population at large but also use them to frame research-based advocacy for the harmonization of such laws with domestic legislation. As lawyers, they have had to work with the legislative branch (with members of Parliament) and the judiciary, such as police officials and magistrates who have the duty to apply the laws, as they strengthen their capacity for women's rights and protection of women as enshrined in CEDAW and the Maputo Protocol. AJS prepared two important research-based advocacy documents, one on the harmonization of Senegalese domestic law with CEDAW and the Maputo Protocol (in 2005), and one on the harmonization of the Family Code with the Constitution and the Conventions ratified by Senegal (in 2009). They use these documents as major advocacy tools with the government of Senegal to realize these rights.

In most of their advocacy campaigns, these women's rights organizations also collaborate with other civil society organizations or with technical and financial partners such as UN agencies or other international organizations. For example, AJS and the Open Society Initiative for West Africa collaborated to translate the legislation on physical and sexual violence into local languages (Wolof) to allow women with limited education to have access to and appropriate the instruments that are meant to protect them.

The RSJ has pioneered several campaigns and has had an important impact on many women's rights achievements such as the 1999 law criminalizing different forms of VAW; RSJ President Safiétou Diop, also noted the need to frame their advocacy towards harmonizing domestic law with international norms that are more conducive to women, since that is the major obstacle in Senegal.

In addition to this, part of the obligation of States Parties is to submit periodic reports to the CEDAW Committee to examine the progress they have made in realizing the rights proclaimed therein. In 2015, the combined third to seventh periodic reports of the government of Senegal were examined by the CEDAW Committee, which stated its concerns and made recommendations relating to family law. Indeed, those recommendations expressed the Committee's concerns about the very long delays in revising the discriminatory provisions contained in Senegalese domestic law, in particular the discriminatory provisions contained in the Family Code, including provisions related to the different minimum ages of marriage for girls and boys, the husband being the head of household, and polygamy (CEDAW Committee /C/SEN/CO/3-7, 7 July 2015). The Committee recommended that Senegal:

- Accelerate, in particular, the revision of the Family Code, with a view to bringing the legislation in conformity with the Convention and ensuring that all discriminatory provisions are repealed, including those related to the different minimum age of marriage for girls and boys (Article 111), the husband being the head of household (Articles 227 and 152) and polygamy (Article 116);
- Strengthen information and awareness-raising campaigns for local, traditional and religious leaders and the general public, especially in rural areas, on the negative effects of discriminatory legal provisions (CEDAW Committee /C/SEN/CO/3-7, 7 July 2015).

Civil society contributes to following up on these recommendations by translating them into action to be taken by the government of Senegal. These governmental actions include sharing the recommendations with the different stakeholders (women's rights organizations, civil society, parliamentarians, and justice officers) so they can jointly determine how to move forward to implement the recommendations. As stakeholders, the women's organizations continue their sensitization activities and documentation of women's experiences of violence, to enable the population to be informed of such issues, but also to keep the pressure on the government to take concrete steps to fulfill its obligations.

Women's organizations have emphasized the need for harmonization between domestic and international law, because that will allow many subsequent positive changes for women and girls. For instance, one of the women's organizations' priority advocacy issues is to raise the minimum legal age of marriage to eighteen from the current sixteen in the Family Code and Penal Code; this would be a significant step towards eradicating the practice of early/child and forced marriage, since the law would specifically prohibit both.

Another priority issue for women's groups is the provision that puts women under the trusteeship of their husbands (Articles 227 and 152 of the Family Code); these grant the man exclusive parental authority and position him as the head of the household. As RSJ President Safiétou Diop stated, this embodies the spirit of the family law in Senegal, which signals the inferiority of women to men; consequently that provision should be specifically targeted. Such provisions reinforce the system of guardianship of men over women and indicate they are not equal partners in marriage. Therefore, repealing these articles will constitute a major step towards achieving equality in the family, especially since the Senegalese Constitution and international law support the equality of rights for men and women and therefore the notion that they should be equal partners in marriage.[18]

Granting men parental authority is based on their traditional role of providers; however, this has changed and now many women are heads of their households, providers, and family caretakers, whether they are divorced women or women who are solely in charge of bringing up their children. Recognizing their status on the same basis as men and securing equal rights for them will allow the government to adapt the family law to correspond with the current situation and needs of women.

Since the review of Senegal by the CEDAW Committee is quite recent, dissemination of these recommendations and specific follow-up have so far been insufficient. However, human rights NGOs use such recommendations in their advocacy through workshops, in the media, or when drafting reports to remind the state of its obligations.

The African regional framework

The Maputo Protocol of the African Charter requires all States Parties to adopt the principle of equality between men and women not only in their constitutions but also in all national legislation (Article 2).

The Maputo Protocol has innovative provisions to promote women's rights, such as its detailed provisions on sexual and reproductive rights, including abortion rights for victims of rape, incest, and pedophilia. The right to be informed about one's state of health and a partner's state of health particularly in the context of sexually transmitted diseases, including HIV infection, is also a unique provision.

The precarious situation of Senegalese women and girls in terms of their sexual and reproductive rights has received international attention through advocacy work by local women's rights organizations. The task force established in 2014 advocated for the abrogation of Senegal's restrictive abortion law, which had resulted in illegal abortions and deaths. This was part of the framework of the "Africa for women's rights" campaign, which was launched by regional and international human rights and women's rights organizations[19] both within and outside Africa to call on African states to ratify international and regional women's human rights protection instruments and to respect them in law and practice.

To respond to its obligations under the Maputo Protocol, Senegal enacted Law No. 2005-18 (2005), on reproductive health, with the recognition that despite the efforts made by the government to improve the population's reproductive health, poor accessibility and quality of the services offered and the persistence of sociocultural factors remained as major constraints. This law was also to correct prior reproductive health documents, which did not provide a clear overview of the nature of the problem.

There are still important measures to be taken for the effective protection of women and girls' sexual and reproductive health, since Senegal continues to maintain one of the most lethal abortion laws, denying abortions in cases of rape, incest, and pedophilia. The former President of AJS, F.K. Camara, denounced Senegal's archaic law on reproductive health and called it one of the deadliest abortion laws.

The task force's report, entitled "I do not want this child, I want to go to school" (FIDH, LSDH, RADDHO 2014), highlights the situation and is the basis for the task force's advocacy, which derives mostly from Article 14 of the Maputo Protocol on sexual and reproductive rights, including the right to medical abortion in cases of rape, pedophilia, incest, and when the life of the fetus and/or the mother are threatened, and Article 12 of CEDAW on women's access to health services, including reproductive health services.

Women's rights organizations have prepared medical, legal, sociological, anthropological, and religious arguments in support of reforming the law; however, they still face strong opposition from religious authorities (both Muslim and Catholic) who oppose any type of abortion (therapeutic or not), even though the task force has the strong support of the judiciary through the Minister of Justice, who has worked to sensitize parliamentarians on the need to reform the Penal Code, the law on reproductive health, and the Code of Medical Ethics. Although this advocacy has not yet led to the reform of the discriminatory provisions, it has at least enabled the taboo around the question to be removed and has led to debates in the public space on a topic that was formerly considered as too private.

Children's rights and women's rights movements have also evoked the African Charter on the Rights and Welfare of the Child, as well as the CRC, in their call to elevate the legal age of marriage to eighteen. Since this is an issue that concerns both girls and women, the human rights movement has strategically come together and advocated for women and girls at the same time.

Lessons learned from the Senegalese family law reform

The process of reform in Senegal has been slow, but it has seen some successes, such as the 1989 law that modified the legal determination of the family's domicile (which previously had been entirely at the husband's discretion), issues of alimony, family abandonment, and women's professional life; the 1999 law criminalizing different forms of VAW in the Penal Code, including domestic violence; the 2001 Constitution that reinforced the principle of equality and acknowledged CEDAW;[20] the 2011 law on parity in fully or partially elective bodies; and the 2013 amendment of the Code of Nationality, which allows Senegalese women to give their nationality to their children. These successes of the women's movement enabled them to oppose the consistent resistance of the pro-Islamists who since 1996 have been proposing a Personal Status Code with CIRCOFS.

However, the picture is far from being perfect. Family law in Senegal is living proof of the sexist laws that still exist in the country after fifty years of independence, thirty years of CEDAW, and more than ten years of the Maputo Protocol. Girls are still subject to early and forced marriage, since the Family Code allows marriage at sixteen for girls and the Penal Code does not criminalize child marriage.[21] Women's parental authority is not recognized, since parental authority is exclusively conferred on men, even though many women today are heads of families and are their families' main support and breadwinner.

One factor in this is the failure of the state and legislators as they tried to achieve a synthesis between the different normative frameworks in family law. This attempt has been an important step towards regulating the sensitive issues relating to the family, which are always politically difficult. However, the Family Code failed in that mission because it has very few allusions to customary law. For instance, on marriage, the consideration of customary law is purely formal, since it concerns only how marriage is to be celebrated and not the substantive rules of marriage that are governed by a single law (Camara 2006). More consideration and weight have been given to the Muslim law regulating issues of marriage and inheritance.

This raises serious questions on the effectiveness of the principle of secularization and democratic values to which the state claims to subscribe. Indeed, according to F.K. Camara (2006), examining the process of elaborating the Family Code indicates that the drafters deliberately intended to give a privileged place to the Arabo-Muslim law.

The process of reforming family law in Muslim contexts is complex, with social, political, and religious challenges, since it requires changing the status quo – the superiority of men in the family. Thus, of all the provisions in the Family Code that are grounded in Muslim law, the Code only consecrates those that are discriminatory and unfavorable to women. For instance, for issues of succession and inheritance, Muslim law is given as the only option.

The composition of the legislature since 1972 also affects the slow pace of achieving meaningful change for women in the family. When the Family Code was approved in 1972, there were only two women serving with eighty male parliamentarians; therefore the voices of women were not heard in that process. This reinforces the saying "What is done without you, for you, is against you." Today, despite the law on parity, women only constitute 26 percent of the Assembly.

Since the passage of the Family Code, the two levels of pressure in Senegal – the government and the religious authorities – have been maintained. Today, references to religion are still made to legitimize what happens inside families. Since 2000, through its advocacy of a Personal Status Code with CIRCOFS and its lobbying of the different religious brotherhoods, the Islamic Superior Council has continued to resist reforms for women's rights.

To some extent, the failure of the current debates to result in reforms is a result of the state's not prioritizing these reforms. During the immediate postcolonial regime, there was more enthusiasm and a manifested political will from President Senghor to reform Senegalese legislation and create a modern family law. At that time, the state stimulated and framed the process; later, during the time of Presidents Wade and Diouf, the state tended towards arbitration and mediation between the feminist/Islamist camps.

The centrality of the debate on religion created by CIRCOFS is also an obstacle to state commitment and productive results because the Senegalese experience shows that the state avoids, at any cost, engaging in issues that religious communities do not agree with. However, there have been valuable successes whenever women used the top-down approach – when they have worked hand-in-hand with members of Parliament to obtain reforms, as they did successfully in 1989.

For RSJ President Safiétou Diop, the major challenge for women is at the legislative and political levels, where they must fight to achieve positions of influence. If women's voices and power at times requiring a decision are not increased, little change will occur for law reforms. The women's movement has been documenting the violence women experience and using this to sensitize women, the government, and other authorities; however, religious opposition is still strong, as is the reticence of the government to engage in fruitful discussions. Therefore, only additional strategies such as representation at times of decision-making and networking with international and regional institutions will allow positive change to happen.

The constant problem of monitoring and follow-up mechanisms must also be resolved, and there are still important procedural gaps to fill. Women have little access to justice, and cases of VAW are treated with a lack of gender sensitivity, with judges preferring to reduce sentences for perpetrators, contributing to a climate of impunity. This also stresses the need for Senegal to engage in harmonizing domestic law with international law, as recommended by the CEDAW Committee in its last examination, and to start this with its most discriminatory laws, such as the Family Code.

Conclusions and recommendations

Family law has been one of the most contested questions in contemporary Muslim countries such as Senegal. Debates around this topic relate specifically to women's position in modern society. However, positive changes in the family law of Muslim countries are possible as have happened in Morocco, Egypt, and elsewhere.

It is clear that the Senegalese experience in law reform, especially family law, has been complicated; however, it has not prevented the women's movement from achieving many successes (see the section "Lessons learned" above). Despite these achievements, there is still a long way to go to achieve equality, and debates and prospects for reform have remained unproductive since 2004. This can be attributed to the lack of political will of the recent political regimes, but also to the debate's focus on religion (due to the pro-Islamists), which created a tension with the women's movement and made debate even more difficult. Advocacy, networking, and strong mobilization have proven to be efficient for women, as has a top-down approach, consisting in first sensitizing and then working with parliamentarians.

Therefore, while Senegal has made important steps towards women's rights, the family remains a space of discrimination for women. Archaic laws that need to be harmonized, religious resistance, and limited political will all contribute to hindering the struggles of the women's movement to achieve family law reform. The lack of respect for women's civil, political, and socio-economic rights also keeps women at the bottom of the ladder, with little power or influence on decisions that concern them. Despite the law on parity, women only constitute 26 percent of members of Parliament. However, there is still hope through the women's rights movement and their advocacy, with the help of the international community, that the laws can be changed for the better for women in Senegal and other Muslim countries.

From the above conclusions, the following recommendations can be made.

For the government of Senegal

- To put on its agenda the issue of family law reform and to create spaces for inclusive debates around family law reform that will gather the views of civil society, religious communities, the population, and all stakeholders;
- To embark on law reform, and to elaborate specific, comprehensive legislation addressing VAW;
- To follow up on the recommendations of the CEDAW Committee with the consultation of civil society and relevant stakeholders, and to harmonize its domestic laws with international law to repeal the discriminatory provisions contained in the Family Code, such as Article 111 on the legal age of marriage, Articles 152 and 227 on men being the heads of households, and to encompass the notion of both sexes having parental authority; and
- To work with local NGOs, such as AJS, to translate the laws into local languages, to remove the language barriers that prevent women from knowing the laws, from being fully informed about their rights, and from understanding the state's obligations towards them.

For the women's movement in Senegal

- In face of the government's inaction, to lead advocacy by documenting and publicizing the need to repeal discriminatory laws and to maintain pressure on the government;
- To propose reforms to the government and stakeholders;
- To strengthen their existing networking among the RSJ, to regroup the eighteen organizations, and to rally other women's rights and human rights NGOs; and
- To utilize top-down strategies, directly lobbying with members of Parliament and the government to achieve change.

For the global campaign

- To address the diversity of legislation in Muslim countries and contexts and the different levels of progress they experience in achieving justice and equality for women through their laws, especially family laws. For instance, the Moroccan legislation on family is more progressive than Senegal's, despite both countries having Muslim majorities. This implies that legal pluralism and secularization in Senegal is not sufficient and not necessarily more conducive to positive change and human rights. The campaign in Morocco has been more aggressive and has received major international support, which gave rise to the government's and Parliament's approval. Therefore, it might be beneficial to use a similar strategy in Senegal to attract political will;

- To advocate for an international comprehensive, specific, legally binding instrument to outlaw VAW in all its forms, to ensure more effective enforcement at country levels; and
- For international NGOs, movements for women's rights, and technical and financial partners to reinforce their support for local civil society organizations and women's rights organizations, to allow them to do their work properly and have meaningful impact at local levels.

Notes

1 Interviews included: Safiétou Diop, President of the Network for the Rehabilitation of Women (Réseau Siguil Jigeen); Penda Diouf Seck, President of the Committee Combating Violence against Women (CLVF); Fatou Kine Camara, member of the Association of Female Senegalese Lawyers (AJS); and Rama Niang, President of Women Education Culture Health and Development in Africa (FECSDA).

2 GESTES is a research and study group based at Gaston Berger University.

3 Diouf is the President of the national Committee Combating Violence Against Women in Senegal.

4 Diop works at the national Committee Combating Violence Against Women in Senegal.

5 The study analyzes about one hundred court decisions made in four regions of Senegal (Dakar, Saint-Louis, Kolda, and Louga) from 1997 to 2013.

6 The Committee was composed of eight members of Parliament, four magistrates of courts and tribunals, a justice of the peace, six cadis (judge in a Sharia court), two presidents of customary courts, two lawyers, a chief clerk, a notary, a bailiff, a municipal agent. The Dean of the Faculty of Law, the Dean of the Faculty of Letters and Human Sciences, a professor of law, and two technical assistance magistrates served on the Committee as experts.

7 These guidelines were included in the report of presentation of the draft law on the Family Code by Youssoupha Ndiaye, President of the Commission of Codification (Y. Ndiaye 1979).

8 In the 1968/1973 legislature in which the Family Code was passed, there were only two women out of eighty deputies (1.6 percent), cf. "Women in the National Assembly of Senegal" by Aissata De in *Democracy where are you? Publication of the COSEF* (Senegalese Women's Council).

9 The respondents were from religious communities and customary law practitioners.

10 Senegalese Progressive Union (UPS), a political party led by President Senghor, which became the Socialist party under President Abdou Diouf's rule.

11 CIRCOFS is the Islamic Committee for the Reform of the Family Code in Senegal, which was set up specifically to advocate for a personal status code.

12 The late Caroline Diop was the only female MP who participated in the voting process related to the 1972 Family Code and remained committed for reforms in favor of women's rights.

13 Interview with Safiétou Diop.

14 For example, African Women Association for Research and Development [AFARD], Senegalese Women's Council [COSEF], Réseau Siguil Jigueen, AJS, CLVF, etc.

15 This section of the Preamble reads as follows: "The Sovereign People of Senegal affirms its adherence to the Declaration of the Rights of Man and of the Citizen of 1789 and to the international instruments adopted by the United Nations and the Organization of African Unity, in particular the Universal Declaration of Human Rights of 10 December 1948, the Convention on the Elimination of All Forms of Discrimination against Women of 18 December 1979, the Convention on the Rights of the Child of 20 November 1989 and the African Charter On Human and Peoples' Rights of 27 June 1981."

16 In 2017, the Committee adopted GR 35 updating GR 19. The first comprehensive international document addressing VAW is the Declaration on the Elimination of VAW, adopted by the UN General Assembly in 1993. According to the Declaration, VAW is "any act of gender-based violence that results in, or is likely to result in, physical, sexual or psychological harm or suffering to women, including threats of such acts, coercion or arbitrary deprivation of liberty, whether occurring in public or in private life."

17 Article 7 (4) of the Senegalese Constitution provides that "All human beings are equal before the law. Men and women are equal in law."

18 Article 7 (4) of the 2001 Constitution of Senegal and Articles 6 of the Maputo Protocol and 16 of CEDAW provide for equality of rights between men and women.

19 The steering committee is composed of FIDH (International Federation of Human Rights), FAS (Women Africa Solidarity), WACOL (Women's Aid Collective), WILDAF (Women in Law and Development in Africa), WLSA (Women and Law in Southern Africa), and ACDHRS (African Center for Democracy and Human Rights Studies).

20 The Preamble of the 2001 Constitution of the Republic of Senegal affirms its adhesion to CEDAW, among other treaties

21 Article 300 of the Penal Code (1965) only punishes sexual acts on a child below the age of thirteen and in connection with the consummation of customary marriage.

References

AJS: Association of Female Senegalese Lawyers (2013) *La Jurisprudence du viol au Sénégal: un déni de justice aux victimes (The Jurisprudence on Rape in Senegal: The Denial of Justice to Victims* (based on decisions collected from 1997 to 2013)) Dakar: AJS.

Brossier, M. (2005) "Débats sur le Code de la Famille au Sénégal" ("Debates on the Family Code in Senegal"), *Autrepart, Revue de sciences sociales au Sud*, No. 41, Paris: Presses de Sciences Po: 7.

Camara, F.K. (2006) "Le Code de la famille du Sénégal ou de l'usage de la religion comme alibi pour la légalisation de l'inégalité genre" ("The Family Code of Senegal or the Use of Religion as an Alibi for the Legalization of Gender Inequality"), First Inter-Network Symposium of the Thematic Program "Aspects of the Rule of Law" of the Agence Universitaire de la Francophonie (*AUF*), Dakar, 25–27 April 2006, Dakar: PUD.

GESTES (2014) *Les Violences Basées Sur Le Genre Au Sénégal: La Prévention Comme Alternative Aux Périls De Sécurité Et De Justice (Gender-Based Violence in Senegal: Prevention as Alternative to Safety and Justice)* Dakar: CRDI.

FIDH, LSDH, RADDHO (2014) "Je ne veux pas de cet enfant je veux aller à l'école: la prohibition de l'interruption volontaire de grossesse au Sénégal" ("I do not want this child, I want to go to school: The Prohibition of Voluntary Termination of Pregnancy in Senegal"), FIDH, LSDH, RADDHO: 7–15.

Mbaye, Kéba (1970) "L'expérience sénégalaise de la réforme du droit" ("The Senegalese Experience in Law Reform"), in *Revue Internationale de droit comparé*, Vol. 22, No.1, Janvier/Mars 1970: 35–42; doi: 10.3406/ridc.1970.17599 (Declaration on the Elimination of Violence against Women 20 December 1993 A/RES/104/48).

Mbow, Penda (2001) "L'islam et la femme sénégalaise" ("Islam and the Senegalese Woman") in *Revue négro-africaine de littérature et de philosophie*, Vol. 7: 66–67.

Ministry of Family and Female Entrepreneurship (Ministère de la Famille et de l'Entreprenariat féminin) (2015) *Stratégie nationale pour l'équité et l'égalité genre* (*Analysis of the Current Situation of Gender Equity and Equality in Senegal*), Dakar: Ministère de la Famille: 25–27.

Ndiaye, Marième (2012), *La Politique Constitutive au Sud: Refonder le droit de la famille au Sénégal et au Maroc* (*The Constitutive Policy in the South: Rebuilding Family Law in Senegal and Morocco*) (Doctoral Thesis): 23-536, Paris: PUF.

Ndiaye, Youssoupha (1979) "Rapport de présentation du projet de loi portant Code de la famille" ("Report Presenting the Draft Law of the Family Code"), in *Le divorce et la séparation de corps*, Dakar: NEA.

UN Women (2012) *La situation des violences faites aux femmes: le mode réponse et soutien aux survivantes dans les régions de Dakar, Diourbel, Fatick, Kaffrine, Kaolack, Louga, Saint-Louis and Thiès* (*A Study on the Situation of Violence against Women: Response and support for survivors in the regions of Dakar, Diourbel, Fatick, Kaffrine, Kaolack, Louga, Saint-Louis and Thiès*), Dakar: UN Women.

10

TURKEY

Gökçeçiçek Ayata and Ayşen Candaş

Introduction

Turkey is regarded as a "staunchly secular" country, while at the same time referred to as a "Muslim democracy." Both of these perceptions cannot be true, since they are contradictory.[1] "Muslim democracy," much like any such descriptions as "Christian," "Jewish," or "Hindu" democracy, is an oxymoron (Candaş 2008), given that a democracy that requires an adjective to qualify its regime type is less than a democracy. Democratic countries are invariably constitutional democracies that recognize equal basic rights and equal membership principles as their permanent features (Habermas 1996 [1992] and 2001). Hence there can be no "Muslim democracies," but countries with predominantly Muslim populations that *may well* be democratized. Turkey is a Muslim-majority country, and while some its people of Muslim background lead secular lives, or are agnostic, irreligious, or atheist, others are devoutly religious and strictly follow its rituals.[2] Diversity is a permanent fact of Turkey (Rawls 1993).

This is also reflected in the status and circumstances of women, which show significant differences in terms of class, economic and political power, ethnicity, rural/urban rift, region, access to social support, and social security, etc. There is a general gap between women's de jure and de facto status[3] (Acar 2010: 15; Ertürk 2016a: 245). Contradictions between legal norms and traditional patriarchal norms, and their continuing clash at law-making processes as well as uneven regional development, all have an impact on violence against women (VAW) (Ertürk 2016a: 247). Migration to the cities, the Justice and Development Party's (*Adalet ve Kalkınma Partisi* – AKP) skillful fusion of neoliberalism and neo-conservatism (Coşar and Yücesan-Özdemir 2012; Balkan and Savran 2002; Savran 2008), and gender aspects of social benefit-distributing policies (Dedeoğlu 2012; İlkkaracan-Ajas et al. 2015; Coşar and Yeğenoğlu 2011; Candaş and Silier 2014; Kandiyoti

2015) impose new burdens on especially disadvantaged women. The intersectionality (Crenshaw 1991) of ethnicity, religious sect, conflict, gender identity, gender orientation, age, and disability, as well as social class position, create compounded and multifaceted entrenched inequalities not only between men and women, but also among women themselves.

While it would not be unfair to depict certain periods in the history of modern Turkey as illiberal secularist, complete de-secularization cannot possibly result in democratization. Turkey is currently ruled by a political party that in the course of its governance has shifted its orientation from the European Union (EU) accession principles – Copenhagen criteria[4] – to one that is ingrained in Islamist ideals and propagates a divisive and sectarian "religious nationalism,"[5] adorned with transnational aspirations. It must, however, be emphasized that legislation does not yet derive its legitimacy from a reference to divine laws; the individual continues to be recognized as the addressee of law. In that sense, legislation in Turkey is – still – secular and addresses women as equal citizens.

The struggle of women to reform family law was, in fact, initiated long before the adoption of the Civil Code in 1926. Feminist historians often cite the late Ottoman modernization as the starting point of democratization and women's struggle (Çakır 1994). While acknowledging this long history of women's struggle, only the last thirty years are within the scope of this study, and half of this time period falls under the rule of the AKP. Prior to the AKP's rise to power in 2002, as well as during its first term in office when the AKP adopted pro-EU policies, the new wave of the women's movement that emerged in 1980s[6] had already managed to make significant impact on the law-making processes.

Prior to the 2000s, the equality norm was not directly challenged.[7] In that sense, the AKP period represents a rupture from the Republican past that promoted women's equality as the norm – though not necessarily from a feminist point of view.

Throughout the 2000s, periods of feminist campaigning that resulted in successes (Anıl et al. 2002, 2005; TCK Kadın Çalışma Grubu 2003; İlkkaracan 2007; İlkkaracan and Erçevik-Amado 2008) also provoked regressive reactions of Islamists, such as calls for criminalizing adultery (Anıl et al. 2005: 13), lowering the age of marriage, and easing the punishments imposed for rape and sexual abuse of minors. Since 2010, a sharp shift towards anti-democratic policies in line with the party's own societal vision became apparent, thus challenging and undermining the equality norm at various levels.

Regardless of the shift in the state's will, research undertaken by Altınay and Arat (2009) revealed that the overwhelming majority of women – 80 percent – demand the egalitarian division of labor at home and outside the home. Furthermore, according to a recent survey (2015),[8] 36.9 percent of women interviewed described themselves as "feminists" and 86 percent indicated that they support organizations that fight for women's rights.

Bowen and colleagues (2015: 656) argued that female labor force participation (LFP) may be less important than family law as an indicator of women's status.

However, in the case of Turkey, LFP as an indicator[9] also verifies[10] the regressive turn[11] that women are facing. The regressive turn in women's status can be traced to the rise of two new trends (Kandiyoti 2015). The first is the rise of government-organized non-governmental organizations (GONGOs) as the means of co-optation; the second is the proliferation of new protectionist policies targeting women that deny their equality and autonomy, and the instrumentalization of these policies for creating "the people of the new Turkey." We must now add a third process – de-institutionalization – caused by the mass closure of NGOs through recent executive orders.[12] So far, this process had the most damaging impact on the Kurdish women's movement (and on the pro-secular teachers' associations).

Research question and scope

The goal of this case study is to analyze the strategies of the women's movement for reforming discriminatory laws. Accordingly, the primary research questions are: in view of gendered discriminatory family laws that sustain VAW, which reform initiatives have been undertaken, what were the strategies employed by the women's movement, and what are the lessons that can be drawn from these campaigns?

We focused on legislation that has a *direct* bearing on the research questions and covered only the following: on the *national* level: Civil Code amendments, Penal Code amendments, Legislation on VAW (Law No. 4320 to Law No. 6284); on the *international* level: the Convention on the Elimination of all forms of Discrimination Against Women (CEDAW) and the Council of Europe Convention on Preventing and Combating Violence against Women and Domestic Violence (Istanbul Convention).

Methodology

The research process for this case study included a *consultative* group that consisted of women with a diversity of expertise. Geographical distribution (i.e., Turkey's seven regions) was taken into account. However, purges, arrests, banning of NGOs, military operations in Kurdish-populated towns, and the clamp-down on the Kurdish movement in particular and the oppositional voices in general had an impact on the research process. *Desktop research* included the compilation and analysis of a list of human rights conventions on women's rights that were signed and ratified by Turkey, reports drafted by academics or women's rights NGOs, and collecting materials such as press releases, campaigns, etc. of the women's rights movement in Turkey. *Interviews* were carried out either face to face or through electronic media with nine women who have played an active role in the thirty-year legal reform, including lawyers/legal experts, NGO representatives, bureaucrats, and feminists.[13] We also organized and held a *national workshop* comprised of experts and members of women's organizations to share the initial findings of the research and receive feedback.

Literature review

Since 1926, when the Turkish Republic codified the Civil Code (borrowed from the Swiss code) replacing the Ottoman family law, Turkey's legal system made a radical break from what Maine called a "status society" and put itself into the path of a "contract society." According to Maine,[14] "while contract societies posit a binding agreement between the individual and the state . . . [status societies emphasize] the standing of a family and are often associated with concepts of honour and shame." All ancient societies were status societies, yet some of them adopted variants of Roman law and continued on the normative legal framework grounded on individual-based legal personhood or a contract model, while some did not.[15] On the cause of the great divergence between the two paths, Maine stated that: "[O]ne steadily carried forward, while the other recoiled from, the series of changes which put an end to the seclusion and degradation of an entire sex" (Bowen et al. 2015: 660).

According to its statutory law, the 2001 and 2002 constitutional amendments, and the Civil Code amendment, Turkey should be considered as a country that formally, in its positive law,[16] established itself as a "contract society" in the sense articulated by Maine.

Duality of legal and customary laws, and the specific paradox of family law

The literature on family law, especially when it deals with Muslim-majority countries where customary law[17] is also the positive law, does not need to draw a distinction between the two (Bowen et al. 2015: 659). This is not the case in Turkey.

The reform of family law in Turkey dates back to the late Ottoman modernization, and a major stride was made in the Republican period when the 1926 statutory law (Civil Code) recognized women as equal citizens, with divorce and inheritance rights (and in 1934 with the right to vote and the right to stand for election). As much as customary law makes a claim to normativity[18] in ruling the family, so does the established gender equality norm make a claim and has sanctioning power. In terms of laws that regulate the family in Turkey, one often observes dualities and contradictions of positive and customary laws. While the positive law sets the norm of gender equality in the family (explicitly added to the Constitution in 2001), customs and traditions continue to make counter-normative claims that derive their authority from an ancient past, reminiscent of Weber's "traditional authority." Thus, the family law in Turkey is *dual*. Depending on the level of democracy practiced in a country, the practice of making law can be understood either as the means of translating patriarchal customary *nomos*[19] into law, or it could be seen as setting gender equality as the legal norm in order to transform customary law – or the patriarchal mentality – accordingly.

The development process of family law is from "status" to "contract" (Serozan et al. 2016: 533). States get less and less involved in regulating the content of the relationships that are handled through family law (ibid.: 534). While the trend towards contract-based law is clear, there are insuperable limits of contractualization, and these are drawn for the benefit of children's and women's wellbeing, since children and women would continue to benefit from positive discrimination (ibid.: 535).

Family law has always been a special branch of law, because the contradictions between religious and secular law arise most concretely in this sphere (ibid.: 536). Yet purely status-based family law (or *nomos*) has been and continues to be impacted by socio-economic and demographic changes as well as changes in production and property relations. Due to major historical processes, the "extended family," which was the direct outcome of the *production-based family* in ancient times, was transformed into *consumption-based nuclear family* – and now that is being replaced by more flexible forms.[20] Stepchildren become part of the new families, and this results in the formation of "collage" families. LGBTQ individuals form new forms of families, called "rainbow families." Sperm banks, artificial insemination, same-sex marriages, and similar developments pave the way for the emergence of yet new forms of families (ibid.: 535–549).

Since family law is the very part of the civil law that is most impacted by the larger socio-economic and demographic changes, it is the most frequently changed part in the body of law (ibid.: 537). At the same time, it is located at a juncture where private law intersects with public law. All these characteristics generate a specific paradox: on the one hand, the relationships that are defined by family law are both horizontal and vertical (as between parents and children) and family law addresses the family as a "closed system" and as "the smallest unit of the social structure." On the other hand, in constitutional democracies individual citizen's rights need to be protected. Insofar as the family is defined as an inflexible unit and a closed system, the drive to protect the family as a unit would inevitably override the intention to protect the individual (ibid.: 550).

In constitutional democracies, family law no longer protects the family. Yet in Turkish law, "the influence of the classical family law structure is still powerful (ibid.: 551). Therefore, despite the changes that have taken place in Turkey's law on the status of women, the changes in the family law have been limited.[21]

According to Serozan and colleagues (2016), in the light of the changing family forms, family law must be rendered flexible to recognize all forms of relationships, from families who want to lead religious lives to those who are "collage" or "rainbow." Accordingly, "the holy halo" framing the concepts of "marriage" and "family" must be removed. Institutions and concepts that are related to family law must be "rescued from religious and ideological obsessions."

Law reform processes: campaigns and dynamics of change

The legal and institutional framework

The provisions of the Constitution, which has been amended many times since its enactment in 1982,[22] that state that the family is based on equality between spouses are of particular importance. Basic legal arrangements concerning family law are included in the Civil Code. The new Civil Code, describing the family as a partnership based on equality between men and women, entered into force on 1 January 2002. As to the Penal Code, while a mentality empowering men, family, and society over women and their bodies was favored in the former text, the new Penal Code, enacted in 2005, abandoned this mindset. The first legislative measure providing for the protection of women against violence (including the removal of the offender from the shared dwelling) is the Law on the Protection of the Family No. 4320, which entered into force in 1998. After the 2007 amendments to that law, it was finally repealed by Law No. 6284 on the Protection of the Family and the Prevention of Violence Against Women, which entered into force in 2012.

Common themes of reform processes

A common theme that emerged during reform processes was the tension between the secular gender-egalitarian legal norm and religious and/or patriarchal customary law. Debates of reform processes concerning adultery, sexual abuse of minors, honor killings, virginity tests, abortion, rape, and child (early and forced) marriage and the increasing involvement of the Directorate of Religious Affairs in providing social policies targeting women involve variations on the theme of this tension. The Republican history of Turkey attests that the existence of a secular constitution by itself is not a guarantee for realizing gender equality. But as it became clear between 2010 and 2017, under the pressure for complete de-secularization, gender equality does not stand a chance. A secular state is a necessary but not a sufficient precondition for an egalitarian gender regime.

Despite the numerous legislative changes since 1926, Turkey has never abandoned the patriarchal norms in its legal system. In the past thirty years, the women's movement did successfully reveal these loopholes and fought with the residues of patriarchal mentality wherever these were expressed in law.

Yet this *proactive phase* of activism was soon replaced by the *reactive period* that the women's movement finds itself in today, as the patriarchy, adorning itself with Islamism, is making a major comeback in social policies targeting women, in the education system, in the suppressed as well as co-opted civil society, and probably soon at the legal level itself. If it is successfully completed, this anti-secular, anti-liberal, anti-women, and anti-democratic "reconstruction period" can end up reversing all the accomplishments that have been made in terms of realizing women's equality. Once the legal reforms of the last decades are reversed, VAW could be "normalized" to comply with the patriarchal and inegalitarian concept of "*fitrat*"[23] or "justice owed to the women."

Advocacy Campaigns

Campaigns Related to International Law

CEDAW

CEDAW and its Optional Protocol entered into force in Turkey on 19 January 1986 and 29 January 2003 respectively.[24] Turkey became a party to CEDAW by entering reservations to its Articles 15(2), 15(4), 16(1/c–d), and 16(1/g) on the grounds that those articles were not compatible with the relevant provisions of the Civil Code in force at the time. Turkey also entered a reservation to Article 29(1), which addresses the authority of the International Court of Justice. In addition to these reservations, Turkey made a declaration to the effect that Article 9(1) of CEDAW does not contradict its Citizenship Law. At the Fourth World Conference on Women (Beijing, 1995), Turkey made a commitment to withdraw its reservations to CEDAW. The reservations to CEDAW Articles 15 and 16 were withdrawn in 1999 in consideration of the proposed amendments to the Civil Code and the draft law. The declaration made with respect to CEDAW Article 9(1) was withdrawn following the amendment to the Citizenship Law in 2008, by which the requirements for acquiring Turkish citizenship by marriage of a woman or a man who is not a Turkish citizen were re-regulated to abolish the inequality. Consequently, only the reservation to Article 29(1), on the authority of the International Court of Justice, is maintained.

The CEDAW process in Turkey cannot be properly understood without taking into account the destruction resulting from the military coup of 12 September 1980. After the coup, all associations, including women's associations, were closed. Until the entry into force of 1982 Constitution and new Law on Associations, it was forbidden to establish an association (Gülbahar and Çakır 1999: 243).

The "Women's Petition" was the first mass action after 1980 (ibid.: 245).[25] On 8 March 1986, "7000 signatures that were collected in the campaign for the implementation [of CEDAW] were submitted to the parliament. In 1987, the Women's Association Against Discrimination was founded to support the implementation of CEDAW" (ibid.: 246).

From the mid-1980s to the 1990s, VAW, forced virginity checks, sexual harassment and rape, the Civil Code, the Penal Code, secularism, and the headscarf ban[26] were the main areas of struggle for the women's movement. The women's movement and activism started in Istanbul, Ankara, and Izmir (the three largest provinces of Turkey) and gradually expanded to other regions. Since the late 1980s, additional women groups have emerged, such as the "feminists in headscarves." Since the 1990s, women's anti-war protests and peace advocacy have surged; the annual 8th of March and 25th of November rallies have become tradition; reproductive and sexual health, employment, and workplace problems have begun to be addressed, and the legal struggle against sexist provisions within the national laws, as well as other matters, has increased. Also, independent women's organizations and municipalities started to open shelters, counseling centers were established to provide legal and psychological support, women's research centers were opened in universities, women collectively attended court hearings, and Kurdish women and LGBTQ groups began to organize. Those periods saw the implementation of several campaigns, such as "No to Virginity Checks," ones against the sexist provisions of the Civil Code and Article 438 of the Penal Code,[27] protests against the reservations entered to European Social Charter, and "Our Bodies are Ours, Say No to Sexual Harassment" (ibid.: 243–277).

In January 1997, women's organizations took part in the CEDAW periodic country review[28] for the first time by preparing a shadow report. From that date onward the women's movement has pursued a policy of preparing shadow reports to the CEDAW Committee, participating in the periodic country review, and monitoring the follow-up of the concluding observations adopted by the Committee.[29] The first legal outcome of the CEDAW periodic country reviews is Law No. 4320 on the Protection of the Family, which provides protective measures such as the removal order from the shared dwelling against the violent offender and the first law to combat VAW in Turkey. Women's organizations, aware of the significance of and the need for protective legislation, launched a campaign after the CEDAW review. They collected signatures in local marketplaces and organized marches (ibid.: 271). Law No. 4320 on the Protection of the Family entered into force on 17 January 1998.

The women's movement consistently reminded the state of its obligations to CEDAW and acted as a watchdog. There have been three important amendments on the articles related to gender equality:

- In 2001, "[Family is] based on equality between the spouses" was added to Article 41 of the Constitution, which stated that "Family is the foundation of the Turkish society." Article 10 of the Constitution on equality before the law states that "everyone is equal before the law without distinction as to language, race, color, gender, political opinion, philosophical view, religion, sect or any such grounds. No privilege shall be granted to any individual, family, group or class. State organs and administrative authorities are obliged to act in compliance with the principle of equality before the law in all their proceedings."
- In 2004, the following amendment was added: "Men and women have equal rights. The State has the obligation to ensure that this equality exists in practice." In this way, the State's obligation to ensure *de facto* equality was constitutionally recognized.
- In 2010, a further addition was made to the same article: "Measures taken for this purpose shall not be interpreted as contrary to the principle of equality."

The women's movement, notably the Women's Constitution Platform group, advocated for two additional amendments to Article 10: (1) that discrimination based on "sexual orientation," "sexual identity," and "marital status" also be banned, and (2) that positive transitory measures for maintaining de facto gender equality be openly structured in the article so that obligations arising from CEDAW could be properly met. The former demand was not approved,[30] while the latter was only partially addressed.[31] The notion of "positive measures" was transformed from its real meaning and started to be used, in practice, as a way of "protecting" women. The government presented practices such as women-only public transportation to the public as "positive discrimination."

The Istanbul Convention

From the onset of the preparation of the Istanbul Convention, the women's movement was involved with women's organizations participating in the meetings held in Turkey.[32] Furthermore, there are organic links with and collaboration between the women's movement and prominent figures – such as Feride Acar and Yakın Ertürk[33] – who hold international human rights mandates. The exchange of experience and information between these figures and the movement has been constant.

Turkey was the first country to sign (11 May 2011) and ratify (14 March 2012) the Istanbul Convention without any reservations. There is no doubt that political will was required to ratify the Convention, but many members of the women's movement point out that this political will was not spontaneously present at that time.[34]

On 8 June 2011, immediately after signing the Convention, pursuant to a Decree Law, the State Ministry Responsible for Women and Family Affairs was replaced by a Ministry of Family and Social Policies, which the government justified on the grounds that woman can only exist within the family, with motherhood being her primary responsibility. Moreover, according to the media reports, two years after the ratification of the Convention, Ayşenur İslam,[35] who was appointed as Minister of Family and Social Policies, attempted to persuade the then-Prime Minister Ahmet Davutoğlu – who had signed the Convention – to withdraw Turkey's signature to the Convention (Armutçu 2014). The authorities have not denied these reports.

The process of nominating a candidate for GREVIO, the committee of independent experts established to monitor the implementation of the Convention, started in December 2014 under the coordination of the Ministry of Family and Social Policies. The Istanbul Convention Monitoring Platform of Turkey (a national entity consisting of about a hundred women and LGBTQ organizations) wrote to the Ministry several times transmitting its suggestions concerning the measures that need to be taken for both the GREVIO candidacy process as well as the implementation of the Convention.[36] However, the Ministry tried to exclude the Platform from the process and cooperated with government-sponsored NGOs (the so-called "GONGOs") that advocated aligning the Convention's implementation with patriarchal customary norms, even though this was against the aim, content, and soul of the Convention. Thanks to the resistance and struggle of the women's movement, Feride Acar was nominated as Turkey's GREVIO candidate.

The women's movement also put great effort into the enactment of the Law No. 6284 on the Protection of the Family and the Prevention of Violence Against Women, which entered into force the year after the signing of the Istanbul Convention. First, a draft law in line with the Istanbul Convention was prepared, but the Ministry did not take it into consideration. Thereafter, a working group of the End Violence Platform, which consists of about three-hundred women's organizations, started to work on the law proposal in order to bring it into conformity with the Convention.

Law No. 6284 became the final legal text built by the limited cooperation between the AKP governments and the independent women's movement.

Campaigns related to domestic law

Civil Code campaign

Although the 1926 Civil Code was a secular legal text, it preserved the male-dominant family model. On 4 October 1992, women's organizations started a nationwide campaign calling for an amendment of the Civil Code. They collected 100,000 signatures, which they submitted to the office of the Speaker of the Parliament (Gülbahar and Çakır 1999: 257–258). Between 2000 and 2001, women's organizations concentrated their efforts. The new Code was adopted by the Parliament on 22 November 2001, and went into force on 1 January 2002 (shortly before the AKP came to power).

A number of achievements had already been reached before the enactment of the new Civil Code. For example, a campaign was launched in August 1990 concerning Article 159, which required a husband's permission for married women to work outside the home, and a petition with 2,500 signatures was submitted to the Constitutional Court. The Constitutional Court annulled the article on 29 November 1990, on the ground that it violated the principle of equality and right to work (ibid.: 243–277). In 1997, the Ministry of Internal Affairs issued a circular replacing the "married/single/widowed/divorced" categories in the marital status section of identity cards with "married" and "single" (ibid.: 271). Not all of the campaigns were able to achieve positive outcomes however. One of these related to the right to choose a family name – a sore spot for the male-dominant system.[37]

The 2002 Civil Code defines the family as a partnership based on equality between women and men. It was successful in challenging patriarchy mainly in two aspects: one is the removal of the concept of the male as head of the family union, and the second is the adoption of an egalitarian matrimonial property regime.[38] The amendments made to the Constitution in 2001, 2004, and 2010 reflect a parallel approach to egalitarian gender relations as codified in the Civil Code.

Penal Code campaign

In the former Penal Code, which entered into force in 1926, the authority over women and women's bodies was vested in men, the family, and the community. Most of the provisions reflecting this viewpoint were not included in the new Code, which entered into force on 1 June 2005.

The Penal Code Campaign was one of the most vibrant events directed by Turkish women, and it paved the way to multiple gains and achievements. Nevertheless, some of the demands of women's groups are still pending: among these are replacing the notion of "honor killings in the name of customary law" with the term "murder," prohibiting virginity checks, including the phrase "sexual orientation" in the anti-discrimination article, etc.

The most significant outcome of these campaigns is the success of diverse groups of women associating to advocate for a collective purpose in an organized way (Eslen-Ziya 2012). The reform processes also created a dynamic public discourse that impacted the minds and decisions of authorities and ordinary people (Ertürk 2016a: 261). The criminalization of marital rape could not have been possible if women had not managed the public discourse so effectively.

The 1990s and early 2000s are not only known by the struggle toward the Civil Code and Penal Code amendments, but also by the start of institutionalization in the area of women's rights (Acuner 2011). The Directorate General on the Status of Women (DGSW) was founded in 1990 to prevent discrimination against women, protect and develop women's human rights, and ensure that women have equal access to rights and opportunities in all walks of social life. The DGSW has functioned under various departments (including the office of the Prime Ministry); in 2011, it was placed under the newly created Ministry of Family and Social Policies. The DGSW has duties within the Parliament. These include both standing (expertise) committees and ad hoc inquiry committees. The standing committees are the Committee on Equal Opportunity for Women and Men, established in 2009, and the Committee on Human Rights Inquiry, established in 1990. Currently, the most active committees are the Parliamentary Committee for Investigating the Factors Threatening the Unity of Families and Divorce Incidents and the Making Recommendations Concerning the Strengthening of the Institution of Family, which was promptly called the "Divorce Committee."

Hülya Gülbahar voiced the prevalent opinion within the women's movement about the key role played by the Divorce Committee, the report of which is perceived as the reflection of the AKP's action plan:

> As women lawyers and activists, we have tried to warn the opposition parties in the parliament to avoid any proposal for legislative amendment or for establishment of a committee . . . The Divorce Committee . . . has presented the government's course of action . . . That report is significant in that it provides an insight into the primary steps to be taken by the government in three main legal texts – Law No. 6284, TCC and TPC – achieved with struggle of 30 years. I'm afraid it's only the beginning.
>
> *(Adalet İçin Hukukçular 2016)*

The report of the Divorce Committee includes various suggestions on many laws. Some of the suggested amendments to the Criminal Code, the Civil Code, and Law No. 6284 on the Prevention of Violence include:

> Children to be married off to their abusers/rapists; promoting juvenile marriage; mediation and reconciliation in both applications of violence and divorce cases; preventing women who were subjected to violence going to the police in the working hours; request for evidence or document for prevention orders given against violence and shortening the term of preventive measure; holding all trials as to the family law in confidentiality; making divorce more difficult; period of limitation for women's right of maintenance; reducing the term of litigation for division of property; in case of death of spouse, 50% share of the wife resulting from property division not to be given; trying to rest psychological counselling services on religious basis.
>
> *(EŞİTİZ 2016)*[39]

The women's organizations made numerous statements against the Committee's report and tried to inform the public about the imminent dangers. The President of the Divorce Committee, AKP Member of Parliament Ayşe Keşir, responded by accusing the women's organizations of forging documents. Women's organizations stated that they rested their claims on the draft report sent by the Committee itself.

The recommendations towards "the marriage of children with their abusers/rapists and encouragement of child/early marriages" suggested in the report, which was initially disavowed by the Divorce Committee, were brought to the agenda through a motion made by some AKP Members of Parliament to amend Article 103 of the Penal Code. This motion proposed amnesty for perpetrators, instigators, and associates of sexual abusers of minors who committed their crime before 16 November 2016. Following the protests of various women's and children's associations (notably the TPC [Turkish Penal Code] 103 Women's Platform), physicians, lawyers, and different sectors of society from across Turkey and the world, the government withdrew the midnight motion of amnesty for sexual abusers.[40] Yet the other amendments to Article 103 were passed. Those amendments may pave the way for seeking consent from the child between twelve and fifteen years of age in the cases of sexual abuse of minors (Arman 2016).

Conclusion

This case study shows that the women's movement in Turkey owes its success in reforming laws on women and family to the various strategies it developed in the course of its struggle and it benefited from a favorable domestic and international environment. An important outcome of this struggle is the movement's impact on public debate on matters related to women's human rights and equality. Every successful campaign brought more legitimacy to the movement, while increasing the movement's leverage against the state.

The most salient strategies women used in their campaigns were situating the movement above political parties and thus forging the solidarity of a diverse coalition; establishing links with international and transnational organizations; tapping the leverage generated and the networks created at the international level to influence the terms of the national public debate; making use of the national network of women at all administrative levels in civil society and of the media; and finally, positioning the movement against the state as a *morally superior* force and not putting the movement in a position to petition to a superior.

Periods of successful reform nevertheless left some pieces of the patriarchal-minded legislation intact, either because certain parts of the law could not be changed due to resistance of the state or because the changes introduced new problems. These loopholes and hooks that patriarchy implanted in pieces of legislation, or managed to keep untouched, were in turn successfully instrumentalized, in politically less fortunate circumstances, to circumvent the level of impact that the egalitarian legislation could have otherwise generated. The lesson to be gathered from this is *the need to approach the legal structure and the implementation processes from a holistic perspective.* Reforming the blatantly inegalitarian articles in the Constitution, or in family law, may not mean much if in that country there is no real hierarchy of norms; unreformed pieces of legislation can be wielded by the practitioners of law to circumvent the constitutional law itself. The law can be divorced from its egalitarian original intent and be subverted to its opposite in the implementation stage or through social policies.

Within a certain international political environment that did not question the validity of gender equality as a norm, within the context of the *acquis* process that was unleashed by the European Union, the state actors had every incentive – particularly between 2001 and 2004 – to agree to reform of gender regime-related laws and regulations.

Yet, since 2010, Turkish politicians have openly stated that "*Women are not and cannot be equal to men; that they should bear five children and not work outside of home.*"[41] Since 2007, bureaucrats of the past era have now been entirely purged from the state, and especially after the 15 July 2016 coup attempt, the last wave of purge has been immense. The new State is now dissolving the structures that are necessary to fight VAW, and is doing so by banning, through executive orders, what was instituted by law.

The women's movement turned itself into a potent democratizing influence and skillfully used the beneficent "window of opportunity" (Tarrow 1996, 1998; McAdam et al. 2001) through 1990s and 2000s to push the state actors to accomplish major reforms in family-related law as well as in the general legal framework.

The heterogeneity of the women's movement was a fact and the success of the women's movement in forging an alliance that was deliberately "above political parties" broadened this heterogeneity. Yet this very success created two separate problems for the women's movement when the state deliberately changed its political will from the norm of gender equality to inequality. First, the rise of the policy of "GONGOization" owes its emergence to the legitimacy generated by the women's movement in the previous decades. Secondly, the heterogeneity began to turn into a liability when the issues of both *ethnicity* and *religion* became very much politicized by the state. Secular, Muslim, Turkish, Kurdish, Sunni, and Alevi identities coexisted side-by-side. The strategy that was keeping them together seems to have been an implicit gag rule on matters of ethnicity and religion. Insofar as this self-imposed gag rule helped diverse groups of women build solidarities on the basis of their common fight against the patriarchy, the women's movement could act in unison.

Yet the tumultuous past decade, or what AKP officials today call the "closing of a 200-year-old parenthesis," shook Turkey's volatile fault lines. As what had previously posed itself as "moderate democratic Islam" reverted to an unconstitutional rule and re-Islamization of a largely secularized society, and simultaneously the stillborn Kurdish "peace process" flared into occupations of towns that were reminiscent of a civil war, the strategies that worked before no longer worked. As one of the participants in the workshop for this study stated, "We need to talk and yet we are afraid to talk to one another fearing we may not be able to ever talk to one another afterwards." The politicization of religion and transformation of the basic structure in accordance with the AKP's understanding of "religion," the failed "peace process," heavy military operations in Kurdish-populated towns, curfews, reports of torture, and the emergency rule[42] that was put in force after July 2016 that resulted in the arrest of Peoples' Democracy Party (HDP) Members of Parliament, the crackdown on civil society, total suppression of the media, arrests of journalists, bans on any kind of political protest, and the mass purges of academics and state employees *politicized everything, while rendering the practice of politics impossible*. This situation muted the Muslim feminists,[43] and circumstantially and through force also the Kurdish feminists, thus reducing the overall women's movement to a purely reactive stance. And KADEM, the GONGO established by Erdoğan's daughter is, at the writing of this report, going on a tour of "Yes" with the President to support the eradication of separation of powers and the institution of a totally arbitrary state.

Thus, the circumstances are now completely transformed and women are finding themselves in tremendously changed domestic and international circumstances. As the AKP turns itself into a party-state, it seems no longer possible for the movement to stand "above all political parties." The larger women's movement is also not ready to formulate an overtly anti-AKP stance, and, in any event, all means of expressing dissent are prohibited. Taking to the streets would now surely result in death at the hands of the security forces. Given the new constraints imposed by the context of the new Turkey, the movement will have to find new strategies to tackle the challenges it faces.

Notes

1 On the inconsistency of the various criticisms leveled against Turkey on secularism, see Somer 2013. It must be noted that referring to Turkey a "Muslim democracy" owes its frequent use to the political Islamists' claim that they are "both Muslim and democrats." Unfortunately, political Islam shed its claim to democracy once it consolidated coercive power in its cadres.
2 On diversity and uneven development in Turkey, see Acar 2010.

3 "In universities one in every four professors is a woman, while almost one out of every four women is illiterate. Similarly, while the number of women working in professional fields such as law, medicine, and academy approaches 40 percent; 39 percent of all women participating in the labour force are unpaid family labour; and the 19.9 percent female labour participation in urban settings is tremendously low to make it impossible to compare it to any Western society" (Acar 2010: 15).

4 The most critical among the Copenhagen criteria is the admissibility condition, which requires a candidate country to ensure the "stability of institutions guaranteeing democracy, the rule of law, human rights and protection of minorities."

5 On religious nationalism, see Juergensmeyer 1993.

6 In 1980, a *coup d'état* took place in Turkey, and civil society could only flourish towards the end of the 1980s, when the political situation in the country began to normalize.

7 Here we especially refer to the interviews the authors of this report conducted with Hülya Gülbahar, a lawyer and prominent women activist, and her views about the trajectory of the equality norm.

8 The survey conducted by Adil Gür in 2015 on a sample of 2,083 women in 116 villages of 26 provinces is unpublished. We have obtained a copy of the survey results (Gür 2015) through correspondence with the researcher.

9 In 2009, the World Bank published a report specifically on the decrease in the female LFP levels in Turkey. While Turkey has experienced important structural and social changes that would be expected to facilitate female LFP, "Female LFP in Turkey is low by international standards and has been decreasing (from 34.3 percent in 1988 to 21.6 percent in 2008). In the 1980s, Turkey enjoyed levels of female LFP that were similar to those of more developed countries, such as Austria, the Netherlands, and Switzerland, induced by the high participation of women in agricultural activities. OECD countries that displayed a similar rate in the 1980s experienced further increases in female participation, while an opposite trend is visible in Turkey. By 2006, Turkey displayed lower levels of female LFP than a number of *Islamic countries of comparable size and level of development* (Figure ES.1)" (World Bank 2009: ii; emphasis added).

10 Similar levels of decrease in female LFP in southern European countries during rapid urbanization processes have been accompanied by an investment in women's education and resulted in higher levels of female LFP, as educated women join the labor force within a decade. In Turkey, however, this is not the case.

11 On the regressive turn, see the interview with the prominent Turkish feminist Şirin Tekeli by Yazıcıoğlu (Tekeli 2016).

12 "Turkey permanently closes hundreds of NGOs – Amnesty International," https://www.amnesty.org/download/Documents/EUR4452082016ENGLISH.pdf.

13 Two of the nine women selected for the interviews (Zozan Özgökçe and Fatma Bostan Ünsal) could not respond due to the purges, arrests, and the state of emergency. Zozan Özgökçe was detained and then released, but the NGO where she had been working for many years was closed down by a recent executive order. Fatma Bostan Ünsal is a Muslim woman and a purged academic, a member of Academics for Peace. Although we also could not interview Canan Arın, she did attend the workshop, where she shared her views. Those interviewed include: Hülya Gülbahar, Selma Acuner, Nazan Moroğlu, İlknur Yüksel, Ayşe Sucu, Açelya Uçan, and Meltem Ağduk.

14 Quoted in Bowen et al. 2015: 659.

15 Ibid.

16 "Positive law" refers to promulgated laws.

17 "Customary law" refers to traditional unwritten rules or practices that have become an intrinsic part of the accepted and expected conduct in a community.

18 "Normativity" refers to society's designating some actions as good or permissible and others as bad or impermissible.

19 "*Nomos*" refers not only to formal laws but to the rules, customs, and traditions people take for granted in their daily activities.

20 Also see Tekeli 1990: 11.

21 There have also been some – limited – changes that have shaped family law to become more open to contractual relations as well, such as prenuptial agreements.

22 On 16 April 2017, a referendum was held to vote for an eighteen-article amendment to the Constitution to transform the political system from a parliamentary one to an executive presidency. It is still a mystery how, having lost all major cities, the AKP still declared itself the winner.

23 Ayşe Sucu, a theologian, argues that "*fitrat*" simply means "human nature" and it does not refer to hierarchical distinctions among human beings – that men and women and every member of the human species share the same "*fitrat*" or nature. Yet the recent and more Salafist interpretations of "*fitrat*," such as the "justice" concept propagated by the state-affiliated Kadın ve Demokrasi Derneği (Women and Democracy Association – KADEM), employ the term "*fitrat*" to refer to the "inferior nature of women." According to this conception, "justice means giving women their due," that their due is not merely different from men's, but is also hierarchically inferior and cannot be equal.

24 In liberal democratic constitutionalism, a principle of the hierarchy of norms is adopted to establish a ranking of legal norms. In accordance with this principle, a legal norm having an inferior authority cannot violate a norm of superior authority. In Turkey, the Constitution is supposed to be in the top rank in the hierarchy of norms. International agreements on fundamental rights and freedoms are superior to the Constitution, in accordance with Article 90 of the Turkish Constitution amended in 2004.

25 In the following years, women continued to demand the implementation of CEDAW and also to secure de facto equality.

26 The women's movement did not only fight for equality and against violence, but also for various other issues. For example, "Women in Black" were arrested in 1989 for protesting the F-type prisons (Gülbahar and Çakır 1999: 249). (F-type prisons are high-security ones containing cells that house one to three inmates. They are used for the detention of political prisoners or those who have received aggravated life sentences. These institutions limit communication among inmates and are based on a strict isolation rule.) At the end of the 1980s, women were in the front line of protests against fossil fuel-based thermal power plants and gold mines (Gülbahar and Çakır 1999: 251).

27 Article 438 of the (former) Penal Code provided a one-third reduction in punishment given to the perpetrator if the rape victim was working as a "prostitute."

28 According to CEDAW Art. 18, States Parties are under obligation to submit periodic reports to the UN CEDAW Committee on the measures adopted by their countries.

29 Women for Women's Human Rights – New Ways, International Advocacy, http://www. wwhr.org/international-advocacy/.

30 Shadow NGO Report on Turkey's Sixth Periodic Report, available at http://tbinternet. ohchr.org/Treaties/CEDAW/Shared%20Documents/TUR/INT_CEDAW_NGO_TUR_46_10193_E.pdf.

31 The shortcomings of those proposed amendments to the Constitution were also known by the state: "Despite the fact that the equality between women and men is ensured by the Constitution, the actual legislative norms do not always allow for real equality . . . [For this reason] the insertion of the following clause is proposed: Women and men have equal rights. The state takes all necessary measures to provide gender equality, including special temporary measures": The Fourth and Fifth Combined Periodic Report of Turkey, available at https://kadininstatusu.aile.gov.tr/uploads/pages/cedaw-ulke-rapor-lari/the-fourth-and-fifth-combined-periodic-report-of-turkey.pdf.

32 Feride Acar, the chairwoman of the Istanbul Convention monitoring mechanism (GREVIO), is the key figure in facilitating the participation of the women's movement in the preparatory works of the Istanbul Convention.

33 Feride Acar was a member of CEDAW Committee – Chair (2003–05),Vice Chair (2001–03), Rapporteur (1999–01) – and Turkish Representative to the Ad Hoc Committee on preventing and combating violence against women and domestic violence (CAHVIO) (2009-2010), and President of GREVIO (since 2015).Yakın Ertürk was the second UN Special Rapporteur on Violence against Women, Its Causes and Consequences (2003–09) as well as holder of other international human rights mandates.
34 Adalet İçin Hukukçular (Legal Experts for Justice) (2016).
35 Ayşenur İslam was in office between 25 December 2013 and 28 August 2015.
36 The Platform's candidates were Canan Arın, Feride Acar, Hülya Gülbahar, Pınar İlkkaracan, Şehnaz Kıymaz, and Yakın Ertürk.
37 A number of applications were made to the European Court of Human Rights (ECHR) on this article. The Court found violations by Turkey and concluded that the relevant article needed to be changed (e.g., *Ünal Tekeli v. Turkey*, Application no. 29865/96 and *Leventoğlu Abdulkadiroğlu v. Turkey*, Application no. 7971/07).
38 Property regime is not retrospective, it does not apply to marriages before 1 January 2002. Women's organizations have worked towards its amendment, but to no avail.
39 Also see Women's Labor and Employment Initiative 2016 and Women for Women's Human Rights – New Ways 2016.
40 For the statements of the TPC 103 Women's Platform in this regard, see TPC (Turkish Penal Code) 103 Women's Platform 2016a, 2016b, and 2016c.
41 See soL 2010; TÜSEV 2012; and Özkan-Kerestecioğlu 2014: 17.
42 The State of Emergency was declared in the immediate aftermath of the failed coup attempt of 15 July 2016.
43 There are significant exceptions, such as Ayşe Sucu, Berrin Sönmez, and Fatma Ünsal, who continue to publish highly critical editorials. But the media is so suppressed that these find expression only in minor newspapers and in Internet-based websites that are followed by like-minded individuals.

References

Acar, Feride (2010) "Türkiye'de Kadınların İnsan Hakları: Uluslararası Standartlar, Hukuk ve Sivil Toplum" (Women's Human Rights in Turkey: International Standards, Law and Civil Society) in Gökçeçiçek Ayata, Sevinç Eryılmaz, and Bertil Emrah Oder (eds.), *Kadın Hakları: Uluslararası Hukuk ve Uygulama* (*Women's Rights: International Law and Practice*), Human Rights Law Studies, Istanbul: İstanbul Bilgi University Press.

Acuner, Selma (2011) "90'lı Yıllar ve Resmi Düzeyde Kurumsallaşmanın Doğuş Aşamaları" (The 90s Years and the Start of Official Institutionalization), in Aksu Bora and Asena Günal (eds.), *90'larda Türkiye'de Feminizm* (*Feminism in Turkey in the 90s*), İstanbul: İletişim Publishing: 125–159.

Adalet İçin Hukukçular (Legal Experts for Justice) (2016) "Av. Hülya Gülbahar: Boşanma Komisyonu Raporu 30 yıllık mücadele ile kazanılmış haklarımızı gasp ediyor," (Lawyer Hülya Gülbahar: Divorce Committee's Report is Hijacking the Rights We Have Won Through 30 Years of Struggle) in *Adalet İçin Hukukçular* (*Legal Experts for Justice*), 27 June 2016.

Altınay, Ayse Gül and Yesim Arat (2009), *Violence Against Women in Turkey: A Nationwide Survey*, İstanbul: Punto.

Anıl, Ela, Canan Arın, Ayşe Berktay-Hacımirzaoğlu, Mehveş Bingöllü, and Pınar İlkkaracan (2002) *The New Legal Status of Women in Turkey*, Istanbul: WWHR-NEW WAYS, Art Press.

———, Canan Arın, Ayşe Berktay-Hacımirzaoğlu, Mehveş Bingöllü, Pınar İlkkaracan, and Liz Erçevik-Amado (2005) *Turkish Civil and Penal Code Reforms from a Gender Perspective: The Success of Two Nation-Wide Campaigns*, Istanbul: WWHR-NEW WAYS, Euromat.

Arman, Ayşe (2016) Gökçeçiçek Ayata interview "Sevinelim mi, Sevinmeyelim mi?" (Shall We Rejoice? Or Not?) in *Hürriyet*, 23 November 2016; www.hurriyet.com.tr/yazarlar/ayse-arman/suc-yok-ama-orgut-uyeligi-var-40286716.

Armutçu, Emel (2014) "Aile Bakanlığı, aile içindeki kadını görebilecek mi?" (Would the Ministry of Family Be Able to See the Individual Woman Existing Within the Family?) in *Hürriyet*, 20 December 2014; www.hurriyet.com.tr/aile-bakanligi-aile-icindeki-kadini-gorebilecek-mi-36322091.

Balkan, Neşecan and Sungur Savran (2002) (eds.) *The Ravages of Neo-Liberalism: Economy, Society and Gender in Turkey*, New York: Nova Science Publishers.

Bowen, Donna L., Valerie M. Hudson, and Perpetua L. Nielsen (2015) "State Fragility and Structural Gender Inequality in Family Law: An Empirical Investigation," *Laws*, 4: 654–672.

Çakır, Serpil (1994, revised and expanded in 2011), *Osmanlı Kadın Hareketi* (*The Ottoman Women's Movement*), İstanbul: Metis Publishing.

Candaş, Ayşen (2008) "Is 'Muslim' Democracy Synonymous with 'Constitutional' Democracy?" in *ResetDOC: Dialogues on Civilizations*, 30 October 2008, www.resetdoc.org/story/is-muslim-democracy-synonymous-with-constitutional-democracy/.

——— and Yıldız Silier (2014) "Quietly Reverting Public Matters into Private Troubles: Gendered and Class-Based Consequences of Care Policies in Turkey," *Social Politics: International Studies in Gender, State & Society*, Vol. 21, No. 1: 103–123.

Coşar, Simten and Metin Yeğenoğlu (2011) "New Grounds for Patriarchy in Turkey? Gender Policy in the Age of AKP," *South European Society and Politics*, Vol. 16, No. 4: 555–573.

Crenshaw, Kimberle (1991) "Mapping the Margins: Intersectionality, Identity Politics, and Violence against Women of Color," *Stanford Law Review*, Vol. 43, No. 6: 1241–1299.

Dedeoğlu, Saniye (2012) "Equality, Protection and Discrimination: Gender Equality Policies in Turkey, Social Politics: International Studies in Gender," *State and Society*, Vol. 19, No. 2: 269–290.

Ertürk, Yakın (2016a) *Violence without Borders: Paradigm, Policy and Praxis Concerning Violence against Women, Women's Learning Partnership Translation Series*, Bethesda, MD: Women's Learning Partnership.

EŞİTİZ – Equality Monitoring Women's Group (2016) "Farkında mıyız? Kadın ve Çocuk Hakları, TBMM Boşanma Komisyonu Aracılığıyla Gasp Edilmeye Çalışılıyor!" ("Are We Aware? The Grand National Assembly's Divorce Committee is Trying to Highjack Women's and Children's Rights") press release on 16 May 2016, on the Report of Divorce Committee, in Women's Labor and Employment Initiative 2016; www.keig.org/wp-content/uploads/2016/05/TBMM-Bo%C5%9Fanma-Komisyonu-Fark%C4%B1nda-m%C4%B1y%C4%B1z.docx.

Eslen-Ziya, Hande (2012) "Türk Ceza Kanunu Değişiminde Kadın Aktivistler: Bir Lobicilik Hikayesi" (Female Activists Playing Role in Amendments to Turkish Penal Code: A Lobby Story), *Journal of Sociological Research*, Vol. 15, No. 1, Spring 2012: 120–149.

Gülbahar, Hülya and Serpil Çakır (1999) "Türkiye'de Kadın Hareketinin Yüz Yılı Kronolojisi" ("Centenary Chronology of Women's Movement in Turkey"), *Türkiye'de Kadın Hareketi'nin Yüzyılı Ajandası – 2000 Ajandası* (*A Century of the Women's Movement in Turkey – 2000 Agenda*), İstanbul: Women's Library and Information Center Foundation Publication, No. 17.

Gür, Adil (2015) "Survey on Women," A&G Survey Research Company.

Habermas, Jurgen (1996 [1992]) *Between Facts and Norms: Contributions to a Discourse Theory of Law and Democracy*, Cambridge: The MIT Press.

——— (2001) "Constitutional Democracy: A Paradoxical Union of Contradictory Principles?" *Political Theory*, Vol. 29: 766–781.

İlkkaracan, Pınar (2007) *Re/Forming the Penal Code in Turkey from a Gender Perspective: The Case of a Successful Campaign*, İstanbul: Women for Women's Human Rights – New Ways.

İlkkaracan, Pınar and Liz Erçevik-Amado (2008) "Good Practices in Legislation on Violence against Women in Turkey and Problems of Implementation," *Expert Paper for Expert Group Meeting on Good Practices in Legislation on Violence against Women United Nations Office at Vienna*, Austria, 26–28 May 2008, EGM/GPLVAW/2008/EP.13.

İlkkaracan-Ajas, İpek, Kijonk Kim, and Tolga Kaya (2015) *The Impact of Public Investment in Social Care Services on Employment, Gender Equality, and Poverty: The Turkish Case*, Research Project Report, Levy Economics Institute of Bard College.

Juergensmeyer, Mark (1993) *The New Cold War? Religious Nationalism Confronts the Secular State, Comparative Studies in Religion and Society*, Berkeley, CA: University of California Press.

Kandiyoti, Deniz (2015) "The Gender Wars in Turkey: A Litmus Test of Democracy?," *Open Democracy*, 30 March 2015; www.opendemocracy.net/5050/deniz-kandiyoti/gender-wars-in-turkey-litmus-test-of-democracy.

McAdam, Doug, Sidney Tarrow, and Charles Tilly (2001) *Dynamics of Contention*, Cambridge: Cambridge University Press.

Özkan-Kerestecioğlu, İnci (2014) "Mahremiyetin Fethi: İdeal Aile Kurgularından İdeal Aile Politikalarına" ("The Conquest of Privacy: From Ideal Family Constructs to Ideal Family Policies"), *Başka Bir Aile Anlayışı Mümkün mü? (Is A Different Family Concept Possible?)*, İstanbul: Heinrich Böll Stiftung Foundation Turkey Office: 17; https://tr.boell.org/sites/default/files/baska_bir_aile_anlayisi_mumkun_mu.pdf.

Rawls, John (1993) *Political Liberalism*, New York: Columbia University Press.

Savran, Gülnur (2008) "SSGSS, Görünmeyen Emek ve Feminist Politika" (SSGHI, Invisible Labour and Feminist Politics), *Amargi*, Vol. 8: 16–19.

Serozan, Rona, Başak Başoğlu, and Berk Kapancı (2016) "Aile Hukukunun Özellikleri İlkeleri ve Gelişimi" (Characteristics, Principles and Development of Family Law), *Istanbul Kültür University Journal of Law Faculty*, Vol. 15, No. 2: 531–560.

soL (2010) "Erdoğan'la açılım buraya kadar: Kadın ve erkek eşit olamaz" ("The Limit of Democratization with Erdogan: Woman and Man Cannot Be Equal") in soL, 20 July 2010; http://haber.sol.org.tr/devlet-ve-siyaset/erdogan-la-acilim-buraya-kadar-kadin-ve-erkek-esit-olamaz-haberi-31112.

Tarrow, Sidney (1996) "States and Opportunities: The Political Structuring of Social Movements," in Doug McAdam, John D. McCarthy, and Mayer N. Zaid (eds.), *Comparative Perspectives on Social Movements*, Cambridge Studies in Social Movements. Cambridge: Cambridge University Press: 41–61.

———— (1998) *Power in Movement: Social Movements and Contentious Politics*, 2nd ed. Cambridge: Cambridge University Press.

TCK Kadın Çalışma Grubu (Women Working Group for the TCP) (2003) *Kadın Bakış Açısından Türk Ceza Kanunu: TCK Tasarısı Değişiklik Talepleri (Turkish Penal Code from the Perspective of Women: Draft TPC Amendment Proposals)*, İstanbul: Women for Women's Human Rights – New Ways.

Tekeli, Şirin (1990) "1980'ler Türkiyesi'nde (sic) Kadınlar" ("Women in Turkey in the 1980s"), in Tekeli Şirin (ed.), *Kadın Bakış Açısından 1980'ler Türkiye'sinde Kadın (Women in Turkey in the 1980s from a Woman's Perspective)*, İstanbul: İletişim Publishing: 7–41.

TPC (Turkish Penal Code) 103 Women's Platform (2016a) "Kadın Örgütlerinden Çağrı: Çocukların tecavüzcülerle, istismarcılarla evlendirilmelerine ilişkin AKP önergesi derhal geri çekilmelidir!" ("Call from Women's Organizations: AKP's Law Proposal Legalizing the Marriage of Children with Their Rapists and Abusers Should Be Immediately Withdrawn!") press release on TPC 103 in Women for Women's Human Rights – New Ways, 18 November 2016; www.kadinininsanhaklari.org/tecavuzmesrulastirilamaz/.

———— (2016b) "Çocuk İstismarı Yasa Taslağı ve Önergesine İtiraz Ediyoruz!" ("We Object to the Child Abuse Law Draft and Proposal!") press release on TPC 103 in Women for Women's Human Rights – New Ways, 21 November 2016; www.kadinininsanhaklari. org/itirazediyoruz/.

———— (2016c) "Yeni Onaylanan TCK 103 Düzenlemesi Uygulamada," ("Recently Passed TPC (Turkish Penal Code) Regulation is Put Into Practice") press release on TPC 103 in Women for Women's Human Rights – New Ways, 25 November 2016; www. kadinininsanhaklari.org/tck103kadin/.

TÜSEV (2012) *Civil Society Monitoring Report 2012 – Case Analysis: Benim Bedenim Benim Kararım (My Body My Decision)* and *Kürtaj Yasaklanamaz (Abortion Cannot Be Banned)*; www.tusev.org.tr/usrfiles/images/BenimBedenimVakaAnaliziENG.06.11.13.pdf.

World Bank (2009) "Female Labor Force Participation in Turkey: Trends, Determinants, and Policy Framework," Report No 48508-TR.

Women for Women's Human Rights – New Ways (2016) "Kadın ve Çocuk hakları, TBMM Boşanma Komisyonu aracılığıyla gasp edilmeye çalışılıyor," ("The Grand National Assembly's Divorce Committee is Trying to Highjack Women's and Children's Rights") in Women for Women's Human Rights – New Ways, 17 May 2016; www. kadinininsanhaklari.org/bosanmakomisyonu/.

Women's Labor and Employment Initiative (2016) "Kadın örgütlerinden TBMM Boşanma Komisyonu Raporu'na tepki yağıyor!" ("Women's Organizations Express Their Protest of the Grand National Assembly's Divorce Committee Report!") in Women's Labor and Employment Initiative; www.keig.org/?p=3230.

PART II

Interviews

INTRODUCTION TO THE INTERVIEWS WITH LEADERS IN THE EGYPTIAN, JORDANIAN, AND MOROCCAN CAMPAIGNS TO REFORM FAMILY LAWS AND ELIMINATE GENDER-BASED VIOLENCE

Haleh Vaziri

Activists have enjoyed varying degrees of success in their efforts to reform personal status codes toward gender equality for Arab women. In three wide-ranging interviews,[1] leaders of reform campaigns in Egypt, Jordan, and Morocco – Hoda Elsadda, Asma Khader, and Rabéa Naciri – recount their experiences working to advocate for women's rights, to change retrograde family laws, and to eliminate gender-based discrimination in their societies. Although these women approach issues of human rights and gender equality from different professional and disciplinary perspectives, they have all worked within civil society as activists, in academia as scholars, and in government as policymakers.

Dr. Hoda Elsadda is Professor of English and Comparative Literature at Cairo University and co-founder of the Women and Memory Forum (WMF), an Egyptian research organization producing knowledge about gender in Arab cultural history. She was a member of the committee that drafted Egypt's Constitution endorsed by the 2014 referendum and the coordinator of the Freedom and Rights Committee.

Asma Khader is Executive Director of the Sisterhood Is Global Institute-Jordan (SIGI/J)[2] and the foremost human rights lawyer in her country. She recently served as one of three official investigators for the UN Human Rights Council's inquiry into abuses during the Libyan conflict. She was appointed to the Senate in October 2013 and elected as Deputy Chief Commissioner by Jordan's Independent Elections Commission in May 2014. Previously, she served as the Minister of Culture for the Hashemite Kingdom and as the President of the Jordanian Women's Union.

Rabéa Naciri is a founding member of the Association Démocratique des Femmes du Maroc (ADFM),[3] one of the largest Moroccan non-governmental organizations focused on women's rights advocacy, and a member of the National Human Rights

Council of Morocco. She is the former Executive Director of the Collectif 95 Maghreb Egalité, a network of women's associations and researchers from Algeria, Morocco, and Tunisia dedicated to preventing gender-based violence.

In their interviews, these three women identify the cultural sources of discriminatory family laws and discuss strategies for grassroots mobilization, advocacy, and policy-making. They also consider the impact of the Arab Spring uprisings and the international human rights discourse on their campaigns to reform family laws, while reflecting on lessons learned during their quest for gender equality.

Notes

1 Hoda Elsadda resides in Cairo and was interviewed through a series of e-mail exchanges; she also completed a detailed questionnaire in November 2017. Asma Khader, based in Amman, was interviewed via telephone on 9 September 2017. Rabéa Naciri lives in Rabat where she was interviewed on 10 December 2017; the interview was conducted in French, and the transcript has been translated into English.
2 Sisterhood Is Global Institute-Jordan (SIGI/J) is WLP's partner organization in Jordan.
3 Association Démocratique des Femmes du Maroc (ADFM) is WLP's partner organization in Morocco.

11

INTERVIEW WITH HODA ELSADDA

When and how did you become engaged in activism for women's human rights in Egypt? What factors – ideas and experiences – have inspired your activism?

My awareness of women's rights issues came as a result of my reading of Arab women's literary narratives. It was not a consequence of personal experience of discrimination as a child or as a young adult, as I was lucky to belong to a supportive and loving family that was also enlightened and progressive. As a teenager, I was an avid reader of fiction in every shape and form: romantic stories, detective stories, biographies, realistic fiction. I was gradually drawn to reading about women's experiences as they interacted with the world, and I came to know of the many struggles and challenges facing them. My consciousness was shaped by Arab and English feminist writers, such as novelist Latifa Elzayyat, who defied societal norms and fought for equality and recognition. Their experiences and insights enabled me to encounter the world outside the prism of my own experience, or beyond the protective circle in which I existed. I chose to study English and comparative literature as an undergraduate and then graduate, and my readings were supplemented with theoretical insights from feminist and post-colonial studies. I acknowledge the influence of Edward Said, whose book *Orientalism* foregrounded the politics of representation, a key issue in feminist theory. He drew attention to the feminization of the colonized and to the significance of this act of discursive violence. I became aware of the power of gendered discourses in perpetuating and maintaining the subordination of the "other" or the "marginalized" or the "weaker link" in society, including women. This introduction to the politics of representation became instrumental to my understanding of, and engagement with, norms, traditions, and ideas that have historically imprisoned women and limited their potential.

When and how did you become involved in efforts to reform Egyptian family law? What factors – ideas and experiences – have motivated your efforts?

In the early nineties, I co-founded a women's studies journal in Arabic called *Hagar*, with the aim of reading and writing Arab cultural history from the women's perspective, or to use current terminology, reading Arab cultural history through a gender lens. My motivation at the time was to encourage the inquiry into Arab and Islamic cultural history to challenge stereotypical representations about the assumed historical victimhood of Arab and Muslim women and to foreground women's agency and power. With this in mind, in 1993, I joined a task force of women's rights activists who worked on revising the marriage certificate template in Egypt. Marriage in Islam is a contractual agreement between two adults that allows for the inclusion of stipulations or conditions that either of the two parties deem important for the future success of the agreement. These stipulations can circumvent or revise the more codified rules that regulate marriage, which vary of course from one country to another and also from one century to another. In Egypt, just to give a brief example, according to Personal Status Law (PSL), a husband enjoys a unilateral right to divorce his wife and is allowed to take a second wife. Throughout Islamic history, women have used the contractual nature of the marriage contract to include conditions to balance power relations in their marriage. Among other things, women have included in their marriage contracts conditions that allow them to divorce their husbands and to restrict the husbands' right to take a second wife. Conditions from earlier periods also included the right to continue to participate in and host literary salons and the right to divorce the husband should he be absent for a period of three months, conditions that reflect social concerns of the time. In the 1990s, the existing marriage contract template issued by the State did not allow for the inclusion of these conditions, and women were discouraged by custom and by state officials from practicing this right.

This project was part of the preparations for the NGO forum of the International Conference on Population and Development that was held in Egypt in 1994. The choice of this particular focus on revising the marriage contract was prompted by a number of considerations. First, there was agreement that the PSL in Egypt was discriminatory, did not do justice to women, and required serious revisions. Second, there was also agreement, based on previous experience, that an attempt to challenge all the discriminatory aspects of the PSL at this historical juncture and in an international conference would not achieve concrete legal gains and would open the gates to violent vilification campaigns against women's rights activists and rights agendas in general, with the usual accusations that rights claims were Westernized, did not represent "our" cultural specificity, and so forth. While these campaigns are not new, and women's rights activists have come to expect them and deal with them in various ways, the agreement was that they were going to be particularly vicious and destructive because of the international attention that the conference was bound to bring to Egypt. Hence the decision was to address the various issues in the PSL in seminars and workshops, but to focus on campaigning to change the marriage contract by lobbying interest groups and organizing tours and discussions all over Egypt to disseminate the project and explain its aims and justifications – i.e., to raise consciousness and mobilize support.

The campaign was an eye-opening experience on more than one level. As we went around the country talking to women, explaining the aim of the campaign, listening to women's views and experiences, two things became very clear. First, there was a knowledge vacuum that needed to be filled, knowledge that empowered women in their struggle. The initial skeptical response to the idea of inserting conditions in the marriage contract was reversed completely once women were informed of the historical precedence since the time of the Prophet. Listening to stories of Muslim women who defied patriarchy and who imposed their will was liberating for many women as it allowed them to question and refute dominant ideas about the unsuitability of rights discourses to their culture. For much too long, patriarchal interpretations of Muslim cultural history have been dominant to the extent that men became the custodians of what culture means and how to define it. I was convinced that this patriarchal domination of "culture" had to be broken by feminist revisions and interpretations of Arab and Muslim culture. Second, despite the fact that the campaign to change the marriage contract was conducted from within an Islamic framework, and with constant references to precedence in Islamic cultural history, there was still a vicious campaign of slander and vilification against the project and the women activists. Hence, the struggle for women's rights cannot be limited to the production of alternative knowledge that empowers, nor can we assume that information as such will transform the power balance: the work of academics and researchers is crucial but not sufficient. The struggle is also about power and authority: who has the power to make which narrative dominant? Who controls the podiums and the media? What does it take to make feminist narratives and points of view mainstream? The power question continues to be a challenge and a key factor in deciphering the dynamics of struggle and change.

How would you characterize the status of Egypt's women in relation to family law? How do specific aspects of the personal status laws affect their lives in the home and in the wider public arena?

In 1956, women in Egypt were granted political and economic rights, but the PSL was kept intact, hence creating an anomalous situation whereby women enjoyed rights of citizenship in the public sphere, but remained subject to the male members of their families in the private sphere. There have been important changes in the PSL since, but the reality remains that women do not enjoy equal citizenship rights. Among the key issues is their unequal ability to end the marriage, despite a modification in 2000 which enabled women to divorce themselves on the basis of *khul'*, a form of divorce that gives women a way out of unsatisfactory relationships, provided that they forfeit their financial rights to alimony or compensation.

The second issue concerns the guardianship of children. Women are only granted guardianship under very strict conditions, and generally male members of the family take priority. This is the case even if the children are in the custody of their mother, hence complicating the mother's everyday life unnecessarily.

What, for you, is the most urgent problem related to family law that affects Egyptian women's status? What aspects of family law do you think are most important to change, and why?

In an article about women's rights in Egypt, I described the efforts to modify the PSL as "a defining hallmark of women's rights activism." This has been the case since the early twentieth century and the struggle of early feminists such as Malak Hifni Nasif (1886–1918) and Hoda Shaarawy (1879–1947). The 1960s saw the appointment of women to leadership positions, but again their potential was circumscribed by the PSL.

In 1974, a popular film, *Urid halan* (*I Want a Solution*), highlighted the discrepancy between a woman's status in the public sphere in comparison with her status in the private sphere. It was based on a true story of a woman who suffered from the discriminatory and unjust nature of the PSL that rendered women prey to abusive relationships. Several initiatives emerged and produced proposals for the modification of the PSL. One of the proposals was championed by Aisha Ratib, Professor of Law at Cairo University and Minister of Social Affairs between 1971 and 1977. The second proposal was presented by the Family Planning Association in Cairo led by Aziza Hussein, a prominent women's rights activist. The timing of these efforts coincided with the first UN Women's Conference in Mexico in 1975 and gained momentum from the international solidarity campaigns and the interest of the Egyptian state to be an active participant in international bodies. Both proposals were subjected to vilification and slander on the grounds of their dissociation from culture and the needs of "authentic" Egyptian women. However, in 1979, Law 44 was passed and drew on some of the proposals presented in the above-mentioned initiatives. The Law introduced very minor reforms to the PSL to protect women from well-documented abuses of the system, particularly the consequences of polygamy, and the social and financial problems faced by women after divorce. Despite the very minor changes introduced by Law 44, it was seen to challenge patriarchal domination and was met with hostility in many quarters. In 1984, Law 44 was declared unconstitutional on procedural grounds, as indeed it was in that respect. In 1985, women's rights activists seized the opportunity to convene the UN conference in Nairobi to lobby for another change in the law, but compromises were made with the conservative segments in society. Starting in 2000, important modifications to the PSL were implemented that improved the conditions of women's access to the legal system, enabled women to obtain a divorce (*khul'*), and facilitated the circumstances of child custody. However, the Egyptian PSL remains patriarchal and not conducive to gender justice.

What are the strategies and tactics that you and other women's human rights activists in Egypt have employed in your efforts to reform family law?

In 1995, a group of academics and activists came together and established the Women and Memory Forum (WMF). Our aim was stated as the production of alternative knowledge in the field of women and gender studies that would challenge dominant stereotypical discourses about women and would potentially empower women and women's rights activists in their struggle for gender justice. WMF was an intellectual and activist project: we believed that the production of feminist knowledge, with specialized research in history, culture, society, law, economics, politics, etc. from a gender lens, constituted the backbone of a strong women's rights movement. As co-founder of the WMF, I carried with me the experience and lessons learnt from my participation in the 1993 campaign to change the template of the marriage contract, where culture and cultural history were key factors in the struggle to raise consciousness and awareness of the importance of introducing the proposed changes to the template. I was convinced that as feminist scholars and activists we should not allow our conservative adversaries to control and manipulate the meaning of culture and that the cultural battle was, and continues to be, at the forefront of women's struggle for justice. Furthermore, and on account of our very complicated and contested history with state feminism in Egypt, where the new nation state endorsed some important legislation that empowered women in the public sphere but its record of manipulation of women's rights issues for political gain undermined women's rights activists' efforts and status in society, we should therefore position ourselves in two interlinked struggles: as agents of change in the battle over gender justice and as agents of change in the battle over democracy and good governance. We should also position ourselves as participants in feminist transnational movements for equality and gender justice.

How we do this and which issues we choose to address and highlight are guided by the expertise in place at the WMF (we are primarily a research group), by our engagement with women's groups actively involved in day-to-day activism, and by the political and social developments in local, regional, and international contexts. Over the course of more than twenty years, we have undertaken many projects: republishing women's forgotten work; creating an oral history archive of women; rewriting folktales from a gender-sensitive perspective; conducting specialized educational workshops to introduce gender theories and approaches to students and activists; revisiting/revising key moments in Arab cultural history from a gender-sensitive perspective; establishing a library and documentation resource center that houses material in Arabic in the field of women and gender studies; and curating exhibitions focusing on women as agents of change (see www.wmf.org.eg).

To go back to the question about work directly focused on reforming family law, we consider that the WMF's research agenda is key to the reformation project, since many of our projects engage with cultural and historical representations that impact directly on cultural attitudes and values regarding the PSL.

Which strategies and tactics have proven most successful for activists? What kinds of obstacles and resistance have you and other activists encountered as you strive to reform family law? How have the events surrounding the "Arab Spring" uprisings affected efforts to reform family law in Egypt?

As noted above, obstacles and resistance to activists' efforts to reform the PSL have traditionally been relegated to cultural factors, the hold of tradition, and the role of religious gate-keepers. One important factor that needs to be highlighted is why these traditional forces have succeeded in dominating the public sphere. Briefly, we need to address the failure of the nation state in delivering on its promises of development and prosperity to the majority of the population; the authoritarian nature of the Egyptian state and its closing-down of political spaces in the face of all social movements, including the women's movement, which had begun to gain momentum in the first half of the twentieth century; the manipulation of social issues, such as women's issues, for political gain; and the ambivalence/complicit role of the ruling elite in institutionalizing and sustaining the role of religion in politics. Against this background, the wave of revolutions that swept the Arab world in 2011 opened up political spaces, although for a short while, that allowed various social actors to interact in public in an unprecedented fashion. These new available spaces for engagement made room for a multiplicity of voices and forces: the good and the bad, the progressive and the conservative, the pro-democracy and the anti-democracy, etc. It was a moment when taboos were broken and real-life issues and political concerns were out in the open. It enabled feminists to mobilize and voice their demands in clear unambiguous terms, and at the same time, enabled conservatives to vent their misogynist views and anti-women sentiments more viciously and on many platforms.

In many ways, the 2012 Egyptian Constitution reflected this rising tide of animosity towards women's rights, as espoused by feminists in Egypt. It was written by a constitutional assembly dominated by an Islamist majority, and in the context of a Shura council dominated by Islamists and a president who was a member of the Muslim Brotherhood. Among other things, the Constitution did not include an article that states that men and women are equal. Feminists and pro-democracy activists regarded this as a serious regression on the previous Constitution and a prelude for more restrictions on women and their rights.

The removal of Morsi from the presidency and the termination of the Islamists' rule in the aftermath of another wave of popular uprisings on 30 June 2013 resulted in another modification of the Constitution, and new constitutional text was endorsed in January 2014. The committee of fifty members appointed to draft a new Constitution consisted of a wide range of representatives of state institutions and social and political figures – experts, in other words, representatives of important, though not all, sectors and forces in society. The committee included five women: three women with a history of feminist activism and one academic and one development expert, both supportive of women's rights agendas. The committee also included pro-feminist men who supported the insertion of women's rights articles in the Constitution. The committee's task was challenging for a number of reasons: it was required to conclude its deliberations and to produce a draft of the Constitution in just sixty days; the political climate was ripe with conflicts and bitter divisions exacerbated by the violent dispersal of the Islamists' occupation of Rabi'a Square in August 2013; there were daily protests on the streets that were not confined to Islamists' fighting against the new political regime, but also various interests groups asserting their demands and voices, and revolutionary groups insisting that the new Constitution reflect the demands of the revolution; the old oligarchy was back in sight as they tried to claw at the perceived gains of the revolution and orchestrated smear campaigns against revolutionary groups and individuals; and the security forces were gaining control over the streets and asserting their role as the "legitimate" users of violence. In the midst of all this, the voice of the revolution demanding bread, freedom, social justice, and dignity resounded loud and clear, and it was heard and echoed around the negotiating tables of the fifty-member committee. The point I am making here is that the opening-up of the political spaces in the aftermath of 2011 empowered the voices for rights and justice, and their influence on the committee cannot be underestimated. The 2014 Constitution consists of many articles that ensure rights and freedoms of citizens, including women. For example, one article relevant to women, Article 11, commits the state to ensuring that men and women are equal in all fields – political, social, economic, legal, and cultural; it commits the state to guarantee women's appropriate representation in elected bodies, their appointment to top public positions and judicial bodies without discrimination, and to protect women from all forms of violence. This constitutional text was possible thanks to the history of activism of women in Egypt: all of the above issues were on the agenda of the women activists for decades, which meant that there was knowledge and expertise that was made available to members of the committee. It was also made possible by the historical moment when rights issues were in the public eye and a revolutionary movement imposed its presence and voice.

Have you explicitly linked efforts to change family law to the struggle against gender-based violence? How so?

As noted earlier, the 2014 Constitution included text that committed the state to combating violence against women. The issue of violence against women became a matter of public debate and attention post-2011 as stories of women experiencing sexual violence on the streets came to the fore, and as more and more radical Islamist figures used their public platforms to spread ideas and values that are demeaning to women. Again, the historical moment and the many incidents and discourses on violence resulted in very important developments in the area of addressing violence against women, an area that previously was taboo. The first significant development can be noted in the media in 2013 as survivors of violent attacks felt empowered to go on live TV and recount their experiences, breaking the social stigma of shame. The second significant development was the insertion of text in the Constitution committing the state to combating violence against women. The third was in June 2014, with the issuance of an anti-sexual harassment decree that criminalized sexual harassment and imposed harsh sentences on offenders. The fourth was the establishment, at Cairo University in September 2014, of the Anti-Sexual Harassment policy and unit, the first of its kind at a national university in Egypt. More universities followed suit as the Cairo University policy and unit became a model to be emulated. Now, women's groups, as well as the National Council of Women, are working on a draft law to combat violence against women to be presented to Parliament for endorsement.

What has been the impact of external factors – international and regional conferences, NGO advocacy, and UN resolutions, among others – on Egyptian activists' efforts to reform family law?

There is no easy answer to this question. The women's movement in Egypt is, and has always been, part of the transnational feminist movement. From the early decades of the twentieth century, Hoda Shaarawy, a leading feminist in Egypt, contributed to regional and international women's meetings and conferences, not only in the West, but also in the Global South. In her memoirs, Hawwa Idriss, a young colleague of Hoda Shaarawy, speaks about her participation in meetings and conferences in Arab countries as well as in India, as the Egyptian Feminist Union, headed by Shaarawy, sought to consolidate ties with like-minded groups and organizations in the West and the Global South and conduct solidarity campaigns on issues related to women and national independence. Feminist activists and scholars are very aware of the role played by Egyptian women in drafting international conventions and covenants. In this sense, the binary of external versus internal needs to be interrogated. The challenge has always been in the way these international ties are manipulated to spread false ideas and perceptions about women's rights activists as Westernized or as isolated from their cultures.

Another way of answering this question would be to consider when and how UN resolutions and international advocacy was beneficial to furthering a women's rights agenda in Egypt. The answer must be historicized. Sylvia Walby has argued that the internationalization of human rights with the emphasis on the responsibilities of states in upholding these rights as a prerequisite for inclusion in the international regime of civilized states has made it possible for feminists across the globe to exert pressure on their respective states to further women's rights agendas. This has also been the situation in Egypt, an authoritarian state that cared about its international status and image and has always sought to present itself as a modern state and a player in the international arena. Since the 1990s, human and women's rights NGOs have used external influence and status as leverage in their campaigns to ensure rights in undemocratic settings. However, this state of affairs does not always work as international leverage can be a double-edged sword. Since 2014, the consequences of the increased terrorist activities in Egypt, the "war on terror," and the catastrophic turn of events in the Arab region have all resulted in muting the power and influence of international human rights discourses in favor of the necessity for security, defeating terrorists, and ensuring stability.

12

INTERVIEW WITH ASMA KHADER

Thank you for agreeing to speak with me, Asma, about your work in women's human rights advocacy and specifically about the campaign to reform Jordan's Personal Status Codes towards the elimination of gender-based violence (GBV). Because you have been a pioneer in these areas, I must ask: When and how did you become an activist in Jordan's movement for women's human rights? What ideas and experiences inspired your activism?

I experienced different milestones in my sensitivity towards gender equality. Perhaps the first time that I became aware of gender differences and inequality was around age eleven, though I could not yet grasp the legal aspects of this problem. At that time, I discovered that I faced some kinds of discrimination because of my sexual identity as a woman, as a girl. I also started to recognize different types of discrimination between boys and girls around me.

Noticing how families addressed parents – that marked the beginning of my sensitivity. Before my brother was born, my parents were addressed as "Abu Asma" and "Umm Asma" – literally, "father of Asma" and "mother of Asma." Then, one second after my brother was born, people called my father "Abu Samir." I was shocked by this shift to my brother's name, "father of Samir," and felt that I had been forgotten the moment he arrived. Of course, that sense of shock made me pay attention to the various types of discrimination between girls and boys, and I started to see more clearly what is "acceptable" for a girl and what is not.

I am fascinated by how early in your life you recognized discrimination for what it is. How did this recognition influence your professional choices?

Yes, that was a very early introduction to gender-based discrimination. Growing up, I felt that I had to study law because defending women's rights would require a powerful tool. As I faced other incidents of discrimination, I was left with the impression that I need to become a lawyer to develop a powerful voice in defense of human rights.

Yet there was no faculty of law in Jordan. So, I decided to study at the nearest university, which at that time was the University of Damascus, with the idea that I would become a women's rights lawyer. When I returned to Jordan, I confronted the reality that most women who needed the court system – who were seeking access to justice – preferred to consult with a male lawyer for many reasons.

A key reason is that most of these women had cases involving family issues. As a civil lawyer, I was not able to handle cases in the family court system. This system of church and Sharia courts had no female judges – no female employees either. There were no female lawyers standing before these courts back then. So, most of my clients at the beginning of my career were men. I was very disappointed.

How did you deal with this situation? When did women start to seek your legal counsel and representation?

As I continued in my career, I discovered that women felt weak vis-à-vis the law and court system. They thought that they should request help from powerful people – that is, men. Women believed that other women, including lawyers, were also weak. It took more than ten years until I became well-known as a lawyer working on human rights and could then represent women in the courts. Several times, judges appointed me as an expert to evaluate damages or to give a technical opinion on issues pertaining to women. Generally, however, I was not able to represent women until a very advanced stage of my career.

So, I entered the field of human rights as an activist, finding ways to defend women's rights other than standing before the court. I should add that not being able to represent women in court early on was the reason I decided to establish legal literacy programs – to raise women's awareness of different aspects of the law. Working with some of my colleagues, I designed a two-week program to cover family, labor, and criminal law, among other areas. The experience opened my eyes once again to discriminatory articles in the laws themselves, in the very text of the laws.

If I understand you correctly, you married your legal career to your women's rights activism, which seemed to work well.

Yes, in fact, this was the only way I could fulfill the goal I had when I chose to study law – to help women. However, they were not knocking on my door in the very early stages of my legal career. So, my colleagues and I decided to open free legal clinics and counseling centers. We opened two centers, one with the Professional Women's Association after a conference on women workers' rights.

We learned that most women workers did not know their rights, and even if they did, they lacked the resources to go to court. So, we provided them with legal aid and counseling for their cases. We then expanded our work to other areas of law where women had great need, including family issues.

Would you say that approaching women's legal concerns from the perspective of workers' rights allowed them to become comfortable speaking to you about their family issues as well?

Yes, and we then opened another legal aid center in Al Wehdat, a Palestinian refugee camp, in conjunction with UNRWA [the United Nations Relief and Works Agency for Palestinian Refugees in the Near East], which was managing seventeen camps in Jordan. Even though we lacked funding, we opened the center and implemented a legal literacy program. I, along with other lawyers from my office, went to these centers on certain days to provide free legal counseling. To be frank, only through these free counseling centers did women start to trust and listen to us as lawyers; they were encouraged to ask for our advice and even to seek redress in court for some cases.

I can see how building that trust would be central in your efforts to help these women because, beyond knowing all the legal rules and regulations, you were eliciting information from them.

Absolutely! To give women the opportunity to talk and to seek help – to encourage them to trust others who are listening because, as you said, their issues are very sensitive – we had to reassure them. They needed to be confident that privacy, respect, and fairness are there. They needed to know that they can put their problems in your hands as a lawyer and then rest easy.

Just the fact that you validated the women's experiences must have been such a source of comfort for them.

Yes, and I think that this was my starting point to understanding deeply the constraints on women – why they were unable to seek access to the justice system and to receive the court's protection in specific cases. You must recognize the social, cultural, and psychological aspects of women's lives. You must understand the lack of choices they have, because as a lawyer – rather than an activist – you may advise a woman that she should go to court and get a divorce, but then you are not responsible for what happens to her and her children.

So, in our legal aid centers, we asked the women who sought our services, "What are you going to do? What will happen to your children? How much money have you saved, and how much can you spend? How much money should the court award you to care for your children?" These questions must be asked so that a woman can weigh her choices – so that she has room to breathe and think clearly about what she wants to do. For example, she may want to attend some sort of vocational training or look for a job before starting the legal process in court.

Because you had this experience of looking at the legal aspects of women's human rights but also taking a more integrated approach to their concerns, I wonder how you would describe the status of Jordanian women in relation to family law as it stands right now.

I can say that many positive developments have occurred in recent years. Before 1976, Ottoman law applied, and the law was based only on Abu Hanifa or the Hanifiyya school of jurisprudence. If there was no specific text applicable to a case, the judge could consult this school of thought and find the solution. Judges had this discretion because the Hanifiyya school is very limited in terms of texts, with only a few articles tackling some major issues.[1] The other source of legal decisions was the knowledge of judges, who were mostly priests in the Christian church courts and sheikhs in the Islamic Sharia courts. Some had no legal degrees and were trained only in religious studies, and all the judges were male.

With the growing presence and strength of female lawyers standing before Sharia and church courts, the media covered these issues more and more. There were other public activities organized within the community – lectures, training and discussions – around the injustices in some provisions of family law. So, in recent years, there were several amendments to the law. In 1976, there was the first Jordanian law. The major amendment was in 2001, and then the latest one was in 2010 that in effect created a new law. In fact, this new law is very similar to the Moroccan law.

How are they similar?

For example, both laws make obtaining a divorce easier for a woman. They both specify that a woman may receive more alimony when her husband divorces her for no legal reason. Moreover, both laws facilitate child custody for the mother. A child can now stay with her/his mother until the age of eighteen. And even if children refuse to join their father, he is still responsible for paying monthly child support to provide for their needs and education.

The previous [Jordanian] law stated that children had to leave their mother when they reach the age of maturity – at thirteen or fourteen years old, when a girl has her first period and when a boy feels that he has become a man. If children refused to leave their mother's custody after the judge verified that they had reached the age of maturity, the police would take them by force to their father's home.

Then, children were asked to join their father and had the option to decline this request. However, if they refused to join him, he would not be responsible for child support; their mother would have to cover the cost of raising children. Finally, in the newest development, the law states that even if children stay with their mother against the will of their father, he is still responsible to pay child support. As you can see, the law has gradually developed during the last twenty to twenty-five years – every few years, one step.

So, this latest progress in the Jordanian law, like that of Morocco, has empowered both women and their children to make certain choices.

Yes, absolutely.

When you look at this progress and consider Jordan's family law, how would you describe its relationship to religion and culture?

To be frank, all the laws in our countries have some roots in religion. In Arab and/ or Muslim-majority countries, religion is either the only source of legislation, the major source, or one of the sources. Laws dealing with different, non-family issues became civil laws, even though the Holy Quran and Hadith discuss such matters as criminal behavior, the economy, and trade, etc. Yet governments typically ignore these aspects of religious texts and opt for civil laws and courts to deal with such matters. Civil laws may be based in part on the Sharia, but they draw on other sources as well. The only law that remains based solely on religion is family law. For Muslims, family law is based on the Sharia, and for Christians, on the Church's texts and teachings. Very simply put, it is patriarchy. The home, a man's castle, is the last bastion for religious people. Men feel that the home is their domain, where they can maintain control over their family members.

You referred to Muslim and Christian sources of family law. I am curious about the differences in the Personal Status Codes for Muslims and Christians in Jordan. Do Muslim and Christian women and their families go to separate courts?

Yes, there are courts for Muslims, the Sharia courts, and there are various Christian courts, one for each sect. Orthodox Christians have their own courts, Catholics have their own courts, and the other eleven sects each have their own courts. In this respect, Jordan is similar to Lebanon.

How do Muslim and Christian women compare in terms of their rights vis-à-vis the family and within the broader society? How do they experience their family and public lives given differences in their Personal Status Codes?

Women experience not only distinctive laws but also different cultures. Christian families may seem more open, and their women may appear freer. Yet the patriarchal mentality is deeply rooted in their culture as well. In my opinion, a careful evaluation of the situation reveals that Muslim women in Jordan and even in most other Arab countries enjoy more rights than Christian women.

Why would you say that is the case?

The reality is that in Sharia courts, a woman can put any conditions in her marriage contract, but a Christian woman cannot do that. In Sharia courts, a woman can ask to be granted a divorce simply because she is not happy with her husband. Among Christian women of certain denominations, divorce is not even known. Obtaining a divorce, and then alimony, is very difficult. For example, if a Christian woman works outside the house or leaves the family home, she will not be awarded alimony. By contrast, if a Muslim woman is mistreated and leaves the family home, her husband is responsible to pay her monthly alimony. Moreover, a Christian woman loses custody of her child at the age of seven in the church courts, whereas Sharia courts allow women to keep custody of their children until age eighteen, and the wife receives alimony in all cases. In short, Muslim courts provide a woman recompense for harmful actions taken by her husband – for example, if he leaves or mistreats her – whereas Christian courts do not generally do so. I think that Islamic law has evolved, while Christian law has stayed where it was in the mid-1980s.

Given their different experiences vis-à-vis family law, have Muslim and Christian women collaborated on reform efforts? Or do they view their status so differently that their approaches to reform have also diverged?

The research we have conducted and the campaigns we have organized tackle both Islamic and Christian laws. As you know, however, Christians in Jordan are only 3 percent of the population. Because the overwhelming majority of Jordanians are Muslims, we have focused more on reforming Islamic family law. In fact, many Christian and Muslim lawyers and activists work together on issues to seek equality and justice in family law.

For example, Christian women have thought that applying their own inheritance laws would be better for them because some provisions of Islamic inheritance laws favor men, who receive double the share given to women. Yet the reality is that according to laws in some Christian denominations, wives do not inherit anything. These women believe that because there is gender equality in many European countries and in the United States, which are predominantly Christian societies, they too will be accorded their rights. What we are trying hard to make clear, however, is that Jordan's Christian women enjoy equality because of civil law. The good news is that within various Christian denominations, churches are revisiting aspects of family law and proposing changes. I think that this development is a positive sign that the reform campaign has affected not only Muslim family law but also Christian Personal Status Codes.

I imagine that as Muslim and Christian women activists work together, they borrow one another's ideas and compare best practices. So, from your perspective, which aspects of family law most urgently need reform?

I think that focusing on a woman's right to work outside of her home is important, as is ensuring that she has control over her income and property. Women often allow themselves to be exploited economically because, as mothers and wives, they want to provide for their families. They will offer shares of their own incomes to secure necessities for their households. As we observed while working with women at our legal aid centers, they tend to regard contributing financially to their households as a duty. Men take advantage of these women: they try to pocket their wives' earnings. While a woman works and strives to support her family, he is using her income to buy land, apartments, cars, and other items in his own name. Then, if the couple divorces or the husband passes away, she inherits none of his property.

Beyond this issue of economic control, women's freedom of movement in society must be protected. If a woman wants to attend a cultural event or political meeting, she should not have to ask her father, brother, or husband for permission. She should not have to tend to all the household chores before going out. If she does not receive support in sharing these responsibilities, then she is not really free to make decisions about where she wants to go and what she wants to do. Though family law reform has had a positive impact on a woman's pursuit of her career, more time and activism are needed for her to be free in her decisions, particularly if she dreams of attaining a high-level position in her field or of becoming a public official. Imagine the negative public perception that would be created if a female politician said that she cannot attend a meeting or travel for work before asking her husband!

I am sure that would not go over well with colleagues and constituents who are counting on her. Her influence on the political process is thus limited.

She lacks genuine free will and is not trusted to make the right decision. She tells herself, "I have children who need me and may not want me to go. So, I feel that I should not attend. But how awful that I cannot decide totally on my own – that I must ask somebody else to make the final decision. My husband could say 'yes' or 'no.'"

You might respond that her husband cannot legally prevent her from leaving the house to do what she wants. However, according to family law, he has the right to divorce simply by telling her, "Go! You are divorced." She is then divorced. He does not even need to go to court. Later, he just has to register the divorce legally. I think that the practice of unilateral divorce by men should be revisited and changed. I believe that both husband and wife should go to court and appear before the judge with their request for a divorce so that they can address all aspects of their relationship and reach a settlement.

Of course, there are many other aspects of family law that need reform. For example, we need a law that stipulates equal distribution of property between the man and woman in case of divorce or death. This rule should apply to women working outside the home and even to non-working women. All women contribute to fulfilling the family's needs, and their household work is an investment of time and energy that allows the value of the family's property to grow.

And a woman contributes to her husband's career as well.

Yes, to his career and to their family. She is working at home for the family. If the husband wanted to hire somebody to do this work, to perform these services, it would cost him a lot.

Now I want to shift our focus to a different but related issue – the impact of family law on the problem of violence against women. As I was preparing for our interview, I read about activists' success in their quest to repeal Article 308 of the Penal Code, which stated that a man guilty of committing rape could be spared from punishment if he agrees to marry his victim.

In fact, our organization, Sisterhood Is Global Institute-Jordan (SIGI/J), initiated and led the coalition to repeal this article; we started this work long ago – during the 1980s – and we were able to achieve our goal just this year [2017]. We are so happy that Article 308 was totally repealed because this resulted from a long and significant campaign comprised of several elements. We conducted research to gauge how much people knew about this article and its impact on women's lives and to learn whether they agreed that it should be abolished. We also raised public awareness; we organized more than 260 lectures and training sessions throughout the country, held meetings with decision-makers in government, lobbied members of parliament, and engaged with media outlets. We used different outlets – newspapers and other publications, radio, television, and social media. And we involved youth and men in our campaign.

How did you engage youth and men in this effort?

We usually work with the Youth Committee to plan the annual Youth Tech Festival, inviting young people to propose one theme related to women's rights that they can address with new technologies. So, this festival combines information technology, young men and women, and a specific theme focused on women's rights. Among those hundreds of young people, many are members of the Youth Committee based in Amman, but we also invite groups from different governorates to participate. We forge coalitions with them on specific issues such as forced marriage, murder in the name of family honor, Article 308, and other forms of GBV. Young people as a group have become very gender-sensitive over the years, and their presence in our campaign was quite important. Parliamentarians may think that they can ignore women voters, but they cannot ignore young men as well.

As you were organizing this coalition, what kind of obstacles did you encounter? Who were your opponents?

Our opponents were traditional people and especially officials espousing a patriarchal mentality. There were those who want to resolve conflict and problems quickly, even if the price of doing so is women's rights, happiness, and future. During this campaign, the Islamists actually voted to abolish Article 308. Of course, their reasons may be based on the perceptions of what is good behavior for a Muslim woman and man, as well as who must be punished if they misbehave by having a sexual relationship without a marriage contract.

Did you need to court or invite the Islamists to participate on your side, or did they do so out of their own logic and self-interest?

We sparked a public debate that spread widely, especially after the proposed draft law was revealed. Some people suggested amendments to Article 308 rather than full repeal, and everyone became engaged in these very tough discussions during the last few years. Jordanians read the articles we published and listened to our interviews. As popular interest increased, media outlets invited public figures to participate in panel discussions and to express their opinions on this issue. I think that all of them, including the Islamists, had to offer an opinion.

Public figures had to be on the record about whether to repeal Article 308.

Yes.

In terms of enlisting youth in this campaign, did you find that young people were relatively unanimous in their position, or did they have diverse opinions? Did they need convincing?

They need to feel that they own the cause, that they believe in it, and that they are not the bad ones who want to destroy girls. I was very encouraged when I heard that they were lecturing at universities and high schools. They were listened to more than any woman.

To be clear, were these were young men speaking at universities and high schools?

Yes, many young men were speaking to their peers around the country. As partners in our coalition, they delivered lectures and screened the film we produced about the issue, ensuring that the discussion continued. So, they played a very interesting role. Amid a group of young women and men, when the men express such sophisticated, gender-sensitive opinions, women will follow.

**What a great way to get something done! Has this kind of effort suc-
ceeded when tackling issues other than the repeal of Article 308? For
example, how has this effort worked with the campaign against crimes
in the name of honor? Have you enjoyed similar success? This problem
seems more intractable than the push to abolish Article 308.**

No, we have not yet enjoyed similar success in dealing with the problem of
so-called honor crimes. At SIGI/J, we have prepared a legal memorandum
regarding amendments to the Penal Code, and one of our concerns has been
initially to limit and ultimately to eliminate the use of "mitigating excuses" in
so-called honor crimes. We sought amendments to Articles 98 and 340 of the
Penal Code, which discuss reduced punishment for a man who kills his female
relative in "the fit of fury" due to an act by the victim. However, the problem
with tightening the legal language about when a man or woman may invoke
"mitigating excuses" for murder or other bodily harm to a victim is that every
person who kills a female relative is now claiming he did so because he caught
her with a strange man. Even if his motive was not truly related to family honor,
he tries to take advantage of this excuse to avoid harsh punishment. Of course,
judges do not believe every man who makes this argument, but the language is
still there to be used.

So, the new amendment makes very clear that a man may invoke "mitigating excuses" for his crime only after he himself sees his wife in bed with another
man. A woman may make the same legal argument if she kills her husband after
catching him with another woman. Yet she must catch him committing adultery in their marital bed – in their bedroom at home – to make this argument,
whereas a husband may claim "mitigating excuses" regardless of where he finds
his wife sleeping with another man. This aspect of the law thus discriminates
against women.[2]

**Who in the government have been your allies on this issue of crimes in
the name of honor? And who have been your opponents or adversaries?**

You can find both allies and adversaries throughout the government and beyond –
in the Parliament, the judiciary, various departments, the police force, and the
media. Everywhere. You can find those who support our cause and others who are
against us. I think that since we started our campaign against so-called honor crimes
twenty-five years ago, the majority in Jordan have gradually come to support our
cause much more than in the past. Of course, we have enjoyed the Royal Family's
support. King Abdullah, Queen Rania, Princess Basma, and other members of the
Royal Family often deliver public remarks and convey other messages about the
need to protect women's rights and to engage women in all aspects of life. They
have played a very positive role, encouraging women to claim their rights and
urging men to take the steps necessary to guarantee those rights.

Shifting to developments in the wider Middle East and North Africa, how would you describe the influence of regional events on your efforts to reform aspects of family law? Did the popular uprisings of the Arab Spring have any impact – positive, negative, or otherwise – on your advocacy campaigns for women's human rights?

Absolutely! Throughout the entire region, people recognized that reforms were urgently needed. Such initiatives as revisions to the Moroccan Constitution, and then later to the Egyptian one, encouraged us to take steps. But we were not able to push for a clear text on gender equality. Article 6 of the Constitution states that all Jordanians are equal under the law, regardless of their language, religion, or race. We tried to add equality between women and men, working through the Royal Commission for Constitutional Amendments; the language was there but suddenly disappeared at the last minute. Then, a new debate started about why the language had disappeared. So, we prepared a memo examining the texts on gender equality in other Muslim countries' constitutions. We considered relevant texts from the constitutions of Indonesia, Malaysia, Turkey, Iran, Bangladesh, and various Arab countries. We saw that most of these constitutions, something like 95 percent of them, include very clear wording on gender equality. Of course, I know that the gap between constitutional texts and implementation is huge, but we proved that at least the wording has been accepted by other countries. Though we did not get the language on gender equality included this time, we will emphasize this point in our future campaigns.

With respect to family law, I was at the Jordanian National Commission for Women when the first draft of the 2010 law came out and then Sharia Law Number 36 was adopted that same year. I reviewed the draft. We proposed many of the articles now in the law and invited the committee drafting this legislation to meet with us. Most committee members were Sharia court judges. We arranged a meeting between them and representatives of the women's movement from different organizations to discuss a proposal I had drafted outlining our concerns. Together, these judges and women's activists reviewed the law's articles one by one. We succeeded in improving many articles. Though we could not push through all our suggestions, we got our most important ones.

Most significantly, we were able to revise the law's provisions on divorce. As you may know, in 2001, a new article in family law was introduced about *khul`a* – a woman divorcing her husband in a way that seems unilateral and without clear cause. The judges deleted this article from their draft of the new law, insisting that men were unhappy with the use of this negative term. It is a tough word because it means "to cast off." The judges were upset that a woman could initiate a divorce the same way a man could – simply by declaring "I am going to divorce you." *Khul`a* is a rough word to introduce between a wife and her husband.

So, what I suggested is that we use wording from the Quran, replacing *khul`a* with "*iftida*", [3] and and the Sharia judges ultimately accepted my recommendation. *Iftida* has the connotation of a woman setting herself free but results in the same outcome as the more negative term *khul`a*. When the judges raised concerns about *iftida*, I responded by saying, "But the Quran uses this wording. If men are unhappy, do they want to protest the Quran?" The judges had no real choice but to agree. My point is that our strategy for introducing amendments to the 2010 family law produced positive results. Of course, there are still other aspects of the law that need improvement. However, we will have the opportunity to address these concerns because this version of the law is temporary; it now needs to be discussed and approved by the Parliament.[4] When this draft law is taken up by members of Parliament, we will need to mobilize public opinion through a campaign. There are some women's organizations that advocate a civil family law for all Jordanians, which I think is a very logical demand. However, I really do believe that we cannot push for this right now. We will need much more time to persuade a majority of the public to accept a civil law. So, we need to focus on improving as much as possible the law we have now, and then we can see what happens in the future.

Your decision to improve the 2010 draft law rather than immediately advocating for a civil law reflects your recognition of the existing cultural and political climate.

Yes, and I should add that we in the women's rights movement need to evaluate our power, the audience for our message, and the influence of other groups in civil society to make progress possible. We must understand the regional context; even though fundamentalist groups, such as ISIS among others, are failing politically and militarily. They remain very strong and have many supporters in the current cultural and social environment. Some of the region's regimes are even adopting forceful religious positions.

I am sure that many of these governments use religion to enhance their legitimacy vis-à-vis the public. Have other external factors had an impact on your efforts to reform family law – for example, international conferences, links with non-governmental organizations outside of Jordan, and UN resolutions?

Absolutely! The open space of the social media has had a significant impact on our activities. We have enjoyed the opportunity to exchange experiences and to learn about the reforms implemented in other Arab, Muslim-majority societies that are similar to Jordan – such as Morocco, Tunisia, and Egypt, where the constitutions are really based on the principle of fifty-fifty for gender equality.

Additionally, UN resolutions and meetings as well as various human rights mechanisms have been important to us. The UN Human Rights Council's process of Universal Periodic Review means that states are questioned about their human rights practices and receive recommendations about how to make improvements. The CEDAW Committee, the Committee on the Rights of the Child, and the Commission on the Status of Women – all these mechanisms allow us to engage with government officials who listen to our concerns and respond to our recommendations, refusing some but accepting others. We use any occasion, resolution, mechanism, or meeting as a tool to advance our reform efforts. We rely on statistics from these organizations to prove the very low level of achievement in women's rights throughout the Arab world. We highlight comparisons between countries in other regions of the world to emphasize how far Arab women lag behind their counterparts in the East and West. We even take advantage of recommendations for reform from the Arab League, despite its weakness. In short, international organizations are important tools for us.

Do you have any additional comments on the campaigns to reform family law and to reduce GBV in Jordan?

I think that building a new type of coalition is most important for reforms to succeed – for instance, talking to men, to associations, to political parties, to media people, and to the academic community, because each of these groups has its own audience, its own followers. They may not listen to me, but they will surely listen to somebody whom they elect or respect. Building broad coalitions means that you will support their just causes and they will support you.

The other significant issue is ownership. Any topic or cause should be owned by a great number of people. You cannot change a law just because a hundred women sign a petition. There must be a movement within the community. People should be talking about this cause and listening to each other in their coffee shops, hearing about it on the radio and everywhere else. For reforms to succeed, people should want to see changes happen.

The third aspect is the need to prepare and produce knowledge – to have relevant statistics and to document cases. Telling a story has much greater impact when you have proof of what happened; the documentation of evidence to support your advocacy is vital. As you know, I think that having a lawyer's mentality is very important for this reform campaign. To design any campaign, you must know what is on your counterpart's mind; you must understand the person in front of you. If you prepare yourself very well to respond to what you think he will say, you have a very powerful tool to win the case. This means that you need to understand the history of an issue, how a law has been implemented correctly and incorrectly. You may turn to comparative legal studies to show that a law was implemented some two or three hundred years ago in Italy or France, for example, or in this or that other country – that the law in question is very old-fashioned and comes from the West. You must also take into consideration the positions of the religious and tribal communities, including evidence from their justice systems that were used in this country years ago. So, you are really constructing your argument in a very scientific way.

And finally, you need to be a very patient person to work towards your objectives and to wait fifteen to twenty years to see them gradually fulfilled!

I can see that you need a lot of patience to engage in coalition building, to enlist support from other interest groups including men and to target your message to the audience you have in mind.

Earlier, you asked who our advisors and allies were, and I just want to tell you that we also seized the moment when the Royal Commission for Judiciary Reform was established. We prepared a memo outlining sixteen demands to make the judicial sector more gender-sensitive. Without reforms to the judiciary, our efforts will not have meaning; justice cannot be for only half the population. So, we suggested that discriminatory practices be abolished, and nine of our sixteen demands were adopted in one way or another by the Commission. This development led His Majesty to make recommendations about our concerns. At this point, the government and Parliament shifted from merely amending Article 308 of the Penal Code to repealing it altogether based on the Royal Commission's recommendation. Catching the moment and knowing our audience and allies – in this instance, prosecutors and judges – were key.

We are now trying to document our experience in this campaign and to translate what we have learned into English as well. We think that documenting and evaluating our campaign will offer many lessons learned. We can identify our successes and failures, so that maybe we can do things better in the future. I look forward to sharing what we have learned in our campaign to reform Jordan's family law in the hope that other women may find our experience useful as they strive toward gender equality in their own communities.

Notes

1 Imam Abu Hanifa of Kufa (699–767 A.D.) established the earliest school of Islamic jurisprudence. His disciples recorded his numerous discussions and opinions, forming the basis of the Hanifiyya school.
2 Jordan's newly amended Penal Code, revisiting and revising Articles 98 and 340 as well as abolishing Article 308, went into force in January 2017.
3 This term is used in Sura Al Baqara (The Cow) 2:229 of the Quran.
4 Because King Abdullah had the Parliament dissolved in November 2009, this 2010 draft law was not debated in this branch of Jordan's government.

13

INTERVIEW WITH RABÉA NACIRI[1]

When and how did you first become involved in the cause of women's human rights in Morocco?

Well, I cannot tell you when I became a women's rights activist, as it happened progressively, through a long process. I started with political activism to stand against all forms of social injustice, thinking that political activism was an efficient and effective way to strive against discrimination. After a few years of activism in a political party, I realized that it was mostly about politics and power, and there was neither clear position-taking nor real action against social injustice, women's rights violations included. All political parties in Morocco, even those claiming to be progressive, adopted a relativistic approach: "We certainly favor the principles of gender equality, but society is not ready for such a change for the time being. We should not jeopardize the chances of revolutionary actors, and so we should wait for society to be ready." I was becoming politically mature. Besides, the contradictions and endless compromises, the double standards, and doublespeak I noticed while working in political parties forced me to distance myself from them. I gave up being an activist in the party, stepped back, and took stock of the situation. I realized that an independent organization targeting mainly women's rights issues is a top priority in Morocco. In the party, we were told that if issues like revolution and class warfare are sorted out, women would subsequently have access to rights. For me, it was the other way round – ensuring women's rights is the revolution that would reshape Moroccan society. It was a progressive process that put me on the path of activism for women's rights.

This path overlapped with an advantageous international context: the United Nations Decade for Women that began with the International Women's Year in 1975, which was all over the media. The whole context paved the way for feminist organizations to emerge in Morocco and Tunisia. These organizations began to observe and study social contradictions through the prism of equality between men and women and their respective roles in society, which was later referred to as "gender relations." A few years later, in 1985, the Association Démocratique des Femmes du Maroc [ADFM] was created. It was the first feminist organization in Morocco. Even though we did not identify as such in the beginning, we were seeking equality between men and women, but our ultimate objective was the revision of the Family Code, which we perceived as totally unacceptable and unfair. I think that the overall context was favorable worldwide, in the Maghreb, and locally. I think it was a set of circumstances occurring in a specific context that pushed us to create ADFM; it took us two years of reflection and discussion.

Regarding the status of Moroccan women with respect to the Family Code, the feminist movement crystallized in the light of the personal status code. In the Arab world, besides Saudi Arabia and the Gulf countries, Morocco had one of the most regressive laws. The law was extremely conservative and patriarchal. To sum up, a woman was bound by the law to obey her husband in return for maintenance. The law even provided that a woman could not visit her family without her husband's permission. As for the spouses' mutual duties, the man was solely obliged to provide financial support, while the woman had several duties towards her husband: to be obedient, to look after the children, and even to breastfeed. Furthermore, a man was free to repudiate his wife without even notifying her.

Feminist organizations were not the first to raise the question of notifying the wife of her repudiation – the magistrates themselves were facing many problems. The husband could leave and set up a second family with his first wife "suspended," neither married nor divorced. Besides, polygamy, although not very common in Morocco, was a question to be raised as a matter of principle.

Later on, permission of a male guardian was abolished for female orphans who wished to marry. A woman, regardless of her age or social status, could not get married without the permission of her father, her brother, or a Muslim adult male who fulfilled the requirements. Nonetheless, the core ideology of the personal status code remained unchanged. For women activists, male guardianship and obedience had to be abolished, women granted the right to divorce, and the minimum age of marriage adjusted to avoid child marriage. We were told that if enacted, our proposals would mark the end of the family and Islam in Morocco. In reality, these provisions were largely overtaken by social practices. In fact, people managed to arrange things, and women were compromising and using subterfuge in order to get divorced, through *khul'* for example, which is divorce with payment to her husband. It is absolutely unacceptable that a woman has to pay her husband in return for her freedom. Surprisingly, women opposed a few amendments, like the abolition of marital guardianship which was perceived as socially accepted by women as well as men. Why? Because they believed that patriarchy ensures protection for women. The amendment on matrimonial guardianship was poorly understood, and so people opposed it. The rest of the amendments were rather well accepted, and the Family Code was revised and reformed. Within a matter of months, all disastrous predictions – that the divorce rate would dramatically increase, for example – were proven to be wrong. On the contrary, the rate of divorce declined. Another provision allows spouses to set up a second contract, separate from the marriage contract, to establish the terms under which assets acquired during marriage would be managed. We were told that it would not work because nobody would consider setting up a contract while celebrating a wedding and that discussing financial matters at this point is socially inappropriate. Nonetheless, these contracts are becoming more common now. I think that the Family Code reform changed numerous things. Are women aware of all these provisions? No, they are not. In the event of a divorce, the wife is left with nothing in the absence of a prior agreement on managing assets acquired during marriage because the Family Code does not include community property. We are still stuck in the outdated philosophy. In the absence of prior agreement, "a woman's property belongs to her, and a man's property belongs to him."

I think that the Moroccan government failed to design and execute a serious communications strategy using the mass media and the school system. It could have introduced the different provisions in a simple, clear, and accessible language. Nevertheless, the Family Code reforms were implemented and assimilated into social practices without any major problems.

Earlier reforms of the Family Code were adopted via *dahir* (royal decree), promulgated by the King as the Commander of the Faithful (*Amir al Mu'minin*). The King has the power to legislate, with the advice of the *ulama*, the scholars of Islamic law. The Family Code was reformed on two occasions, on which the King was advised by Islamic jurists. The Personal Status Code, first adopted in 1958, was written by a committee of the *ulama*. For the minor reform of 1993, the King promulgated the law after consulting the *ulama*.

The new Family Code was adopted by Parliament in 2004. This event marked a break with the old legal and institutional traditions in Morocco. The King, acting within his constitutional prerogatives, assigned a committee that in addition to Islamic legal scholars, included doctors, sociologists, and others. It was an attempt to go beyond the restrictions of a literal interpretation of Islamic law and Sharia. Additionally, the women's movement requested the participation of women in the process. For the first time, three female members were assigned to the committee. Changes covered not only provisions but the reform's institutional procedures. In fact, although *dahirs* are usually promulgated directly, this time the committee communicated their findings and proposals to the King, who submitted the document and the reform proposal to Parliament. We were going beyond the mere interpretation of Islamic law (*'ijtihad*) into a broader perspective. We broke that principle by involving people of different backgrounds and disciplines and by referring the bill to Parliament – a non-religious and secular institution that embodies the sovereignty of the people. Debating the bill in Parliament and revising its amendments wiped away the image of the Family Code as a branch of Islamic law. We now have a law that resembles other secular laws, subjected to the same legislative procedure in Parliament. It was the end of an era where only jurisconsults were entitled to discuss, advise, and interpret the Quran; enacting laws is now more modern and democratic.

Today, fourteen years since the first reform, discussions and initiatives are starting to resurface, indicating that it is time to resume the debate. Every law should be discussed and evaluated according to its social impact, ideology, and objectives. The Family Code is intended to resolve social issues. It should be reviewed if it fails to tackle social problems or worsens them.

We have pointed out some of the current issues that need to be resolved urgently. The first issue is child marriage. The Family Code does not discriminate between girls and boys – the age for both is eighteen. Nevertheless, the code has a loophole that allows the Family Affairs judge to grant exemptions. It does not take more than a legal procedure to authorize child marriage. Fourteen years later, child marriage is mobilizing the masses and has become one of the most publicized topics in Morocco. Luckily, annual statistics on the implementation of the Family Code in courts are now available, and we can see that, since the reform, the number of exemption requests approved is increasing. Most exemption requests are filed to authorize the marriage of underage girls. According to a recent survey, the vast majority of Moroccans call for banning underage marriage exemptions. It is still problematic for many people who think that the exemption permits girls who get pregnant outside marriage to solve the problem. In Morocco, sexual relations outside marriage are prohibited, and a child born out of wedlock is considered illegitimate and cannot be filiated by his biological father even if he consents. The fact is that most of the time, the family forces the girl into a marriage they know is doomed to fail, just to preserve honor.

The second issue is polygamy. Polygamy is not very common in Morocco and was subjected to terms and conditions in the Family Code. With the emergence of Islamic movements in Morocco and in other Arab countries, polygamy has become significantly more socially acceptable. Indeed, polygamous men used to be more discreet in general, especially in urban areas where this practice was not socially acceptable. Nowadays, polygamy is praised, and even the current Minister of Human Rights boasts about having two wives. The revalorization of polygamy in some environments resulted in the increase of such marriages. The conditions established by the Family Code are not strict enough. For example, we had a case where a judge authorized a polygamous marriage because the first wife had diabetes. In another incident that sparked public outrage in Morocco, a polygamous marriage was approved because the wife gave birth to girls only. Although such incidents probably existed in the past, we simply did not know about them, but now everything goes public thanks to social media.

The next sensitive issue is Article 49, which allows spouses to set, separately from the marriage contract, an agreement about the management of assets acquired during marriage. The provision is discriminatory, given that well-off women capable of imposing a separate agreement are a minority. All those who lack funds and access to information will end up on the street in the case of divorce. Revision of this provision is very challenging. We need strategies that improve women's conditions, and they should also be feasible and realistic enough to be taken into account.

Legal guardianship of children is another problematic issue. This provision can be easily modified to grant guardianship to women and men, which they exercise as they wish. Moreover, one of the reforms considered revolutionary, not only in Morocco but also in other Arab countries, is placing the family under the joint responsibility of the spouses. We eliminated "head of the family" in the revised code, and replaced it with "joint responsibility towards children." Yet legal guardianship remains solely granted to the father. Granting legal guardianship to the mother is subjected to strict and limited conditions.

The last issue is divorce. Today, we have four different procedures for divorce. The reform resulted in new provisions aiming to ensure better access for women to divorce, yet the old procedures remain unchanged. The types are divorce by mutual consent, then divorce for irreconcilable differences, repudiation, and at-fault divorce that may be filed by the wife if she provides evidence to prove her case. These four types of divorce are ineffective. Additionally, divorce in exchange for compensation is still accepted. We have then five types of divorce, but statistics reveal that only two types are commonly chosen. Divorce for irreconcilable differences tops the list and replaces the other types because it is suitable for both spouses. I think that we should now re-examine and simplify divorce procedures. Divorce with mutual consent should be kept, and at-fault divorce should not be replaced by divorce for irreconcilable differences, as is the case currently.

Tunisia and Morocco are the only Muslim countries to debate the issue of equal inheritance. The current debate was launched by feminists in a hostile regional context, especially with the emergence of Islamic movements. It was difficult to raise public awareness about the issue, but we managed to do so. We have published many books, convened workshops, and appeared on TV talk shows. The issue is being widely debated. Changing the inheritance regime in Morocco is obviously not around the corner yet, but it is not regarded as taboo anymore.

The National Human Rights Council and UN Women each recently carried out surveys at the regional level. Twenty percent of Moroccans, especially women, embrace equal inheritance. The inheritance issue is definitely our ultimate challenge. Those who are familiar with Islamic law and Sharia know the fierce resistance on this issue – on the grounds that inheritance is clearly explained in the Quran. In reality, the reason is purely economic. Men are still privileged over women in terms of inheritance.

Sharia, which provides the chief issue in reform of family laws in all Arab countries, is a human effort of centuries of interpretation of the words and habits of the Prophet and the Quran. Morocco follows the Maliki school to adapt interpretation in the Moroccan context.[2] However, most family legislation has little to do with Sharia. It is a perpetual effort of reinterpretation according to the local evolution of each country. It was only after independence in 1958 that we secured a unified and transcribed code, the Mudawana, that addressed all Moroccans, be they men or women. Before the code, each region lived by its own interpretation. Patriarchy is widespread in Morocco. But it is not specific to Muslim societies. It is entrenched across the world and in a variety of contexts, and it is the underlying obstacle to change. We should bear in mind that change is inevitable when it comes to relations among individuals and social groups.

What strategies did the activists use to reform the family law?

It took almost twenty years for the Family Code to be reformed. I could say that Moroccan feminists used all possible and imaginable strategies, but one of the things highlighted is knowledge. We cannot change such an important law that structures families, social relations, and beyond without thorough knowledge of the context and the situation of women as well as family relations. Consequently, there was a significant number of studies, surveys, and discussions with women, because feminist activists in Morocco, specifically at ADFM and other associations, have always used an approach that not only condemned but suggested solutions, which is much harder. It is true that they went through a phase of condemnation, which was healthy and it was the starting phase of the creation process of ADFM which was the first association (others were created later). We started the condemnation phase by being vocal about what we could no longer accept. Rapidly, we moved to the next step, the more difficult one, that was based on asking "What do we propose?" We thought, maybe wrongly, that we should not only call for changing the divorce regulations, for example, in order to grant women the right to divorce. These were not real suggestions; we went beyond that. We created parallel and alternative provisions. There was a significant amount of work that was done in the framework of "Collectif 95 Maghreb Égalité," where we united our efforts and synergy as feminist movements to work across the three Maghreb countries – Algeria, Morocco, and Tunisia. It took many days and nights of work, conflicts, and arguments, so that we could come up with a shared vision regarding what we suggest to change the Family Code, despite the differences between the three countries. Therefore, we elaborated, in the early 1990s, a hundred measures and provisions to reform family laws in the Maghreb. This little compendium was magnificent. We started with all the provisions that we considered discriminatory or unacceptable, and we suggested alternatives. This work, which took a significant amount of time and effort, inspired all mobilizations in Morocco as well as Algeria. It was taken on by numerous associations, and many provisions in the Moroccan Family Code are based directly or indirectly on this work. It was widely distributed in Morocco and internationally – in the Maghreb region, Arab countries, and Muslim-majority countries. It was the first step. Although knowledge is necessary to make our voices heard, we had to be excellent. People had to give us their ear, and to be heard, we needed to provide coherent and well-argued proposals. That was the first strategy: the one based on excellence in proposals. Moreover, we used the *Dalil* (*Guidebook*), which reintroduced the alternative suggestions of the hundred measures in the first document – the alternative to the Family Code – and justified every reform proposal. For example, to address the question of why reforming the minimum age of marriage is necessary, we pointed to international law and changes in society as well as analyzing Islamic texts and relevant data. We used a three-level argumentation: sociological, socio-economic, and Muslim law from a doctrinal point of view, and also international law on human rights used by women's rights movements, to push the Moroccan state into ratifying the Convention on the Elimination of All Forms of Discrimination against Women (CEDAW) addition to the revised Family Code. Ratification of CEDAW was to hold the Moroccan government internationally accountable. We struggled for the ratification, which took place in 1993 but was not officially announced before 2000 or 2001; according to the Moroccan Constitution, a law is only effective and applicable in Morocco once it is published in the Official Bulletin.

We used knowledge, the strategy of excellence – we would not allow ourselves to talk drivel. It would be fatal for a feminist movement already attacked from all sides, taxed, and accused of all imaginable evils. In my association [ADFM], we strived to stick to this strategy in all our work, so that if there was a point of view, decision-makers, those who create opinions, the media, and the other associations knew very well that when ADFM released a proposal, a document, or a statement, we were generally heard, given the amount of work behind it.

The second strategy ensured that there is a wide agreement in terms of numbers, because as we say, numbers are power. It takes a large number of alliances, stakeholders who subscribe to our proposals and accept them. The second strategy was networking. Today it is much harder, but then, despite the differences, we could work together to create multiple synergistic relationships related to these proposals. We worked not only with feminist but also human rights organizations, development-oriented organizations, and several civic initiatives that agreed with us on those matters. Networking was therefore very important, as was searching for alliances with political left-wing parties or at least with parties claiming to be socially aware, and with trade unions, given their capacity to mobilize. For instance, during demonstrations and sit-ins, the presence of unions was very useful, especially women trade unionists, who played an important role. It was not a women's rights-oriented network – we called it "the associations field." It was one association of organizations that believed in democratic development, including gender equality, community development, and citizen participation. The network was professionalized and gathered dozens of organizations. ADFM was among the organizations that built the network. Initially, we thought we lacked time and the means to expand, but we made the right move by founding that movement. One of ADFM's members was the president of the network which was very useful later on, when we were attacked by Islamists during the large mobilizations that started in 1998.

The third strategy was the capacity to access information. We had what we called "brothers and sisters" in chambers, administrations, ministries, and Parliament. We were aware of all that was happening. Sometimes, we knew what was happening when it came to women's rights matters by the end of the government council. We worked in an intuitive way, according to our good sense. When we work for twenty years on an issue, we end up building contacts. And most of all, at ADFM we have always worked with men; even if they were not members, they have always been sympathetic to our thinking, to our advocacy and to our consultations. We even included the *ulama*. For instance, we relied on three well-known and respected *ulama*, who publicly supported us during the confrontations of 1998 to 2002. At least, two of them did so through their writings.

Finally, we always considered the media strategy to be important. Then, print media still played a major role. We had great contacts, many friends, and interactions with a particular newspaper that ranked first among Arabic-language readers. We also had other options, including a magazine that still exists, "femmes du Maroc" that was almost a tribune for the feminist movement – in every issue, there was something on the Family Code. Considering all the activities that we organized, we were also present on TV – maybe not on public national television but on the second channel, which had a more modern approach. We benefited from significant media exposure, taking advantage of every opportunity to plan press conferences. And beginning in 1998, when Islamists led a campaign against us, the press was really interested. The conflict between the modernist faction of Moroccan society and the Islamic or conservative faction caught the interest of the media, which soon took part in favor of our discourse. We had relays amongst athletes, and filmmakers made amazing movies that highlighted in one way or another some problems related to the Family Code – for example, the film *A la recherché du mari de ma femme*, among others. These movies inspired public debate.

Concurrently, there were positive changes in the political context. Beginning in 1998, in the context of a profound economic crisis when King Hassan II was said to be sick, Morocco transitioned from an administrative technocratic government to an opening to the socialist party in a coalition led by the head of government, a major opponent who spent years in jail. We therefore had happy years from 1998 to 2002 – a four-year period that was supposed to be favorable. A socialist party can be supportive when in opposition, but once it joins the government, things become more difficult.

Yet this period was favorable only because we knew the majority of members of government, including my husband. Half of the ministers were our friends in political parties. The women's movement was therefore able to introduce and advocate comprehensive proposals – in particular, the national plan for women's integration in development that was presented to and approved by the new progressive, center-left government coalition.

However, at the same time, the evolving Islamic movement was politically recognized. They created their own party and had a legal existence. At that moment, the women's movement and the Family Code reform proposals faced fierce opposition. Yet the Islamic mobilization against us actually served us well. It pushed a lot of people, institutions, and social structures to take a position. Because Moroccan society is complex, there are very old organizational traditions, trade unions, and political parties, unlike some Arab countries that have no intermediate structures between state and citizens. It is very important to know about these structures and their ins and outs, to know how to approach and influence them. This complexity of Moroccan society played in our favor, because as soon as Islamists mobilized against the feminist movement that was only composed of a few hundred people but whose influence outnumbered its activists, society was galvanized. People were horrified to find out that Islamists were active and in large numbers. It was the end of the 1990s; now things have changed, unfortunately. Then people were scared; it was a shock because in Morocco, we were not familiar with such movements. This led several institutions to position themselves on the side of the women's movement. We received significant support, even from people and institutions that we did not expect to side with us – for example, the Rotary Club, entrepreneurs, the employers' union, and banks – but who were curious about the collision between the modernists and Islamists or conservatives. The shock pushed society to react, to seek information. Even institutions that usually do not become involved in such debates took an interest and tried to understand the issues. We were invited on a daily basis to talk here, to facilitate a conference there. We travelled across Morocco. It was a very powerful mobilization. The main lesson I learned as I travelled through the country was not to fear confrontation, especially with the Islamists. Conflict, as long as it remains peaceful, will always be beneficial and fruitful for change. The absence of debate and reaction is much worse.

Let me refer to a recent example: in 2015, when the Human Rights Council – a constitutional institution whose president is assigned by the King and whose members' names are published in the Official Bulletin – issued a report on the state of parity and equality in Morocco. It pointed out that the provisions on inheritance were unfair and unequal. This time, fingers were pointed at the Constitutional Council. However, I found out that one year later, I was right to think that they would be proud that the Human Rights Council was responsible for submitting this matter to public debate. There were conflicts – the head of the Islamic government stood against the Human Rights Council. Yet today, the debate on gender equality in inheritance has made its way out of the closet and has reached the public space. I think that a fruitful conflict should not be feared, if individuals can express themselves freely and they respect the rules of democratic debate.

How are the Family Code reforms related to combating violence?

I would say that they are directly related. The Family Code as a whole is mere violence against women. When a woman is repudiated without being notified, when she is ousted because she does not have the right to remain in the family house that most often belongs to or is rented under the name of the man because a woman is not allowed to possess or to sign a lease agreement, that is violence. When she is repudiated without receiving alimony and she cannot have her husband summoned to appear in court, that is violence. When a father does not authorize his daughter to get married because she works and gives him her salary, when she cannot get married as long as her father is alive, that is violence. The entire Family Code was economic, psychological, and sexual violence, since it obliged the wife to obey her husband. There was even a provision called "*bayt al ta'ah*" [literally, "house of obedience"] that permits a husband to force his wife to return to the matrimonial house when she takes refuge in her parents' house. At that time, we were not focusing on violence; our main concerns were about rights, discrimination, and abuse of human dignity and women's liberties that we perceived as absolutely intolerable. Later on, we obviously addressed the issue of violence against women. Thanks to the efforts of the women's movement, violence against women is now publicly denounced by ministers. Women's achievements are celebrated, and we are even given flowers on trains and in offices. Combating violence against women is widely accepted in society. However, violent practices are not decreasing. We prioritized the Family Code because it was a crucial problem. Once it was reformed, official initiatives multiplied, with a willingness to talk about women's rights and the Family Code – it was the pride of Morocco. The Moroccan government and its ambassadors celebrated the Family Code. The barrier caved in to clear the way for positive initiatives, and, as a matter of fact, the institutionalization of similar issues such as equity and equality started after the Family Code reforms. There was progress in terms of women's political involvement, the Nationality Law, and other issues.

In 2004, we created an interesting network, Anaruz, that gathers all counseling centers providing support for women victims of violence. On a political level, we had to introduce the Family Code and the penal code reforms in public debates. The penal code was reformed later. We managed to demonstrate that some provisions of the Family Code constitute violence against women. For example, depriving a woman of her right to alimony is economic violence; throwing a woman out of the matrimonial house is violence too. We even added hampering the right of women to travel as violence. The first official survey on the prevalence of violence against women in 2009 referred to the findings of Anaruz. Since it was the very first official survey, they called for the women's movement to participate in the conceptualization; I was invited to participate in designing the questionnaire.

The obstacles to reform did not arise from the general public – quite the opposite. They arose from the well-educated political elites, even left-wingers. It was such a disillusion. One of our strategies was to directly address first-rank leaders such as party chairmen. Sometimes, it was ridiculous. At other times, we were in tears knowing that these people would someday rule the country. There was a great deal of incompetence and ignorance. The women's movement became a shining example to follow. It was the first social movement to develop innovative work plans and mobilization strategies. The notion of advocacy was nonexistent in Morocco, except for trade unions that operate within a regulated, legal, and institutional framework where the Ministry of Employment, along with the employers' association and trade unions, cooperate to solve problems. The women's movement helped expand the scope of citizenship: citizens directly address the government and hold it accountable. Regrettably, intellectuals did not play a significant role in our countries. A few works were published, but that was less frequent with time. In the 1960s, we had intellectuals who, through their works, stimulated analytical thinking. In the 1980s and 1990s, 80 percent of Moroccan women could not read or write.

As a matter of fact, the problem was not relevant to this large public; it only emerged when we were confronted by the Islamic movement in the late 1990s. For a long period, we faced resistance amongst political elites, mostly right-wingers and to a lesser extent, left-wingers, whose support was taken for granted. We have been through tough times. The resistance crystallized by the end of the 1990s as the Islamic movement started to dominate. Obstacles were of all kinds, notably financial, given that associational life in the Maghreb was different from that in the Middle East in terms of traditions. Work was mainly based on volunteering, and associational work is not professionalized: 90 percent of the work is done by volunteers who are in charge of decision-making, paperwork, research, and their daily implementation.

Paradoxically, we managed to move ahead despite adversity. Now that things are much easier, we struggle to cope with the current national and regional context. We had to make sacrifices, but we believed that our cause was just and we eventually reached our goals. Some of our demands were not approved; nonetheless, it remains a revolutionary achievement in terms of the Family Code provisions, but especially in terms of the process itself – we broke the myth that the Family Code is unchangeable within the religious identity of Moroccan families. Nowadays, reviewing some of the provisions seems feasible. Obstacles, as I said earlier, arose from the political and intellectual elite of the country.

What about the external context?

When you travel to a foreign country and notice the same issues or a situation worse than in Morocco – you see women fighting, mobilizing in order to bring change – you gain strength. We witnessed the golden age of the United Nations and the international feminist movement back in the 1980s until the conference of 1995. Later on, the movement suffered a setback. But at that moment, it was strong enough to impose incredible progress during both the human rights and the 1995 world conferences. All that ardor and mobilization on the international level were relayed to Morocco on TV through satellite channels. All of these factors helped us gain distant but powerful allies. We could not assume that Moroccan feminists were the only ones demanding reforms. For instance, the 1995 world conference in Beijing was covered by all international media channels, not only because it was the largest but also because it was held in Beijing, and China, back then, was still a closed country. We therefore received significant media coverage. We started to gain regular exposure, we were invited everywhere. We learned much from others, and we were extremely confident that if they succeeded, why can't we? We used to invite other organizations, in difficult times, to send letters to political parties and to the royal cabinet to claim changes. It worked in the difficult context of 1998 and especially in 1999–2000, when we were subject to attacks from the Islamist party; there was a great feeling of solidarity. Yet I am delighted to notice the current recovery, when the public is regaining interest in this issue thanks to the ongoing campaign against harassment. The media coverage of harassment will draw attention to violence against women and women's rights. The question of violence, especially sexual, is frequently addressed on TV. The four UN Conferences on Women between 1975 and 1995 and the preparatory conferences helped us mobilize, and that was of great support. The Moroccan diaspora, including women who settled in different countries of Europe, were very supportive and helped raise awareness through petitions and others actions, especially in France, Belgium, and the Netherlands. They provided great support in favor of the Family Code reforms and the Nationality Law. The first generation of women who moved to Europe to join their spouses now have daughters who studied in Europe and were raised in an egalitarian environment. The female diaspora mobilized, raised awareness, and held the government accountable by writing to the royal cabinet.

What about the role of the media?

In the beginning, before confrontations, mobilizations, and counter-mobilizations, the media was our main means of reaching the public. The media not only creates public awareness, but it also puts politicians under pressure. We privileged the Moroccan news agency because it shares information with all press organizations. We gained the loyalty of five or six journalists, some of whom were men. Some newspapers would spontaneously organize roundtables, invite intellectuals and high-profile people to debate certain topics related to the Family Code, and publish the debate. There were plenty of initiatives that played a crucial role. Reforming the Family Code was nothing but a mere fantasy before turning this goal into a serious political issue. It is possible that without the role of media and Islamic mobilization, we would not have reached the critical mass that led to the reforms.

Gaining the loyalty of media outlets required that we make an extra effort by doing part of their job for them. Press releases issued by ADFM were comprehensive but concise; they never exceeded one page. We wanted to grab the media's attention without being sensational. Besides, the messenger is as important as the message. We recently adopted a strategy in this regard, with women working on the Nationality Law and with the Soulaliyates ["women of collective lands"]. We tried to transmit messages via different channels, in a way that the public does not associate a message with a specific profile, by picking celebrities who are not feminists. Discussions were held about who is going to speak and why, according to the messenger's public influence. In the beginning, we used to work rather intuitively, but when it came to media, the approach was more reasoned and rational.

For the Mudawana, we had recourse to male public figures through religious scholars. We sometimes picked bearded men, which was surprising because they were first mistaken for Islamists, but with a different discourse. We also chose men wearing the traditional *djellaba* to break the stereotype of Westernized feminists, as characterized by the media. Personally, I limited my media appearances to ensure diverse messages and messengers.

What about the role and influence of Islamic women's associations?

I think that the question relates to the Family Code reform process. We should note that there was no such thing as feminist women at that point; they only emerged when the Islamic Party became structured and official. Feminists were there, but they could not make their voices heard because they were not operating in well-structured entities. Once the party was organized, activists of the female wing of the party started to position themselves in a feminist organization backing the "Unification and Reform" movement, but they were not very active. They were probably token women, as in progressive parties. Afterwards, Islamists thought it would benefit them to take advantage of the current context and the emergence of the feminist movement. Integrating women's associations in the party structures was instrumentalized. A women's branch was created in the party, but they were smart enough to predict that women would not be very productive in the party and therefore created Islamic women's associations, which increased in numbers later on. Many of these associations were simply helping within their communities by distributing soup and clothes and doing circumcisions, mostly charity work. Others, by contrast, became strategically involved in the questions raised by the feminists. In the beginning, they complied with the positions taken by their parties. There was a general feeling that their role was to amplify the voices of men. By the way, political quotas were favored by the Islamic parties mostly because they were ahead of secular parties in seeing the advantages of having women representing them in Parliament and on local councils. Women were the spokespersons of men in Parliament. Indeed, the women, who were initially their party's tokens, began to claim exposure as they gained access to Parliament and the related responsibilities. Some female Islamists tried to distance themselves from their party's official positions. This contradiction is likely to be fruitful in the long run. The Islamist parties thought that they were capable of instrumentalizing women by assigning them to strategic positions (ministers, members of Parliament, local representatives, party leaders, etc.); but they were only digging their own graves as their instruments turned against them. Women would increasingly claim more responsibilities and demand respectful treatment. They would give up their role of being tokens. They would build on their experiences, becoming more studious and eager to learn. They would expand their capacity and gain access to a wide range of environments and points of view – and they will therefore end up making a U-turn. It will definitely take time, but some of them have already started to open up and to hold a rational discourse. They are no longer subscribing unconditionally to their parties' positions. Initially, women were extremely hostile to the feminist movement and to the Family Code reforms – the current Minister of Women's Affairs even stated that polygamy benefited women more than men. They even struggled to maintain the marriageable age as fifteen. Today, society is calling to ban underage marriage, yet some women still defend it.

Notes

1   This chapter was translated from the original French version by Nadia Labidi.
2   Imam Malik ibn Anas (711–795 C.E.) founded this school of Islamic jurisprudence during the eighth century. It relies on the Quran and Hadiths as primary sources. Unlike other jurisprudential schools, however, it also considers the consensus of the people of Medina to be a valid source of Islamic law.

14

CONCLUSION

Reflections on recent progress and reversals in the war to curb violence against women

Ann Elizabeth Mayer

We see much to applaud when we review recent developments showing how the concept "violence against women" (VAW) can be used by feminists in advocating for family law reform to advance women's human rights. These developments are illuminated in the case studies and interviews in this volume and are assessed in Ertürk's comparative overview, for which her book provides a valuable historical framework (Ertürk 2016). This chapter will attempt to assess where we now stand and will also warn about new setbacks and the threat of VAW on the Internet.

Using VAW as a concept enables us to identify how acts of violence are linked to patterns in the discriminatory treatment of women in a variety of domains. For example, it enables us to discredit the old idea that VAW within the confines of the family belongs in a zone of privacy that should be off-limits to governmental intervention. We find no mention of VAW in the text of CEDAW, which was produced back in 1979 – a major deficiency in our basic women's human rights document. Not till the late 1980s did the General Recommendations compensate for CEDAW's original failure to grapple with VAW as a factor in discrimination against women. The UN did not squarely address VAW until 1993, when it produced the Declaration on the Elimination of Violence against Women. As awareness grew of the need to grapple with VAW, declarations and conventions were adopted, and many national laws following similar principles were enacted.

Now that VAW is widely understood as a harmful phenomenon, it has become harder to defend practices that segments of society long viewed as completely normal human behavior. For example, some countries have had laws that offer rapists exoneration for their crimes if they marry their victims. Viewed through the prisms of patriarchal systems that prioritize family honor and ignore the harms caused to the rape victim, such cancellations of rapists' criminal liability make sense; aggravating the suffering of the victim by having her marry and live with the man who assaulted her is discounted. With the VAW concept in the foreground, feminists denounced the failure to take into account the violations of the victim's human rights (Sengupta 2017a).

With a spreading appreciation that VAW is criminal, movements condemning "marry the rapist" laws have been proliferating. Countries such as Egypt, Morocco, and Tunisia have recently decided to cancel the local versions of these laws. In Morocco, the change followed an international scandal that broke out when Amina al-Filali, a sixteen-year-old rape victim, was forced to marry her twenty-three-year-old rapist to "restore her family's honor." After seven months of wretchedness as his wife, al-Filali committed suicide by swallowing rat poison. A wave of outraged protests led to the abandonment of the marry-your-rapist principle in Morocco (Al Jazeera 2014).

The most recent victories have been in Jordan and in Lebanon. The July 2017 Jordanian reform was acclaimed by Salma Nims, the secretary general of the Jordanian National Commission for Women, who asserted that it was "a victory for the women's movement and human rights movement in Jordan" (Su 2017).

After a campaign that employed shocking visuals to mobilize support, in August 2017 Lebanon repealed its "marry-your-rapist law." Ghida Anani, the founder of ABAAD, a Lebanese women's rights organization, praised the repeal as "the first step to changing the mind-set and traditions." ABAAD had hung bloodied and torn wedding gowns around Beirut and put up billboards with the caption "A white dress doesn't cover up rape" (Sengupta 2017b). The spectacle of white gowns ripped and bloodied conveyed the brutality of VAW, attracting international attention and opprobrium. This made it easier to convey the need for reforms. Even in strongly patriarchal milieus, exposés of the brutality of VAW have the capacity to reach people's consciences.

Similarly, in Pakistan distressing images changed attitudes. Saba Qaiser, a young Pakistani woman, was shot in the head and thrown into a river to drown by her father and uncle to "save the family honor." Saba's offense had been that, shortly before she married a man who had initially won her family's approval, she disregarded the last-minute intervention of her uncle, who declared that she should marry his brother-in-law instead. Her family deemed this a shameful act. After being shot and tossed in the river, Saba somehow managed to summon help, after which she was conveyed to a hospital. Confident that they would not be punished, Saba's family would probably have tried to kill her a second time, but for the publicity that transformed the would-be honor killing into a cause celebre. Sharmeen Obaid-Chinoy, a Pakistani filmmaker and feminist activist, made a documentary film on this case called *A Girl in the River: The Price of Forgiveness.* Not only did the film win high praise, but Obaid-Chinoy won an Oscar for the Best Documentary Short category.

With an international spotlight on the case and widespread criticisms circulating, the Pakistani Prime Minister Nawaz Sharif proclaimed that he wanted the relevant laws to be changed (Hassan 2016). Pakistan did pass legislation in 2016 that called for mandatory prison sentences of twenty-five years for honor killings, but not without opposition from conservative forces and those who associated the old rules on honor killings with upholding Islamic morality. To mollify the opponents, the original version of the 2016 law was modified to allow the killer to escape the death penalty if the woman's relatives agreed to pardon him (Boone 2016).

Experience shows that feminist activism can make striking progress in open political environments where women's rights NGOs can operate without risking prosecution or shutdowns. The impressive accomplishments of Brazilian feminists are detailed in the Brazil chapter. They have achieved great things despite working in a country in which patriarchal norms were deeply embedded – achievements that demonstrate how campaigns against VAW can succeed where feminists are not intimidated, forcibly silenced, or imprisoned. Conversely, women's rights activists in countries such as Iran and Saudi Arabia have faced daunting odds.

While it is gratifying to tally the progress that has been achieved, we should also recognize certain ominous trends. Activists need to confront the possibility that recent measures designed to deter VAW can be reversed, as forces hostile to women's rights gain ground in politics and reassert their patriarchal visions. Iran, Russia, Turkey, and the US offer dramatic illustrations of how fragile women's gains can be, once regimes come to power that decide to cater to the forces of patriarchal reaction. Reviewing these examples, one can discern a perverse linkage of policies reversing progress towards eradicating VAW and policies aimed at intimidating members of the LGBTQ community and stripping them of hard-won rights. Of course, expanding the rights of women and members of the LGBTQ community threatens to erode patriarchal domination and to unsettle the old religious rules that validated it.

Iran provided an early example of how improvements in women's status provoked the ire of conservatives, leading to the progress being suddenly reversed in the wake of a political upheaval. In an interview, Iran's Minister of Women's Affairs prior to the Islamic Revolution, Mahnaz Afkhami, reminisced about Iran's successes advancing women's rights and their cancellation in the wake of the Islamic Revolution (Khorasani 2008). Hard work and background research by the Women's Organization of Iran (WOI) led to the reform of Article 179 of Iran's Penal Code on honor killings. Over the following decades, the WOI's research and methods for law reforms had impact in other countries, including Brazil and Jordan. The WOI was assisted by advice from Françoise Giroud, the French Minister of Women's Affairs, on the revocation of articles similar to Iran's Article 179 in the French civil and penal codes. That is, far from being an isolated endeavor, the Iranian campaign against laws condoning honor crimes had international connections and ramifications, showing how feminists collaborated and shared, despite being on different sides of national and cultural borders.

In addition to the reforms in Iran's laws on honor killings, a striking achievement in the area of women's rights came in the form of dramatic reforms in Iranian family law in the breakthrough 1967 Family Protection Act and later amendments. As discussed in the Iran chapter, this law significantly improved women's rights in the family, including in areas relevant for domestic violence cases.

In reacting to how this 1967 reform has been portrayed, Afkhami argues that the role of Iran's dynamic feminist movement has typically been underplayed. The Act tends to be dismissed as a measure imposed by an autocratic monarch obsessed with imitating the West and eager to win plaudits by posing as a supporter of women's emancipation. In reality, records of the work that led to this historic legal change show that the Shah kept his distance from the project and that the Act came into being as a result of tireless negotiations by Iranian feminists, the WOI playing a major role. Some of the more radical proposed reforms had to be abandoned when they proved to be too bold, too controversial; but reactionaries were not placated. In February 1979, shortly after the Shah's ouster and the installation of the Islamic revolutionary regime, Ayatollah Khomeini announced that the Act was suspended.

In the light of subsequent reversals, Afkhami wondered if the reformers should have been even more cautious. With the benefit of hindsight, she concluded that they had moved too fast in the direction of modernity, progress, equality, and women's rights, not considering whether they were putting a great strain on Iran's social fabric that would lead to reaction (ibid.).

Observing how progressive reforms to advance gender equality have engendered potent backlash in the MENA region, Afkhami pointed out how politicians have found it politically profitable to play to populist forces eager to turn the clock back, basing their legitimacy not on advancing women's rights but on upholding a vision of tradition. She commented that advancing women's equality was formerly considered a point of pride, but that now legitimacy is often being based on programs at odds with such equality (ibid.).

Thus, in the wake of the 1979 Islamic Revolution, Iran's ruling theocrats based their legitimacy on their professed dedication to upholding Islamic law, which the post-revolutionary Constitution explicitly ranked above human rights. Frequent tough clampdowns on feminist groups and publications made it dangerous for feminists to challenge the setbacks to women's rights (Mir-Hosseini 2016).

As in the period before the Revolution, Iran's laws and policies on the legality of abortion continued to exhibit complications and ambivalence; the shifting positions did not exhibit the classic liberal-conservative splits that are characteristic of abortion policies in countries with Christian heritages.

In other areas, the changes – such as using the threat of criminal penalties to force women to wear the approved form of Islamic dress – were dramatic, as detailed in the chapter on Iran. Not surprisingly, the ruling clerics, whose version of Islamic law accommodated wife-beating, were not concerned with eliminating VAW. Although studies of VAW in post-revolutionary Iran are limited and statistics are not as complete as one would wish, as the Iran chapter shows and as other studies indicate, VAW has continued to pose serious problems (Adineh et al. 2016; Hajnasiri et al. 2016; Rasoulian et al. 2014).

The concealing dress, like the chador required by Iran's theocracy, might connote pristine morality for some, but it could also serve to cloak evidence of domestic violence, as was shown in a 2015 scandal involving an Iranian TV presenter, Azadeh Namdari. As one partner in a celebrity couple with regime connections, she boasted of being proud to wear the chador, which she claimed brought her blessings. Namdari was frequently shown in photographs beaming while swathed in her chador, her smiling husband at her side. The image of domestic bliss was shattered when she shared on Instagram a photo of her bruised face after a pummeling by her husband. After the scandal exploded, reports surfaced of her husband's earlier history of assaulting women. In the aftermath of the embarrassing publicity, her marriage ended without her husband being punished. Iranians were shocked by this incident, but reactions to Namdari's decision to publicize her injuries were mixed, with some praising her courage and others condemning her for revealing a private matter (Shahrabi 2015).

In an intriguing coda to this scandal, Namdari was subsequently embarrassed when a photo taken in Switzerland caught her off-guard: she became the center of a second scandal in 2017 when she was surreptitiously photographed at an outdoor dining venue unveiled and drinking what appeared to be a bottle of Feldschlösschen beer (Gaffey 2017). Although Namdari had acted as an apologist for Iran's rules on Islamic dress, it turned out that underneath the chador there was a woman with non-conforming values.

A counterpart case occurred in Saudi Arabia involving the TV news anchor Rania al-Baz, showing how VAW thrives under the cover of rules upholding the patriarchal family and strict Islamic morality.

Rania al-Baz – always carefully veiled – had been used to being beaten by her violent and sadistic husband. Like many other victims of VAW, she was fearful of losing custody of her children if she got a divorce and therefore felt obliged to put up with her husband's intensifying abuse. At last, after a particularly savage beating came close to killing her and left her hospitalized in a coma for several days, she allowed photographs of her hideously bruised and swollen face to be published. This exposé of her husband's brutality caused a sensation, with Saudi opinion being divided on whether al-Baz was brave to publicize her suffering or whether it was shameful for a woman to "betray" her husband in this manner. Although even in Saudi Arabia this murderous beating was deemed wrongful, al-Baz felt obliged to waive any claim for compensation and pardon her husband as part of a deal to secure a divorce and custody of her children (Vulliamy 2005).

It is significant that both the Namdari and al-Baz photos provoked dismay and controversy. When the once-beautiful faces of women celebrities were displayed after being disfigured by abusive husbands, both opponents and defenders of VAW realized that the old consensus supporting wife-beating was crumbling. The visuals mobilized both women's rights activists who condemned VAW and the forces seeking to uphold traditions of male domination who wanted to quell the growing movement calling for an end to domestic violence.

Responding to changing attitudes, even reactionaries have become reluctant to articulate the premise that women's defective nature requires physical chastisement at the hands of men, whose nature made them superior beings. Thus, instead of exalting men's right to inflict pain and humiliation on women, they now tend to invoke the need to uphold abstract values such as religion, morality, tradition, and the sanctity of the family – as if it were self-evident that patterns of VAW were furthering these ideals.

At the same time that VAW has become a point of contention, controversies rage regarding LGBTQ rights. Where the rights of gay men are concerned, Iran has adhered to an ideologized version of tradition and Islamic morality to underpin a repressive agenda. Iran harshly punishes adult gay men found guilty of nothing more than having consensual sexual relations (Human Rights Watch 2010).

Paradoxically, when compared with many other regimes that condemn gays on religious grounds, Iran is willing to accommodate transgender individuals. Iran supports sex-reassignment surgeries for Iranians who claim they are attracted to members of the "wrong" sex. The official line is that an individual's transitioning from a gender that is a bad fit to one that is more in accordance with the patient's true nature is perfectly licit. Sex-reassignment surgeries have been become common in Iran. One must recognize the coercive element behind such surgeries, because when a gay man "chooses" sex reassignment, this may only be out of fear of being hanged if he does not transition (Bahreini 2009).

Iran's reaction against previous liberalization and its adoption of retrograde policies affecting women is not unique and is also not peculiar either to Muslim countries or to countries in the Global South. Analogous political reversals in Russia and the US have led them to adopt policies inimical to the rights of women and sexual minorities. Trends in Turkey, discussed in more detail in the chapter on Turkey, embody a particularly dramatic turnaround in governmental policies, which have taken it from assertive laicism and sponsorship of reforms to advance women's rights to an embrace of Islamist policies and promotion of the idea that women belong in domestic and child-rearing roles.

Those observing Iran's 1979 Islamic Revolution probably did not look north towards the Soviet Union and anticipate an analogous triumph of reactionary religious politics. The USSR's atheistic communist system, in place since the 1917 Russian Revolution, seemed to be firmly entrenched. Communism had called for creating an egalitarian society and unshackling women from old strictures. In the early years after the 1917 Revolution, many steps were taken to advance women's rights and welfare, including liberalizing grounds for divorce, granting women reproductive rights, and opening job opportunities that enabled women to live independently of men (Ghodsee 2017).

With the 1989 fall of the USSR, after a short democratic opening, power was consolidated in the hands of a kleptocratic elite that relied on ruthless repression to maintain control. The new autocracy that emerged under Vladimir Putin became closely associated with the Russian Orthodox Church, which had previously been reduced to a beleaguered, marginal institution. Needing a rationale for monopolizing power, Putin, who had worked as an officer in the USSR's KGB and since 1999 variously served as prime minister and president, resorted to appeals to Russian tradition and the Russian Orthodox Church, currently led by clerics who hold reactionary views on women and gay men. This entailed significant self-reinvention for someone who had spent his earlier career as a communist stalwart.

As a sign of the government's recommitment to Russian Orthodoxy, the grandiose Cathedral of Christ the Savior near the Kremlin, which was demolished under Stalin as part of his campaign against Christianity, was rebuilt at great expense in 1995–2000. Putin attends services and celebrations there with fanfare and publicity – as when cameras covered his visit to the cathedral to venerate with ostentatious manifestations of piety the bones of Russia's revered St. Nicholas, which were on special loan to Moscow from Italy (YouTube n.d.).

As part of his call for returning to traditional values – meaning Russian values as they stood prior to the communist era – Putin's regime has vilified supposed Western degeneracy while promoting policies at odds with feminist principles and also demonizing gay men. Given the reactionary trends in Russia, it was not surprising that, as of 2017, Russia had failed to sign or ratify the 2011 Istanbul Convention on preventing and combating VAW and domestic violence. Russian feminists could briefly congratulate themselves on bucking the trends and scoring a legal victory in 2016 when a provision was added to the criminal code that punished VAW. This was a noteworthy accomplishment in a country where domestic violence was both rife and generally condoned, and where the local folklore had long promoted the nostrum "If he beats you, it means he loves you" (Litvinova 2016).

In a disturbing development in 2017, this progressive measure was canceled and replaced by a law that decriminalized VAW. Those trying to defend the revision described it as merely decriminalizing VAW in cases where it did not cause "substantial bodily harm" and where the violence did not occur more than once a year. The change would, however, look ominous to anyone who appreciated the implications of quickly backtracking after enacting a law criminalizing VAW. When a Kremlin spokesperson asserted that family conflicts do "not necessarily constitute domestic violence," critical observers would realize that "domestic violence" was likely to be narrowly defined so that supposedly normal levels of wife-beating would not fall in the VAW category (Stanglin 2017).

After the implosion of the USSR, gay sex was briefly decriminalized in Russia, which did not mean an end to discrimination and persecution targeting sexual minorities. At the regional level, various "gay propaganda laws" were introduced starting in 2003. Eventually, in 2013 a law was adopted at the national level that banned "the promoting of nontraditional sexual relationships among minors" and "creating a distorted image of the social equivalence of traditional and nontraditional sexual relationships." Consequently, it became criminal to share information on homosexuality that portrayed it as one of the natural variations in human sexuality. This meant that gay men, if they challenged anti-gay prejudices, could be deemed to be engaging in criminal activity. This law was vehemently denounced by human rights groups, which viewed it as being aimed at stifling educational initiatives and human rights activism on behalf of the LGBTQ community (Chan 2017). Meanwhile, the national government has failed to intervene in the region of Chechnya as the local regime has carried out savage pogroms against gay men and those merely suspected of being gay (Kramer 2017).

As Putin has moved to the right, other figures in Russian politics have followed his lead. One is Yelena Mizulina, a Russian politician who was not originally a proponent of reaction but who has become notorious for sponsoring the national "gay propaganda law." Among other things, with her new-found religiosity, she has proposed an amendment to the Russian Constitution that would make the Russian Orthodox Church the basis of Russia's national and cultural identity (Mostovshchikov 2015).

Unlike Brazilian women's rights activists, who have been able to achieve great things, their Russian counterparts, under the growing repression of the post-communist era, have seen short-lived advances being reversed (McIntosh Sundstrom 2002). Complicating the Russian picture is the emergence of a fake feminism that is allied with the Putin regime and aims to whitewash women's problems, including domestic violence. According to Nadezda Azhgikhina, a prominent journalist and writer, government-organized non-governmental organizations (GONGOs) pretending to speak for Russian feminism proclaim the virtues of modern Russian life, promoting the idea that "[t]here is no discrimination, nor thousands of victims of domestic violence, or forced marriage and honor killings in the North Caucasus, nor misogyny, aggression, and sexism in the society" (Azhgikhina 2017).

In this hostile environment, some Russian feminists have resorted to outrageous stunts to draw attention to women's actual grievances. The punk band Pussy Riot is the most infamous such group after their provocative performance of a song mocking Putin in 2012 in the Cathedral of Christ the Savior in Moscow, for which two band members received prison sentences and were vilified in the media (Rutenberg 2016).

One study proposes that Pussy Riot amounts to a kind of "informal feminism" that emerged in reaction to the Putin regime's repression of NGO feminism and that its stunts "are a logical reaction to the Kremlin's masculinity-based nation-rebuilding scheme, which was a cover for crude homophobic misogyny" (Johnson 2014).

When one considers that in 2012, Pussy Riot members received prison sentences for a stunt in a cathedral while "normal" wife-beating was decriminalized in 2017, one appreciates what Putin's embrace of Russian traditions implied in terms of policies affecting women.

If one compares recent trends in Russia and in the US, one notices that in both countries there is a backlash against women's rights, and in both the leaders seek to placate religious conservatives by degrading women's rights.

In 1964, the US Civil Rights Act, which was primarily intended to curb racial discrimination, offered US women important protections, even though it fell short of affording women the equality that they had sought for decades. Uneven progress towards expanding US women's rights characterized the decades that followed. Women experienced some grievous setbacks, as when conservatives successfully mobilized to defeat the Equal Rights Amendment in 1984 and blocked ratification of CEDAW, leaving US women cut off from participation in the CEDAW system. As part of the see-sawing, important advances were occasionally made, such as the

1994 Violence Against Women Act, but these were often balanced by conservative victories, especially in the form of regressive measures such as court rulings and legal enactments that were designed to curb women's access to abortion and contraception (see Talbot 2017).

The bitter conflicts over US women's right to abortion intensified after 1973, when the Supreme Court confronted a Texas statute that, like most contemporaneous state laws, banned all abortions except where they were needed to save the life of the mother. Not appreciating the enormous backlash that it would create, the Court ruled in the famous *Roe v. Wade* case that such blanket restrictions on abortion rights were unconstitutional. In crude summary, the decision, which acknowledged that states had interests that justified certain regulations, provided that, at least in the early months of pregnancy, the appropriate person to make the decision about the wisdom of terminating a pregnancy was the pregnant woman herself.

US conservatives reacted with dismay and fury to the Supreme Court decision. Not coincidentally, the groups opposing liberalized access to abortion tended to be ones that were opposed to women's rights in general and that espoused patriarchal modes of thinking. Over the decades, organizations dedicated to weakening and overturning *Roe v. Wade* succeeded in mobilizing strong backing for schemes designed to restrict access to abortion, imposing onerous procedural hurdles and burdensome requirements on doctors and facilities that provided abortion services (Redden 2013).

The coalition loosely known as the "Religious Right" figured prominently in the fight to ban abortion. This name had applied originally to an alliance of Protestant denominations committed to defending traditional morality, but it later came to include conservative Catholics who are out of sympathy with Pope Francis and his outlook. In a Jesuit publication in 2017, Antonio Spadaro, a prominent Vatican priest, complained that some Catholics were embracing ideas popular among Protestant fundamentalists. Looking at the US political scene, he bemoaned the alliance between Evangelical fundamentalists and Catholic Integralists, accusing them of ignoring the teachings of Jesus and instead showing a preoccupation with abortion and same-sex marriage while seeking to supplant US secularism with "a theocratic type of state" (Collins 2017). Taking a similar line, Massimo Faggioli, a professor of historical theology at Villanova University, has argued that American Catholicism is deviating from the mainstream European and Latin American models and has fallen "into the hands of the religious right" (Horowitz 2017).

In the campaign of this right-wing coalition of Protestants and Catholics to reshape US laws according to their values and to force women back into the roles of homemakers and child-bearers, one saw echoes of the campaign of Iran's ruling theocrats to push women back into domestic roles. While the prospects for the emergence of an actual US theocratic state may seem remote, nonetheless, the growing political clout of US religious forces that are eager to enforce rigid patriarchal norms causes justifiable alarm among women and sexual minorities, who are standing in the forefront of those with much to lose.

The Religious Right was able to influence the outcome of the November 2016 presidential election, overwhelmingly supporting Donald Trump. The twice-divorced Trump, while enjoying a flamboyantly sybaritic life as a real estate mogul who invested in gambling casinos and beauty pageants, went out of his way to flaunt his libertine inclinations and sexual adventures. Moreover, his disregard for religion was patent. His attitude was signaled when he revealed that his favorite book was *The Fountainhead* by the stridently atheist philosopher Ayn Rand. Trump stated that he identified with the book's hero, Howard Roark, a self-centered and egotistic architect, who in the story violently rapes the lead female character, an assault celebrated in the novel as emblematic of male dynamism and power (Kilgore 2016).

Nonetheless, as his political ambitions grew, Trump recognized that political profit was to be gained from claiming to support the narrow views of Christian morality endorsed by the Religious Right, a morality that involved curbing the rights and freedoms of women and sexual minorities. Having once supported abortion rights, he proclaimed his backing for abortion bans and in March 2016 even went so far as to assert that "some kind of punishment" should be imposed on women for having abortions – this before being warned that he risked being labeled too extreme and quickly walking back his comment (Flegenheimer and Haberman 2016).

There was widespread astonishment as members of the Religious Right continued to back Trump throughout 2016 as more exposés of Trump's crudely profane and sexist language came to light, along with reports of numerous alleged sexual assaults. His own words and actions exposed his unapologetically lewd machismo. In October 2016, a videotape revealed Trump's boasting of assaulting beautiful women and liking to "[g]rab 'em by the pussy," which provoked widespread denunciations and led many to assume – wrongly – that conservatives would turn their backs on him (Mathis-Lilley 2016).

In contrast to those who condoned Trump's sexual predations, feminists expressed outrage. Women staged massive protest marches in many US cities after Trump's inauguration (Rosner et al. 2017). Fury over Trump's sexual assaults subsequently metastasized and led to vigorous campaigns in many countries to combat sexual harassment, exposing the vast scope of the problem in the process.

In the face of all this, a group of influential evangelical pastors came to the White House in July 2017 to lay hands on Trump and utter prayers, thereby blessing his leadership and confirming suspicions that ambitions for political power and a chance to revive patriarchal privilege were driving their positions (Pulliam Bailey 2017).

Meanwhile, in a peculiar twist, both Trump and US religious conservatives have discovered a model leader in Vladimir Putin. Habitually harshly critical of people he deals with, Trump has had only kind words and praise for Putin. In similar fashion, having once been fervid opponents of Russia, which under communism was viewed as the nemesis of Christianity, members of the Religious Right have hailed Putin as a champion of Christian values (Peters 2017). For those on the right, the fact that Putin and Trump show a mutual admiration for each other enhances both of their heroic images.

Not surprisingly, soon after the Trump administration took over, measures started to be taken that were detrimental to women's rights and to programs to curb VAW. On his first Monday in office, Trump signed an executive order banning international NGOs receiving US funding from providing any abortion services or offering information about abortions, thereby gratifying conservatives determined to curb women's reproductive freedoms (Boseley 2017). As Ulla Müller, president and CEO of EngenderHealth, observed, the cutting-off of funding for women's health services would have terrible consequences for the human rights of women in poor countries, a special concern being girls who would be forced out of school and into marriage if they could not avoid or terminate pregnancies (ibid.).

Significantly, in 2017 under the Trump presidency, steps were taken that would eviscerate programs under the Violence Against Women Act, entailing massive cuts to funding needed to aid survivors of sexual assault and domestic violence (Wise McClatchy 2017). In addition, in July 2017, Trump's Department of Education under Betsy DeVos, a pillar of the right-wing Republican faction, launched initiatives to re-examine policies that under President Obama had been designed to provide for improved handling of reports of sexual violence occurring on campus and to make it easier for victims to make effective complaints (Drexler 2017). DeVos met with representatives of men's rights groups, who maintained that the rates of rape and domestic violence were being exaggerated. All indications were that she would push for revisions of Obama's policies that, according to her office, were denying due process to men accused of rape, changes that would make it much more difficult to establish that a rape had been committed (Redden 2017).

This indicated that the efforts that had been made over several years to devise ways to curb the plague of sexual assaults occurring on college campuses would be impeded. Although in the abstract it seemed legitimate to question whether investigations of campus rape cases were always being conducted in a manner that was equally fair to accusers and alleged perpetrators, the fact that DeVos was serving a president who had a history of sexual predation would lead one to expect that the changed proceedings would cast doubt on the veracity of rape charges and make it easier for campus rapists to escape punishment.

The efforts by Putin's supporters to whitewash women's problems, including domestic violence, had a parallel in the Trump administration's decision in 2017 to remove a 2014 report on sexual violence from the White House website. Called "Rape and Sexual Assault: Renewed Call to Action," the report had been produced under the Obama administration by the White House Council on Women and Girls. In the main, it comprised statistics on sexual violence and examined how the criminal justice system and college campuses could improve their efforts to combat sexual violence (Vagianos 2017). Obviously, no administration that was committed to reducing VAW would have chosen to remove such a report.

The phenomenon of fake feminism under Putin has already been referred to. Not surprisingly, under Trump there is a similar attempt to present governmental policies affecting women in a positive light. In this connection, Trump's daughter Ivanka has played a salient role, portraying her father as a champion of women and offering anodyne and superficial remarks in favor of women's empowerment. While some seem impressed, feminists who examine Ivanka Trump's record see through the spin. As Alana Moceri has written:

> Ivanka Trump embodies a right-wing fantasy of what feminism should be. In fact, it's a brilliant tactic: instead of a full frontal assault on feminism, a la feminazi, they claim the term via hollowed out platitudes about women's empowerment. Then all they need is the perfect spokesperson, a wealthy, pretty and well-dressed blonde who dutifully pays lip service to putting motherhood above all else.
>
> This fake feminism is infuriating and dangerous. It undermines the slow slog towards progress we've been making in favor of less funding for women's healthcare, a nearly all-male presidential cabinet and a president who not only says crude things about women but has been accused of sexual assault and harassment more than 15 times.
>
> *(Moceri 2017; see also Valenti 2017)*

Like the feminist community, members of the US LGBTQ community had reason to lament the Trump takeover. In the decades preceding Trump's presidency, they had made important progress, no longer being forced to disguise their sexual orientations and winning respect and acceptance in politics and the professions, including in the military. Despite during his campaign having promised to be protective of LGBTQ rights, once in office Trump reversed course. He decided in February 2017 to revoke the previous guidance to public schools that allowed transgender students to use bathrooms of their choice. In July 2017, he sent out a tweeted announcement that clashed with existing military policy, proclaiming that transgender people would be barred from serving in the military in any capacity (Hirschfeld Davis and Cooper 2017). Trump's ban was a calculated attempt to solidify his support among religious factions determined to uphold the rigid gender binary that they believed was mandated by the Bible (ibid.).

In an era when there is a consistent disposition to assume that advances in human rights come from the West while the rest of the world lags behind, it was enlightening to contrast the regressive steps taken under Trump in 2017 with the progressive measures being taken in Pakistan in the same year to advance the rights of transgender people. In August 2017, the Pakistani Parliament was preparing to enact a law recognizing transgender people as equal citizens and providing for penalties for discrimination and violence against them. The proposed legislation may reflect the influence of a long cultural tradition in the region in which the idea of an intermediate sexual category had won acceptance (Zahra-Malik 2017).

In a further sign that the Trump administration would be stripping sexual minorities of their rights, in July 2017, Trump's Justice Department took the position that the Civil Rights Act did not afford protection from discrimination based on a person's sexual orientation, stripping gays of legal protections that they had enjoyed under previous interpretations of the law. In addition, Sam Brownback, a vigorous foe of gay rights who had attracted attention for opposing gay marriage while governor of Kansas, was nominated to be the US ambassador for international religious freedom (Shear and Savage 2017). It was obvious that he would be using his office to press the idea that "religious freedom," construed as a person's freedom to discriminate against gays when following religious dictates, outranked gays' human rights. Trump's nomination of Brownback for this prominent position was another indication that he would strip members of the LGBTQ community of hard-won gains in efforts to retain the support of the Religious Right (Bruni 2017).

As is discussed more thoroughly in the chapter on Turkey, without anything like the political upheavals in Iran in 1979 and in Russia in 1989, in the 2000s Turkey under the leadership of Recep Tayyip Erdoğan, who denies that women and men can be equal and calls for Turkish women to have a minimum of three children, has undergone a remarkable reorientation. While not expressly repudiating Kemal Ataturk's principle of laicism, which is stipulated in the constitution, in recent years the increasingly despotic Erdoğan has been pushing an Islamist agenda. The consequences have been highly detrimental for women's rights and for prospects of combating and reducing VAW. As in Iran, the patriarchal values shaping the Islamization program are being reasserted as a reaction against progressive legal reform measures. The latter embodied principles endorsed by Turkish women's organizations that had long fought to bring Turkish law into conformity with CEDAW. The Islamist counter-measures have included initiatives to lower the age of marriage and to reduce penalties for raping or sexually abusing minors. Anxious to suppress the women's movement, Erdoğan has lashed out against feminist leaders and NGOs. Meanwhile, Turkey, which had witnessed a burgeoning of campaigns for enhancing LGBTQ rights, has been clamping down on LGBTQ activism. In November 2017, the Turkish capital Ankara banned all LGBTQ events, and similar bans were subsequently adopted elsewhere. Where the treatment of the human rights of women and members of the LGBTQ community was concerned, Turkey's political climate was coming to resemble that of its two big neighbors, Iran and Russia.

But there is even more to worry about than these reactionary trends. A new form of VAW has recently metastasized – online attacks on women that prove that ferocious, threatening expressions of misogyny in postings on the Internet can be turned into weapons at least as powerful as an angry man's fists. The kind of online abuse that is often called "trolling" has become extensively employed by the alt-right in its fascist-inflected campaigns on behalf of White nationalism, patriarchal values, and subjugation of women (Stein 2016).

Misogynist trolling can harm its immediate targets but also serves to intimidate other women from speaking out against oppression. Kara Alaimo, a female professor, recently wrote about her own experiences of being vilified online and commented on studies of Internet trolling. Among the things she reports are that a high proportion of online abuse is directed at women – especially black women – and that the attacks tend to be personal – as opposed to rational arguments against positions that the targets articulated. The threat of trolling scares off many women who would otherwise want to post; 49 percent of women age eighteen to twenty-nine said they censored themselves after witnessing the trolling of others (Alaimo 2017).

Women whose views offend men on the right are particularly likely to be the targets of savage online insults and dehumanizing profanity, which often include threats of rape. Thus, after being inundated by protracted, sadistic trolling, Lindy West, a prominent feminist author and performer, abandoned Twitter. In 2016, she wrote about her experience of being savaged online:

> Largely, the people harassing me online are guys, and my male colleagues don't experience the same kind of violent, sexualized, gendered harassment that my female colleagues experience . . . I've come to realize it's a culture problem. The platform is just the vehicle for this ingrained systemic misogyny that we're steeped in from birth to the point where men think of women as a scapegoat for their feelings. There's something behind the decision to choose to lash out at a woman. The answer to how to fix internet trolling is like fixing sexism. How do you do that?
>
> *(Andrews 2016)*

In 2017, West wrote that the abuse that she and others endured on Twitter amounted to "a grand-scale normalization project, disseminating libel and disinformation . . . and ultimately greasing the wheels for Donald Trump's ascendance to the US presidency" (Fallon 2017).

One can easily imagine how a young woman who would like to make postings supporting Lindy West's feminist positions would, out of fear of being trolled, decide instead to remain mute on the sidelines. Of course, scaring women into silence is exactly the kind of result that misogynist trolls would celebrate.

It might be imagined that this is a problem that besets US women more than women elsewhere, but even in countries where Internet use is less common, women have disturbing, frightening experiences with online trolling, discovering that online threats and attacks can serve as a new form of VAW. In Pakistan, where women suffer from high levels of sexual and domestic violence, women have had to deal with online trolling. According to a 2017 report, there were more than 136 million mobile phone users and 34 million Internet users in Pakistan. The report noted the troubling fact that offline violence was becoming increasingly connected to online abuse, harassment, and blackmail, with women bearing the brunt of such attacks. A student based in Lahore, Eman Suleman, articulately described becoming a target of voluminous, lurid threats from Pakistani men after launching a campaign to challenge the stigmatization around menstruation. Eventually, the trolling forced her to go offline, and she explained her reaction:

> I'm more scared of online harassment than offline harassment. When there are three to four people harassing you in a public space, it's easier to handle them. When there are thousands of people harassing you online – people you can't see – you don't know what they're like, you don't know if their threats are empty or real, and it becomes really frightening.
>
> *(Toppa 2017)*

Recognizing this problem, the Lahore-based Digital Rights Foundation set up Pakistan's first cyber-harassment helpline, a nationwide initiative to provide legal and psychological support to women facing cases involving online black-mail, revenge porn, cyber stalking, and harassment. This commendable initiative deserves to be emulated elsewhere.

In the same way that the problems of Internet trolling designed to silence women's voices know no national boundaries, so the challenge of combating VAW is shared by societies of the most diverse cultural and religious heritages. As the studies presented in this volume demonstrate, around the globe women's rights advocacy has promoted progressive reforms in family laws and discredited policies that demean women and accommodate VAW. Unfortunately, recent trends to re-entrench patriarchal bias in family laws threaten to erase previous gains. Evidence shows that governments of countries that have in some instances been in the forefront of advancing aspects of women's rights can shift course and embark on projects to curtail women's rights, including discarding measures that were designed to end VAW. With political shifts, governments can suddenly undergo changes that lead to relying on retrograde, patriarchal versions of religion as pillars of legitimacy, empowering reactionary forces in the process. Fortunately, there is now an international coalition of women's rights activists that, one hopes, can be mobilized for the hard work to remove the obstacles that still stand in the way of guaranteeing women's equality and security.

References

Adineh, H.A., Z. Almasi, M.E. Rad, I. Zareban, and A.A. Moghaddam (2016) "Prevalence of Domestic Violence against Women in Iran: A Systematic Review," *Epidemiology* (Sunnyvale), Vol. 6: 276; doi: 10.4172/2161-1165.1000276; www.omicsonline.org/open-access/prevalence-of-domestic-violence-against-women-in-iran-a-systematic-review-2161-1165-1000276.php?aid=83878.

Al Jazeera (2014) "Morocco Repeals 'Rape Marriage Law': Controversial Article Previously Allowed Rapists to Avoid Charges if They Married Their Victims," *Al Jazeera*, 22 January 2014; www.aljazeera.com/news/africa/2014/01/morocco-repeals-rape-marriage-law-2014123254643455.html.

Alaimo, Kara (2017) "How Not to Communicate: Lessons from Trolls," *Bloomberg*, 28 August 2017; www.bloomberg.com/view/articles/2017-08-28/how-not-to-communicate-lessons-from-trolls.

Andrews, Becca (2016) "How to Fight Fat Shaming, Internet Trolls, and Rape Culture: Lindy West Gives Us Her Best Advice," *Mother Jones*, 23 May 2016; www.motherjones.com/media/2016/05/lindy-west-talks-abortion-fat-shaming-trolls-and-rape-culture/.

Azhgikhina, Nadezda (2017) "In Russia, Are Fake Feminist Groups Back in Action? The Goals of 'Fem Fest' Seemed to be Less Rallying Russian Women and More Demonstrating to the West that Russian Feminists Exist," *The Nation*, 29 March 2017; www.thenation.com/article/in-russia-are-fake-feminist-groups-back-in-action/.

Bahreini, Raha (2009) "Perversion to Pathology: Discourses and Practices of Gender Policing in the Islamic Republic of Iran," *Muslim World Journal of Human Rights*, Vol. 5, No. 1; https://philpapers.org/rec/BAHFPT.

Boone, Jon (2016) "Pakistan Makes 'Honour Killings' Punishable by Mandatory Prison Time," *The Guardian*, 6 October 2016; www.theguardian.com/world/2016/oct/06/pakistan-honor-killing-law-prison-sentence#img-1.

Boseley, Sarah (2017) "How Trump Signed a Global Death Warrant for Women," *The Guardian*, 21 July 2017; www.theguardian.com/global-development/2017/jul/21/trump-global-death-warrant-women-family-planning-population-reproductive-rights-mexico-city-policy.

Bruni, Frank (2017) "America's Worst (and Best) Places to Be Gay," *The New York Times*, 27 August 2017; www.nytimes.com/interactive/2017/08/25/opinion/sunday/worst-and-best-places-to-be-gay.html?mcubz=0.

Chan, Sewell (2017) "Russia's 'Gay Propaganda' Laws Are Illegal, European Court Rules," *The New York Times*, 20 June 2017; www.nytimes.com/2017/06/20/world/europe/russia-gay-propaganda.html.

Collins, Charles (2017) "Jesuit Journal Close to Pope Says 'Manichean Vision' Behind Trump," *Crux*, 13 July 2017; https://cruxnow.com/vatican/2017/07/13/jesuit-journal-close-pope-says-manichean-vision-behind-trump/.

Drexler, Peggy (2017) "Betsy DeVos' Huge Step Back For College Women's Safety," *CNN*, 13 July 2017; www.cnn.com/2017/07/13/opinions/devos-reexamining-campus-sexual-assault-protections-drexler/index.html.

Ertürk, Yakın (2016) *Violence Without Borders: Paradigm, Policies, and Praxis Concerning Violence Against Women*, Bethesda, MD: Women's Learning Partnership for Rights, Development, & Peace.

Fallon, Claire (2017) "Lindy West on How Rape Joke Proponents Paved the Way for Trump," *Huffington Post*, 18 April 2017; www.huffingtonpost.com/entry/lindy-west-on-how-rape-joke-proponents-paved-the-way-for-trump_us_58efd2c6e4b0bb9638e2733d.

Flegenheimer, Matt and Maggie Haberman (2016) "Donald Trump, Abortion Foe, Eyes 'Punishment' for Women, Then Recants,'" *The New York Times*, 30 March 2016; www.nytimes.com/2016/03/31/us/politics/donald-trump-abortion.html.

Gaffey, Conor (2017) "Hijab or Not: Iran TV Host, Unveiled and Beer-Drinking, Criticized as a "Hypocrite" . . . After Leaked Images Appear Online," *Newsweek*, 26 July 2017; www.newsweek.com/women-iran-iran-hijab-azadeh-namdari-642012.

Ghodsee, Kristen R. (2017) "Why Women Had Better Sex Under Socialism," *The New York Times*, 12 August 2017; www.nytimes.com/2017/08/12/opinion/why-women-had-better-sex-under-socialism.html.

Hajnasiri, Hamideh, Reza Ghanei Gheshlagh, Kourosh Sayehmiri, Farnoosh Moafi, and Mohammad Farajzadeh (2016) "Domestic Violence among Iranian Women: A Systematic Review and Meta-Analysis," *Iran Red Crescent Medical Journal*, Vol. 18,

No. 6, June: e34971; doi: 10.5812/ircmj.34971, PMCID: PMC5006439; www.ncbi.nlm.nih.gov/pmc/articles/PMC5006439/.

Hassan, Yasmeen (2016) "A Girl in the River's Oscar Win Gives Pakistan Chance to End Honour Killings," *The Guardian*, 4 March 2016; www.theguardian.com/global-development/2016/mar/04/a-girl-in-the-river-oscar-win-pakistan-end-honour-killings.

Hirschfeld Davis, Julie and Helene Cooper (2017) "Trump Says Transgender People Will Not Be Allowed in the Military," *The New York Times*, 26 July 2017; www.nytimes.com/2017/07/26/us/politics/trump-transgender-military.html.

Horowitz, Jason (2017) "A Vatican Shot Across the Bow for Hard-Line U.S. Catholics," *The New York Times*, 2 August 2017; www.nytimes.com/2017/08/02/world/europe/vatican-us-catholic-conservatives.html.

Human Rights Watch (2010) "Iran: Discrimination and Violence against Sexual Minorities: Laws, Policies Put Already Vulnerable People at Even Greater Risk," Human Rights Watch, 15 December 2010; www.hrw.org/news/2010/12/15/iran-discrimination-and-violence-against-sexual-minorities.

Johnson, Janet Elise (2014) "Pussy Riot as a Feminist Project: Russia's Gendered Informal Politics," *Nationalities Papers, The Journal of Nationalism and Ethnicity*, Vol. 42, Issue 4: 583–590; www.tandfonline.com/doi/abs/10.1080/00905992.2014.916667?src=recsys&journalCode=cnap20.

Khorasani, Noushin Ahmadi (2008) "The Fate of the Family Protection Law/Noushin Ahmadi Khorasani's Interview with Mahnaz Afkhami, the Second Woman Minister in Iran," The Feminist School, 14 October 2008; www.feministschool.com/english/spip.php?article158.

Kilgore, Ed (2016) "Donald Trump's Role Model Is an Ayn Rand Character," *New York Magazine*, 12 April 2016; http://nymag.com/daily/intelligencer/2016/04/trumps-role-model-is-an-ayn-rand-character.html.

Kramer, Andrew E. (2017) "'They Starve You. They Shock You': Inside the Anti-Gay Pogrom in Chechnya," *The New York Times*, 21 April 2017; www.nytimes.com/2017/04/21/world/europe/chechnya-russia-attacks-gays.html.

Litvinova, Daria (2016) "'If He Beats You, It Means He Loves You': Domestic Violence is Again on the Agenda in Russia, as Lawmakers and Religious Leaders Call for Battery Within Families to be Decriminalized," *The Moscow Times*, 5 August 2016; https://themoscowtimes.com/articles/if-he-beats-you-it-means-he-loves-you-54866.

Mathis-Lilley, Ben (2016) "Trump Was Recorded in 2005 Bragging about Grabbing Women 'by the Pussy,'" *Slate*, 7 October 2016; www.slate.com/blogs/the_slatest/2016/10/07/donald_trump_2005_tape_i_grab_women_by_the_pussy.html.

McIntosh Sundstrom, Lisa (2002) "Women's NGOs in Russia: Struggling from the Margins," *ResearchGate*, March 2002; www.researchgate.net/publication/242389697.

Mir-Hosseini, Ziba (2016) "The Islamic Republic's War on Women," *Foreign Policy*, 29 August 2016; http://foreignpolicy.com/2016/08/29/the-islamic-republics-war-on-women-iran-feminism/.

Moceri, Alana (2017) "Ivanka Trump Is an Anti-Feminist in Feminist Clothing," *Huffington Post*, 28 April 2017; www.huffingtonpost.com/entry/ivanka-is-no-feminist-shes-trumps-mini-me_us_5900ae10e4b06feec8ac9243.

Mostovshchikov, Egor (2015) "Yelena Mizulina: The Creation of a Conservative," *Open Democracy*, 28 May 2015; www.opendemocracy.net/egor-mostovshikov/yelena-mizulina-creation-of-conservative.

Peters, Jeremy W. (2017) "A Reverence for Putin on the Right Buys Trump Cover," *The New York Times*, 14 July 2017; www.nytimes.com/2017/07/14/us/politics/putin-trump-conservatives.html.

Pulliam Bailey, Sarah (2017) "Photo Surfaces of Evangelical Pastors Laying Hands on Trump in the Oval Office," *The Washington Post*, 12 July 2017; www.washingtonpost. com/news/acts-of-faith/wp/2017/07/12/photo-surfaces-of-evangelical-pastors-laying-hands-on-trump-in-the-oval-office/?utm_term=.46177de155f2.

Rasoulian, M., S. Habib, J. Bolhari, M. Hakim Shooshtari, M. Nojomi, and Sh. Abedi (2014) "Risk Factors of Domestic Violence in Iran, Research Article," *Journal of Environmental and Public Health*, Vol. 2014, Article ID 352346; http://dx.doi. org/10.1155/2014/352346.

Redden, Molly (2013) "Pro-Lifers Aren't Even Trying to Make Abortion Restrictions Sound Nice Anymore," *The New Republic*, 27 August 2013; https://newrepublic.com/ article/114480/abortion-laws-without-rape-exceptions-are-proliferating.

——— (2017) "Betsy DeVos to Overhaul 'Failed' Guidelines on Campus Sexual Assault," *The Guardian*, 8 September 2017; www.theguardian.com/education/2017/sep/07/ betsy-devos-campus-sexual-assault-policy.

Rosner, Elizabeth, Doree Lewak, and Stephanie Pagones (2017) "Millions of Women in 'Pussyhats' Protest Trump Around the World," *New York Post*, 21 January 2017; http:// nypost.com/2017/01/21/women-descend-on-dc-to-push-back-against-trump/.

Rutenberg, Jim (2016) "A Warning for Americans from a Member of Pussy Riot," *The New York Times*, 4 December 2016; www.nytimes.com/2016/12/04/business/rutenberg-lessons-in-free-speech-from-pussy-riot.html.

Sengupta, Somini (2017a) "One by One, Marry-Your-Rapist Laws Are Falling in the Middle East," *The New York Times*, 22 July 2017; www.nytimes.com/2017/07/22/ world/middleeast/marry-your-rapist-laws-middle-east.html?mcubz=0.

——— (2017b) "Lebanon Repeals Its Marry-Your-Rapist Law," *The New York Times*, 16 August 2017,;www.nytimes.com/2017/08/16/world/middleeast/lebanon-rapists-marriage-law-repeal.html?mcubz=0.

Shahrabi, Shima (2015) "Iranian TV Star Sparks National Debate on Domestic Violence," *Iranwire*, 27 March 2015; https://iranwire.com/en/features/972.

Shear, Michael D. and Charlie Savage (2017) "In One Day, Trump Administration Lands 3 Punches against Gay Rights," *The New York Times*, 28 July 2017; www.nytimes. com/2017/07/27/us/politics/white-house-lgbt-rights-military-civil-rights-act.html.

Stanglin, Doug (2017) "Russia Parliament Votes 380–3 to Decriminalize Domestic Violence," *USA TODAY*, 27 January 2017; www.usatoday.com/story/news/2017/01/27/russian-parliament-decrimiinalizes-domestic-violence/97129912/.

Stein, Joel (2016) "How Trolls are Ruining the Internet," *TIME*, 18 August 2016; http:// time.com/4457110/internet-trolls/.

Su, Alice (2017) "Activists in Jordan Celebrate the Repeal of a 'Marry the Rapist' Law," *AP TIME*, 1 August 2017; http://amp.timeinc.net/time/4883487/jordan-marry-rapist-law/?source=dam.

Talbot, Margaret (2017) "Why its Become So Hard to Get an Abortion" *The New Yorker*, 3 April 2017: 86–91; www.newyorker.com/magazine/2017/04/03/why-its-become-so-hard-to-get-an-abortion.

Toppa, Sabrina (2017) "Abuse in Pakistan: 'I'm More Scared of Harassment Online than Offline,'" *The Guardian*, 9 August 2017; www.theguardian.com/global-development-professionals-network/2017/aug/09/abuse-in-pakistan-im-more-scared-of-harassment-online-than-offline.

Vagianos, Alanna (2017) "White House Quietly Removes Sexual Assault Report from Website," *Huffington Post*, 30 August 2017; www.huffingtonpost.com/entry/white-house-quietly-removes-sexual-assault-report-from-website_us_59a6c322e4b084581a14 ab59?ncid=inblnkushpmg00000009.

Valenti, Jessica (2017) "Where is Ivanka Trump's 'Concern for Women's Rights' When You Need It?" *The Guardian*, 31 August 2017; www.theguardian.com/commentis free/2017/aug/31/ivanka-trump-womens-rights-wage-gap.

Vulliamy, Ed (2005) "Breaking the Silence," *The Guardian*, 5 October 2005; www. theguardian.com/media/2005/oct/05/broadcasting.saudiarabia.

Wise McClatchy, Lindsay (2017) "Massive Cuts to Violence Against Women Programs Just 'Technical,' White House Says," *DC*, 25 May 2017; www.mcclatchydc.com/news/ politics-government/white-house/article152705234.html.

YouTube (n.d.) "Russia: Putin Visits the Relics of St. Nicholas in the Christ the Saviour Cathedral," *Ruptly TV*; www.youtube.com/watch?v=v5rXRphNU7A.

Zahra-Malik, Mehreen (2017) "Transgender Pakistanis Win Legal Victories, but Violence Goes On," *The New York Times*, 19 August 2017; www.nytimes.com/2017/08/19/ world/asia/pakistan-transgender-bill.html.

INDEX